DATE DUE

Programming Language Processors in Java

We work with leading authors to develop the
strongest educational materials in computer science,
bringing cutting-edge thinking and best learning
practice to a global market.

Under a range of well-known imprints, including
Prentice Hall, we craft high quality print and
electronic publications which help
readers to understand and apply their content,
whether studying or at work.

To find out more about the complete range of our
publishing please visit us on the World Wide Web at:
www.pearsoneduc.com

Programming Language Processors in Java

COMPILERS AND INTERPRETERS

DAVID A WATT
University of Glasgow, Scotland
and
DERYCK F BROWN
The Robert Gordon University, Scotland

An imprint of **Pearson Education**

Harlow, England · London · New York · Reading, Massachusetts · San Francisco · Toronto · Don Mills, Ontario · Sydney
Tokyo · Singapore · Hong Kong · Seoul · Taipei · Cape Town · Madrid · Mexico City · Amsterdam · Munich · Paris · Milan

7/04

42641722

Pearson Education Limited
Edinburgh Gate
Harlow
Essex, CM20 2JE
England

and Associated Companies throughout the world

Visit us on the World Wide Web at:
http://www.pearsoneduc.com

First published 2000

ISBN 0 130 25786 9

British Library Cataloguing in Publication Data
A catalogue record for this book is available from the British Library.

Library of Congress Cataloging-in-Publication Data
Watt, David A. (David Anthony)
      Programming language processors in Java : compilers and interpreters / David A. Watt
and Deryck F. Brown
           p.   cm.
      Includes bibliographical references.
      ISBN 0–13–025786–9 (case)
      1. Java (Computer program language) 2. Compilers (Computer programs) 3.
Interpreters (Computer programs) I. Brown, Deryck F. II. Title.

      QA76.73.J38 W385 1999
      005.4´53–dc21   99–050395

10 9 8 7 6 5 4 3 2
04 03 02 01 00

Typeset by 7
Printed an bound in Great Britain by Biddles Ltd, *www.biddles.co.uk*

Contents

Trademark notice

The following are trademarks or registered trademarks of their respective companies:
Ada is a trademark of the US Department of Defense – Ada Joint Program Office; Intel
80386 and Pentium are trademarks of Intel Corporation; Java, JavaCC, and JDK are
trademarks of Sun Microsystems, Inc.; JBuilder is a trademark of Borland International,
Inc.; PowerPC is a trademark of International Business Machines Corporation; SPARC
is a trademark of SPARC International, Inc.; UNIX is a trademark licensed through
X/Open Company Ltd.

Preface

The subject of this book is the implementation of programming languages. Programming language processors are programs that process other programs. The primary examples of language processors are compilers and interpreters.

Programming languages are of central importance in computer science. They are the most fundamental tools of software engineers, who are completely dependent on the quality of the language processors they use. There is an interplay between the design of programming languages and computer instruction sets: compilers must bridge the gap between high-level languages and machine code. And programming language design itself raises strong feelings among computer scientists, as witnessed by the proliferation of language paradigms. Imperative and object-oriented languages are currently dominant in terms of actual usage, and it is on the implementation of such languages that this book focuses.

Programming language implementation is a particularly fascinating topic, in our view, because of its close interplay between theory and practice. Ever since the dawn of computer science, the engineering of language processors has driven, and has been vastly improved by, the development of relevant theories.

Nowadays, the principles of programming language implementation are very well understood. An experienced compiler writer can implement a simple programming language about as fast as he or she can type. The basic techniques are simple yet effective, and can be lucidly presented to students. Once the techniques have been mastered, building a compiler from scratch is essentially an exercise in software engineering.

A textbook example of a compiler is often the first complete program of its size seen by computer science students. Such an example should therefore be an exemplar of good software engineering principles. Regrettably, many compiler textbooks offend these principles. This textbook, based on a total of about twenty-five years' experience of teaching programming language implementation, aims to exemplify good software engineering principles at the same time as explaining the specific techniques needed to build compilers and interpreters.

The book shows how to design and build simple compilers and interpreters using the object-oriented programming language Java. The reasons for this choice are two-fold. First, object-oriented methods have emerged as a dominant software engineering technology, yielding substantial improvements in software modularity, maintainability, and reusability. Secondly, Java itself has experienced a prodigious growth in popularity since its appearance as recently as 1994, and that for good technical reasons: Java is simple, consistent, portable, and equipped with an extremely rich class library. Soon we can expect all computer science students to have at least some familiarity with Java.

A programming languages series

This is the fourth of a series of books on programming languages:

- *Programming Language Concepts and Paradigms*

- *Programming Language Syntax and Semantics*

- *Programming Language Processors*

- *Programming Language Processors in Java*

Programming Language Concepts and Paradigms studies the concepts underlying programming languages, and the major language paradigms that use these concepts in different ways; in other words, it is about language design. *Programming Language Syntax and Semantics* shows how we can formally specify the syntax (form) and semantics (meaning) of programming languages. *Programming Language Processors* studies the implementation of programming languages, examining language processors such as compilers and interpreters, and using Pascal as the implementation language. *Programming Language Processors in Java* likewise studies the implementation of programming languages, but now using Java as the implementation language and object-oriented design as the engineering principle; moreover, it introduces basic techniques for implementing object-oriented languages.

This series attempts something that has not previously been achieved, as far as we know: a broad study of all aspects of programming languages, using consistent terminology, and emphasizing connections likely to be missed by books that deal with these aspects separately. For example, the concepts incorporated in a language must be defined precisely in the language's semantic specification. Conversely, a study of semantics helps us to discover and refine elegant and powerful new concepts, which can be incorporated in future language designs. A language's syntax underlies analysis of source programs by language processors; its semantics underlies object code generation and interpretation. Implementation is an important consideration for the language designer, since a language that cannot be implemented with acceptable efficiency will not be used.

The books may be read as a series, but each book is sufficiently self-contained to be read on its own, if the reader prefers.

Content of this book

Chapter 1 introduces the topic of the book. It reviews the concepts of high-level programming languages, and their syntax, contextual constraints, and semantics. It explains what a language processor is, with examples from well-known programming systems.

Chapter 2 introduces the basic terminology of language processors: translators, compilers, interpreters, source and target languages, and real and abstract machines. It goes on to study interesting ways of using language processors: interpretive compilers, portable compilers, and bootstrapping. In this chapter we view language processors as 'black boxes'. In the following chapters we look inside these black boxes.

Chapter 3 looks inside compilers. It shows how compilation can be decomposed into three principal phases: syntactic analysis, contextual analysis, and code generation. It also compares different ways of designing compilers, leading to one-pass and multi-pass compilation.

Chapter 4 studies syntactic analysis in detail. It decomposes syntactic analysis into scanning, parsing, and abstract syntax tree construction. It introduces recursive-descent parsing, and shows how a parser and scanner can be systematically constructed from the source language's syntactic specification.

Chapter 5 studies contextual analysis in detail, assuming that the source language exhibits static bindings and is statically typed. The main topics are identification, which is related to the language's scope rules, and type checking, which is related to the language's type rules.

Chapter 6 prepares for code generation by discussing the relationship between the source language and the target machine. It shows how target machine instructions and storage must be marshaled to support the higher-level concepts of the source language. The topics covered include data representation, expression evaluation, storage allocation, routines and their arguments, garbage collection, and the run-time organization of simple object-oriented languages.

Chapter 7 studies code generation in detail. It shows how to organize the translation from source language to object code. It relates the selection of object code to the semantics of the source language. As this is an introductory textbook, only code generation for a stack-based target machine is covered. (The more difficult topics of code generation for a register-based machine, and code transformations are left to more advanced textbooks.)

Chapter 8 looks inside interpreters. It gives examples of interpreters for both low-level and high-level languages.

Chapter 9 concludes the book. It places the implementation of a programming language in the context of the language's life cycle, along with design and specification. It also discusses quality issues, namely error reporting and efficiency.

There are several possible orders for studying the main topics of this book. The chapter on interpretation can be read independently of the chapters on compilation. Within the latter, the chapters on syntactic analysis, contextual analysis, and code generation can be read in any order. The following diagram summarizes the dependencies between chapters.

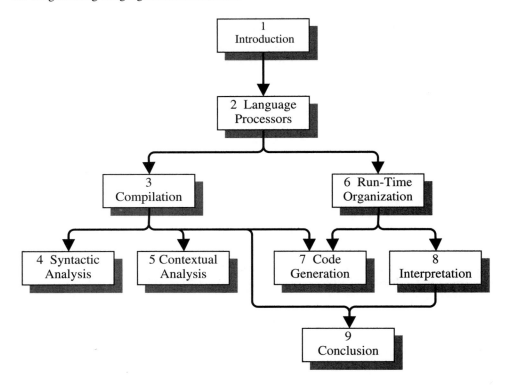

Examples and case studies

The methods described in this textbook are freely illustrated by examples. In Chapter 2, the examples are of language processors for real programming languages. In the remaining chapters, most examples are based on smaller languages, in order that the essential points can be conveyed without the reader getting lost in detail.

A complete programming language is a synthesis of numerous concepts, which often interact with one another in quite complicated ways. It is important that the reader understands how we cope with these complications in implementing a complete programming language. For this purpose we use the programming language Triangle as a case study. An overview of Triangle is given in Section 1.4. A reader already familiar with a Pascal-like language should have no trouble in reading Triangle programs. A complete specification of Triangle is given in Appendix B; this includes a formal specification of its syntax, but is otherwise informal.

We designed Triangle for two specific purposes: to illustrate how a programming language can be formally specified (in the companion textbook *Programming Language Syntax and Semantics*), and to illustrate how a programming language can be implemented. Ideally we would use a real programming language, such as Pascal or Java, for these purposes. In practice, however, real languages are excessively complicated. They contain many features that are tedious but unilluminating to specify and to implement.

Although Triangle is a model language, it is rich enough to write interesting programs and to illustrate basic methods of specification and implementation. Finally, it can readily be extended in various ways (such as adding new types, new control structures, or packages), and such extensions are a basis for a variety of projects.

Educational software

A Triangle language processor is available *for educational use* in conjunction with this textbook. The Triangle language processor consists of: a compiler for Triangle, which generates code for TAM (Triangle Abstract Machine); an interpreter for TAM; and a disassembler for TAM. The tools are written entirely in Java, and will run on any computer equipped with a JVM (Java Virtual Machine). You can download the Triangle language processor from our Web site:

```
www.dcs.gla.ac.uk/~daw/books/PLPJ/
```

Exercises and projects

Each chapter of this book is followed by a number of relevant exercises. These vary from short exercises, through longer ones (marked *), up to truly demanding ones (marked **) that could be treated as projects.

A typical exercise is to apply the methods of the chapter to a very small toy language, or a minor extension of Triangle.

A typical project is to implement some substantial extension to Triangle. Most of the projects are gathered together at the end of Chapter 9; they require modifications to several parts of the Triangle compiler, and should be undertaken only after reading up to Chapter 7 at least.

Readership

This book and its companions are aimed at junior, senior, and graduate students of computer science and information technology, all of whom need some understanding of the fundamentals of programming languages. The books should also be of interest to professional software engineers, especially project leaders responsible for language evaluation and selection, designers and implementors of language processors, and designers of new languages and extensions to existing languages.

The basic prerequisites for this textbook are courses in programming and data structures, and a course in programming languages that covers at least basic language concepts and syntax. The reader should be familiar with Java, and preferably at least one other high-level language, since in studying implementation of programming languages it is important not to be unduly influenced by the idiosyncrasies of a particular language. All the algorithms in this textbook are expressed in Java.

The ability to read a programming language specification critically is an essential skill. A programming language implementor is forced to explore the entire language, including its darker corners. (The ordinary programmer is wise to avoid these dark corners!) The reader of this textbook will need a good knowledge of syntax, and ideally some knowledge of semantics; these topics are briefly reviewed in Chapter 1 for the benefit of readers who might lack such knowledge. Familiarity with BNF and EBNF (which are commonly used in language specifications) is essential, because in Chapter 4 we show how to exploit them in syntactic analysis. No knowledge of formal semantics is assumed.

The reader should be comfortable with some elementary concepts from discrete mathematics – sets and recursive functions – as these help to sharpen understanding of, for example, parsing algorithms. Discrete mathematics is essential for a deeper understanding of compiler theory; however, only a minimum of compiler theory is presented in this book.

This book and its companions attempt to cover all the most important aspects of a large subject. Where necessary, depth has been sacrificed for breadth. Thus the really serious student will need to follow up with more advanced studies. Each book has an extensive bibliography, and each chapter closes with pointers to further reading on the topics covered by the chapter.

Acknowledgments

Most of the methods described in this textbook have long since passed into compiler folklore, and are almost impossible to attribute to individuals. Instead, we shall mention people who have particularly influenced us personally.

For providing a stimulating environment in which to think about programming language issues, we are grateful to colleagues in the Department of Computing Science at the University of Glasgow, in particular Malcolm Atkinson, Muffy Calder, Quintin Cutts, Peter Dickman, Bill Findlay, John Hughes, John Launchbury, Hermano Moura, John Patterson, Simon Peyton Jones, Fermin Reig, Phil Trinder, and Phil Wadler. We have also been strongly influenced, in many different ways, by the work of Peter Buneman, Luca Cardelli, Edsger Dijkstra, Jim Gosling, Susan Graham, Tony Hoare, Jean Ichbiah, Mehdi Jazayeri, Robin Milner, Peter Mosses, Atsushi Ohori, Bob Tennent, Jim Welsh, and Niklaus Wirth.

We wish to thank the reviewers for reading and providing valuable comments on an earlier draft of this book. Numerous cohorts of undergraduate students taking the *Programming Languages 3* module at the University of Glasgow made an involuntary but essential contribution by class-testing the Triangle language processor, as have three cohorts of students taking the *Compilers* module at the Robert Gordon University.

We are particularly grateful to Tony Hoare, editor of the Prentice Hall International Series in Computer Science, for his encouragement and advice, freely and generously offered when these books were still at the planning stage. If this book is more than just another compiler textbook, that is partly due to his suggestion to emphasize the connections between compilation, interpretation, and semantics.

Glasgow and Aberdeen   D.A.W.
July, 1999   D.F.B.

CHAPTER ONE

Introduction

In this introductory chapter we start by reviewing the distinction between low-level and high-level programming languages. We then see what is meant by a programming language processor, and look at examples from different programming systems. We review the specification of the syntax and semantics of programming languages. Finally, we look at Triangle, a programming language that will be used as a case study throughout this book.

1.1 Levels of programming language

Programming languages are the basic tools of all programmers. A programming language is a formal notation for expressing algorithms. Now, an algorithm is an abstract concept, and has an existence independent of any particular notation in which it might be expressed. Without a notation, however, we cannot express an algorithm, nor communicate it to others, nor reason about its correctness.

Practicing programmers, of course, are concerned not only with expressing and analyzing algorithms, but also with constructing software that instructs machines to perform useful tasks. For this purpose programmers need facilities to enter, edit, translate, and interpret programs on machines. Tools that perform these tasks are called *programming language processors*, and are the subject of this book.

Machines are driven by programs expressed in **machine code** (or *machine language*). A machine-code program is a sequence of *instructions*, where each instruction is just a bit string that is interpreted by the machine to perform some defined operation. Typical machine-code instructions perform primitive operations like the following:

* Load an item of data from memory address 366.

* Add two numbers held in registers 1 and 2.

* Jump to instruction 13 if the result of the previous operation was zero.

In the very early days of computing, programs were written directly in machine code. The above instructions might be written, respectively, as follows:

* 0000 0001 0110 1110

1

- 0100 0000 0001 0010

- 1100 0000 0000 1101

Once written, a program could simply be loaded into the machine and run.

Clearly, machine-code programs are extremely difficult to read, write, and edit. The programmer must keep track of the exact address of each item of data and each instruction in storage, and must encode every single instruction as a bit string. For small programs (consisting of thousands of instructions) this task is onerous; for larger programs the task is practically infeasible.

Programmers soon began to invent symbolic notations to make programs easier to read, write, and edit. The above instructions might be written, respectively, as follows:

- LOAD x

- ADD R1 R2

- JUMPZ h

where LOAD, ADD, and JUMPZ are symbolic names for operations, R1 and R2 are symbolic names for registers, x is a symbolic name for the address of a particular item of data, and h is a symbolic name for the address of a particular instruction. Having written a program like this on paper, the programmer would prepare it to be run by manually translating each instruction into machine code. This process was called *assembling* the program.

The obvious next step was to make the machine itself assemble the program. For this process to work, it is necessary to standardize the symbolic names for operations and registers. (However, the programmer should still be free to choose symbolic names for data and instruction addresses.) Thus the symbolic notation is formalized, and can now be termed an ***assembly language***.

Even when writing programs in an assembly language, the programmer is still working in terms of the machine's instruction set. A program consists of a large number of very primitive instructions. The instructions must be written individually, and put together in the correct sequence. The algorithm in the mind of the programmer tends to be swamped by details of registers, jumps, and so on. To take a very simple example, consider computing the area of a triangle with sides a, b, and c, using the formula:

$$\sqrt{(s \times (s - a) \times (s - b) \times (s - c))}$$
where $s = (a + b + c) / 2$

Written in assembly language, the program must be expressed in terms of individual arithmetic operations, and in terms of the registers that contain intermediate results:

```
LOAD R1 a;   ADD R1 b;   ADD R1 c;   DIV R1 #2;
LOAD R2 R1;
LOAD R3 R1;   SUB R3 a;   MULT R2 R3;
LOAD R3 R1;   SUB R3 b;   MULT R2 R3;
```

```
LOAD R3 R1;    SUB R3 c;    MULT R2 R3;
LOAD R0 R2;    CALL sqrt
```

Programming is made very much easier if we can use notation similar to the familiar mathematical notation:

```
let s = (a+b+c)/2
in sqrt(s*(s-a)*(s-b)*(s-c))
```

Today the vast majority of programs are written in programming languages of this kind. These are called *high-level languages*, by contrast with machine languages and assembly languages, which are *low-level languages*. Low-level languages are so called because they force algorithms to be expressed in terms of primitive instructions, of the kind that can be performed directly by electronic hardware. High-level languages are so called because they allow algorithms to be expressed in terms that are closer to the way in which we conceptualize these algorithms in our heads. The following are typical of concepts that are supported by high-level languages, but are supported only in a rudimentary form or not at all by low-level languages:

• *Expressions:* An expression is a rule for computing a value. The high-level language programmer can write expressions similar to ordinary mathematical notation, using operators such as '+', '−', '*', and '/'.

• *Data types:* Programs manipulate data of many types: primitive types such as truth values, characters, and integers, and composite types such as records and arrays. The high-level language programmer can explicitly define such types, and declare constants, variables, functions, and parameters of these types.

• *Control structures:* Control structures allow the high-level language programmer to program selective computation (e.g., by if- and case-commands) and iterative computation (e.g., by while- and for-commands).

• *Declarations:* Declarations allow the high-level language programmer to introduce identifiers to denote entities such as constant values, variables, procedures, functions, and types.

• *Abstraction:* An essential mental tool of the programmer is abstraction, or separation of concerns: separating the notion of *what* computation is to be performed from the details of *how* it is to be performed. The programmer can emphasize this separation by use of named procedures and functions. Moreover, these can be parameterized with respect to the entities on which they operate.

• *Encapsulation* (or *data abstraction*): Packages and classes allow the programmer to group together related declarations, and selectively to hide some of them. A particularly important usage of this concept is to group hidden variables together with operations on these variables, which is the essence of object-oriented programming.

Section 1.5 suggests further reading on the concepts of high-level programming languages.

1.2   Programming language processors

A *programming language processor* is any system that manipulates programs expressed in some particular programming language. With the help of language processors we can run programs, or prepare them to be run.

This definition of language processors is very general. It encompasses a variety of systems, including the following:

- *Editors*. An editor allows a program text to be entered, modified, and saved in a file. An ordinary text editor lets us edit any textual document (not necessarily a program text). A more sophisticated kind of editor is one tailored to edit programs expressed in a particular language.

- *Translators* and *compilers*. A translator translates a text from one language to another. In particular, a compiler translates a program from a high-level language to a low-level language, thus preparing it to be run on a machine. Prior to performing this translation, a compiler checks the program for syntactic and contextual errors.

- *Interpreters*. An interpreter takes a program expressed in a particular language, and runs it immediately. This mode of execution, omitting a compilation stage in favor of immediate response, is preferred in an interactive environment. Command languages and database query languages are usually interpreted.

In practice, we use all the above kinds of language processor in program development. In a conventional programming system, these language processors are usually separate tools; this is the 'software tools' philosophy. However, most systems now offer integrated language processors, in which editing, compilation, and interpretation are just options within a single system. The following examples contrast these two approaches.

Example 1.1   Language processors as software tools

The 'software tools' philosophy is well exemplified by the UNIX operating system. Indeed, this philosophy was fundamental to the system's design.

Consider a UNIX user developing a chess-playing application in Java, using the Sun Java Development Kit (JDK). The user invokes an editor, such as the screen editor vi, to enter and store the program text in a file named (say) Chess.java:

```
vi Chess.java
```

Then the user invokes the Java compiler, javac:

```
javac Chess.java
```

This translates the stored program into object code, which it stores in a file named Chess.class. The user can now test the object-code program by running it using the interpreter, java:

```
java Chess
```

If the program fails to compile, or misbehaves when run, the user reinvokes the editor to modify the program; then reinvokes the compiler; and so on. Thus program development is an edit–compile–run cycle.

There is no direct communication between these language processors. If the program fails to compile, the compiler will generate one or more error reports, each indicating the position of the error. The user must note these error reports, and on reinvoking the editor must find the errors and correct them. This is very inconvenient, especially in the early stages of program development when errors might be numerous.

□

The essence of the 'software tools' philosophy is to provide a small number of common and simple tools, which can be used in various combinations to perform a large variety of tasks. Thus only a single editor need be provided, one that can be used to edit programs in a variety of languages, and indeed other textual documents too.

What we have described is the 'software tools' philosophy in its purest form. In practice, the philosophy is compromised in order to make program development easier. The editor might have a facility that allows the user to compile the program (or indeed issue any system command) without leaving the editor. Some compilers go further: if the program fails to compile, the editor is automatically reinvoked and positioned at the first error.

These are *ad hoc* solutions. A fresh approach seems preferable: a fully integrated language processor, designed specifically to support the edit–compile–run cycle.

Example 1.2   Integrated language processor

Borland JBuilder is a fully integrated language processor for Java, consisting of an editor, a compiler, and other facilities. The user issues commands to open, edit, compile, and run the program. These commands may be selected from pull-down menus, or from the keyboard.

The editor is tailored to Java. It assists with the program layout using indentation, and it distinguishes between Java keywords, literals and comments using color. The editor is also fully integrated with the visual interface construction facilities of JBuilder.

The compiler is integrated with the editor. When the user issues the 'compile' command, and the program is found to contain a compile-time error, the erroneous phrase is highlighted, ready for immediate editing. If the program contains several errors, then the compiler will list all of them, and the user can select a particular error message and have the relevant phrase highlighted.

The object program is also integrated with the editor. If the program fails at run-time, the failing phrase is highlighted. (Of course, this phrase is not necessarily the one that contains the logical error. But it would be unreasonable to expect the language processor to debug the program automatically!)

□

1.3 Specification of programming languages

Several groups of people have a direct interest in a programming language: the *designer* who invented the language in the first place; the *implementors*, whose task it is to write language processors; and the much larger community of ordinary *programmers*. All of these people must rely on a common understanding of the language, for which they must refer to an agreed ***specification*** of the language.

Several aspects of a programming language need to be specified:

- ***Syntax*** is concerned with the form of programs. A language's syntax defines what tokens (symbols) are used in programs, and how phrases are composed from tokens and subphrases. Examples of phrases are commands, expressions, declarations, and complete programs.

- ***Contextual constraints*** (sometimes called *static semantics*) are rules such as the following. *Scope rules* determine the scope of each declaration, and allow us to locate the declaration of each identifier. *Type rules* allow us to infer the type of each expression, and to ensure that each operation is supplied with operands of the correct types. Contextual constraints are so called because whether a phrase such as an expression is well-formed depends on its context.

- ***Semantics*** is concerned with the meanings of programs. There are various points of view on how we should specify semantics. From one point of view, we can take the meaning of a program to be a mathematical function, mapping the program's inputs to its outputs. (This is the basis of *denotational semantics*.) From another point of view, we can take the meaning of a program to be its behavior when it is run on a machine. (This is the basis of *operational semantics*.) Since this book is about language processors, i.e., systems that run programs or prepare them to be run, we shall prefer the operational point of view.

When a programming language is specified, there is a choice between formal and informal specification:

- An ***informal specification*** is one written in English or some other natural language. Such a specification can be readily understood by any user of the programming language, if it is well-written. Experience shows, however, that it is very hard to make an informal specification sufficiently precise for all the needs of implementors and programmers; misinterpretations are common. Even for the language designer, an informal specification is unsatisfactory because it can too easily be inconsistent or incomplete.

- A ***formal specification*** is one written in a precise notation. Such a specification is more likely to be unambiguous, consistent, and complete, and less likely to be misinterpreted. However, a formal specification will be intelligible only to people who understand the notation in which the specification is written.

In practice, most programming language specifications are hybrids. Syntax is usually specified formally, using BNF or one of its variants, because this notation is easy and widely understood. But contextual constraints and semantics are usually specified informally, because their formal specification is more difficult, and the available notations are not yet widely understood. A typical language specification, with formal syntax but otherwise informal, may be found in Appendix B.

1.3.1   Syntax

Syntax is concerned with the form of programs. We can specify the syntax of a programming language formally by means of a ***context-free grammar***. This consists of the following elements:

- A finite set of ***terminal symbols*** (or just *terminals*). These are atomic symbols, the ones we actually enter at the keyboard when composing a program in the language. Typical examples of terminals in a programming language's grammar are '>=', 'while', and ';'.

- A finite set of ***nonterminal symbols*** (or just *nonterminals*). A nonterminal symbol represents a particular class of phrases in the language. Typical examples of nonterminals in a programming language's grammar are Program, Command, Expression, and Declaration.

- A ***start symbol***, which is one of the nonterminals. The start symbol represents the principal class of phrases in the language. Typically the start symbol in a programming language's grammar is Program.

- A finite set of ***production rules***. These define how phrases are composed from terminals and subphrases.

Grammars are usually written in the notation *BNF* (Backus–Naur Form). In BNF, a production rule is written in the form $N ::= \alpha$, where N is a nonterminal symbol, and where α is a (possibly empty) string of terminal and/or nonterminal symbols. Several production rules with a common nonterminal on their left-hand sides:

$N ::= \alpha$

$N ::= \beta$

...

may be grouped as:

$N ::= \alpha \mid \beta \mid ....$

The BNF symbol '::=' is pronounced 'may consist of', and '|' is pronounced 'or alternatively'.

Example 1.3   Mini-Triangle syntax

Mini-Triangle is a toy programming language that will serve as a running example here and elsewhere. (It is a subset of Triangle, the language to be introduced in Section 1.4.)

Here is a trivial Mini-Triangle program:

```
! This is a comment. It continues to the end-of-line.
let
    const m ~ 7;
    var n: Integer
in
    begin
    n := 2 * m * m;
    putint(n)
    end
```

Here we present the context-free grammar of Mini-Triangle.

The terminal symbols of Mini-Triangle include:

```
begin       const   do      else    end     if
in          let     then    var     while
;           :       :=      ~       (       )
+           -       *       /       <       >       =
\
```

(These are emboldened in the production rules below, for emphasis.)

The nonterminal symbols of Mini-Triangle include:

Program (start symbol)
Command   single-Command
Expression   primary-Expression
V-name
Declaration   single-Declaration
Type-denoter
Operator   Identifier
Integer-Literal

The production rules are:

Program	::=	single-Command	(1.1)
Command	::=	single-Command	(1.2a)
	|	Command **;** single-Command	(1.2b)
single-Command	::=	V-name **:=** Expression	(1.3a)
	|	Identifier **(** Expression **)**	(1.3b)
	|	**if** Expression **then** single-Command	(1.3c)
		else single-Command	
	|	**while** Expression **do** single-Command	(1.3d)
	|	**let** Declaration **in** single-Command	(1.3e)
	|	**begin** Command **end**	(1.3f)

Expression	::=	primary-Expression	(1.4a)
			Expression Operator primary-Expression	(1.4b)
primary-Expression	::=	Integer-Literal	(1.5a)
			V-name	(1.5b)
			Operator primary-Expression	(1.5c)
			(Expression)	(1.5d)
V-name	::=	Identifier	(1.6)
Declaration	::=	single-Declaration	(1.7a)
			Declaration ; single-Declaration	(1.7b)
single-Declaration	::=	**const** Identifier ~ Expression	(1.8a)
			var Identifier : Type-denoter	(1.8b)
Type-denoter	::=	Identifier	(1.9)
Operator	::=	+ | – | * | / | < | > | = | \	(1.10a–h)
Identifier	::=	Letter | Identifier Letter | Identifier Digit	(1.11a–c)
Integer-Literal	::=	Digit | Integer-Literal Digit	(1.12a–b)
Comment	::=	! Graphic* eol	(1.13)

Production rule (1.3f) tells us that a single-command may consist of the terminal symbol 'begin', followed by a command, followed by the terminal symbol 'end'.

Production rule (1.3a) tells us that a single-command may consist of a value-or-variable-name, followed by the terminal symbol ': =', followed by an expression.

A value-or-variable-name, represented by the nonterminal symbol V-name, is the name of a declared constant or variable. Production rule (1.6) tells us that a value-or-variable-name is just an identifier. (More complex value-or-variable-names can be written in full Triangle.)

Production rules (1.2a–b) tell us that a command may consist of a single-command alone, or alternatively it may consist of a command followed by the terminal symbol ';' followed by a single-command. In other words, a command consists of a sequence of one or more single-commands separated by semicolons.

In production rules (1.11a–c), (1.12a–b), and (1.13):

- eol stands for an end-of-line 'character';
- Letter stands for one of the lowercase letters 'a', 'b', …, or 'z';
- Digit stands for one of the digits '0', '1', …, or '9';
- Graphic stands for a space or visible character.

The nonterminals Letter, Digit, and Graphic each represents a set of single characters. Specifying them formally is simple but tedious, for example:

Digit   ::=   **0** | **1** | **2** | **3** | **4** | **5** | **6** | **7** | **8** | **9**

☐

Each context-free grammar generates a language, which is a set of strings of terminal symbols. We define this language in terms of syntax trees and phrases. Consider a particular context-free grammar G.

A **syntax tree** of G is an ordered labeled tree such that: (a) the terminal nodes are labeled by terminal symbols; (b) the nonterminal nodes are labeled by nonterminal symbols; and (c) each nonterminal node labeled by N has children labeled by $X_1, \ldots, X_n$ (in order from left to right) such that $N ::= X_1 \ldots X_n$ is a production rule. More specifically, an *N-tree* of G is a syntax tree whose root node is labeled by N.

A **phrase** of G is a string of terminal symbols labeling the terminal nodes (taken from left to right) of a syntax tree. More specifically, an *N-phrase* of G is a string of terminal symbols labeling the terminal nodes of an *N*-tree.

A **sentence** of G is an *S*-phrase, where S is the start symbol. The **language** generated by G is the set of all sentences of G.

Example 1.4   Mini-Triangle syntax trees

Figures 1.1 through 1.3 show some Mini-Triangle syntax trees. Some of the nonterminal symbols have been abbreviated. The syntax trees of identifiers, operators and literals have been elided, being of little interest.

From the syntax tree of Figure 1.1 we can see that the following is an expression (formally, an Expression-phrase):

```
d + 10 * n
```

Note that this expression will be evaluated like '(d+10)*n', since Mini-Triangle's binary operators all have the same precedence. This is implicit in production rule (1.4b), and in the shape of the syntax tree.

From the syntax tree of Figure 1.2 we can see that the following is a single-command (formally, a single-Command-phrase):

```
while b do begin n := 0; b := false end
```

From the syntax tree of Figure 1.3 we can see that the following is a program (formally, a sentence or Program-phrase):

```
let var y: Integer in y := y + 1
```

☐

A grammar like that of Example 1.3 has two roles:

- The grammar tells us, for each form of phrase, what its subphrases are. For example, a Mini-Triangle assignment command (1.3a) has two subphrases: a value-or-variable-name and an expression. A Mini-Triangle if-command (1.3c) has three subphrases: an expression and two (sub)commands. The way in which a program is composed from phrases and subphrases is called its ***phrase structure***.

• The grammar also tells us the order in which the subphrases must be written, and the terminal symbols with which they must be delimited. For example, a Mini-Triangle assignment command (1.3a) consisting of a value-or-variable-name V and an expression E must be written in the form '$V := E$'. A Mini-Triangle if-command (1.3c) consisting of an expression E and subcommands C_1 and C_2 must be written in the form 'if E then C_1 else C_2'. Moreover, the grammar tells us that C_1 and C_2 must be *single*-commands (in order to avoid ambiguity).

Because of its concentration on concrete syntactic details, a grammar such as this specifies what we call the ***concrete syntax*** of the language. The concrete syntax is important to the programmer who needs to know exactly how to write syntactically well-formed programs.

But concrete syntax has no influence on the *semantics* of the programs. For example, whether the assignment command is written in the form '$V := E$' or '$V \leftarrow E$' or '$E \rightarrow V$' or 'set $V = E$' or 'assign E to V' does not affect how the command will be executed. These are all different in terms of concrete syntax, but all the same in terms of phrase structure.

When specifying semantics, it is convenient to concentrate on phrase structure alone. This is the point of ***abstract syntax***. A grammar specifying abstract syntax generates only a set of ***abstract syntax trees*** (ASTs). Each nonterminal node of an AST is labeled by a production rule, and it has exactly one subtree for each subphrase. The grammar does not generate sentences, for terminal symbols have no real role in abstract syntax.

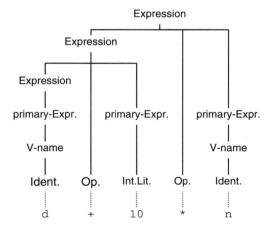

Figure 1.1 Syntax tree of a Mini-Triangle expression.

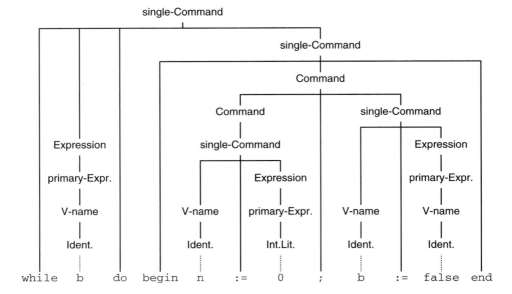

Figure 1.2 Syntax tree of a Mini-Triangle single-command.

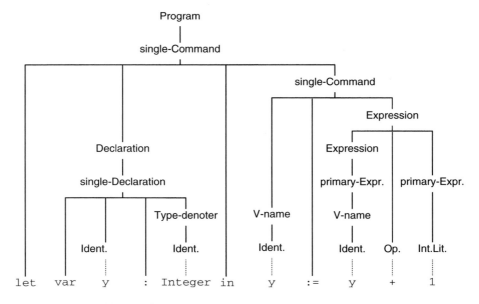

Figure 1.3 Syntax tree of a Mini-Triangle program.

Example 1.5   Mini-Triangle abstract syntax

Here we present a grammar specifying the abstract syntax of Mini-Triangle. This will specify only the phrase structure of Mini-Triangle. Distinctions between commands and single-commands, between declarations and single-declarations, and between expressions and primary-expressions, will be swept away.

The nonterminal symbols are:

```
Program  (start symbol)
Command
Expression
V-name
Declaration
Type-denoter
```

The production rules are:

Program	::=	Command	Program	(1.14)
Command	::=	V-name **:=** Expression	AssignCommand	(1.15a)
	|	Identifier **(** Expression **)**	CallCommand	(1.15b)
	|	Command **;** Command	SequentialCommand	(1.15c)
	|	**if** Expression **then** Command **else** Command	IfCommand	(1.15d)
	|	**while** Expression **do** Command	WhileCommand	(1.15e)
	|	**let** Declaration **in** Command	LetCommand	(1.15f)
Expression	::=	Integer-Literal	IntegerExpression	(1.16a)
	|	V-name	VnameExpression	(1.16b)
	|	Operator Expression	UnaryExpression	(1.16c)
	|	Expression Operator Expression	BinaryExpression	(1.16d)
V-name	::=	Identifier	SimpleVname	(1.17)
Declaration	::=	**const** Identifier **~** Expression	ConstDeclaration	(1.18a)
	|	**var** Identifier **:** Type-denoter	VarDeclaration	(1.18b)
	|	Declaration **;** Declaration	SequentialDeclaration	(1.18c)
Type-denoter	::=	Identifier	SimpleTypeDenoter	(1.19)

Production rules in the abstract syntax look much like those in the concrete syntax. In addition, we give each production rule a suitable label, as shown above right. We will use these labels to label the nonterminal nodes of ASTs.

Figures 1.4 through 1.6 show some Mini-Triangle ASTs, corresponding to the (concrete) syntax trees of Figures 1.1 through 1.3, respectively.

The AST of Figure 1.5 represents the following command:

```
while b do begin n := 0; b := false end
```

This AST's root node is labeled WhileCommand, signifying the fact that this is a while-command. The root node's second child is labeled SequentialCommand, signifying the fact that the body of the while-command is a sequential-command. Both children of the SequentialCommand node are labeled AssignCommand.

When we write down the above command, we need the symbols 'begin' and 'end' to bracket the subcommands 'n := 0' and 'b := false'. These brackets distinguish the above command from:

```
while b do n := 0; b := false
```

whose meaning is quite different. (See Exercise 1.5.) There is no trace of these brackets in the abstract syntax, nor in the AST of Figure 1.5. They are not needed because the AST structure itself represents the bracketing of the subcommands.

A program's AST represents its phrase structure explicitly. The AST is a convenient structure for specifying the program's contextual constraints and semantics. It is also a convenient representation for language processors such as compilers. For example, consider again the assignment command 'while E do C'. The meaning of this command can be specified in terms of the meanings of its subphrases E and C. The translation of this command into object code can be specified in terms of the translations of E and C into object code. The command is represented by an AST with root node labeled 'While-Command' and two subtrees representing E and C, so the compiler can easily access these subphrases.

In Chapter 3 we shall use ASTs extensively to discuss the internal phases of a compiler. In Chapter 4 we shall see how a compiler constructs an AST to represent the source program. In Chapter 5 we shall see how the AST is used to check that the program satisfies the contextual constraints. In Chapter 7 we shall see how to translate the program into object code.

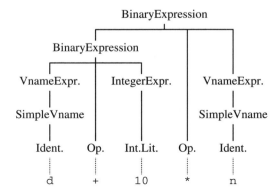

Figure 1.4 Abstract syntax tree of a Mini-Triangle expression.

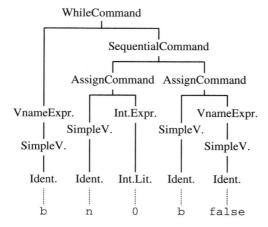

Figure 1.5 Abstract syntax tree of a Mini-Triangle command.

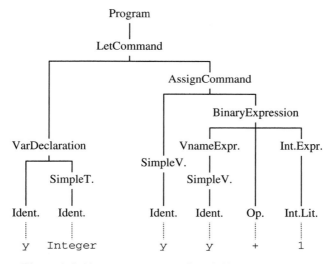

Figure 1.6 Abstract syntax tree of a Mini-Triangle program.

1.3.2   Contextual constraints

Contextual constraints are things like scope rules and type rules. They arise from the possibility that whether a phrase is well-formed or not may depend on its context.

Every programming language allows identifiers to be declared, and thereafter used in ways consistent with their declaration. For instance, an identifier declared as a constant can be used as an operand in an expression; an identifier declared as a variable can be used either as an operand in an expression or on the left-hand side of an assignment; an identifier declared as a procedure can be used in a procedure call; and so on.

The occurrence of an identifier *I* at which it is declared is called a **binding occurrence**. Any other occurrence of *I* (at which it is used) is called an **applied occurrence**. At its binding occurrence, the identifier *I* is bound to some entity (such as a value, variable, or procedure). Each applied occurrence of *I* then denotes that entity. A programming language's rules about binding and applied occurrences of identifiers are called its **scope rules**.

If the programming language permits the same identifier *I* to be declared in several places, we need to be careful about which binding occurrence of *I* corresponds to a given applied occurrence of *I*. The language exhibits **static binding** if this can be determined by a language processor without actually running the program; the language exhibits **dynamic binding** if this can be determined only at run-time. In fact, nearly all major programming languages do exhibit static binding; only a few languages (such as Lisp and Smalltalk) exhibit dynamic binding.

Example 1.6   Triangle scope rules

Mini-Triangle is too simplistic a language for static binding to be an issue, so we shall use Triangle itself for illustration. In the following Triangle program outline, binding occurrences of identifiers are underlined, and applied occurrences are italicized:

```
let
    const m ~ 2;
    var n: Integer;
    func f (i: Integer) : Integer ~
        i * m
in
    begin
    ...;
    n := f(n);              (1)
    ...
    end
```

Each applied occurrence of m denotes the constant value 2. Each applied occurrence of n denotes a particular variable. Each applied occurrence of f denotes a function that doubles its argument. Each applied occurrence of i denotes that function's argument. Each applied occurrence of Integer denotes the standard type *int*, whose values are integer numbers.

Triangle exhibits static binding. The function call at point (1) above doubles its argument. Imagine a call to f in a block where m is redeclared:

```
let
    const m ~ 3
```

```
in
    ... f(n) ...          (2)
```

The function call at point (2) also doubles its argument, because the applied occurrence of m inside the function f always denotes 2, regardless of what m denotes at the point of call.

In a language with dynamic binding, on the other hand, the applied occurrence of m would denote the value to which m was *most recently* bound. In such a language, the function call at (1) would double its argument, whereas the function call at (2) would *triple* its argument.

□

Every programming language has a universe of discourse, the elements of which we call **values**. Usually these values are classified into **types**. Each operation in the language has an associated **type rule**, which tells us the expected operand type(s), and the type of the operation's result (if any). Any attempt to apply an operation to a wrongly-typed value is called a *type error*.

A programming language is **statically typed** if a language processor can detect all type errors without actually running the program; the language is **dynamically typed** if type errors cannot be detected until run-time.

Example 1.7   Mini-Triangle type rules

Mini-Triangle is statically typed. Consider the following program outline:

```
let
    var n: Integer
in
    begin
    ...
    while n > 0 do          (1)
        n := n - 1;          (2)
    ...
    end
```

The type rule of '>' is:

   If both operands are of type *int*, then the result is of type *bool*.

Thus the expression 'n > 0' at point (1) is indeed of type *bool*. Although we cannot tell in advance what particular values n will take, we know that such values will always be integers. Likewise, although we cannot tell in advance what particular values the expression 'n > 0' will take, we know that such values will always be truth values.

The type rule of 'while *E* do *C*' is:

   E must be of type *bool*.

Thus the while-command starting at point (2) is indeed well-typed.

The type rule of '−' is:

If both operands are of type *int*, then the result is of type *int*.

Thus the expression 'n − 1' at point (2) is indeed of type *int*.

The type rule of '*V* : = *E*' is:

V and *E* must be of equivalent type.

Thus the assignment command at point (2) is indeed well-typed.

In a dynamically-typed language, each variable, parameter, etc., may take values of any type. For example, a given variable x might contain an integer or a truth value or a value of some other type. The same variable might even contain values of different types at different times. Thus we could not tell in advance what *type* of value x will contain, never mind what individual value. It follows that we could not tell in advance whether evaluating an expression such as 'x + 1' will satisfy the type rule of '+'.

The fact that a programming language is statically typed implies the following:

* Every well-formed expression *E* has a unique type *T*, which can be inferred without actually evaluating *E*.

* Whenever *E* is evaluated, it will yield a value of type *T*. (Evaluation of *E* might fail due to overflow or some other run-time error, or it might diverge, but its evaluation will never fail due to a type error.)

In this book we shall generally assume that the source language exhibits static binding and is statically typed.

1.3.3   Semantics

Semantics is concerned with the meanings of programs, i.e., their behavior when run. Many notations have been devised for specifying semantics formally, but so far none has achieved widespread acceptance. Here we show how to specify the semantics of a programming language informally.

Our first task is to specify, *in general terms*, what will be the semantics of each class of phrase in the language. We may specify the semantics of commands, expressions, and declarations as follows:

* A command is executed to update variables. [It may also have the side effect of performing input–output.]

* An expression is evaluated to yield a value. [It may also have the side effect of updating variables.]

- A declaration is elaborated to produce bindings. [It may also have the side effect of allocating [and initializing] variables.]

In each case, the text in brackets is applicable only in certain languages.

Our remaining task is to systematically specify the semantics of each specific form of command, expression, declaration, and so on. Here we should follow the language's abstract syntax. In the abstract syntax there is one production rule for each form of phrase; in the semantics there should be one (or occasionally more than one) clause for each form of phrase.

Example 1.8   Mini-Triangle semantics

We specified the abstract syntax of Mini-Triangle in Example 1.5. Here we specify the semantics of Mini-Triangle, following the structure of the abstract syntax.

A *command* C is executed in order to update variables. (This includes input–output.)

The assignment-command '$V := E$' is executed as follows. The expression E is evaluated to yield a value v; then v is assigned to the value-or-variable-name V.   (1.20a)

The call-command '$I (E)$' is executed as follows. The expression E is evaluated to yield a value v; then the procedure bound to I is called with v as its argument.   (1.20b)

The sequential command 'C_1; C_2' is executed as follows. First C_1 is executed; then C_2 is executed.   (1.20c)

The if-command 'if E then C_1 else C_2' is executed as follows. The expression E is evaluated to yield a truth-value t; if t is true, C_1 is executed; if t is false, C_2 is executed.   (1.20d)

The while-command 'while E do C' is executed as follows. The expression E is evaluated to yield a truth-value t; if t is true, C is executed, and then the while-command is executed again; if t is false, execution of the while-command is completed.   (1.20e)

The let-command 'let D in C' is executed as follows. The declaration D is elaborated to produce bindings b; C is executed, in the environment of the let-command overlaid by the bindings b. The bindings b have no effect outside the let-command.   (1.20f)

Note that clauses (1.20a–f) correspond respectively to production rules (1.15a–f) of the abstract syntax.

Note also that clauses (1.20d) and (1.20e) assume that evaluation of E will yield a truth-value. Likewise, clause (1.20a) assumes that evaluation of E will yield a value of the same type as V. These assumptions are justified if the command is well-typed.

An *expression E* is evaluated to yield a value.

The expression '*IL*' yields the value of the integer-literal *IL*.   (1.21a)

The expression '*V*' yields the value of the value-or-variable-name *V*.   (1.21b)

The unary expression '*O E*' yields the value obtained by applying unary
operator *O* to the value yielded by the expression *E*.   (1.21c)

The binary expression 'E_1 *O* E_2' yields the value obtained by applying binary operator *O* to the values yielded by the expressions E_1 and E_2.   (1.21d)

Note that clauses (1.21a–d) correspond respectively to production rules (1.16a–d) of
the abstract syntax.

Note also that expressions have no side effects in Mini-Triangle.

A *value-or-variable-name V* may be identified *either* to yield a value *or* to assign a
value to a variable (as required by the context).

A simple value-or-variable-name *I* yields a value as follows. If *I* is bound
to a value, it yields that value. If *I* is bound to a variable, it yields the
value contained in that variable.   (1.22)

A simple value-or-variable-name *I* is assigned a value *v* as follows. If *I* is
bound to a variable, it updates that variable to contain *v*.   (1.23)

A *declaration D* is elaborated to produce bindings; it may also have the side effect of
allocating variables.

The constant declaration 'const *I* ~ *E*' is elaborated by binding *I* to the
value yielded by the expression *E*.   (1.24a)

The variable declaration 'var *I* : *T*' is elaborated by binding *I* to a newly
allocated variable, whose initial value is undefined. The variable will be
deallocated on exit from the block containing the variable declaration.   (1.24b)

The sequential declaration 'D_1 ; D_2' is elaborated by elaborating D_1 followed by D_2, and combining the bindings they produce. D_2 is elaborated
in the environment of the sequential declaration, overlaid by the bindings
produced by D_1.   (1.24c)

Note that clauses (1.24a–c) correspond respectively to production rules (1.18a–c) of
the abstract syntax.

☐

In Chapter 7 we shall use the semantics of Mini-Triangle to build a code generator
for Mini-Triangle. In Chapter 8 we shall use the semantics to build a Mini-Triangle
interpreter.

1.4   Case study: the programming language Triangle

In this book we shall use small examples – such as the toy language Mini-Triangle – to illustrate various implementation methods without getting lost in details. Nevertheless, it is also important to illustrate how these methods can be applied to realistic programming languages.

A major language like Pascal or Java is just *too* complicated for the purposes of an introductory textbook. Instead we shall use *Triangle*, a small but realistic programming language, as a case study. Triangle is a Pascal-like language, but generally simpler and more regular. Here we give a brief overview of Triangle. (A complete description may be found in Appendix B.)

Triangle commands are similar to Pascal's, but for simplicity there is only one conditional command and one iterative command. Unlike Pascal, Triangle has a let-command with local declarations.

Example 1.9   Triangle commands

The following illustrates the Triangle if-command and let-command:

```
if x > y then
   let const xcopy ~ x
   in
      begin x := y; y := xcopy end
else
```

Note the empty else-part. (It is actually a skip command.)

$\square$

Triangle expressions are richer than Pascal's, but free of side effects. Conditional expressions, let-expressions with local declarations, and aggregates (record and array expressions) are all provided. A function body is just an expression. For simplicity, only three primitive types (denoted by the identifiers `Boolean`, `Char`, and `Integer`), and two forms of composite type (records and arrays), are provided. Unlike Pascal, Triangle is type-complete, i.e., no operations are arbitrarily restricted in the types of their operands. Thus values of any type may be passed as parameters, returned as function results, assigned, and compared using the binary operators '=' and '\='.

Example 1.10 Triangle expressions

The following illustrates a Triangle let-expression and if-expression:

```
let
    const taxable ~ if income > allowance
                    then income - allowance
                    else 0
in
    taxable / 4
```

The following illustrates Triangle record and array types and aggregates:

```
let
    type  Date ~ record
                    m: Integer, d: Integer
                 end;
    const days ~ [31, 28, 31, 30, 31, 30,
                  31, 31, 30, 31, 30, 31];
    var    today: Date
in
    ...
    if today.d < days[today.m - 1]
    then {m ~ today.m, d ~ today.d + 1}
    else if today.m \= 12
    then {m ~ today.m + 1, d ~ 1}
    else {m ~ 1, d ~ 1}
    ...
    if today = {m ~ 2, d ~ 29} then ... else ...
```

Here days is declared to be a constant of type 'array 12 of Integer', i.e., an array with elements 31, 28, 31, etc. The first if-expression yields a value of the record type Date, representing the day after today. The second if-expression illustrates record comparison.

□

Triangle declarations of different kinds may be mixed freely. Constant, variable, and type declarations have been illustrated in Examples 1.9 and 1.10. A Triangle constant declaration may have any expression, of any type, on its right-hand side. This expression must be evaluated at run-time, but thereafter the constant identifier's value is fixed. (The Triangle constant declaration is more general than Pascal's, where the right-hand side is restricted to be a constant.)

Triangle has procedure and function declarations. A procedure body is just a command, which may be (but not necessarily) a let-command. Likewise, a function body is just an expression, which may be (but not necessarily) a let-expression. Functions are free of side effects.

Procedures and functions may have constant, variable, procedural, or functional parameters. These have uniform semantics: in each case the formal-parameter identifier is simply bound to the corresponding argument, which is a value, variable, procedure, or function, respectively.

Example 1.11 Triangle procedures and functions

The following function and procedure implement operations on a type `Point`:

```
type Point ~ record
                x: Integer,
                y: Integer
            end;

func projection (pt: Point) : Point ~
        { x ~ pt.x, y ~ 0 - pt.y };

proc moveup (yshift: Integer, var pt: Point) ~
        pt.y := pt.y + yshift;

...
var p: Point; var q: Point;
...
moveup(3, var p);
q := projection(p)
```

□

Triangle has the usual variety of operators, standard functions, and standard procedures. These behave exactly like ordinary declared functions and procedures; unlike Pascal, they have no special type rules or parameter mechanisms. In particular, Triangle operators behave exactly like functions of one or two parameters.

Example 1.12 Triangle operators

The Triangle operator '/\' (logical conjunction) is, in effect, declared as follows:

```
func /\ (b1: Boolean, b2: Boolean) : Boolean ~
        if b1 then b2 else false
```

The expression 'a /\b' is, in effect, a function call:

```
/\(a, b)
```

and the more complicated expression '(n > 0) /\ (sum/n > 40)' likewise:

```
/\(>(n, 0), >(/(sum, n), 40))
```

Note that the above declaration of /\ implies that both operands of /\ are evaluated before the function is called. (Some other programming languages allow *short-circuit evaluation*: the second operand of /\ is skipped if the first operand evaluates to *false*.)

□

A complete informal specification of Triangle may be found in Appendix B. Each section is devoted to a major construct, e.g., commands, expressions, or declarations. Within the section there are subsections describing the intended *usage* of the construct, its *syntax* (expressed in BNF), its *semantics* (and contextual constraints), and finally *examples*. Browse through Appendix B, attempting to fill the gaps in your understanding of Triangle left by the brief overview here. Appendix B is intended to serve as a model of a carefully written informal specification of a programming language. Nevertheless, if you read carefully, you might well find loopholes!

1.5   Further reading

This book assumes that you are familiar with the basic concepts of high-level programming languages, including those summarized in Section 1.1. A detailed study of these concepts, using terminology consistent with this book, may be found in the companion textbook by Watt (1990). Some other good textbooks cover similar material, including those by Ghezzi and Jazayeri (1987), Sethi (1988), and Tennent (1981).

A very brief review of syntax and semantics was given in Section 1.3. A much fuller treatment may be found in the companion textbook by Watt (1991). The advantages and disadvantages of formal and informal specification are discussed in detail, as are various methods for formally specifying syntax, contextual constraints, and semantics. There is an introduction to formal semantics. Formal specifications of the syntax and semantics of Triangle are given as case studies.

A typical and recent example of a programming language specification is that of Java (Gosling *et al.* 1996). Java's syntax is specified formally in BNF, but its contextual constraints and semantics are specified informally. This specification is by no means easy reading.

Exercises

1.1   In this chapter editors, compilers, and interpreters have been cited as kinds of language processor. Can you think of any other kinds of language processor?

1.2*   Recall Examples 1.1 and 1.2. Write a similar critical account of any other programming system with which you are familiar.

1.3**   Design an editor tailored to your favorite programming language.

        (*Hints:* Think of the editing operations you perform most frequently on your programs. You probably delete or replace complete symbols more often than individual characters, and you probably delete or replace complete phrases –

expressions, commands, declarations – rather than individual lines. You probably spend a lot of time on chores such as good layout. Also think of the
common syntactic errors that might reasonably be detected immediately.)

1.4   According to the context-free grammar of Mini-Triangle in Example 1.3,
which of the following are Mini-Triangle expressions?

(a) `true`

(b) `sin(x)`

(c) `-n`

(d) `m >= n`

(e) `m - n * 2`

Draw the syntax tree and AST of each one that *is* an expression.

Similarly, which of the following are Mini-Triangle commands?

(f) `n := n + 1`

(g) `halt`

(h) `put(m, n)`

(i) `if n > m then m := n`

(j) `while n > 0 do n := n-1`

Similarly, which of the following are Mini-Triangle declarations?

(k) `const pi ~ 3.1416`

(l) `const y ~ x+1`

(m) `var b: Boolean`

(n) `var m, n: Integer`

(o) `var y: Integer; const dpy ~ 365`

1.5   Draw the syntax tree and AST of the Mini-Triangle command:

```
while b do n := 0; b := false
```

cited at the end of Example 1.5. Compare with Figures 1.2 and 1.5.

1.6   According to the syntax and semantics of Mini-Triangle in Examples 1.3 and
1.8, what value is written by the following Mini-Triangle program? (The standard procedure `putint` writes its argument, an integer value.)

```
let
   const m ~ 2;
   const n ~ m + 1
in
   putint(m + n * 2)
```

(*Note:* Do not be misled by your knowledge of any other languages.)

guage Processors

In this book we shall study two particularly important kinds of language processor: translators (particularly compilers) and interpreters. In this chapter we start by reviewing the basic ideas of translation and interpretation, which will already be familiar to most readers. Then we build on these basic ideas to explore the more sophisticated ways in which language processors can be used. A language processor is itself a program, and thus can be processed (translated or interpreted) in just the same way as an ordinary program. The ultimate development of this idea is bootstrapping, whereby a language processor is used to process itself!

In this chapter we view translators and interpreters as 'black boxes'; we concentrate on what they do rather than how they do it. In subsequent chapters we shall look inside them to see how they work.

2.1 Translators and compilers

A *translator* is a program that accepts any text expressed in one language (the translator's *source language*), and generates a semantically-equivalent text expressed in another language (its *target language*).

Example 2.1 Translators

Here are some diverse examples of translators:

(a) A Chinese-into-English translator: This is a program that translates Chinese texts into English. The source and target languages of this translator are both natural languages.

   Natural-language translation is an advanced topic, related to artificial intelligence, and well beyond the scope of this textbook. We shall restrict our attention to translators whose source and target languages are programming languages.

(b) A Java-into-C translator: This is a program that translates Java programs into C. The source language is Java, and the target language is C.

26

(c)   A Java-into-x86[1] compiler: This is a program that translates Java programs into x86 machine code. The source language is Java, and the target language is x86 machine code.

(d)   An x86 assembler: This is a program that translates x86 assembly-language programs into x86 machine code. The source language is x86 assembly language, and the target language is x86 machine code.

An **assembler** translates from an assembly language into the corresponding machine code. An example is the x86 assembler of Example 2.1(d). Typically, an assembler generates one machine-code instruction per source instruction.

A **compiler** translates from a high-level language into a low-level language. An example is the Java-into-x86 compiler of Example 2.1(c). Typically, a compiler generates several machine-code instructions per source command.

Assemblers and compilers are the most important kinds of programming language translator, but not the only kinds. We sometimes come across *high-level translators* whose source and target languages are both high-level languages, such as the Java-into-C translator of Example 2.1(b). A *disassembler* translates a machine code into the corresponding assembly language. A *decompiler* translates a low-level language into a high-level language. (See Exercise 2.1.)

Here the translated texts are themselves programs. The source language text is called the **source program**, and the target language text is called the **object program**.

Before performing any translation, a compiler checks that the source text really is a well-formed program of the source language. (Otherwise it generates error reports.) These checks take into account the *syntax* and the *contextual constraints* of the source language. Assuming that the source program is indeed well-formed, the compiler goes on to generate an object program that is semantically equivalent to the source program, i.e., that will have exactly the desired effect when run. Generation of the object program takes into account the *semantics* of the source and target languages.

Translators, and other language processors, are programs that manipulate programs. Several languages are involved: not only the source language and the target language, but also the language in which the translator is itself expressed! The latter is called the *implementation language*.

To help avoid confusion, we shall use **tombstone diagrams** to represent ordinary programs and language processors, and to express manipulations of programs by language processors. We shall use one form of tombstone to represent an ordinary program, and distinctive forms of tombstone to represent translators and interpreters.

---

[1]   We use the term x86 to refer to the family of processors represented by the Intel 80386 processor and its successors.

An ordinary program is represented by a round-topped tombstone, as shown in Figure 2.1. The head of the tombstone names the program *P*. The base of the tombstone names the implementation language *L*, i.e., the language in which the program is expressed.

Figure 2.1 Tombstone representing a program *P* expressed in language *L*.

Example 2.2   Tombstone diagrams representing programs

The following diagrams show how we represent:

(a)   A program named `sort` expressed in Java.

(b)   A program named `sort` expressed in x86 machine code. (By convention, we abbreviate 'x86 machine code' to 'x86'.)

(c)   A program named `graph` expressed in Basic.

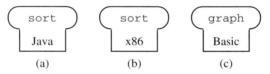

Programs run on machines. A machine that executes machine code *M* is represented by a pentagon inside which *M* is named, as shown in Figure 2.2.

Figure 2.2 Tombstone representing a machine *M*.

Example 2.3   Tombstone diagrams representing machines

The following diagrams show how we represent:

(a)   An x86 machine.

(b)   A Power PC (PPC) machine.

(c)   A SPARC machine.

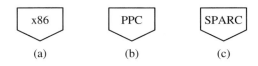

| (a) | (b) | (c) |

A program can run on a machine only if it is expressed in the appropriate machine code. Consider running a program *P* (expressed in machine code *M*) on machine *M*. We represent this by putting the *P* tombstone on top of the *M* pentagon, as shown in Figure 2.3.

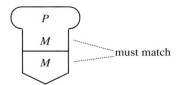

Figure 2.3 Running program *P* on machine *M*.

Example 2.4   Tombstone diagrams representing program execution

The following diagrams show how we represent:

(a)   Running program `sort` (expressed in x86 machine code) on an x86 machine.

(b)   Running program `sort` (expressed in PPC machine code) on a PPC machine.

(c)   Attempting to run program `sort` (expressed in PPC machine code) on an x86 machine. Of course, this will not work; the diagram clearly shows that the machine code in which the program is expressed does not match the machine on which we are attempting to run the program.

(d)   Attempting to run program `sort` (expressed in Java) on an x86 machine. This will not work either; a program expressed in a high-level language cannot run immediately on any machine. (It must first be translated into machine code.)

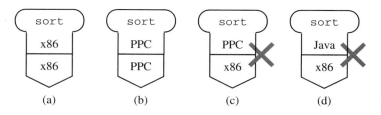

We have now introduced the elementary forms of tombstone. There are also distinctive forms of tombstone to represent different kinds of language processor. A translator is represented by a T-shaped tombstone, as shown in Figure 2.4. The head of the tombstone names the translator's source language S and target language T, separated by an arrow. The base of the tombstone names the translator's implementation language L.[2]

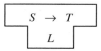

Figure 2.4 Tombstone representing an S-into-T translator expressed in language L.

Example 2.5   Tombstones representing translators

The following diagrams show how we represent:

(a)   A Java-into-x86 compiler, expressed in C.

(b)   A Java-into-x86 compiler, expressed in x86 machine code.

(c)   A Java-into-C translator, expressed in C++.

(d)   An x86 assembler, which translates from x86 assembly language into x86 machine code, and is itself expressed in x86 machine code.

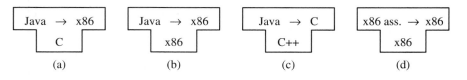

---

[2]   Although we use tombstones of different shapes to represent ordinary programs, translators, and interpreters, the base of a tombstone always names the implementation language. Compare Figures 2.1, 2.4, and 2.6.

An *S*-into-*T* translator is itself a program, and can run on machine *M* only if it is expressed in machine code *M*. When the translator runs, it translates a source program *P*, expressed in the source language *S*, to an equivalent object program *P*, expressed in the target language *T*. This is shown in Figure 2.5. (The object program is shaded gray, to emphasize that it is newly generated, unlike the translator and source program, which must be given at the start.)

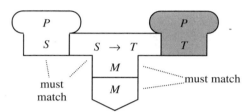

Figure 2.5 Translating a source program *P* expressed in language *S* to an object program expressed in language *T*, using an *S*-into-*T* translator running on machine *M*.

Example 2.6   Compilation

The following diagram represents compilation of a Java program on an x86 machine. Using the Java-into-x86 compiler, we translate the source program `sort` to an equivalent object program, expressed in x86 machine code. Since the compiler is itself expressed in x86 machine code, the compiler will run on an x86 machine.

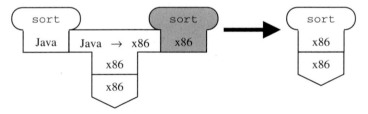

The second stage of the diagram shows the object program being run, also on an x86 machine.

A *cross-compiler* is a compiler that runs on one machine (the *host machine*) but generates code for a dissimilar machine (the *target machine*). The object program must be generated on the host machine but downloaded to the target machine to be run. A cross-compiler is a useful tool if the target machine has too little memory to accommodate the compiler, or if the target machine is ill-equipped with program development aids. (Compilers tend to be large programs, needing a good programming environment to develop, and needing ample memory to run.)

Example 2.7   Cross-compilation

The following diagram represents cross-compilation of a Java program to enable it to run on a Power PC microprocessor. Using a Java-into-PPC cross-compiler, we translate the source program `sort` to an equivalent object program, expressed in PPC machine code. Since the compiler is itself expressed in x86 machine code, the compiler runs on an x86 machine.

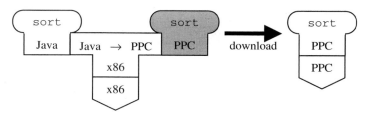

The second stage of the diagram shows the object program being run on a PPC machine, having been downloaded from the x86.

□

The behavior of a translator can be summarized by a few simple rules, which are clearly evident in Figure 2.5:

- A translator (like any other program) can run on a machine *M* only if it is expressed in machine code *M*.

- The source program must be expressed in the translator's source language *S*.

- The object program is expressed in the translator's target language *T*.

- The object program is semantically equivalent to the source program. (We emphasize this by giving the source and object programs the same name.)

Example 2.8   Illegal translator interactions

The following tombstone diagrams illustrate what we *cannot* do with a translator:

(a)   A C compiler cannot translate a Java source program.

(b)   A translator expressed in x86 machine code cannot run on a PPC machine.

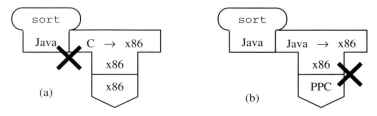

Similarly, it should be clear that a translator expressed in C or Java cannot run on any machine. (It must first be translated into machine code.)

□

A *two-stage translator* is a composition of two translators. If we have an *S*-into-*T* translator and a *T*-into-*U* translator, we can compose them to make a two-stage *S*-into-*U* translator. The source language *S* is translated to the target language *U* not directly, but via an intermediate language *T*.

We can easily generalize this idea to multiple stages. An *n-stage translator* is a composition of *n* translators, and involves *n*–1 intermediate languages.

Example 2.9   *Two-stage compilation*

Given a Java-into-C translator and a C-into-x86 compiler, we can compose them to make a two-stage Java-into-x86 compiler, as shown below. The Java source program is translated into C, which is then compiled into x86 machine code.

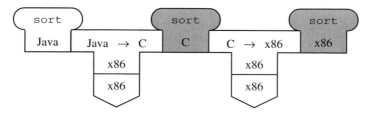

The two-stage compiler is functionally equivalent to a Java-into-x86 compiler.

□

A translator is itself a program, expressed in some language. As such, it can be translated into another language.

Example 2.10 *Compiling a compiler*

Suppose we have a Java-into-x86 compiler expressed in C. We cannot run this compiler at all, because it is not expressed in machine code. But we can treat it as an ordinary source program to be translated by a C-into-x86 compiler:

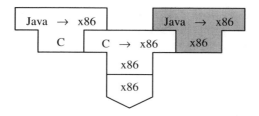

The object program is a Java-into-x86 compiler expressed in x86 machine code (shaded gray). We can now use this to compile Java programs, as illustrated in Example 2.6.

□

More generally, all language processors are themselves programs, and as such can be manipulated by other language processors. For example, language processors can be translated (as in Example 2.10) or interpreted. We shall see the importance of this later in the chapter.

2.2   Interpreters

A compiler allows us to prepare a program to be run on a machine, by first translating the program into machine code. The program will then run at full machine speed. This method of working is not without disadvantages, however: the entire program must be translated before it can even start to run and produce results. In an interactive environment, *interpretation* is often a more attractive method of working. Thus we come to a new kind of language processor, an interpreter, that also allows us to run programs.

An **interpreter** is a program that accepts any program (the *source program*) expressed in a particular language (the *source language*), and runs that source program immediately.

An interpreter works by fetching, analyzing, and executing the source program instructions, *one at a time*. The source program starts to run and produce results as soon as the first instruction has been analyzed. The interpreter does *not* translate the source program into object code prior to execution.

Interpretation is sensible when most of the following circumstances exist:

• The programmer is working in interactive mode, and wishes to see the results of each instruction before entering the next instruction.

• The program is to be used once and then discarded (i.e., it is a 'throw-away' program), and therefore running speed is not very important.

• Each instruction is expected to be executed only once (or at least not very frequently).

• The instructions have simple formats, and thus can be analyzed easily and efficiently.

Interpretation is very slow. Interpretation of a source program, in a high-level language, can be up to 100 times slower than running an equivalent machine-code program. Therefore interpretation is not sensible when:

• The program is to be run in production mode, and therefore speed is important.

• The instructions are expected to be executed frequently.

• The instructions have complicated formats, and are therefore time-consuming to analyze. (This is the case in most high-level languages.)

Example 2.11 Interpreters

Here are some well-known examples of interpreters:

(a)   A Basic interpreter: Basic has expressions and assignment commands like other high-level languages. But its control structures are low-level: a program is just a sequence of commands linked by conditional and unconditional jumps. A Basic interpreter fetches, analyzes, and executes one command at a time.

(b)   A Lisp interpreter: Lisp is a very unusual language in that it assumes a common data structure (trees) for both code and data. Indeed, a Lisp program can manufacture new code at run-time! The Lisp program structure lends itself to interpretation. (See also Exercise 2.10.)

(c)   The UNIX command language interpreter (*shell*): A UNIX user instructs the operating system by entering textual commands. The *shell* program reads each command, analyzes it to extract a command-name together with some arguments, and executes the command by means of a system call. The user can see the results of a command before entering the next one. The commands constitute a command language, and the *shell* is an interpreter for that command language.

(d)   An SQL interpreter: SQL is a database query language. The user extracts information from the database by entering an SQL query, which is analyzed and executed immediately. This is done by an SQL interpreter within the database management system.

An interpreter is represented by a rectangular tombstone, as shown in Figure 2.6. The head of the tombstone names the interpreter's source language. The base of the tombstone (as usual) names the implementation language.

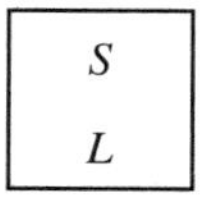

$$\boxed{\begin{array}{c} S \\ \hline L \end{array}}$$

Figure 2.6 Tombstone representing an S interpreter expressed in language L.

Example 2.12 Tombstones representing interpreters

The following diagrams show how we represent:

(a)   A Basic interpreter, expressed in x86 machine code.

(b)   An SQL interpreter, expressed in x86 machine code.

(c)   The UNIX shell (command language interpreter), expressed in C.

(d)   The UNIX shell, expressed in SPARC machine code.

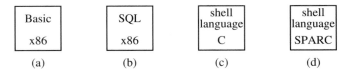

Basic	SQL	shell language	shell language
x86	x86	C	SPARC
(a)	(b)	(c)	(d)

An *S* interpreter is itself a program, and can run on machine *M* only if it is expressed in machine code *M*. When the interpreter runs, it runs a source program *P*, which must be expressed in source language *S*. We say that *P* runs *on top of* the *S* interpreter. This is shown in Figure 2.7.

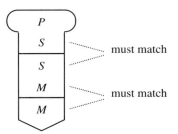

Figure 2.7 Interpreting a program *P* expressed in language *S*, using an *S* interpreter running on machine *M*.

Example 2.13

The following diagrams show how we represent:

(a)   Running program `graph` (expressed in Basic) on top of a Basic interpreter, which itself runs on an x86 machine.

(b)   Running program `chess` (expressed in Lisp) on top of a Lisp interpreter, which itself runs on an x86 machine.

(c)   Attempting to run program `chess` (expressed in Lisp) on top of a Basic interpreter. Of course, this will not work; the diagram clearly shows that the language in which the program is expressed does not match the interpreter's source language.

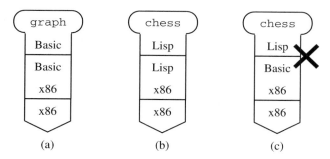

(a)   (b)   (c)

2.3   Real and abstract machines

The interpreters mentioned in Example 2.12 were all for (relatively) high-level languages. But interpreters for low-level languages are also useful.

Example 2.14 Hardware emulation

Suppose that a computer engineer has designed the architecture and instruction set of a radical new machine, Ultima. Now, actually constructing Ultima as a piece of hardware will be an expensive and time-consuming job. Modifying the hardware to implement design changes will likewise be costly. It would be wise to defer hardware construction until the engineer has somehow tested the design. But how can a paper design be tested?

There is a remarkably simple method that is both cheap and fast: we write an interpreter for Ultima machine code. E.g., we could write the interpreter in C:

We can now translate the interpreter into some machine code, say *M*, using the C compiler:

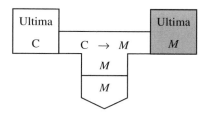

This gives us an Ultima interpreter expressed in *M* machine code (shaded gray above). Now we can run Ultima machine-code programs on top of the interpreter, which itself runs on *M*, as shown below left:

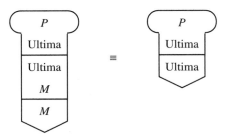

In all respects except speed, the effect is the same as running the programs on Ultima itself, as shown above right.

This kind of interpreter is often called an *emulator*. It cannot be used to measure the emulated machine's absolute speed, because interpretation slows everything down. But emulation can still be used to obtain useful quantitative information: counting memory cycles, estimating the degree of parallelism, and so on. It can also be used to obtain qualitative information about how well the architecture and instruction set meet the needs of programmers.

□

Running a program on top of an interpreter is functionally equivalent to running the same program directly on a machine, as illustrated in Example 2.14. The user sees the same behavior in terms of the program's inputs and outputs. The two processes are even similar in detail: an interpreter works in a fetch–analyze–execute cycle, and a machine works in a fetch–decode–execute cycle. The only difference is that an interpreter is a software artifact, whereas a machine is a hardware artifact (and therefore much faster).

Thus a machine may be viewed as an interpreter implemented in hardware. Conversely, an interpreter may be viewed as a machine implemented by software. We sometimes call an interpreter an ***abstract machine***, as opposed to its hardware counterpart, which is a ***real machine***. An abstract machine is functionally equivalent to a real machine if they both implement the same language *L*. This is summarized in Figure 2.8.

A related observation is that there is no fundamental difference between machine codes and other low-level languages. By a machine code we just mean a language for which a hardware interpreter exists.

Figure 2.8 An abstract machine is functionally equivalent to a real machine.

2.4   Interpretive compilers

A compiler may take quite a long time to translate a source program into machine code, but then the object program will run at full machine speed. An interpreter allows the program to start running immediately, but it will run very slowly (up to 100 times more slowly than the machine-code program).

An **interpretive compiler** is a combination of compiler and interpreter, giving some of the advantages of each. The key idea is to translate the source program into an *intermediate language*, designed to the following requirements:

• it is intermediate in level between the source language and ordinary machine code;

• its instructions have simple formats, and therefore can be analyzed easily and quickly;

• translation from the source language into the intermediate language is easy and fast.

Thus an interpretive compiler combines fast compilation with tolerable running speed.

Example 2.15 Interpretive compilation

Sun Microsystems' Java Development Kit (JDK) is an implementation of an interpretive compiler for Java. At its heart is the Java Virtual Machine (JVM), a powerful abstract machine.

JVM-code is an intermediate language oriented to Java. It provides powerful instructions that correspond directly to Java operations such as object creation, method call, and array indexing. Thus translation from Java into JVM-code is easy and fast. Although powerful, JVM-code instructions have simple formats like machine-code instructions, with operation fields and operand fields, and so are easy to analyze. Thus JVM-code interpretation is relatively fast: 'only' about ten times slower than machine code.

JDK consists of a Java-into-JVM-code translator and a JVM-code interpreter, both of which run on some machine *M*:

A Java program *P* is first translated into JVM-code, and then the JVM-code object program is interpreted:

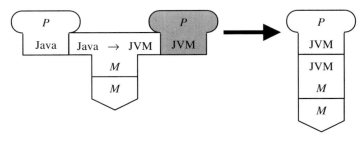

Interpretive compilers are very useful language processors. In the early stages of program development, the programmer might well spend more time compiling than running the program, since he or she is repeatedly discovering and correcting simple syntactic, contextual, and logical errors. At that stage fast compilation is more important than fast running, so an interpretive compiler is ideal. (Later, and especially when the program is put into production use, the program will be run many times but rarely recompiled. At that stage fast running will assume paramount importance, so a compiler that generates efficient machine code will be required. In Java, this problem is typically addressed by a so-called *just-in-time compiler*. See Section 2.8 and Exercise 2.7.)

2.5   Portable compilers

A program is *portable* to the extent that it can be (compiled and) run on any machine, without change. We can measure portability roughly by the proportion of code that remains unchanged when the program is moved to a dissimilar machine. Portability is an economic issue: a portable program is more valuable than an unportable one, because its development cost can be spread over more copies.

The language in which the program is expressed has a major impact on its portability. At one extreme, a program expressed in assembly language cannot be moved to a dissimilar machine unless it is completely rewritten, so its portability is 0%. A program expressed in a high-level language is much more portable. Ideally, it only needs to be recompiled when moved to a dissimilar machine, in which case its portability is 100%. However, this ideal is often quite elusive. For example, a program's behavior might be altered (perhaps subtly) by moving it to a machine with a different character set or different arithmetic. Written with care, however, application programs expressed in high-level languages should achieve 95–99% portability.

Similar points apply to language processors, which are themselves programs. Indeed, it is particularly important for language processors to be portable because they are especially valuable and widely-used programs. For this reason language processors are commonly written in high-level languages such as Pascal, C, and Java.

Unfortunately, it is particularly hard to make compilers portable. A compiler's function is to generate machine code for a particular machine, a function that is machine-dependent by its very nature. If we have a C-into-x86 compiler expressed in a high-level language, we should be able to move this compiler quite easily to run on a dissimilar machine, but it will still generate x86 machine code! To change the compiler to generate different machine code would require about half the compiler to be rewritten, implying that the compiler is only about 50% portable.

It might seem that highly portable compilers are unattainable. However, the situation is not quite so gloomy: a compiler that generates intermediate language is potentially much more portable than a compiler that generates machine code.

Example 2.16 A portable compiler kit

Consider the possibility of producing a portable Java compiler kit. Such a kit would consist of a Java-into-JVM-code translator, expressed both in Java and in JVM-code, and a JVM-code interpreter, expressed in Java:

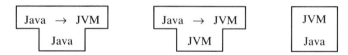

How can we make this work? It seems that we cannot compile Java programs until we have an implementation of JVM-code, and we cannot use the JVM-code interpreter until we can compile Java programs! Fortunately, a small amount of work can get us out of this chicken-and-egg situation.

Suppose that we want to get the system running on machine *M*, and suppose that we already have a compiler for a suitable high-level language, such as C, on this machine.

Then we rewrite the interpreter in C:

and then compile it:

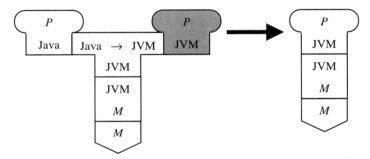

Now we have an interpretive compiler, similar to the one described in Example 2.15. There is one difference: the compiler itself, being expressed in JVM-code, has to run on top of the JVM-code interpreter:

The JVM-code interpreter is much smaller and simpler than the compiler, so rewriting the interpreter is an easy job (a few days' work for an experienced programmer). Consequently, our example compiler kit as a whole would be about 95% portable. If no suitable high-level language is available, it is even feasible to rewrite the interpreter in assembly language.

Notice that the compiler expressed in Java is not actually needed to bootstrap the portable compiler. It would, however, be used to generate the compiler expressed in JVM-code. It would also prove to be useful in later development of the compiler after the initial move to machine M.

The Java compiler in Example 2.16 must be interpreted, so compilation of a Java source program will be slow. However, the compiler can be improved by bootstrapping, as we shall see in Section 2.6.1.

2.6 Bootstrapping

A language processor, such as a translator or interpreter, is a program that processes programs expressed in a particular language (the source language). The language processor is expressed in some implementation language.

Now suppose that the implementation language *is* the source language: the language processor can be used to process itself! This process is called ***bootstrapping***. The idea seems at first to be paradoxical, but it can be made to work. Indeed, it turns out to be extremely useful. In this section we study several kinds of bootstrapping.

2.6.1   Bootstrapping a portable compiler

In Sections 2.4 and 2.5 we looked at interpretive and portable compilers. These work by translating from the high-level source language into an intermediate language, and then interpreting the latter.

A portable compiler can be bootstrapped to make a true compiler – one that generates machine code – by writing an intermediate-language-into-machine-code translator.

Example 2.17 Bootstrapping an interpretive compiler to generate machine code

Suppose that we have made a portable Java compiler kit into an interpretive compiler running on machine *M*, as described in Example 2.16. We can use this to build an efficient Java-into-*M* compiler, as follows.

First, we write a JVM-code-into-*M* translator, in Java:

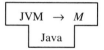

(This is a substantial job, but only about half as much work as writing a complete Java-into-*M* compiler.) Next, we compile this translator using the existing interpretive compiler:

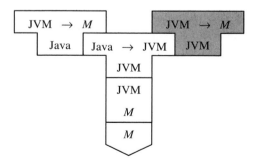

This gives a JVM-code-into-*M* translator expressed in JVM-code itself.

Next, we use this translator to translate *itself* :

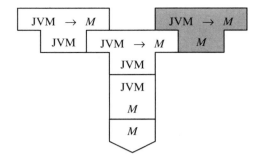

This, the actual bootstrap, gives a JVM-code-into-M translator expressed in machine code M.

Finally, we translate the Java-into-JVM-code translator into machine code:

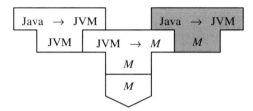

Now we have implemented a two-stage Java-into-M compiler:

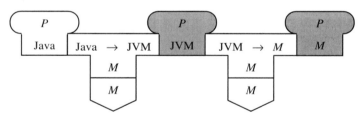

Moreover, the compiler is expressed in machine code, so compilation of a Java source program is much faster than in Example 2.16.

□

2.6.2 Full bootstrap

We have seen that a program, if it is to be portable, should be written in a suitable high-level language, L. That implies a commitment to the language L throughout the program's lifetime. If we wish to make a new version of the program (e.g., to remove known bugs, or to make it more efficient), we must edit the L source program and recompile it. In other words, the program is maintainable only as long as an L compiler is available.

Exactly the same point applies to a language processor expressed in *L*. In Example 2.10, we saw how a Java compiler, expressed in C, could be translated into machine code by a C compiler (and thus enabled to run). However, this Java compiler can be maintained only as long as a C compiler is available. If we wish to make a new version of the Java compiler (e.g., to remove known bugs, or to generate better-quality machine code), we will need a C compiler to recompile the Java compiler.

In general, a compiler whose source language is *S*, expressed in a different high-level language *L*, can be maintained only as long as a compiler for *L* is available. This problem can be avoided by writing the *S* compiler in *S* itself! Whenever we make a new version of the *S* compiler, we use the old version to compile the new version. The only difficulty is how to get started: how can we compile the *first* version of the *S* compiler? The key idea is to start with a subset of *S* – a subset just large enough to be suitable for writing the compiler. The method is called ***full bootstrap*** – since a whole compiler is to be written from scratch.

Example 2.18   Full bootstrap

Suppose that we wish to build an Ada compiler for machine *M*. Now Ada is a very large language, so it makes sense to build the compiler incrementally. We start by selecting a small subset of Ada that will be adequate for compiler writing. (The Pascal-like subset of Ada would be suitable.) Call this subset Ada-S.

We write version 1 of our Ada-S compiler in C (or any suitable language for which a compiler is currently available):

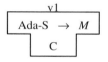

We compile version 1 using the C compiler:

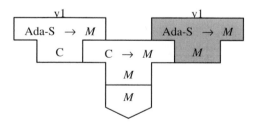

This gives an Ada-S compiler for machine *M*. We can test it by using it to compile and run Ada-S test programs.

But we prefer not to rely permanently on version 1 of the Ada-S compiler, because it is expressed in C, and therefore is maintainable only as long as a C compiler is available. Instead, we make version 2 of the Ada-S compiler, expressed in Ada-S itself:

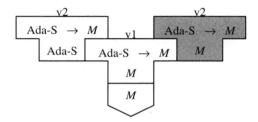

This rewriting of the compiler is not a hard job, because all the algorithms and data structures have already been developed and tested in version 1. (In fact, we could have wisely anticipated the rewriting, by refraining from using C features with no direct counterparts in Ada-S.)

Now we use version 1 to compile version 2:

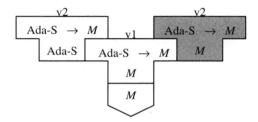

As usual, we can test version 2 of the Ada-S compiler by using it to compile and run Ada-S test programs. We have now broken our dependency on C, because the version-2 Ada-S compiler is expressed in Ada-S itself.

Finally, we extend the Ada-S compiler to a (full) Ada compiler, giving version 3:

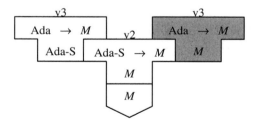

and compile it using version 2:

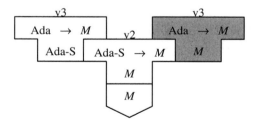

This gives us an Ada compiler expressed in Ada itself. (Actually it is expressed in a subset of Ada, but that does not matter.) This compiler can be used to maintain itself by using version 3 to compile version 4, and so on.

2.6.3   Half bootstrap

Suppose that we have a compiler that runs on a machine *HM*, and generates *HM*'s machine code; now we wish to move the compiler to run on a dissimilar machine *TM*. In this transaction *HM* is called the *host machine*, and *TM* is called the *target machine*.

If the compiler is expressed in a high-level language for which we have a compiler on *TM*, just getting the compiler to run on *TM* is straightforward, but we would still have a compiler that generates *HM*'s machine code. It would, in fact, be a cross-compiler.

To make our compiler generate *TM*'s machine code, we have no choice but to rewrite part of the compiler. As we shall see in Chapter 3, one of the major parts of a compiler is the *code generator*, which does the actual translation into the target language. Typically the code generator is about half of the compiler. If our compiler has been constructed in a modular fashion, it is not too difficult to strip out the old code generator, which generated *HM*'s machine code; then we can substitute the new code generator, which will generate *TM*'s machine code.

If the compiler is expressed in its own source language, this process is called a **half bootstrap** – since roughly half the compiler must be modified. It does not depend on any compiler or assembler being already available on the target machine – indeed, it depends *only* on the host machine compiler!

Example 2.19 Half bootstrap

Suppose that we have a Ada compiler that generates machine code for machine *HM*. The compiler is expressed in Ada itself, and in *HM*'s machine code:

We wish to bootstrap this compiler to machine *TM*. To be precise, we want a compiler that runs on *TM* and generates *TM*'s machine code.

First, we modify the compiler's code generator to generate *TM*'s machine code:

We compile the modified compiler, using the original compiler, to obtain a cross-compiler:

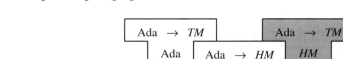

How do we test the cross-compiler? We can run it on *HM* to compile Ada test programs into *TM*'s machine code, and then download the object programs to *TM* to be run:

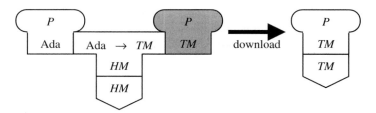

(Visual inspection of the object code is also a good idea, but practicable only for small test programs.)

Once we are satisfied that the cross-compiler is correct, we can use it to compile *itself* into *TM*'s machine code (the actual bootstrap):

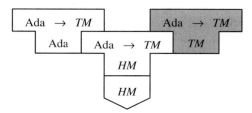

Finally, we download the Ada-into-*TM* compiler (expressed in both Ada and *TM*'s machine code) to the target machine *TM*, and subsequently maintain it there.

2.6.4   Bootstrapping to improve efficiency

The efficiency of an ordinary program can be measured with respect to either time or space: how fast does it run, and how much storage space does it require?

When we discuss the efficiency of a compiler, the situation is more complicated. We can measure the efficiency of the compiler itself, and we can measure the efficiency of the object programs it generates.

In this chapter, we are not concerned with techniques for generating efficient object programs. But we can show that bootstrapping is a useful *strategy* for taking a simple compiler and upgrading it to generate more efficient object programs. The basic idea is to use the existing version of the compiler to compile the new version, and to do this repeatedly to make better and better versions.

Example 2.20 Bootstrapping to improve object code

Suppose that we have an Ada compiler, version 1, that generates slow machine code. Version 1 is expressed in slow machine code, as well as in Ada:

In the diagrams we will use notation like M_{fast} and M_{slow} to indicate fast and slow machine code, respectively. (Note that M_{fast} and M_{slow} are the same language, the machine code M; the subscripts are merely indications of code *quality*.)

When we compile Ada programs, both the version-1 compiler and its object programs will be slow. (Why?) Our objective is to make a fast compiler that generates fast object programs.

First, we modify version 1 to make a version-2 compiler that generates faster machine code:

v2
| Ada → M_{fast} |
| Ada |

We can use version 1 to compile version 2:

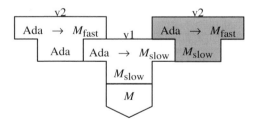

This gives us a better compiler, which we can use to compile Ada programs:

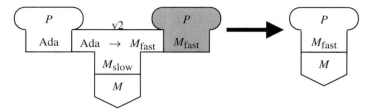

Compilation will still be slow (since the compiler is expressed in slow machine code), but the object program will be fast (since the generated machine code is fast).

The final stage of bootstrapping is to use version 2 to compile itself:

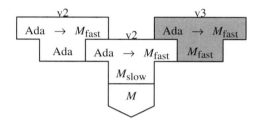

This gives us version 3, a fast compiler that generates fast object programs:

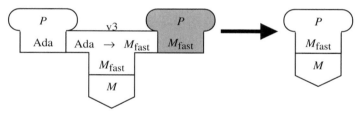

In practice, the bootstrapping steps illustrated in Example 2.20 would be used many times, as the compiler is gradually improved to generate better and better object code.

2.7   Case study: the Triangle language processor

The Triangle language processor will be used as a case study throughout this book. It consists of a compiler, an interpreter, and a disassembler. We will study how they work in the following chapters. Here we examine the Triangle language processor's overall structure. (See Figure 2.9.)

The compiler translates Triangle source programs into TAM code. *TAM* (Triangle Abstract Machine) is an abstract machine, implemented by an interpreter. TAM has been designed to facilitate the implementation of Triangle – although it would be equally suitable for implementing Algol, Pascal, and similar languages. Like JVM-code (Example 2.15), TAM's primitive operations are more similar to the operations of a high-level language than to the very primitive operations of a typical real machine. As a consequence, the translation from Triangle into TAM code is straightforward and fast.

The Triangle-into-TAM compiler and the TAM interpreter together constitute an interpretive compiler, much like the one described in Example 2.15. (See Exercise 2.2.) The TAM disassembler translates a TAM machine code program into *TAL* (Triangle Assembly Language). It is used to inspect the object programs produced by the Triangle-into-TAM compiler.

Figure 2.9 The compiler, interpreter, and disassembler components
of the Triangle language processor.

2.8   Further reading

A number of authors have used tombstone diagrams to represent language processors and their interactions. The formalism was fully developed, complete with mathematical underpinnings, by Earley and Sturgis (1970). Their paper also presents an algorithm that systematically determines all the tombstones that can be generated from a given initial set of tombstones.

A case study of compiler development by full bootstrap may be found in Wirth (1971). A case study of compiler development by half bootstrap may be found in Welsh and Quinn (1972). Finally, a case study of compiler improvement by bootstrapping may be found in Ammann (1981). Interestingly, all these three case studies are interlinked: Wirth's Pascal compiler was the starting point for the other two developments.

Bootstrapping has a longer history, the basic idea being described by several authors in the 1950s. (At that time compiler development itself was still in its infancy!) The first well-known application of the idea seems to have been a program called `eval`, which was a Lisp interpreter expressed in Lisp itself (McCarthy *et al.* 1965).

Sun Microsystems' Java Development Kit (JDK) consists of a compiler that translates Java code to JVM code, a JVM interpreter, and a number of other tools. The compiler (`javac`) is written in Java itself, having been bootstrapped from an initial version written in C. The interpreter (java) is written in C, for efficiency. Most web browsers contain an embedded JVM interpreter to allow them to run Java software downloaded from the Internet. For a comprehensive account of the Java Virtual Machine, see Lindholm and Yellin (1999).

Java software has to be highly portable, especially applets that may be downloaded from a host computer and run on any computer connected to the Internet. In this context, the use of an interpretive compiler makes sense, but for some applications the run-time performance penalty is excessive. This observation has led to the appearance of JIT (just-in-time) compilers. A JIT compiler translates program code into machine code just when it is loaded into memory for execution. In particular, a Java JIT compiler translates JVM code into machine code each time a class is loaded. Since classes are loaded dynamically (during execution), JIT compilation also happens dynamically. Portability is not affected, since Java software is still stored on the host computer and downloaded to the user's computer as JVM code; the JIT compiler runs on the user's computer. If a user does not have a JIT compiler, the same Java software can still be run (albeit more slowly) using the JVM interpreter embedded in the user's Internet browser.

Some Java JIT compilers are even more dynamic than suggested in the previous paragraph. They keep track of the number of calls to individual methods, and translate only the most frequently-executed methods into machine code. The less frequently-executed methods remain as JVM code and are still interpreted. This more complex scheme seems to yield a good tradeoff between compilation time and execution time. Just-in-time compilation is explained in a paper by Adl-Tabatabai *et al.* (1998).

Exercises

2.1*   Consider each of the following (hypothetical) translators. Do you think the translator might be useful in practice? Explain your answer. Also, what difficulties could be anticipated in making it generate a good-quality object program?

(a)   a Java-into-C translator;

(b)   a C-into-Java translator;

(c)   an assembly-language-into-Pascal decompiler.

2.2   From the description of the Triangle language processor in Section 2.7, use tombstone diagrams to show:

(a)   compiling a Triangle source program *P*;

(b)   running the object program;

(c)   disassembling the object program.

2.3   Assume that you have the following: a machine *M*; a C compiler that runs on machine *M* and generates machine code *M*; and a Java-into-C translator expressed in C. Use tombstone diagrams to represent these language processors. Also show how you would use these language processors to:

(a)   compile and run a program *P* expressed in C;

(b)   compile the Java-into-C translator into machine code;

(c)   compile and run a program *Q* expressed in Java.

2.4   Assume that you have the following: a machine *M*; a C compiler that runs on machine *M* and generates machine code *M*; a TAM interpreter expressed in C; and a Pascal-into-TAM compiler expressed in C. Use tombstone diagrams to represent these language processors. Also show how you would use these language processors to:

(a)   compile the TAM interpreter into machine code;

(b)   compile the Pascal-into-TAM compiler into machine code;

(c)   compile and run a program *P* expressed in Pascal.

2.5   The Gnu compiler kit uses a machine-independent register transfer language, RTL, as an intermediate language. The kit includes translators from several high-level languages (such as C, C++, Pascal) into RTL, and translators from RTL into several machine codes (such as Alpha, PPC, SPARC). It also includes an RTL 'optimizer', i.e., a program that translates RTL into more efficient RTL. All of these translators are expressed in C.

(a)   Show how you would install these translators on a SPARC machine, given a C compiler for the SPARC.

Now show how you would use these translators to:

(b)   compile a program *P*, expressed in Pascal, into SPARC machine code;

(c)   compile the same program, but using the RTL optimizer to generate more efficient object code;

(d)   cross-compile a program *Q*, expressed in C++, into PPC machine code.

2.6   The Triangle language processor (see Section 2.7) is expressed entirely in Java. Use tombstone diagrams to show how the compiler, interpreter, and disassembler would be made to run on machine *M*. Assume that a Java-into-*M* compiler is available.

2.7   Draw tombstone diagrams to illustrate the use of a Java JIT (just-in-time) compiler. Show what happens when a Java program *P* is compiled and stored on a host machine *H*, and subsequently downloaded for execution on the user's machine U. Assume that a JIT compiler is available that runs on and generates code for machine U.

2.8*   Suppose that you have designed a language C+, which is C extended with packages. (A package is just a named group of global declarations, some of which are designated as exported by the package; the remaining declarations are visible only inside the package. So packages are intended to support a modern programming discipline, rather than adding new functionality to the language.)

A two-stage C-into-M compiler is available, consisting of a C-into-RTL translator and an RTL-into-M translator. The two-stage compiler is available both in C and in machine code M. Machine M is also available.

Suggest *two* different strategies for implementing C+. What are the advantages and disadvantages of each strategy?

2.9*   Suppose that an ambitious new programming language, Utopia, has been designed to meet the needs of all programmers everywhere. Rather than a single language, it is actually a series of nested sublanguages Utopia-1, Utopia-2, and Utopia-3. The smallest sublanguage Utopia-1 has roughly the functionality of C; Utopia-2 has some extra features; and the full language Utopia-3 supports a variety of advanced features such as concurrency.

The motivations for defining the sublanguages were as follows. Some implementors might prefer to develop compilers for the sublanguages only; whereas more ambitious implementors will aim to develop compilers for the full language. Programmers who do not need the functionality of the full language can use a compiler for a sublanguage (and such a compiler will be smaller and faster than a compiler for the full language); but they can easily graduate to the full language if the need arises, without having to rewrite any of their existing programs.

You are required to develop a complete set of compilers for Utopia-1, Utopia-2, and Utopia-3. What strategy would you adopt? You may assume that a C compiler is available. (*Note:* There are several possible strategies. Weigh their advantages and disadvantages carefully.)

2.10*   Consider a programming language that allows code to be manufactured at run-time (such as Lisp, Example 2.11(b)).

(a)   What would be unusual about the *specification* of this language?

(b)   Why would this language normally be implemented by means of an *interpreter*?

(c)   Suppose, nevertheless, that a *compiler* is to be designed for this language. What would be unusual about this compiler?

CHAPTER THREE

Compilation

In this chapter we study the internal structure of compilers. A compiler's basic function is to translate a high-level source program to a low-level object program, but before doing so it must check that the source program is well-formed. So compilation is decomposed into three *phases*: syntactic analysis, contextual analysis, and code generation. In this chapter we study these phases and their relationships. We also examine some possible compiler designs, each design being characterized by the number of passes over the source program or its internal representation, and discuss the issues underlying the choice of compiler design.

In this chapter we restrict ourselves to a shallow exploration of compilation. We shall take a more detailed look at syntactic analysis, contextual analysis, and code generation in Chapters 4, 5, and 7, respectively.

3.1 Phases

Inside any compiler, the source program is subjected to several transformations before an object program is finally generated. These transformations are called *phases*. The three principal phases of compilation are as follows:

- *Syntactic analysis:* The source program is parsed to check whether it conforms to the source language's syntax, and to determine its phrase structure.

- *Contextual analysis:* The parsed program is analyzed to check whether it conforms to the source language's contextual constraints.

- *Code generation:* The checked program is translated to an object program, in accordance with the semantics of the source and target languages.

The three phases of compilation correspond directly to the three parts of the source language's specification: its syntax, its contextual constraints, and its semantics. [1]

---

[1] Some compilers include a fourth phase, code optimization. Lexical analysis is sometimes treated as a distinct phase, but in this book we shall treat it as a sub-phase of syntactic analysis.

Between the phases we need to represent the source program in such a way as to reflect the analysis already done on it. A suitable choice of representation is an abstract syntax tree (AST). The AST explicitly represents the source program's phrase structure. Its subtrees will correspond to the phrases (commands, expressions, declarations, etc.) of the source program. Its leaf nodes will correspond to the identifiers, literals, and operators of the source program. All other terminal symbols in the source program can be discarded after syntactic analysis.

We can conveniently summarize the phases of a compiler by means of a data flow diagram.[2] Figure 3.1 shows the data flow diagram of a typical compiler. It shows the successive transformations effected by the three phases. It also shows that syntactic and contextual analysis may generate error reports, which will be transmitted to the programmer.

Let us now examine the three principal phases in more detail. We shall follow a tiny Triangle program through all the phases of compilation. The source program is shown in Figure 3.2, and the results of successive transformations in Figures 3.3, 3.4, and 3.7.

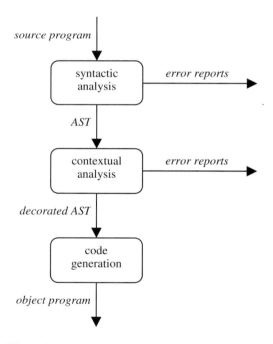

Figure 3.1 Data flow diagram for a typical compiler.

---

[2]   A data flow diagram summarizes data flows and transformations in a system. An arrow represents a data flow, and is labeled by a description of the data. A rounded box represents a transformation, and is labeled accordingly.

In order to be concrete, we shall explain these transformations as implemented in the Triangle compiler that is our case study. It should be understood, however, that another Triangle compiler could implement the transformations in a different way. The main purpose of this section is to explain *what* transformations are performed, not *how* they are implemented. In Section 3.2.2 we shall emphasize this point by sketching an alternative Triangle compiler with a very different design, which nevertheless performs essentially the same processing on the source program.

3.1.1   Syntactic analysis

The purpose of syntactic analysis is to determine the source program's phrase structure. This process is called ***parsing***. It is an essential part of compilation because the subsequent phases (contextual analysis and code generation) depend on knowing how the program is composed from commands, expressions, declarations, and so on.

The source program is parsed to check whether it conforms to the source language's syntax, and to construct a suitable representation of its phrase structure. Here we assume that the chosen representation is an AST.

Example 3.1   Triangle AST

Syntactic analysis of the Triangle source program of Figure 3.2 yields the AST of Figure 3.3. As we shall be studying the compilation of this program in some detail, let us examine those parts of the AST that are numbered in Figure 3.3.

(1)   The program is a let-command. It consists of a declaration ('var n: Integer; var c: Char' in the source program) and a subcommand ('c := '&'; n := n+1'). This is represented by an AST whose root node is labeled 'LetCommand', and whose subtrees represent the declaration and subcommand, respectively.

(2)   This is a variable declaration. It consists of an identifier (n) and a type-denoter (Integer).

(3)   This also is a variable declaration. It consists of an identifier (c) and a type-denoter (Char).

(4)   This is a sequential command. It consists of two subcommands ('c := '&'' and 'n := n+1').

(5)   This is an assignment command. It consists of a value-or-variable-name on the left-hand side (n) and an expression on the right-hand side (n+1).

(6)   This value-or-variable-name is just an identifier (n).

(7)   This is an expression that applies an operator ('+') to two subexpressions.

(8)   This expression is a value-or-variable-name (n).

(9)   This expression is an integer-literal (1).

□

```
! This program is useless
! except for illustration.
let
    var n: Integer;
    var c: Char
in
    begin
    c := '&';
    n := n+1
    end
```

Figure 3.2 A Triangle source program.

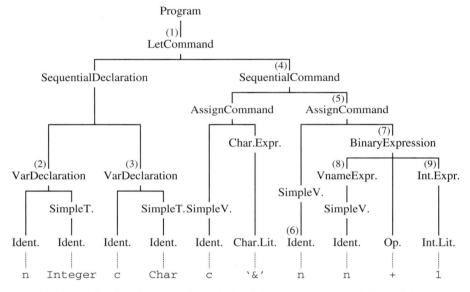

Figure 3.3 AST after syntactic analysis of the source program of Figure 3.2.

In general, the AST has terminal nodes that correspond to identifiers, literals, and operators in the source program, and subtrees that represent the phrases of the source program. Blank space and comments are not represented in the AST, because they contribute nothing to the source program's phrase structure. Punctuation and brackets also have no counterparts in the AST, because they serve only to separate and enclose phrases of the source program; once the source program has been parsed, they are no longer needed. For example, the 'begin' and 'end' brackets in Figure 3.2 serve only to enclose the sequential command 'c := '&'; n := n+1', thus ensuring that the sequential command as a whole is taken as the body of the let-command. The AST's very structure represents this bracketing perfectly well.

If the source program contains syntactic errors, it has no proper phrase structure. In that case, syntactic analysis generates error reports instead of constructing an AST.

3.1.2 Contextual analysis

In contextual analysis the parsed program is further analyzed, to determine whether it conforms to the source language's contextual constraints:

- The source language's scope rules allow us, at compile-time, to associate each applied occurrence of an identifier (e.g., in an expression or command) with the corresponding declaration of that identifier, and to detect any undeclared identifiers. (Here we are assuming that the source language exhibits static binding.)

- The source language's type rules allow us, at compile-time, to infer the type of each expression and to detect any type errors. (Here we are assuming that the source language is statically typed.)

If the parsed program is represented by its AST, then contextual analysis will yield a **decorated AST**. This is an AST enriched with information gathered during contextual analysis:

- As a result of applying the scope rules, each applied occurrence of an identifier is linked to the corresponding declaration. We show this diagrammatically by a dashed arrow.

- As a result of applying the type rules, each expression is decorated by its type T. We show this diagrammatically by marking the expression's root node ': T'.

Example 3.2   Triangle contextual analysis

Triangle exhibits static binding and is statically typed. Contextual analysis of the AST of Figure 3.3 yields the decorated AST of Figure 3.4.

The contextual analyzer checks the declarations as follows:

(2)   It notes that identifier n is declared as a variable of type *int*.

(3)   It notes that identifier c is declared as a variable of type *char*.

The contextual analyzer checks the second assignment command as follows:

(6)   At this applied occurrence of identifier n, it finds the corresponding declaration at (2). It links this node to (2). From the declaration it infers that n is a variable of type *int*.

(8)   Here, similarly, it infers that the expression n is of type *int*.

(9)   This expression, being an integer-literal, is manifestly of type *int*.

(7)   Since the operator '+' is of type $int \times int \rightarrow int$, it checks that the left and right subexpressions are of type *int*, and infers that the whole expression is of type *int*.

(5)   It checks that the left-hand side of the assignment command is a variable, and that the right-hand side is an expression of equivalent type. Here both (6) and (7) are of type *int*, so the assignment command is indeed well-typed.

In this way the contextual analyzer verifies that the source program satisfies all the contextual constraints of Triangle.

□

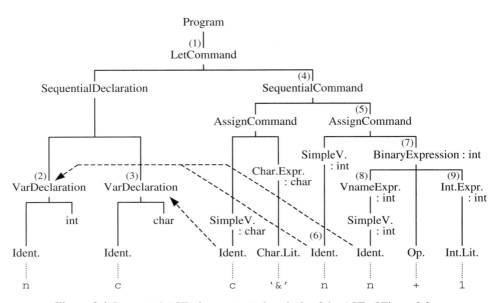

Figure 3.4 Decorated AST after contextual analysis of the AST of Figure 3.3.

If the source program does not satisfy the source language's contextual constraints, contextual analysis generates error reports.

Example 3.3   Detection of Triangle contextual errors

Figures 3.5 and 3.6 illustrate how contextual analysis will detect violations of scope rules and type rules. This particular Triangle program contains three contextual errors:

(1)   The expression of this while-command is not of type *bool*.

(2)   Identifier m is used but not declared.

(3)   In this application of operator '>', which is of type *int* × *int* → *bool*, one subexpression has the wrong type.

□

```
let
    var n: Integer
in  ! ill-formed program
    while n/2 do
        m := 'n' > 1
```

Figure 3.5 An ill-formed Triangle source program.

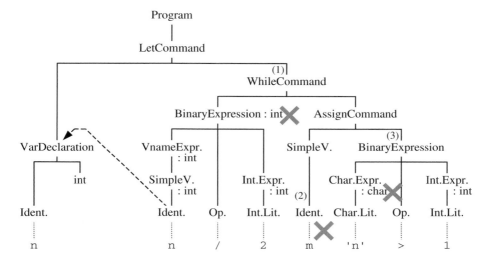

Figure 3.6 Discovering errors during contextual analysis of the Triangle program of Figure 3.5.

3.1.3   Code generation

After syntactic and contextual analysis, the source program has been thoroughly checked and is known to be well-formed. Code generation is the final translation of the checked program to an object program, in accordance with the source and target languages' semantics.

A pervasive issue in code generation is the treatment of identifiers that are declared and/or used in the source program. In semantic terms, a declaration *binds* an identifier to some sort of entity. For example:

- A constant declaration such as 'const m ~ 7' binds the identifier m to the value 7. The code generator must then replace each applied occurrence of m by the value 7.

- A variable declaration such as 'var b: Boolean' binds the identifier b to some address (storage cell), which is decided by the code generator itself. The code generator must then replace each applied occurrence of b by the address to which it is bound.

A rather different issue for the compiler designer is the exact nature of the target language: should the compiler generate machine code or the assembly language of the target machine? Actually, the choice has only minor influence on the structure of the compiler, and we shall not pursue the issue in this book. When presenting examples of object code, however, we always write instructions mnemonically (as in Figure 3.7), since this is considerably more readable than the equivalent binary machine code.

```
PUSH   2
LOADL  38
STORE  1[SB]
LOAD   0[SB]
LOADL  1
CALL   add
STORE  0[SB]
POP    2
HALT
```

Figure 3.7 Object program after code generation from Figure 3.4.

Example 3.4   TAM code generation

Code generation from the decorated AST of Figure 3.4 yields the TAM object program of Figure 3.7.

The code generator processes the declarations as follows:

(2)   It allocates an address for the variable n, say 0[SB]. It stores that address at node (2), for later retrieval.[3]

(3)   It similarly allocates an address for the variable c, say 1[SB]. It stores that address at node (3), for later retrieval.

The code generator processes the second assignment command as follows:

(8)   By following the link to the declaration of n, it retrieves this variable's address, namely 0[SB]. Then it generates the instruction 'LOAD 0[SB]'. (When executed, this instruction will fetch the current value of that variable.)

(9)   It generates the instruction 'LOADL 1'. (When executed, this instruction will fetch the literal value 1.)

---

[3]   Here '0[SB]' means address 0 relative to the base register SB – but you will be able to follow this example without knowing TAM's addressing mechanism.

(7) It generates the instruction 'CALL *add*'. (When executed, this instruction will add the two previously-fetched values.)

(5) By following the link to the declaration of n, it retrieves this variable's address, namely 0[SB]. Then it generates the instruction 'STORE 0[SB]'. (When executed, this instruction will store the previously-computed value in that variable.)

In this way the code generator translates the whole program into object code.

□

3.2 Passes

In the previous section we examined the principal phases of compilation, and the flow of data between them. In this section we go on to examine and compare alternative compiler designs.

In designing a compiler, we wish to decompose it into modules, in such a way that each module is responsible for a particular phase. In practice there are several ways of doing so. The design of the compiler affects its modularity, its time and space requirements, and the number of passes over the program being compiled.

A *pass* is a complete traversal of the source program, or a complete traversal of an internal representation of the source program (such as an AST). A *one-pass* compiler makes a single traversal of the source program; a *multi-pass* compiler makes several traversals.

In practice, the design of a compiler is inextricably linked to the number of passes it makes. In this section we contrast multi-pass and one-pass compilation, and summarize the advantages and disadvantages of each.

3.2.1 Multi-pass compilation

One possible compiler design is shown by the structure diagram[4] of Figure 3.8.

The compiler consists of a top-level driver module together with three lower-level modules, the syntactic analyzer, the contextual analyzer, and the code generator. First, the compiler driver calls the syntactic analyzer, which reads the source program, parses it, and constructs a complete AST. Next, the compiler driver calls the contextual

---

[4] A structure diagram summarizes the modules and module dependencies in a system. The higher-level modules are those near the top of the structure diagram. A connecting line represents a dependency of a higher-level module on a lower-level module. This dependency consists of the higher-level module using the services (e.g., types or methods) provided by the lower-level module.

analyzer, which traverses the AST, checks it, and decorates it. Finally, the compiler driver calls the code generator, which traverses the decorated AST and generates an object program.

In general, a compiler with this design makes at least three passes over the program being compiled. The syntactic analyzer takes one pass, and the contextual analyzer and code generator take at least one pass each.

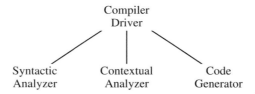

Figure 3.8 Structure diagram for a typical multi-pass compiler.

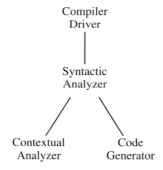

Figure 3.9 Structure diagram for a typical one-pass compiler.

3.2.2   One-pass compilation

An alternative compiler design is for the syntactic analyzer to control the other phases of compilation, as shown in Figure 3.9. A compiler with this design makes a single pass over the source program.

Contextual analysis and code generation are performed 'on the fly' during syntactic analysis. As soon as a phrase (e.g., expression, command, or declaration) has been parsed, the syntactic analyzer calls the contextual analyzer to perform any necessary checks. It also calls the code generator to generate any object code. Then the syntactic analyzer continues parsing the source program.

Example 3.5   One-pass compilation

A one-pass Triangle compiler would work as follows. Consider the following Triangle source program:

```
! This program is useless
! except for illustration.
let
    var n: Integer(1);
    var c: Char(2)
in
    begin
    c(3) := '&'(4)(5);
    n(6) := n+1(7)(8)
    end
```

This is identical to the source program of Figure 3.2, but some of the key points in the program have been numbered for easy reference. At these points the following actions are taken:

(1)   After parsing the variable declaration 'var n: Integer', the syntactic analyzer calls the contextual analyzer to record the fact (in a table) that identifier n is declared to be a variable of type *int*. It then calls the code generator to allocate and record an address for this variable, say 0[SB].

(2)   After parsing the variable declaration 'var c: Char', the syntactic analyzer similarly calls the contextual analyzer to record the fact that identifier c is declared to be a variable of type *char*. It then calls the code generator to allocate and record an address for this variable, say 1[SB].

(3)   After parsing the value-or-variable-name c, the syntactic analyzer infers (by calling the contextual analyzer) that it is a variable of type *char*. It then calls the code generator to retrieve its address, 1[SB].

(4)   After parsing the expression '&', the syntactic analyzer infers that it is of type *char*. It then calls the code generator to generate instruction 'LOADL 38'.

(5)   After parsing the assignment command 'c := '&'', the syntactic analyzer calls the contextual analyzer to check type compatibility. It then calls the code generator to generate instruction 'STORE 1[SB]', using the address retrieved at point (3).

(6)   After parsing the value-or-variable-name n, the syntactic analyzer infers (by calling the contextual analyzer) that it is a variable of type *int*. It then calls the code generator to retrieve the variable's address, 0[SB].

(7)   While parsing the expression n+1, the syntactic analyzer infers (by calling the contextual analyzer) that the subexpression n is of type *int*, that the operator '+' is of type *int* $\times$ *int* $\rightarrow$ *int*, that the subexpression 1 is of type *int*, and hence that the whole expression is of type *int*. It calls the code generator to generate instructions 'LOAD 0[SB]', 'LOADL 1', and 'CALL *add*'.

(8)   After parsing the assignment command 'n := n+1', the syntactic analyzer calls
the contextual analyzer to check type compatibility. It then calls the code generator
to generate instruction 'STORE 0[SB]'.

□

3.2.3   Compiler design issues

The choice between one-pass and multi-pass compilation is one of the first and most
important design decisions for the compiler writer. It is not an easy decision, for both
designs have important advantages and disadvantages. We summarize the main issues
here.

• *Speed* is an issue where a one-pass compiler wins. Construction and subsequent
traversals of the AST (or other internal program representation) is a modest time
overhead in any multi-pass compiler. If the AST is stored on disk, however, the
input–output overhead is likely to be large, even dominating compilation time.

• *Space* might also seem to favor a one-pass compiler. A multi-pass compiler must find
memory to store the AST. But the situation is not really so clear-cut. In a multi-pass
compiler, only one of the principal modules (syntactic analyzer, contextual analyzer,
and code generator) is active at a time, so their code can share memory. In a one-pass
compiler, all these modules are active throughout compile-time, so they must be co-
resident in memory. As a result, the code of a one-pass compiler occupies more memory than the code of a multi-pass compiler.

Of course, a very large source program will give rise to a very large AST, perhaps
occupying more memory than the compiler itself. Fortunately, modern programming
languages allow larger programs to be decomposed into compilation units, which are
compiled separately; and individual compilation units tend to be moderately-sized.
(See also Exercises 3.5 and 3.6.)

• *Modularity* favors the multi-pass compiler. In a one-pass compiler, the syntactic
analyzer not only parses the source program but also coordinates the contextual analyzer and code generator. That is to say, it calls these modules, and maintains the data
passed to and from them. In practice, the coordinating code may swamp the syntactic
analysis code. In a multi-pass compiler, each module (including the syntactic
analyzer) is responsible for a single function.

• *Flexibility* is an issue that favors the multi-pass compiler. Once the syntactic analyzer
has constructed the AST, the contextual analyzer and code generator can traverse the
AST in any convenient order. In particular, the code generator can translate phrases
out of order, and sometimes this allows it to generate more efficient object code. A
one-pass compiler is restricted to check and translate the phrases in exactly the order
in which they appear in the source program.

• Semantics-preserving *transformations* of the source program or object program are
performed by some compilers in order to make the object code as efficient as

possible. (These are the so-called 'optimizing' compilers.) Such transformations generally require analysis of the whole program prior to code generation, so they force a multi-pass design on the compiler.

- *Source language properties* might restrict the choice of compiler design. A source program can be compiled in one pass only if every phrase (e.g., command or expression) can be compiled using only information obtained from the preceding part of the source program. This requirement usually boils down to whether identifiers must be declared before use. If they must be declared before use (as in Pascal, Ada, and Triangle), then one-pass compilation is possible in principle. If identifiers need not be declared before use (as in Java and ML), then multi-pass compilation is required.

Example 3.6   *Pascal compiler design*

In Pascal, the usual rule is that identifiers must be declared before use. Thus an applied occurrence of an identifier can be compiled in the sure knowledge that the identifier's declaration has already been processed (or is missing altogether).

Consider the following Pascal block:

```
var n: Integer;
procedure inc;
    begin
    n := n+1
    end;

begin
n := 0; inc
end
```

When a Pascal one-pass compiler encounters the command 'n := n+1', it has already processed the declaration of n. It can therefore retrieve the type and address of the variable, and subject the command to contextual analysis and code generation.

Suppose, instead, that the declaration of n *follows* the procedure. When the Pascal one-pass compiler encounters the command 'n := n+1', it has not yet encountered the declaration of n. So it cannot subject the command to contextual analysis and code generation. Fortunately, the compiler is not obliged to do so: it can safely generate an error report that the declaration of n is either misplaced or missing altogether.

□

Example 3.7   *Java compiler design*

The situation is different in Java, in which variable or method declarations need not be in any particular order. The following Java class is perfectly well-formed:

```
class Example {

    void inc() { n = n + 1; }

    int n;

    void use() { n = 0; inc(); }
}
```

The command 'n = n + 1;' cannot be subjected to contextual analysis and code generation until the variable declaration 'int n;' has been processed. A Java compiler must therefore process variable declarations in one pass, and the commands and expressions inside a method body in a later pass.

□

3.3   Case study: the Triangle compiler

In Section 2.7 we introduced our case study, the Triangle language processor. This consists of a compiler, an interpreter, and a disassembler. In this section we look more closely at the Triangle compiler, explaining its design.

The Triangle compiler has the usual three phases of syntactic analysis, contextual analysis, and code generation, as shown in the data flow diagram of Figure 3.1. It has three passes, having the outline structure shown in Figure 3.8. The syntactic analyzer, contextual analyzer, and code generator modules take one pass each, communicating via an AST that represents the source program. This was illustrated in Examples 3.1, 3.2, and 3.4.

Omitting minor details, the compiler driver looks like this:

```
public class Compiler {

    public static void compileProgram (...) {
        Parser parser = new Parser(...);
        Checker checker = new Checker(...);
        Encoder generator = new Encoder(...);

        // Call the syntactic analyzer to parse the source program and
        // construct theAST...
        Program theAST = parser.parse();

        // Call the contextual analyzer to check and decorate theAST...
        checker.check(theAST);

        // Call the code generator to translate theAST to an object program...
        generator.encode(theAST);
    }
```

```
public static void main (String[] args) {
    ...
    compileProgram(...);
}
}
```

A one-pass Triangle compiler would have been perfectly feasible, so the choice of a three-pass design needs to be justified. The Triangle compiler is intended primarily for educational purposes, so simplicity and clarity are paramount. Efficiency is a secondary consideration; in any case, efficiency arguments for a one-pass compiler are inconclusive, as we saw in Section 3.2.3. So the Triangle compiler was designed to be as modular as possible, allowing the different phases to be studied independently of one another.

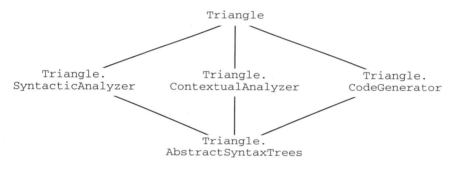

Figure 3.10 Structure diagram for the Triangle compiler.

A detailed structure diagram of the Triangle compiler is given in Figure 3.10, showing the main classes and packages. Here are brief explanations of the packages and the main classes they contain:

• The `Triangle.AbstractSyntaxTrees` package contains classes defining the AST data structure. There is a class for each Triangle construct, e.g., `AssignCommand`, `IfCommand`, `BinaryExpression`, `ConstDeclaration`, `VarDeclaration`, etc. Each class contains a constructor for building the AST for that construct, and a visitor method used by the contextual analyzer and the code generator to traverse the AST. The other parts of the compiler are allowed to manipulate the fields of the AST objects directly.

• The `Triangle.SyntacticAnalyzer` package contains the `Parser` class (and some classes of no concern here). The parser parses the source program, and constructs the AST. It generates an error report if it detects a syntactic error.

• The `Triangle.ContextualAnalyzer` package contains the `Checker` class. The checker traverses the AST, links applied occurrences of identifiers to the corresponding declarations, infers the types of all expressions, and performs all necessary type checks. It decorates the AST with these types. It generates an error report if it detects a contextual error.

- The `Triangle.CodeGenerator` package contains the `Encoder` class. The encoder traverses the decorated AST, allocates addresses to variables, and generates TAM object code.

- The `Triangle` package contains the `Compiler` class. The compiler simply drives the three phases of the compilation, as described above.

Diagrams describing the complete design of the Triangle compiler are given in Appendix D. In later chapters we shall continue this case study by looking inside the individual packages and their classes. Detailed documentation about the contents of each class can also be found at our Web site (see Preface, page).

3.4 Further reading

The textbook by Aho *et al.* (1985) offers a comprehensive treatment of all aspects of compilation. Chapter 1 discusses compiler designs in general; Chapter 2 presents a complete example of one-pass compilation; Chapter 11 discusses compiler design issues; and Chapter 12 looks at several case studies of real compilers.

This book concentrates on multi-pass compilation, in the interests of clarity and modularity. Other authors, such as Hoare (1973), have stressed the advantages of one-pass compilation. Welsh and McKeag (1980) devote a large part of their textbook to one-pass compilation. As a case study they develop a complete compiler for a subset of Pascal. Welsh and Hay (1986) is a complete one-pass Pascal compiler, together with an interpreter. That book is a fine example of literate programming.

The idea of using abstract syntax as a basis for compilation seems to be due to McCarthy (1963). Despite the attractions of this idea, it has received scant attention in most compiler textbooks.

Many internal representations other than ASTs are possible, of course. Lower-level internal representations tend to be more convenient for code generation to real machine code. A prominent example of this is the Gnu compiler kit, which uses a machine-independent but low-level intermediate language RTL. We can then construct 'front-ends' translating a variety of high-level languages to RTL, and 'back-ends' translating RTL to a variety of target machine codes. (See Exercise 2.5.) If we have m front-ends and n back-ends, we can combine these $m+n$ components to make mn distinct compilers. This is a major saving of effort.

Exercises

3.1 In Examples 3.2 and 3.4, the first assignment command 'c := '&'' was ignored. Describe how this command would have been subjected to contextual analysis and code generation.

3.2 The Mini-Triangle source program below left would be compiled to the object program below right:

```
let
  const m ~ 7;
  var x: Integer          PUSH   1
in
  x := m * x              LOADL  7
                          LOAD   0[SB]
                          CALL   mult
                          STORE  0[SB]
                          POP    1
                          HALT
```

Describe the compilation in the same manner as Examples 3.1, 3.2, and 3.4. (You may ignore the generation of the PUSH, and POP instructions.)

3.3 The Mini-Triangle source program below contains several contextual errors:

```
let
  var a: Logical;
  var b: Boolean;
  var i: Integer
in
  if i then b := i = 0 else b := yes
```

In the same manner as Example 3.3, show how contextual analysis will detect these errors.

3.4* Choose a compiler with which you are familiar. Find out and describe its phases and its pass structure. Draw a data flow diagram (like Figure 3.1) and a structure diagram (like Figure 3.8 or Figure 3.9).

3.5 Consider a source language, like Fortran or C, in which the source program consists of one or more distinct subprograms – a main program plus some procedures or functions. Design a compiler that uses ASTs, but (assuming that individual subprograms are moderately-sized) requires only a moderate amount of memory for ASTs.

3.6*   The Triangle compiler would be unable to translate a very large source program, because of the memory required to store its AST. Consider the following proposal to redesign the compiler to improve its handling of very large source programs.

One procedure/function body is to be (completely) compiled at a time. Whenever the compiler has parsed a procedure/function declaration and constructed its AST, it breaks off to perform contextual analysis and code generation on the procedure/function body's AST, and then prunes the AST leaving a stub in place of the procedure/function body. Then the compiler resumes parsing the source program.

Would such a restructuring of the compiler be feasible? If *no*, explain why not. If *yes*, work through the following small source program, showing the steps that would be taken by the compiler, along the same lines as Example 3.5:

```
let
   var n: Integer;
   proc inc () ~
       n := n + 1
in
   begin n := 0; inc() end
```

CHAPTER FOUR

Syntactic Analysis

In Chapter 3 we saw how compilation can be decomposed into three principal phases, one of which is syntactic analysis. In this chapter we study syntactic analysis, and further decompose it into scanning, parsing, and abstract syntax tree construction. Section 4.1 explains this decomposition.

The main function of syntactic analysis is to parse the source program in order to discover its phrase structure. Thus the main topic of this chapter is parsing, and in particular the simple but effective method known as recursive-descent parsing. Section 4.3 explains how parsing works, and shows how a recursive-descent parser can be systematically developed from the programming language's grammar. This development is facilitated by a flexible grammatical notation (EBNF) and by various techniques for transforming grammars, ideas that are introduced in Section 4.2.

In a multi-pass compiler, the source program's phrase structure must be represented explicitly in some way. This choice of representation is a major design decision. One convenient and widely-used representation is the abstract syntax tree. Section 4.4 shows how to make the parser construct an abstract syntax tree.

In parsing it is convenient to view the source program as a stream of tokens: symbols such as identifiers, literals, operators, keywords, and punctuation. Since the source program text actually consists of individual characters, and a token may consist of several characters, scanning is needed to group the characters into tokens, and to discard other text such as blank space and comments. Scanning is the topic of Section 4.5.

4.1   Subphases of syntactic analysis

Syntactic analysis in a compiler consists of the following subphases:

- *Scanning* (or *lexical analysis*): The source program is transformed to a stream of *tokens*: symbols such as identifiers, literals, operators, keywords, and punctuation. Comments, and blank spaces between tokens, are discarded. (They are present in the source program mainly for the benefit of human readers.)

- *Parsing:* The source program (now represented by a stream of tokens) is parsed to determine its phrase structure. The parser treats each token as a terminal symbol.

- *Representation of the phrase structure:* A data structure representing the source program's phrase structure is constructed. This representation is typically an abstract syntax tree (AST).

The first two subphases are present in every compiler. The third subphase is absent in a one-pass compiler, which has no need to construct an explicit representation of the source program's phrase structure.

Example 4.1   Syntactic analysis of Mini-Triangle

We shall use Mini-Triangle to illustrate syntactic analysis in a compiler. A context-free grammar of Mini-Triangle was given in Example 1.3.

Syntactic analysis of a small Mini-Triangle source program is shown in Figures 4.1 through 4.4.

Scanning transforms the source program of Figure 4.1 to the stream of tokens shown in Figure 4.2. Blanks (spaces, ends-of-lines, etc.) and comments (introduced by '!') have been discarded. Each identifier, literal, and operator is treated as a single token.

Parsing determines the phrase structure of the stream of tokens, i.e., identifies its commands, expressions, declarations, etc. Figure 4.3 illustrates the effect of parsing.

Finally, the parser can be made to construct an AST that explicitly represents the source program's phrase structure. This is illustrated in Figure 4.4.

□

4.1.1   Tokens

The interface between the scanner and the parser is a stream of tokens. A ***token*** is an atomic symbol of the source program. A token may consist of several characters, but these characters have little or no individual significance. For example, the letters of the keyword 'let' clearly have no individual significance; they serve only to distinguish this keyword from similarly-spelled identifiers like 'lot' and 'led'. The letters of an identifier also have no individual significance, except to distinguish between different identifiers.

As well as tokens, the source program may contain blank space and comments. These are not themselves tokens because they are completely insignificant. Part of the scanner's function is to discard blank space and comments.[1]

Tokens may be classified according to their kind, as shown in Figure 4.2. For example, the tokens 'y' and 'Integer' are of kind *identifier*, '1' is of kind *integer-*

---

[1]   However, spaces in character-literals and string-literals (in languages that have them) form part of tokens, and must *not* be discarded.

literal, and '+' is of kind *operator*. The criterion for classifying tokens is simply this: all tokens of the same kind can be freely interchanged without affecting the program's phrase structure. Thus the identifier 'y' could be replaced by 'x' or 'banana', and the integer-literal '1' by '7' or '100', without affecting the program's phrase structure. On the other hand, the token 'let' could not be replaced by 'lot' or 'led' or anything else; 'let' is the only token of its kind.

Each token is completely described by its *kind* and *spelling*. Thus a token can be represented simply by an object with these two fields. The different kinds of token can be represented by small integers.

```
let var y: Integer
in  !new year
    y := y+1
```

Figure 4.1 A Mini-Triangle source program.

let	*var*	*ident.*	*colon*	*ident.*	*in*	*ident.*	*bec-omes*	*ident.*	*op.*	*intlit.*	*eot*
let	var	y	:	Int-eger	in	y	:=	y	+	1	

Figure 4.2 The program of Figure 4.1 represented by a stream of tokens.

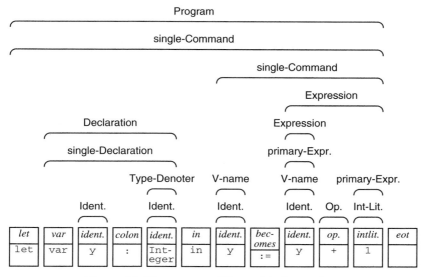

Figure 4.3 The program of Figure 4.1 after parsing.

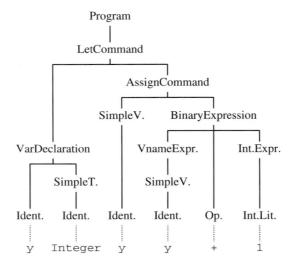

Figure 4.4 The program of Figure 4.1 represented by an AST.

Example 4.2   Tokens of Mini-Triangle

Mini-Triangle tokens could be represented by objects of the following class:

```java
public class Token {

   public byte kind;
   public String spelling;

   public Token (byte kind, String spelling) {
      this.kind = kind;
      this.spelling = spelling;
   }

   // Constants denoting different kinds of token:
   public final static byte
         IDENTIFIER =   0,
         INTLITERAL =   1,
         OPERATOR   =   2,
         BEGIN      =   3,      // begin
         CONST      =   4,      // const
         DO         =   5,      // do
         ELSE       =   6,      // else
         END        =   7,      // end
         IF         =   8,      // if
         IN         =   9,      // in
         LET        =  10,      // let
```

```
    THEN          = 11,        // then
    VAR          , = 12,        // var
    WHILE         = 13,        // while
    SEMICOLON     = 14,        // ;
    COLON         = 15,        // :
    BECOMES       = 16,        // :=
    IS            = 17,        // ~
    LPAREN        = 18,        // (
    RPAREN        = 19,        // )
    EOT           = 20;        // end of text
}
```

Note that a token of kind EOT represents the end of the source text. In both scanning and parsing of the source program, the existence of this token will prove convenient.

Only the kind of each token will be examined by the parser, since different tokens of the same kind do not affect the source program's phrase structure. The spellings of some tokens (identifiers, literals, operators) will be examined by the contextual analyzer and/or code generator, so their spellings must be retained and eventually incorporated into the AST. The spellings of other tokens (such as 'let') will never be examined after scanning. Nevertheless, it is convenient to have a uniform representation for all tokens.

4.2 Grammars revisited

In Section 1.3.1 we briefly reviewed context-free grammars, and showed how a grammar generates a set of *sentences*. Each sentence is a string of terminal symbols. An (unambiguous) sentence has a unique *phrase structure*, embodied in its syntax tree.

In Section 4.3 we shall see, not only how parsers work, but also how parsers can be systematically developed from context-free grammars. The development is clearest if we use an extension of BNF called *EBNF*, which is effectively BNF plus regular expressions. EBNF lends itself to a variety of transformations that can be used to mould a programming language's grammar into a form suitable for parser development. In this section we briefly review regular expressions and EBNF, before presenting some useful grammar transformations.

4.2.1 Regular expressions

A *regular expression* (RE) is a convenient notation for expressing a set of strings of terminal symbols. The main features of the RE notation are:

- '|' separates alternatives;

- '*' indicates that the previous item may be repeated zero or more times;

- '(' and ')' are grouping parentheses.

The notation is summarized in Table 4.1, and illustrated by Example 4.3 below.

Table 4.1 Regular expressions.

	Regular expression	This regular expression generates …
empty	ε	just the empty string
singleton	t	just the string consisting of t alone
concatenation	$X\,Y$ (or $X \cdot Y$)	the concatenation of any string generated by X and any string generated by Y
alternative	$X \mid Y$	any string generated either by X or by Y
iteration	$X*$	the concatenation of zero or more of the strings generated by X
grouping	(X)	any string generated by X

Note: X and Y are arbitrary regular expressions; t is any terminal symbol.

Example 4.3   Regular expressions

Here are some REs. Each generates a set of strings of letters, as shown:

M r | M s   – generates {**Mr, Ms**}

M (r | s)   – generates {**Mr, Ms**}

p s* t   – generates {**pt, pst, psst, pssst**, …}

b a (n a)*   – generates {**ba, bana, banana, bananana**, …}

M (r | s)*   – generates {**M, Mr, Ms, Mrr, Mrs, Msr, Mss, Mrrr**, …}

An RE generates a set of strings of terminal symbols, in other words a language. However, REs are capable of generating only very simple languages, called ***regular languages***. Within programming languages, sublanguages such as identifiers and literals are typically regular languages.

On the other hand, complete programming languages invariably exhibit ***self-embedding***. In Mini-Triangle, for example, the expression 'a*(b+c)/d' contains an embedded subexpression, 'b+c'; and the command 'if x > y then m := x else m := y' contains an embedded subcommand, 'm := x'. Self-embedding allows us to write arbitrarily complex expressions, commands, and suchlike.

In summary:

- A regular language – a language that does not exhibit self-embedding – can be generated by an RE.

- A language that does exhibit self-embedding cannot be generated by any RE. To generate such a language, we must write recursive production rules in either BNF or EBNF.

4.2.2   Extended BNF

EBNF (Extended BNF) is a combination of BNF and REs. An EBNF production rule is of the form $N ::= X$, where N is a nonterminal symbol and X is an **extended RE**, i.e., an RE constructed from both terminal and nonterminal symbols.

Unlike BNF, the right-hand side of an EBNF production rule may use not only '|' but also '*' and '(' and ')'. Unlike an ordinary RE, the right-hand side may contain nonterminal symbols as well as terminal symbols. Thus we can write recursive production rules, and an EBNF grammar is capable of generating a language with self-embedding.

Example 4.4   Grammar expressed in EBNF

Consider the following EBNF grammar:

Expression	::=	primary-Expression (Operator primary-Expression)*
primary-Expression	::=	Identifier
	|	(Expression)
Identifier	::=	**a** | **b** | **c** | **d** | **e**
Operator	::=	**+** | **-** | ***** | **/**

This grammar generates expressions such as:

```
e
a + b
a - b - c
a + (b * c)
a * (b + c) / d
a - (b - (c - (d - e)))
```

Because the production rules defining Expression and primary-Expression are mutually recursive, the grammar can generate self-embedded expressions.

□

EBNF combines the advantages of both BNF and REs. It is equivalent to BNF in expressive power. Its use of RE notation makes it more convenient than BNF for specifying some aspects of syntax.

4.2.3   Grammar transformations

EBNF is a much more flexible notation than BNF. In particular, grouping of alternatives '(...|...|...)' and iteration '*' make it easy to perform useful transformations on a grammar expressed in EBNF. Here we introduce and illustrate some possible transformations. Later, in Section 4.3.4, we shall see how they are used in practice.

Left factorization

Suppose that we have alternatives of the form:

$$X\ Y \mid X\ Z$$

where X, Y, and Z are arbitrary (extended) REs. We can replace these alternatives by the equivalent extended RE:

$$X\ (Y \mid Z)$$

The REs $X\ Y \mid X\ Z$ and $X\ (Y \mid Z)$ are equivalent in the sense that they generate exactly the same languages. This fact was illustrated by the first two REs in Example 4.3.

Example 4.5   Left factorization

Many programming languages have alternative forms of if-command:

```
single-Command    ::=   V-name := Expression
                  |     if Expression then single-Command
                  |     if Expression then single-Command
                            else single-Command
```

This production rule can be left-factorized as follows:

```
single-Command    ::=   V-name := Expression
                  |     if Expression then single-Command
                           (ε | else single-Command)
```

◻

Right factorization is the mirror-image of left factorization, but is less useful in practice.

Elimination of left recursion

Suppose that we have a production rule of the form:

$$N ::= X \mid N\ Y$$

where N is a nonterminal symbol, and X and Y are arbitrary extended REs. This production rule is ***left-recursive***. We can replace it by the equivalent EBNF production rule:

$$N ::= X\ (Y)^*$$

These production rules are equivalent in the sense that they generate exactly the same languages. The production rule $N ::= X \mid N\ Y$ states that an N-phrase may consist either of an X-phrase or of an N-phrase followed by a Y-phrase. This is just a roundabout way of stating that an N-phrase consists of an X-phrase followed by any number of Y-phrases. The production rule $N ::= X\ (Y)*$ states the same thing more concisely.

Example 4.6   Elimination of left recursion

The syntax of Triangle identifiers is expressed in BNF as follows:

Identifier	::=	Letter
	|	Identifier Letter
	|	Identifier Digit

This production rule is a little more complicated than the form shown above, but we can left-factorize it:

Identifier	::=	Letter
	|	Identifier (Letter | Digit)

and now eliminate the left recursion:

Identifier	::=	Letter (Letter | Digit)*

$\square$

As illustrated by Example 4.6, it is possible for a more complicated production rule to be left-recursive:

$$N ::= X_1 \mid \ldots \mid X_m \mid N\ Y_1 \mid \ldots \mid N\ Y_n$$

However, left factorization gives us:

$$N ::= (X_1 \mid \ldots \mid X_m) \mid N\ (Y_1 \mid \ldots \mid Y_n)$$

and now we can apply our elimination rule:

$$N ::= (X_1 \mid \ldots \mid X_m)\ (Y_1 \mid \ldots \mid Y_n)*$$

Substitution of nonterminal symbols

Given an EBNF production rule $N ::= X$, we may substitute X for any occurrence of N on the right-hand side of another production rule.

If we substitute X for *every* occurrence of N, then we may eliminate the nonterminal N and the production rule $N ::= X$ altogether. (This is possible, however, only if $N ::= X$ is nonrecursive and is the only production rule for N.)

Whether we actually choose to make such substitutions is a matter of convenience. If N occurs in only a few places, and if X is uncomplicated, then elimination of $N ::= X$ might well simplify the grammar as a whole.

Example 4.7   Substitution

Consider the following production rules, taken from a BNF grammar of Pascal:

single-Command	::=	**for** Control-Variable **:=** Expression To-or-Downto
		Expression **do** single-Command
	|	…
Control-Variable	::=	Identifier
To-or-Downto	::=	**to**
	|	**downto**

It makes sense to eliminate Control-Variable and To-or-Downto by substitution:

single-Command	::=	**for** Identifier **:=** Expression (**to** | **downto**)
		Expression **do** single-Command
	|	…

The nonterminal To-or-Downto was present in the first place only because grouping of alternatives '(…|…)' is not possible in BNF. The nonterminal Control-Variable was present only to act as a 'semantic clue' – to emphasize the role this particular identifier plays in the for-command – and not for any grammatical reason. Eliminating such nonterminals simplifies the grammar.

4.2.4   Starter sets

The ***starter set*** of an RE X, written *starters*$[\![X]\!]$, is the set of terminal symbols that can start a string generated by X. For example:

$$starters[\![\mathbf{h\,i\,s}\,|\,\mathbf{h\,e\,r}\,|\,\mathbf{i\,t\,s}]\!] \quad = \{\mathbf{h, i}\}$$
$$starters[\![(\mathbf{r\,e})^*\,\mathbf{s\,e\,t}]\!] \quad = \{\mathbf{r, s}\}$$

since '$(\mathbf{r\,e})^*\,\mathbf{s\,e\,t}$' generates the set of strings {**set**, **reset**, **rereset**, …}.

The following is a precise and complete definition of *starters:*

starters$[\![\varepsilon]\!]$	$= \{\;\}$	
starters$[\![t]\!]$	$= \{t\}$	where t is a terminal symbol
starters$[\![X\,Y]\!]$	$= starters[\![X]\!] \cup starters[\![Y]\!]$	if X generates ε
starters$[\![X\,Y]\!]$	$= starters[\![X]\!]$	if X does not generate ε
starters$[\![X\,|\,Y]\!]$	$= starters[\![X]\!] \cup starters[\![Y]\!]$	
starters$[\![X^*]\!]$	$= starters[\![X]\!]$	

(where X and Y stand for arbitrary REs).

We can easily generalize this to define the starter set of an extended RE. There is only one case to add:

$$starters[\![N]\!] \qquad = \quad starters[\![X]\!] \qquad\qquad \text{where } N \text{ is a nonterminal}$$
$$\text{symbol defined by}$$
$$\text{production rule } N ::= X$$

In Example 4.4:

$$starters[\![\text{Expression}]\!] = starters[\![\text{primary-Expression}$$
$$\text{(Operator primary-Expression)}*\,]\!]$$
$$= starters[\![\text{primary-Expression}]\!]$$
$$= starters[\![\text{Identifier}]\!] \cup starters[\![\,(\text{ Expression })\,]\!]$$
$$= starters[\![\mathbf{a} \mid \mathbf{b} \mid \mathbf{c} \mid \mathbf{d} \mid \mathbf{e}]\!] \cup \{\,(\,\}$$
$$= \{\mathbf{a}, \mathbf{b}, \mathbf{c}, \mathbf{d}, \mathbf{e}, \,(\,\}$$

4.3 Parsing

In this section we are concerned with analyzing sentences in some grammar. Given an input string of terminal symbols, our task is to determine whether the input string is a sentence of the grammar, and if so to discover its phrase structure. The following definitions capture the essence of this.

With respect to a particular context-free grammar G:

• **Recognition** of an input string is deciding whether or not the input string is a sentence of G.

• **Parsing** of an input string is recognition of the input string plus determination of its phrase structure. The phrase structure can be represented by a syntax tree, or otherwise.

We assume that G is **unambiguous**, i.e., that every sentence of G has exactly one syntax tree. The possibility of an input string having several syntax trees is a complication we prefer to avoid.

Parsing is a task that humans perform extremely well. As we read a document, or listen to a speaker, we are continuously parsing the sentences to determine their phrase structure (and then determine their meaning). Parsing is subconscious most of the time, but occasionally it surfaces in our consciousness: when we notice a grammatical error, or realize that a sentence is ambiguous. Young children can be taught consciously to parse simple sentences on paper.

In this section we are interested in *parsing algorithms*, which we can use in syntactic analysis. Many parsing algorithms have been developed, but there are only two basic parsing strategies: *bottom-up parsing* and *top-down parsing*. These strategies are characterized by the order in which the input string's syntax tree is reconstructed. (In fact, a parser need not construct a syntax tree explicitly, but it is convenient to explain these parsing strategies in terms of constructing a syntax tree.)

In the following subsections we compare bottom-up parsing and top-down parsing, then we introduce a particular top-down parsing algorithm known as *recursive descent*. We shall use the following simple grammar as a running example to illustrate different parsing techniques.

Example 4.8   Grammar of micro-English

Here is the grammar of a tiny fragment of English, which we shall call *micro-English*:

Sentence	::=	Subject Verb Object **.**	(4.1)
Subject	::=	**I** | **a** Noun | **the** Noun	(4.2a–c)
Object	::=	**me** | **a** Noun | **the** Noun	(4.3a–c)
Noun	::=	**cat** | **mat** | **rat**	(4.4a–c)
Verb	::=	**like** | **is** | **see** | **sees**	(4.5a–d)

The terminal symbols (shown in bold) are words such as 'I' and 'me', and the punctuation mark '.'. The nonterminal symbols are Sentence (the start symbol), Subject, Object, Noun, and Verb.

The following are among the sentences generated by the micro-English grammar:

the cat sees a rat .

I like the mat .

the cat likes me .

I sees the cat .

The last example is of course ungrammatical in English, but is grammatical in micro-English. (See Exercise 4.8.)

Some non-sentences in this grammar are '**me sees the cat .**' ('me' is not a subject), '**I see like a cat .**' ('like' can be used only as a verb), and '**I the mat see .**' (verb and object are out of order).

□

4.3.1   The bottom-up parsing strategy

Bottom-up parsing of an input string works as follows. The parser examines the terminal symbols of the input string, in order from left to right, and reconstructs the syntax tree from the *bottom* (terminal nodes) *up* (towards the root node).

Example 4.9   Bottom-up parsing of micro-English

Recall the grammar of micro-English (Example 4.8). Consider the following input string, consisting of six terminal symbols:

the cat sees a rat .

Bottom-up parsing of this input string proceeds as follows:

(1)   The first input terminal symbol is 'the'. The parser cannot do anything with this terminal symbol yet, so it moves on to the next input terminal symbol, 'cat'. Here it can apply the production rule 'Noun ::= **cat**' (4.4a), forming a Noun-tree with the terminal symbol 'cat' as subtree:

(Input terminal symbols not yet examined by the parser are shaded gray.)

(2)   Now the parser can apply the production rule 'Subject ::= **the** Noun' (4.2c), combining the input terminal symbol '**the**' and the adjacent Noun-tree into a Subject-tree:

(3)   Now the parser moves on to the next input terminal symbol, '**sees**'. Here it can apply the production rule 'Verb ::= **sees**' (4.5d), forming a Verb-tree:

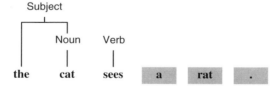

(4)   The next input terminal symbol is '**a**'. The parser cannot do anything with this terminal symbol yet, so it moves on to the following input terminal symbol, '**rat**'. Here it can apply the production rule 'Noun ::= **rat**' (4.4c), forming a Noun-tree:

(5)   Now the parser can apply the production rule 'Object ::= **a** Noun' (4.3b), combining the input terminal symbol '**a**' and the adjacent Noun-tree into an Object-tree:

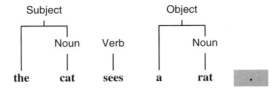

(6)   The next (and last) input terminal symbol is '.'. With this the parser can apply the production rule 'Sentence ::= Subject Verb Object .' (4.1), combining the adjacent Subject-tree, Verb-tree, Object-tree, and input terminal symbol '.' into a Sentence-tree:

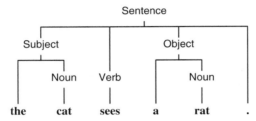

The parser has reduced the entire input string to a Sentence-tree. In other words, it has successfully parsed a sentence.

☐

Consider a particular context-free grammar G. Each production rule is of the form $N ::= X_1 \ldots X_n$, where N is a nonterminal symbol of G, and each X_i is a terminal or nonterminal symbol of G.

In general, a bottom-up parser for G works as follows. When it encounters a sequence of terminal symbols and trees that match the right-hand side of a production rule $N ::= X_1 \ldots X_n$, it may combine these terminal symbols and trees into a single N-tree. The latter tree is then available for further matching. Parsing succeeds when and if the whole of the input string has been reduced to a single S-tree, where S is the start symbol of G.

How does the parser choose what to do at each step? This is an important issue, since a wrong choice can lead the parser into a blind alley. At step (5) in Example 4.9, the parser might have chosen to apply 'Subject ::= **a** Noun' (instead of the correct 'Object ::= **a** Noun'):

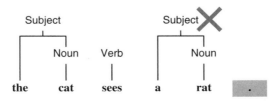

In this case, the trees would *not* match the right-hand side of the production rule 'Sentence ::= Subject Verb Object .', nor indeed any other production rule, so the parser would be unable to make further progress. Having parsed a subject and verb, the parser has reached a state in which it should parse an object, not another subject. In general, a bottom-up parser must, when choosing what to do next, take into account whatever information is available: the next input terminal symbol, and the state it has reached as a result of previous parsing steps.

4.3.2 The top-down parsing strategy

Top-down parsing of an input string works as follows. The parser examines the terminal symbols of the input string, in order from left to right, and reconstructs its syntax tree from the *top* (root node) *down* (towards the terminal nodes).

Example 4.10 Top-down parsing of micro-English

Recall the grammar of micro-English (Example 4.8). Consider once more the input string:

the cat sees a rat .

Top-down parsing starts by making a root node labeled Sentence. Then it proceeds as follows:

(1)   The parser must decide which production rule to apply at the Sentence-node. In fact there is only one production rule with Sentence on the left-hand side, so it has no choice but to apply 'Sentence ::= Subject Verb Object .' (4.1):

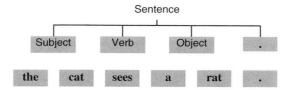

This step has made four stubs, i.e., nodes not yet connected to the input string. (The symbols labeling the stubs, as well as the input terminal symbols not yet examined, are shaded gray in the diagram.)

(2)   Now the parser considers the leftmost stub, the node labeled Subject. It must decide which production rule to apply to it. There are three to choose from, but it should be clear that the appropriate one is 'Subject ::= **the** Noun' (4.2c). This step connects up the first input terminal symbol '**the**', and makes a new stub labeled Noun:

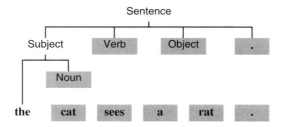

(3)   The leftmost stub is now the node labeled Noun, and the parser must decide which production rule to apply to it. If it chooses 'Noun ::= **cat**' (4.4a), it can connect the next input terminal symbol '**cat**' to the tree:

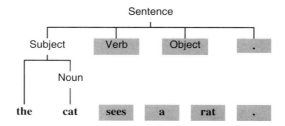

(4)   The leftmost stub is now the node labeled Verb. If the parser chooses to apply the production rule 'Verb ::= **sees**' (4.5d), it can connect the input terminal symbol '**sees**' to the tree:

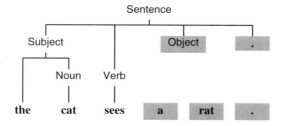

(5)   The leftmost stub is now the node labeled Object. There are three production rules to choose from, but it should be clear that the appropriate production rule is 'Object ::= **a** Noun' (4.3b). This step connects up the next input terminal symbol '**a**', and makes a new stub labeled Noun:

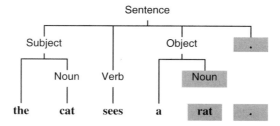

(6)   The leftmost stub is now the (second) node labeled Noun. If the parser chooses to apply production rule 'Noun ::= **rat**' (4.4c), it can connect the input terminal symbol '**rat**' to the tree. This step leaves the parser with a stub labeled '.' that matches the next (and last) input terminal symbol:

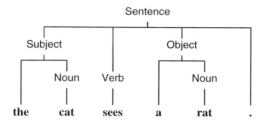

Thus the parser has successfully parsed the input string.

Consider a particular context-free grammar G. In general, a top-down parser for G starts with just a stub for the root node, labeled by S (the start symbol of G). At each step, the parser takes the leftmost stub. If the stub is labeled by terminal symbol t, the parser connects it to the next input terminal symbol, which must be t. (If not, the parser has detected a syntactic error.) If the stub is labeled by nonterminal symbol N, the parser chooses one of the production rules $N ::= X_1...X_n$, and grows branches from the node labeled by N to new stubs labeled X_1, …, X_n (in order from left to right). Parsing succeeds when and if the whole input string is connected up to the syntax tree.

How does the parser choose which production rule to apply at each step? In the micro-English top-down parser the choices are easy. For example, the parser can always choose which of the production rules 'Subject ::= …' to apply simply by examining the next input terminal symbol: if the terminal symbol is '**I**', it chooses 'Subject ::= **I**'; or if the terminal symbol is '**the**', it chooses 'Subject ::= **the** Noun'; or if the terminal symbol is '**a**', it chooses 'Subject ::= **a** Noun'. Unfortunately, some grammars make the choice more difficult; and some grammars are completely unsuited to this parsing strategy.

4.3.3   Recursive-descent parsing

The bottom-up and top-down parsing strategies outlined in the previous subsections are the basis of a variety of parsing algorithms. We observed that a parser often has to choose which production rule to apply next. A particular way of making such choices gives rise to a particular parsing algorithm.

Several parsing algorithms are commonly used in compilers. Here we describe just one, which is both effective and easy to understand.

Recursive descent is a top-down parsing algorithm. A recursive-descent parser for a grammar G consists of a group of methods parse$N$, one for each nonterminal symbol

N of *G*. The task of each method parse*N* is to parse a single *N*-phrase. These **parsing methods** cooperate to parse complete sentences.

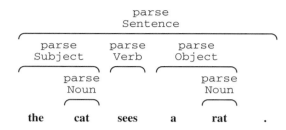

Figure 4.5 Recursive-descent parsing of a micro-English sentence.

Example 4.11 Recursive-descent parser for micro-English

Let us develop a recursive-descent parser for micro-English, expressed in Java.

The grammar of micro-English (Example 4.8) has nonterminal symbols Noun, Verb, Subject, Object, and Sentence. So the parsing methods will be:

```
private void parseNoun ();
// Parse a noun, i.e., 'cat', 'mat', or 'rat'.

private void parseVerb ();
// Parse a verb, e.g., 'like' or 'sees'.

private void parseSubject ();
// Parse a subject, e.g., 'I' or 'a rat'.

private void parseObject ();
// Parse an object, e.g., 'me' or 'a rat'.

private void parseSentence ();
// Parse a complete sentence.
```

These methods should cooperate to parse the input string '**the cat sees a rat .**' as shown in Figure 4.5. The method parseSentence parses the whole input string, but delegates most of the work to methods parseSubject, parseVerb, and parseObject, before itself accepting the last terminal '**.**'. The method parseSubject itself accepts the terminal '**the**', before delegating the rest of its work to method parseNoun. The latter simply accepts '**cat**'. And so on.

Comparison of Figure 4.5 with the same sentence's syntax tree (at the end of Example 4.10) shows that the methods have, in effect, discovered the sentence's phrase structure. Thus they really do constitute a parser.

Now let us see how to implement the parser. We need a class to contain all of the parsing methods; let us call it `Parser`. This class will also contain an instance variable, `currentTerminal`, that will range over the terminal symbols of the input string. (For example, given the input string of Figure 4.5, `currentTerminal` will first contain '**the**', then '**cat**', then '**sees**', etc., and finally '**.**'.) The `Parser` class, containing `currentTerminal`, is declared as follows:

```
public class Parser {

    private TerminalSymbol currentTerminal;

    ...  // Auxiliary methods will go here.

    ...  // Parsing methods will go here.
}
```

The current terminal is accessed by the following auxiliary method of the `Parser` class:

```
private void accept (TerminalSymbol expectedTerminal) {
    if (currentTerminal matches expectedTerminal)
        currentTerminal = next input terminal;
    else
        report a syntactic error²
}
```

The parser will call '`accept(t)`' when it expects the current terminal to be *t*, and wishes to check that it is indeed *t*, before fetching the next input terminal.

The parsing methods themselves are implemented as follows. (For easy reference, the corresponding production rules of the grammar are reproduced on the right.)

First, method `parseSentence`:

```
private void parseSentence () {        Sentence ::=
    parseSubject();                        Subject
    parseVerb();                           Verb
    parseObject();                         Object
    accept('.');                           .
}
```

This is easy to understand. According to the production rule, a sentence consists of a subject, verb, object, and period, in that order. Therefore `parseSentence` should encounter the subject, verb, object, and period, in that same order. It calls methods `parseSubject`, `parseVerb`, and `parseObject`, one after another, to parse the subject, verb, and object, respectively. Finally it calls `accept` to check that the (now) current terminal is indeed a period.

---

² This type style indicates a command or expression not yet refined into Java. We will use this convention to suppress minor details.

Now, method `parseSubject`:

```
private void parseSubject () {                      Subject ::=
    if (currentTerminal matches 'I')
        accept ('I');                                    I
    else                                                 |
    if (currentTerminal matches 'a') {
        accept ('a');                                    a
        parseNoun();                                     Noun
    } else                                               |
    if (currentTerminal matches 'the') {
        accept ('the');                                  the
        parseNoun();                                     Noun
    } else
        report a syntactic error
}
```

This is a little more complicated. According to the production rule, a subject must have one of three forms: 'I', 'a Noun', or 'the Noun'. Method `parseSubject` must decide which form it is, and the only way to decide is to inspect the current terminal. On entry to `parseSubject`, the current terminal should contain the first terminal of the subject. If the current terminal is 'I', then clearly the subject is of the form 'I'; if the current terminal is 'a', then presumably the subject is of the form 'a Noun'; if the current terminal is 'the', then presumably the subject is of the form 'the Noun'; otherwise the subject is ill-formed.

Now method `parseNoun`:

```
private void parseNoun () {                         Noun ::=
    if (currentTerminal matches 'cat')
        accept ('cat');                                  cat
    else                                                 |
    if (currentTerminal matches 'mat')
        accept ('mat');                                  mat
    else                                                 |
    if (currentTerminal matches 'rat')
        accept ('rat');                                  rat
    else
        report a syntactic error
}
```

This is straightforward. According to the production rule, a noun must be 'cat', 'mat', or 'rat', and `parseNoun` simply checks the contents of `currentTerminal` to discover which it is. If `currentTerminal` does not contain one of these alternatives then the noun is ill-formed.

Method `parseObject` is analogous to `parseSubject`, and `parseVerb` to `parseNoun`, so we omit the details here. (See Exercise 4.6.)

The parser is initiated using the following method:

```
public void parse () {
    currentTerminal = first input terminal;
    parseSentence();
    check that no terminal follows the sentence
}
```

This parser does not actually construct a syntax tree. But it does (implicitly) determine the input string's phrase structure. For example, `parseNoun` whenever called finds the beginning and end of a phrase of class **Noun**, and `parseSubject` whenever called finds the beginning and end of a phrase of class **Subject**. (See Figure 4.5.)

□

In general, the methods of a recursive-descent parser cooperate as follows:

• The variable `currentTerminal` will successively contain each input terminal. All parsing methods have access to this variable.

• On entry to method `parseN`, `currentTerminal` is supposed to contain the first terminal of an *N*-phrase. On exit from `parseN`, `currentTerminal` is supposed to contain the input terminal immediately following that *N*-phrase.

• On entry to method `accept` with argument *t*, `currentTerminal` is supposed to contain the terminal *t*. On exit from `accept`, `currentTerminal` is supposed to contain the input terminal immediately following *t*.

If the production rules are mutually recursive, then the parsing methods will also be mutually recursive. For this reason (and because the parsing strategy is top-down), the algorithm is called *recursive descent*.

4.3.4   Systematic development of a recursive-descent parser

A recursive-descent parser can be *systematically* developed from a (suitable) context-free grammar, in the following steps:

(1) Express the grammar in EBNF, with a single production rule for each nonterminal symbol, and perform any necessary grammar transformations. In particular, always eliminate left recursion, and left-factorize wherever possible.

(2) Transcribe each EBNF production rule $N ::= X$ to a parsing method `parseN`, whose body is determined by X.

(3) Make the parser consist of:

   • a private variable `currentToken`;

   • private parsing methods developed in step (2);

- private auxiliary methods `accept` and `acceptIt` (to be explained later), both of which call the scanner;

- a public `parse` method that calls `parseS` (where *S* is the start symbol of the grammar), having first called the scanner to store the first input token in `currentToken`.

Example 4.12 Recursive-descent parser for Mini-Triangle

Consider the language Mini-Triangle whose BNF grammar was given in Example 1.3. We systematically develop a Mini-Triangle parser as follows.

Step (1) is to express the grammar in EBNF, performing any necessary transformations. Recall production rules (1.2a–b):

    Command   ::=   single-Command
                 | Command ; single-Command

The left recursion here is a BNF device for specifying a sequence of single-commands separated by semicolons. By eliminating the left recursion, we can specify this more directly using the '*' notation of EBNF:

    Command   ::=   single-Command (; single-Command)*

Now recall production rule (1.6):

    V-name   ::=   Identifier

We can simplify the grammar (for parsing purposes) by substituting Identifier for V-name wherever it appears on the right-hand side of a production rule, such as (1.3):

    single-Command   ::=   Identifier := Expression
                      | Identifier (Expression)
                      | if Expression then single-Command
                                 else single-Command
                      | ...

The first two alternatives above can now be left-factorized:[3]

    single-Command   ::=   Identifier (:= Expression | (Expression))
                      | if Expression then single-Command
                                 else single-Command
                      | ...

---

[3] Distinguish carefully between '(' and ')', which are EBNF grouping parentheses, and the emboldened '(' and ')', which are terminal symbols of the source language. We will consistently use this typography to distinguish between EBNF symbols and any terminal symbols that happen to resemble them.

These transformations are justified because they will make the grammar more suitable for parsing purposes. After making similar transformations to other parts of the grammar, we obtain the following complete EBNF grammar of Mini-Triangle:

Program	::=	single-Command	(4.6)
Command	::=	single-Command (**;** single-Command)*	(4.7)
single-Command	::=	Identifier (**:=** Expression | **(** Expression **)**)	(4.8)
	|	**if** Expression **then** single-Command	
		else single-Command	
	|	**while** Expression **do** single-Command	
	|	**let** Declaration **in** single-Command	
	|	**begin** Command **end**	
Expression	::=	primary-Expression	(4.9)
		(Operator primary-Expression)*	
primary-Expression	::=	Integer-Literal	(4.10)
	|	Identifier	
	|	Operator primary-Expression	
	|	**(** Expression **)**	
Declaration	::=	single-Declaration (**;** single-Declaration)*	(4.11)
single-Declaration	::=	**const** Identifier ~ Expression	(4.12)
	|	**var** Identifier **:** Type-denoter	
Type-denoter	::=	Identifier	(4.13)

We have excluded production rules (1.10) through (1.13), which specify the syntax of operators, identifiers, literals, and comments, all in terms of individual characters. This part of the syntax is called the language's *lexicon* (or *microsyntax*). The lexicon is of no concern to the parser, which will view each identifier, literal, and operator as a single token. Instead, the lexicon will later be used to develop the scanner, in Section 4.5.

We shall assume that the scanner returns tokens of class `Token`, defined in Example 4.2. Each token consists of a kind and a spelling. The parser will examine only the kind of each token.

Step (2) is to convert each EBNF production rule to a parsing method. The parsing methods will be as follows:

```
private void parseProgram ();
private void parseCommand ();
private void parseSingleCommand ();
private void parseExpression ();
private void parsePrimaryExpression ();
private void parseDeclaration ();
private void parseSingleDeclaration ();
```

```
private void parseTypeDenoter ();
private void parseIdentifier ();
private void parseIntegerLiteral ();
private void parseOperator ();
```

Here is method parseSingleDeclaration:

```
private void parseSingleDeclaration () {
    switch (currentToken.kind) {          single-Declaration ::=

    case Token.CONST:
        {
            acceptIt();                   const
            parseIdentifier();            Identifier
            accept(Token.IS);             ~
            parseExpression();            Expression
        }
        break;

    case Token.VAR:                                    |

        {
            acceptIt();                   var
            parseIdentifier();            Identifier
            accept(Token.COLON);          :
            parseTypeDenoter();           Type-denoter
        }
        break;

    default:
        report a syntactic error
    }
}
```

Note the use of the auxiliary method acceptIt, which unconditionally fetches the next token from the source program. The following is also correct:

```
    case Token.VAR:
        {
            accept(Token.VAR);            var
            parseIdentifier();            Identifier
            accept(Token.COLON);          :
            parseTypeDenoter();           Type-denoter
        }
        break;
```

Here 'accept(Token.VAR);' would check that the current token is of kind Token.VAR. In this context, however, such a check is redundant.

Now here is method parseCommand:

```
private void parseCommand () {          Command ::=
    parseSingleCommand();                   single-Command
    while (currentToken.kind
            == Token.SEMICOLON)
    {                                       (
        acceptIt();                             ;
        parseSingleCommand();                   single-Command
    }                                       )*
}
```

This method illustrates something new. The EBNF notation '(; single-Command)*' signifies a sequence of zero or more occurrences of '; single-Command'. To parse this we use a while-loop, which is iterated zero or more times. The condition for continuing the iteration is simply that the current token is a semicolon.

Method `parseDeclaration` is similar to `parseCommand`. The remaining methods are as follows:

```
private void parseProgram () {          Program ::=
    parseSingleCommand();                   single-Command
}

private void parseSingleCommand () {    single-Command ::=
    switch (currentToken.kind) {

    case Token.IDENTIFIER:
        {
            parseIdentifier();                  Identifier
            switch (currentToken.kind) {        (
            case Token.BECOMES:
                {
                    acceptIt();                     :=
                    parseExpression();              Expression
                }
                break;

            case Token.LPAREN:                  |
                {
                    acceptIt();                     (
                    parseExpression();              Expression
                    accept(Token.RPAREN);           )
                }
                break;

            default:
                report a syntactic error
            }                                   )
        }
        break;
```

```
        case Token.IF:                              |
            {
                acceptIt();                         if
                parseExpression();                  Expression
                accept(Token.THEN);                 then
                parseSingleCommand();               single-Command
                accept(Token.ELSE);                 else
                parseSingleCommand();               single-Command
            }
            break;

        case Token.WHILE:                           |
            {
                acceptIt();                         while
                parseExpression();                  Expression
                accept(Token.DO);                   do
                parseSingleCommand();               single-Command
            }
            break;

        case Token.LET:                             |
            {
                acceptIt();                         let
                parseDeclaration();                 Declaration
                accept(Token.IN);                   in
                parseSingleCommand();               single-Command
            }
            break;

        case Token.BEGIN:                           |
            {
                acceptIt();                         begin
                parseCommand();                     Command
                accept(Token.END);                  end
            }
            break;

        default:
            report a syntactic error
        }
    }

    private void parseExpression () {     Expression ::=
        parsePrimaryExpression();             primary-Expression
        while (currentToken.kind
                == Token.OPERATOR) {              (
```

```
            parseOperator();                        Operator
            parsePrimaryExpression();               primary-Expression
        }                                           )*
    }

    private void parsePrimaryExpression () {
        switch (currentToken.kind) {                primary-Expression ::=
        case Token.INTLITERAL:
            parseIntegerLiteral();                      Integer-Literal
            break;

        case Token.IDENTIFIER:                      |
            parseIdentifier();                          Identifier
            break;

        case Token.OPERATOR:                        |
            {
                parseOperator();                        Operator
                parsePrimaryExpression();               primary-Expression
            }
            break;

        case Token.LPAREN:                          |
            {
                acceptIt();                             (
                parseExpression();                      Expression
                accept(Token.RPAREN);                   )
            }

            break;

        default:
            report a syntactic error
    }

    private void parseTypeDenoter () {              Type-denoter ::=
        parseIdentifier();                              Identifier
    }
```

The nonterminal symbol Identifier corresponds to a single token, so the method parseIdentifier is similar to accept:

```
    private void parseIdentifier () {
        if (currentToken.kind == Token.IDENTIFIER)
            currentToken = scanner.scan();
        else
            report a syntactic error
    }
```

The methods `parseIntegerLiteral` and `parseOperator` are analogous.[4]

Step (3) is to assemble the complete parser:

```
public class Parser {

    private Token currentToken;

    private void accept (byte expectedKind) {
        if (currentToken.kind == expectedKind)
            currentToken = scanner.scan();
        else
            report a syntactic error
    }

    private void acceptIt () {
        currentToken = scanner.scan();
    }

    ...   // Parsing methods, as above.

    public void parse () {
        currentToken = scanner.scan();
        parseProgram();
        if (currentToken.kind != Token.EOT)
            report a syntactic error
    }
}
```

The parser reads the next input token by calling the scanner. The method call 'scanner.scan()' constructs the next token from the input and returns it. (This will be explained in Section 4.5.)

Note the following points:

• The parser examines only the kind of the current token, ignoring its spelling.

• After parsing the program, `parse` checks that the token following the program is the end-of-text.

• The parsing methods are mutually recursive (because the production rules are mutually recursive). For example, `parseCommand` calls `parseSingleCommand`, which may call `parseCommand` recursively.

□

---

[4] Later we shall enhance method `parseIdentifier` to construct an AST terminal node containing the identifier's spelling. It would be wrong to write simply 'accept(Token.IDENTIFIER);', because this would discard the identifier token, including its spelling. The same point applies to `parseIntegerLiteral`, and `parseOperator`.

Having worked through a complete example, let us now study in general terms how we systematically develop a recursive-descent parser from a suitable grammar. The two main steps are: (1) express the grammar in EBNF, performing any necessary transformations; and (2) convert the EBNF production rules to parsing methods. It will be convenient to examine these steps in reverse order.

Converting EBNF production rules to parsing methods

Consider an EBNF production rule $N ::= X$. We convert this production rule to a parsing method named parse$N$. This method's body will be derived from the extended RE X:

```
private void parseN () {
    parse X
}
```

Here 'parse X' is supposed to parse an X-phrase, i.e., a terminal string generated by X. (And of course the task of method parse$N$ is to parse an N-phrase.)

Next, we perform stepwise refinement on 'parse X', decomposing it according to the structure of X. (In the following, X and Y stand for arbitrary extended REs.)

- We refine 'parse ε' to a dummy statement.

- We refine 'parse t' (where t is a terminal symbol) to:

  ```
  accept(t);
  ```

  In a situation where the current terminal is already known to be t, the following is also correct and more efficient:

  ```
  acceptIt();
  ```

- We refine 'parse N' (where N is a nonterminal symbol) to a call of the corresponding parsing method:

  ```
  parseN();
  ```

- We refine 'parse $X\ Y$' to:

  ```
  {
      parse X
      parse Y
  }
  ```

The reasoning behind this is simple. The input must consist of an X-phrase followed by a Y-phrase. Since the parser works from left to right, it must parse the X-phrase and then parse the Y-phrase.

This refinement rule is easily generalized to 'parse $X_1 \ldots X_n$'.

- We refine 'parse $X\,|\,Y$' to:

```
switch (currentToken.kind) {
cases in starters⟦X⟧ :
    parse X
    break;
cases in starters⟦Y⟧ :
    parse Y
    break;
default:
    report a syntactic error
}
```

The reasoning behind this is also straightforward. The input must consist of either an X-phrase or a Y-phrase. The parser must parse one of these, and it must decide immediately which it will be. It should choose 'parse X' only if the current token is one that can start an X-phrase (since otherwise 'parse X' would certainly fail). And likewise it should choose 'parse Y' only if the current token is one that can start a Y-phrase. We can express these conditions abstractly in terms of the starter sets of X and Y, and concretely in terms of Java case labels.

The parser will work correctly only if *starters*⟦X⟧ and *starters*⟦Y⟧ are disjoint. Otherwise the parser could not know whether to parse an X-phrase or a Y-phrase. In fact, if token t is in both *starters*⟦X⟧ and *starters*⟦Y⟧, the switch-statement will contain two occurrences of '**case** t:', and will fail to compile. (See Example 4.15.)

This refinement rule is easily generalized to 'parse X_1 | … | X_n'.

• We refine 'parse X*' to:

```
while (currentToken.kind is in starters⟦X⟧)
    parse X
```

The reasoning behind this is as follows. The input must consist of zero or more consecutive X-phrases. The parser must repeatedly parse X-phrases, and it does this by means of a while-loop. Before each iteration, it must decide whether to terminate or to continue parsing X-phrases. It should continue only if the current token is one that can start an X-phrase (since otherwise 'parse X' would certainly fail).

The parser will work correctly only if *starters*⟦X⟧ is disjoint from the set of tokens that can follow X* in this particular context. Suppose that some token t is in *starters*⟦X⟧ and can also follow X*. When the current token is t, the parser will continue parsing X-phrases even when it should terminate. (See Example 4.16.)

The following examples illustrate the stepwise refinement of parsing methods.

Example 4.13 Stepwise refinement of `parseCommand`

Let us follow the stepwise refinement of the method `parseCommand` of Example 4.12, starting from production rule (4.7):

```
Command ::= single-Command (; single-Command)*
```

We start with the following outline of the method:

```
private void parseCommand () {
    parse single-Command (; single-Command)*
}
```

Now we refine 'parse single-Command (; single-Command)*' to:

```
parseSingleCommand ();
parse (; single-Command)*
```

Now we refine 'parse (; single-Command)*' to:

```
while (currentToken.kind == Token.SEMICOLON)
    parse (; single-Command)
```

since *starters*⟦*;* single-Command⟧ = { *;* }.

Finally we refine 'parse (; single-Command)' to:

```
{
    acceptIt ();
    parseSingleCommand ();
}
```

In this situation we know already that the current token is a semicolon, so 'accept-It();' is a correct alternative to 'accept(Token.SEMICOLON);'.

□

Example 4.14 *Stepwise refinement of* parseSingleDeclaration

Let us also follow the stepwise refinement of the method parseSingleDeclaration of Example 4.12, starting from production rule (4.11):

single-Declaration ::= **const** Identifier ~ Expression
                | **var** Identifier **:** Type-denoter

We start with the following outline of the method:

```
private void parseSingleDeclaration () {
    parse const Identifier ~ Expression | var Identifier : Type-denoter
}
```

Now we refine 'parse **const** ... | **var** ...' to:

```
switch (currentToken.kind) {

case Token.CONST:
    parse const Identifier ~ Expression
    break;
```

```
case Token.VAR:
    parse var Identifier : Type-denoter
    break;

default:
    report a syntactic error
}
```

since *starters*⟦**const** ...⟧ = {**const**} and *starters*⟦**var** ...⟧ = {**var**}. Fortunately, these starter sets are disjoint.

Finally, we refine 'parse **const** Identifier ~ Expression' to:

```
{
    acceptIt();
    parseIdentifier();
    accept(Token.IS);
    parseExpression();
}
```

and 'parse **var** Identifier : Type-denoter' similarly, as shown in Example 4.12.

□

In defining how to refine 'parse $X \mid Y$' and 'parse X^*', we stated certain conditions that must be satisfied. These conditions are:

- If the grammar contains $X \mid Y$, *starters*⟦X⟧ and *starters*⟦Y⟧ must be disjoint.
- If the grammar contains X^*, *starters*⟦X⟧ must be disjoint from the set of tokens that can follow X^* in this particular context.

A grammar that satisfies both these conditions is called an ***LL(1) grammar***.

Recursive-descent parsing is suitable *only* for LL(1) grammars.

Not all programming language grammars are LL(1). In practice, however, nearly every programming language grammar can easily be transformed to make it LL(1), without changing the language it generates. Why this should be so is a matter for conjecture, but often a language designer will consciously design the new language's syntax to be suitable for recursive-descent parsing.

The following examples illustrate grammars that are not LL(1). However, simple transformations of these grammars are sufficient to make them LL(1).

Example 4.15 Non-LL(1) grammar for Mini-Triangle

Recall production rules (1.3a–f) in the original grammar of Mini-Triangle:

single-Command   ::=   V-name **:=** Expression
            | Identifier **(** Expression **)**
            | **if** Expression **then** single-Command
                      else single-Command
            | ...

The relevant starter sets are:

$starters[\![$V-name **:=** Expression$]\!]$ $= \; starters[\![$V-name$]\!]$
                                         $= \; \{$Identifier$\}$

$starters[\![$Identifier **(** Expression **)** $]\!]$ $= \; \{$Identifier$\}$

$starters[\![$**if** Expression **then** ...$]\!]$ $= \; \{$**if**$\}$

The first two are *not* disjoint, so the grammar is not LL(1).

What would happen if we tried to develop a parsing method directly from the above production rule? The parsing method would turn out as follows:

```
private void parseSingleCommand () {
    switch (currentToken.kind) {

    case Token.IDENTIFIER: {
            parseVname();
            accept(Token.BECOMES);
            parseExpression();
        }
        break;

    case Token.IDENTIFIER: {
            parseIdentifier();
            accept(Token.LPAREN);
            parseExpression();
            accept(Token.RPAREN)
        }
        break;

    case Token.IF:
        ...

    default:
        ...
    }
}
```

This parser is clearly incorrect, and will not compile due to the duplicate case label.

Fortunately the problematic production rule can easily be transformed, by substitution and left factorization, to solve this particular problem. This was done in Example 4.12.

□

Example 4.16 Non-LL(1) grammar for Algol

Consider the following production rules taken from a grammar of Algol:

Block   ::=   **begin** Declaration (**;** Declaration)* **;** Command **end**

Declaration   ::=   **integer** Identifier (**,** Identifier)*

Here *starters*⟦**;** Declaration⟧ = {**;**}, and the set of terminals that can follow '(**;** Declaration)*' in this context is {**;**}. These sets are not disjoint, so the grammar is not LL(1).

If we tried to develop a parsing method directly from the production rule defining Block, we would get:

```
private void parseBlock () {
    accept(Token.BEGIN);
    parseDeclaration();
    while (currentToken.kind == Token.SEMICOLON)
    {
        acceptIt();
        parseDeclaration();
    }
    accept(Token.SEMICOLON);
    parseCommand();
    accept(Token.END);
}
```

This is clearly incorrect. Iteration will continue as long as the current token is a semicolon. But this might be the semicolon that separates the declarations from the command, e.g., the second semicolon in:

```
begin integer i; integer j; i := j+1 end
```

Then `parseBlock` would attempt to parse the command 'i := j+1' as a declaration.

Fortunately, we can transform the production rule defining Block:

Block ::= **begin** Declaration **;** (Declaration **;**)* Command **end**

This does not affect the generated language, but leads to the following correct parsing method:

```
private void parseBlock () {
    accept(Token.BEGIN);
    parseDeclaration();
    accept(Token.SEMICOLON);
    while (currentToken.kind == Token.INTEGER)
    {
        parseDeclaration();
        accept(Token.SEMICOLON);
    }
```

```
    parseCommand();
    accept(Token.END);
}
```

This eliminates the problem, assuming that *starters*⟦Declaration **;** ⟧ is disjoint from *starters*⟦Command⟧.

⬜

The above examples are quite typical. Although the LL(1) condition is quite restrictive, in practice most programming language grammars can be transformed to make them LL(1) and thus suitable for recursive-descent parsing.

Performing grammar transformations

Left factorization is essential in some situations, as illustrated by the following example.

Example 4.17 Left factorization

In Example 4.12, the production rule 'V-name ::= Identifier' was eliminated. The occurrences of V-name on the right-hand sides of (1.3a) and (1.5b) were simply replaced by Identifier, giving:

```
single-Command    ::=   Identifier := Expression
                   |     Identifier ( Expression )
                   |     if Expression then single-Command
                              else single-Command
                   |     ...
```

The starter sets are not disjoint:

> *starters*⟦Identifier **:=** Expression⟧   = {Identifier}
>
> *starters*⟦Identifier **(** Expression **)** ⟧   = {Identifier}

However, the substitution created an opportunity for left factorization:

```
single-Command    ::=   Identifier (:= Expression | ( Expression ))
                   |     if Expression then single-Command
                              else single-Command
                   |     ...
```

This is an improvement, since now the relevant starter sets *are* disjoint:

> *starters*⟦ **:=** Expression⟧   = { **:=** }
>
> *starters*⟦ **(** Expression **)** ⟧   = { **(** }

⬜

Left recursion must always be eliminated if the grammar is to be LL(1). The following example shows why.

Example 4.18 Left recursion elimination

Recall production rules (1.2a–b) in the grammar of Mini-Triangle:

    Command   ::=   single-Command
                   | Command ; single-Command

In Example 4.12 we eliminated this left recursion, yielding:

    Command   ::=   single-Command (; single-Command)*

What would happen if we omitted this transformation? First we would compute the relevant starter sets:

    starters⟦single-Command⟧   = { Identifier, **if**, **while**, **let**, **begin**}
    starters⟦Command ; single-Command⟧ = { Identifier, **if**, **while**, **let**, **begin**}

Then we would write the parsing method like this:

```
private void parseCommand () {
    switch (currentToken.kind) {

    case Token.IDENTIFIER:
    case Token.IF:
    case Token.WHILE:
    case Token.LET:
    case Token.BEGIN:
        parseSingleCommand();
        break;

    case Token.IDENTIFIER:
    case Token.IF:
    case Token.WHILE:
    case Token.LET:
    case Token.BEGIN:   {
            parseCommand();
            accept(Token.SEMICOLON);
            parseSingleCommand();
        }
        break;

    default:
        report a syntactic error
    }
}
```

This method cannot tell which way to go if the current token is an identifier, 'if', 'while', 'let', or 'begin'. It simply does not have the information required to make a correct decision. (In fact, this method will fail to compile due to the duplicate case labels.)

In general, a grammar that exhibits left recursion cannot be LL(1). Any attempt to convert left-recursive production rules directly into parsing methods would result in an incorrect parser. It is easy to see why. Given the left-recursive production rule:

$$N ::= X \mid N\ Y$$

we find:

$$starters[\![N\ Y]\!]\ = starters[\![N]\!]\ = starters[\![X]\!] \cup starters[\![N\ Y]\!]$$

so $starters[\![X]\!]$ and $starters[\![N\ Y]\!]$ cannot be disjoint.

4.4 Abstract syntax trees

A recursive-descent parser determines the source program's phrase structure *implicitly*, in the sense that it finds the beginning and end of each phrase. In a one-pass compiler, this is quite sufficient for the syntactic analyzer to know when to call the contextual analyzer and code generator. In a multi-pass compiler, however, the syntactic analyzer must construct an *explicit* representation of the source program's phrase structure. Here we shall assume that the representation is to be an AST.

4.4.1   Representation

The following example illustrates how we can define ASTs in Java.

Example 4.19 Abstract syntax trees of Mini-Triangle

Figure 4.4 shows an example of a Mini-Triangle AST. Below we summarize all possible forms of Mini-Triangle AST, showing how each form relates to one of the production rules of the Mini-Triangle abstract syntax (Example 1.5):

- Program ASTs (P):

$$
\begin{array}{c}
\text{Program} \\
\mid \qquad (1.14) \\
C
\end{array}
$$

- Command ASTs (C):

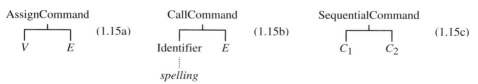

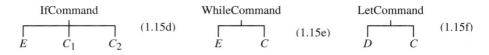

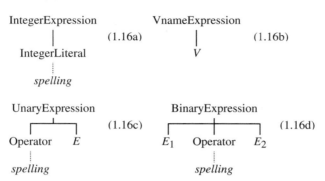

- Expression ASTs (E):

- V-name ASTs (V):

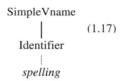

- Declaration ASTs (D):

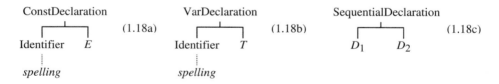

- Type-denoter ASTs (T):

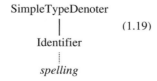

Each AST node has a tag that determines what (if any) subtrees that node has. For example:

- A node with tag 'IfCommand' is the root of a **Command** AST with three subtrees: an **Expression** AST and two **Command** ASTs.

- A node with tag 'ConstDeclaration' is the root of a Declaration AST with two subtrees: an Identifier AST and an Expression AST.

- A node with tag 'Identifier' is the root of an Identifier AST. This is just a terminal node, whose only content is its spelling.

We need to define Java classes that capture the structure of Mini-Triangle ASTs. We begin by introducing an abstract class, called AST, for all abstract syntax trees:

```
public abstract class AST {
    ...
}
```

Every node in the AST will be an object of a subclass of AST.

- Program ASTs:

```
public class Program extends AST {
    public Command C;                // body of program
    ...
}
```

Program has only a single form, consisting simply of a Command, so the class Program simply contains an instance variable for the command that is the body of the program.

For each nonterminal in the Mini-Triangle abstract syntax that has several forms (such as Command), we introduce an *abstract* class (such as Command), and several concrete subclasses.

- Command ASTs:

```
public abstract class Command extends AST { ... }

public class AssignCommand extends Command {
    public Vname V;                  // left-side variable
    public Expression E;             // right-side expression
    ...
}

public class CallCommand extends Command {
    public Identifier I;             // procedure name
    public Expression E;             // actual parameter
    ...
}

public class SequentialCommand extends Command {
    public Command C1, C2;           // subcommands
    ...
}
```

```
public class IfCommand extends Command {
    public Expression E;              // if condition
    public Command C1, C2;            // true and false commands
    ...
}

public class WhileCommand extends Command {
    public Expression E;              // loop condition
    public Command C;                 // body of loop
    ...
}

public class LetCommand extends Command {
    public Declaration D;             // block declarations
    public Command C;                 // body of block
    ...
}
```

Command is a subclass of AST, and defines any features that are common to all Command ASTs. The root node of any particular Command AST will be an object of some subclass of Command. We introduce a concrete class for each distinct form of command in the abstract syntax: AssignCommand, IfCommand, WhileCommand, etc. Each of these concrete classes is a subclass of Command, and contains instance variables for the subtrees of the corresponding form of command. For example, AssignCommand contains instance variables of class Vname and Expression.

For each of the remaining nonterminals (Expression, V-name, Declaration, and Type-denoter), we similarly introduce an abstract class and a group of concrete subclasses.

- Expression ASTs:

```
public abstract class Expression extends AST { ... }

public class UnaryExpression extends Expression {
    public Operator O;                // unary operator symbol
    public Expression E;              // operand
    ...
}

public class BinaryExpression extends Expression {
    public Operator O;                // binary operator symbol
    public Expression E1, E2;         // left and right operands
    ...
}
```

- V-name ASTs:

```
public abstract class Vname extends AST { ... }
```

```
public class SimpleVname extends Vname {
    public Identifier I;           // value-or-variable name
    ...
}
```

- Declaration ASTs:

```
public abstract class Declaration extends AST { ... }

public class ConstDeclaration extends Declaration {
    public Identifier I;           // constant name
    public Expression E;           // constant value
    ...
}

public class VarDeclaration extends Declaration {
    public Identifier I;           // variable name
    public TypeDenoter T;          // variable type
    ...
}

public class SequentialDeclaration extends Declaration
{
    public Declaration D1, D2;     // subdeclarations
    ...
}
```

- Type-denoter ASTs:

```
public abstract class TypeDenoter extends AST { ... }

public class SimpleTypeDenoter extends TypeDenoter {
    public Identifier I;           // type name
    ...
}
```

Finally we introduce an abstract class, Terminal, to represent the terminal nodes in the AST. A terminal node corresponds to a token (identifier, integer-literal, or operator) in the Mini-Triangle source program. The only data at a terminal node is the spelling of that token, so the Terminal class includes an instance variable for the spelling. We then introduce concrete classes for each distinct kind of terminal node (Identifier, IntegerLiteral, Operator).

- Terminal nodes:

```
public abstract class Terminal extends AST {
    public String spelling;        // token spelling from scanner
    ...
}

public class Identifier extends Terminal { ... }
```

```
public class IntegerLiteral extends Terminal { ... }

public class Operator extends Terminal { ... }
```

In order to construct an AST, each concrete class must also define a suitable constructor. For example, the constructor for the `AssignCommand` class would be defined as follows:

```
public AssignCommand (Vname V, Expression E) {
    this.V = V;
    this.E = E;
}
```

and the constructor for the `Identifier` class would be defined as follows:

```
public Identifier (String spelling) {
    this.spelling = spelling;
}
```

□

The Java representation of ASTs illustrated in Example 4.19 is not the only possibility. Exercise 4.16 suggests an alternative representation.

To make the syntactic analyzer construct the AST, we must augment the parser with calls to the constructors of the various concrete classes. This is explained next.

4.4.2   Construction

It is straightforward to make a recursive-descent parser construct an AST to represent the source program's phrase structure. We enhance the parser as follows:

- We make each method parse*N*, as well as parsing an *N*-phrase, return that phrase's AST as its result.

- We make the body of parse*N* construct the *N*-phrase's AST by combining the ASTs of any subphrases (or by creating a terminal node).

Thus, for production rule $N ::= X$:

```
private ASTN parseN () {
    ASTN itsAST;
    parse X, at the same time constructing itsAST
    return itsAST;
}
```

where AST_N is the abstract subclass of AST corresponding to nonterminal N.

Example 4.20 Construction of Mini-Triangle ASTs

Here we enhance the Mini-Triangle parser of Example 4.12, to construct an AST representing the source program. The enhanced parsing methods will be as follows:

```
private Program        parseProgram ();
private Command        parseCommand ();
private Command        parseSingleCommand ();
private Expression     parseExpression ();
private Expression     parsePrimaryExpression ();
private Declaration    parseDeclaration ();
private Declaration    parseSingleDeclaration ();
private TypeDenoter    parseTypeDenoter ();
private Identifier     parseIdentifier ();
private IntegerLiteral parseIntegerLiteral ();
private Operator       parseOperator ();
```

Each returns an AST of the appropriate class.

Here is the enhanced method `parseSingleDeclaration` (with the enhancements italicized for emphasis):

```
private Declaration parseSingleDeclaration () {
    Declaration declAST;
    switch (currentToken.kind) {

    case Token.CONST: {
        acceptIt();
        Identifier iAST = parseIdentifier();
        accept(Token.IS);
        Expression eAST = parseExpression();
        declAST = new ConstDeclaration(iAST, eAST);
    }
        break;

    case Token.VAR: {
        acceptIt();
        Identifier iAST = parseIdentifier();
        accept(Token.COLON);
        TypeDenoter tAST = parseTypeDenoter();
        declAST = new VarDeclaration(iAST, tAST);
    }
        break;

    default:
        report a syntactic error
    }
    return declAST;
}
```

This method is fairly typical. It has been enhanced with a local variable, declAST, in which the AST of the single-declaration will be stored. The method eventually returns this AST as its result. Local variables iAST, eAST, and tAST are introduced where required to contain the ASTs of the single-declaration's subphrases.

Here is the enhanced method parseCommand:

```
private Command parseCommand () {
    Command c1AST = parseSingleCommand();
    while (currentToken.kind == Token.SEMICOLON) {
        acceptIt();
        Command c2AST = parseSingleCommand();
        c1AST = new SequentialCommand(c1AST, c2AST);
    }
    return c1AST;
}
```

This method contains a loop, arising from the iteration '*' in production rule (4.7), which in turn was introduced by eliminating the left recursion in (1.2a–b). We must be careful to construct an AST with the correct structure. The local variable c1AST is used to accumulate this AST.

Suppose that the command being parsed is 't := x; x := y; y := t'. Then after the method parses 't := x', it sets c1AST to the AST for 't := x'; after it parses 'x := y', it updates c1AST to the AST for 't := x; x := y'; and after it parses 'y := t', it updates c1AST to the AST for 't := x; x := y; y := t'.

Here is an outline of the enhanced method parseSingleCommand:

```
private Command parseSingleCommand () {
    Command comAST;
    switch (currentToken.kind) {

    case Token.IDENTIFIER: {
        Identifier iAST = parseIdentifier();
        switch (currentToken.kind) {
        case Token.BECOMES: {
            acceptIt();
            Expression eAST = parseExpression();
            comAST = new AssignCommand(iAST, eAST);
        }
        break;
        case Token.LPAREN: {
            acceptIt();
            Expression eAST = parseExpression();
            accept(Token.RPAREN);
            comAST = new CallCommand(iAST, eAST);
        }
        break;
```

```
                    default:
                        report a syntactic error
                    }
            }
            break;

        case Token.IF:
            ...
        case Token.WHILE:
            ...
        case Token.LET: {
                acceptIt();
                Declaration dAST = parseDeclaration();
                accept(Token.IN);
                Command cAST = parseSingleCommand();
                comAST = new LetCommand(dAST, cAST);
            }
            break;

        case Token.BEGIN: {
                acceptIt();
                comAST = parseCommand();
                accept(Token.END);
            }
            break;

        default:
            report a syntactic error
        }
        return comAST;
}
```

If the single-command turns out to be of the form 'begin C end', there is no need to construct a new AST, since the 'begin' and 'end' are just command brackets. So in this case the method immediately stores C's AST in comAST.

The method parseIdentifier constructs an AST terminal node:

```
    private Identifier parseIdentifier () {
        Identifier idAST;
        if (currentToken.kind == Token.IDENTIFIER) {
            idAST = new Identifier(currentToken.spelling);
            currentToken = scanner.scan();
        } else
            report a syntactic error
        return idAST;
    }
```

The methods parseIntegerLiteral and parseOperator do likewise.

The complete parser is:

```
public class Parser {

    private Token currentToken;

    ...  // Auxiliary methods.

    ...  // Enhanced parsing methods, as above.

    public Program parse () {
        currentToken = scanner.scan();
        Program progAST = parseProgram();
        if (currentToken.kind != Token.EOT)
            report a syntactic error
        return progAST;
    }

}
```

4.5 Scanning

The purpose of scanning is to recognize tokens in the source program. Scanning is somewhat analogous to parsing, but works at a finer level of detail. In parsing, the terminal symbols are tokens, which are to be grouped into larger phrases such as expressions and commands. In scanning, the terminal symbols are individual characters, which are to be grouped into tokens.

As well as tokens, the source program contains **separators**: blank space, comments, and the like. Separators serve to separate tokens, and to assist human readers of the program. But only tokens contribute to the program's phrase structure.

We can systematically develop a scanner in much the same way as a parser. We start with a **lexical grammar** specifying the source language's lexicon. This grammar's terminal symbols are individual characters, and its nonterminal symbols include Token and Separator. The lexical grammar must not exhibit self-embedding.

We develop the scanner as follows:

(1) Express the lexical grammar in EBNF, performing any necessary grammar transformations.

(2) Transcribe each EBNF production rule $N ::= X$ to a scanning method scan$N$, whose body is determined by X.

(3) Make the scanner consist of:

- a private variable currentChar;

- private auxiliary methods `take` and `takeIt`;

- private scanning methods developed in step (2), enhanced to record each token's kind and spelling;

- a public `scan` method that scans 'Separator* Token', discarding any separators but returning the token that follows them.

The scanning methods will be analogous to the parsing methods we met in Section 4.3. On entry to scan*N*, `currentChar` is supposed to contain the first character of a character sequence of kind *N*; on exit, `currentChar` is supposed to contain the character immediately following that character sequence.

Likewise, the auxiliary methods `take` and `takeIt` are analogous to the parser's auxiliary methods `accept` and `acceptIt`. Both `take` and `takeIt` will fetch the next character from the source text and store it in `currentChar`; however, `take` will do so only if its argument character matches `currentChar`.

The method `scan` is supposed to fetch the next token from the source program, each time it is called. But the next token might turn out to be preceded by some separators. This is the reason for scanning 'Separator* Token'. In this we are assuming that the source language has a conventional lexicon: separators may be used freely between tokens. (Most modern programming languages do follow this convention.)

Example 4.21 Scanner for Mini-Triangle

The lexical grammar of Mini-Triangle is partly given by production rules (1.10) through (1.13). We add production rules for Token and Separator:

Token	::=	Identifier | Integer-Literal | Operator |	(4.14)
		; | : | : = | ~ | (|) | eot	
Identifier	::=	Letter | Identifier Letter | Identifier Digit	(4.15)
Integer-Literal	::=	Digit | Integer-Literal Digit	(4.16)
Operator	::=	+ | – | * | / | < | > | = | \	(4.17)
Separator	::=	Comment | space | eol	(4.18)
Comment	::=	! Graphic* eol	(4.19)

In these production rules:

- space stands for a space character;

- eol stands for an end-of-line 'character';

- eot stands for an end-of-text 'character'.

(Visible characters can be expressed as themselves in (E)BNF, but these invisible characters cannot.) Also:

- Digit stands for one of the digits '0', '1', ..., or '9';

- Letter stands for one of the lowercase letters 'a', 'b', ..., or 'z';

- Graphic stands for a space or visible character.

Each of these nonterminals represents a group of single characters. Specifying them formally would be straightforward but tedious.

Note a very important point: the nonterminal symbol Identifier actually encompasses both identifiers and keywords. It turns out that any attempt to distinguish between identifiers and keywords in the lexical grammar gets us into difficulties. (See Exercise 4.18 for the reason.) We shall return to this point later.

Let us now develop a scanner for Mini-Triangle. A class definition for `Token` was given in Example 4.2.

Step (1) is to express the lexical grammar in EBNF and make any necessary transformations. We eliminate left recursion in (4.15) and (4.16), giving:

Identifier	::=	Letter (Letter | Digit)*	(4.20)
Integer-Literal	::=	Digit Digit*	(4.21)

Now we can simplify the lexical grammar by substitution and left factorization:

Token	::=	Letter (Letter | Digit)* | Digit Digit* |	(4.22)
		+ | - | * | / | < | > | = | \ |	
		; | : (= | ε) | ~ | (|) | eot	
Separator	::=	! Graphic* eol | space | eol	(4.23)

Step (2) is to convert the production rules to scanning methods, as below. (For the moment, ignore the code in italics: it anticipates enhancements to be made in step (3).)

```
private byte scanToken () {                    Token ::=
   switch (currentChar) {

   case 'a': case 'b': case 'c':
   ...        case 'y': case 'z':
      takeIt();                                Letter
      while (isLetter(currentChar)
            || isDigit(currentChar))
         takeIt();                             (Letter | Digit)*
      return Token.IDENTIFIER;

   case '0': case '1': case '2':
   case '3': case '4': case '5':
   case '6': case '7': case '8':
   case '9':                              |
      takeIt();                                Digit
      while (isDigit(currentChar))
         takeIt();                             Digit*
      return Token.INTLITERAL;
```

```
      case '+': case '-': case '*':
      case '/': case '<': case '>':
      case '=': case '\\':                    |
          takeIt();                              + | - | * | / | < | > | = | \
          return Token.OPERATOR;

      case ';':                               |
          takeIt();                              ;
          return Token.SEMICOLON;

      case ':':                               |
          takeIt();                              :
          if (currentChar == '=') {
              takeIt();                          ( =
              return Token.BECOMES;
          }
          else                                |
              return Token.COLON;               ε )

      case '~':                               |
          takeIt();                              ~
          return Token.IS;

      case '(':                               |
          takeIt();                              (
          return Token.LPAREN;

      case ')':                               |
          takeIt();                              )
          return Token.RPAREN;

      case '\000':                            |
          return Token.EOT;                      eot

      default:
          report a lexical error
      }
}

private void scanSeparator () {        Separator ::=
    switch (currentChar) {
    case '!': {
          takeIt();                              !
          while (
              isGraphic(currentChar))
              takeIt();                          Graphic*
              take('\n');                        eol
      }
      break;
```

```
case ' ': case '\n':
   takeIt();
   break;
}
```
                                                    |
                                                  space | eol

```
}
```

The auxiliary methods isDigit, isLetter, and isGraphic (not shown here) perform the obvious tests.

Step (3) is to assemble the complete scanner, and make it determine the token's kind and spelling. We can easily make scanToken return a small integer representing the token's kind; the necessary enhancements are italicized above. We can also make the auxiliary methods take and takeIt store the current character in the token's spelling (before fetching the next source character).

Here is the complete scanner, including the auxiliary methods:

```
public class Scanner {

   private char currentChar = first source character;

   // Kind and spelling of the current token:
   private byte currentKind;
   private StringBuffer currentSpelling;

   private void take (char expectedChar) {
      if (currentChar == expectedChar) {
         currentSpelling.append(currentChar);
         currentChar = next source character;
      } else
         report a lexical error
   }

   private void takeIt () {
      currentSpelling.append(currentChar);
      currentChar = next source character;
   }

   private boolean isDigit (char c) {
      ...  // Returns true iff the character c is a digit.
   }

   private boolean isLetter (char c) {
      ...  // Returns true iff the character c is a letter.
   }

   private boolean isGraphic (char c) {
      ...  // Returns true iff the character c is a graphic.
   }
```

```
   private byte scanToken () {
      ...  // As above.
   }

   private void scanSeparator () {
      ...  // As above.
   }

   public Token scan () {
      while (currentChar == '!'
             || currentChar == ' '
             || currentChar == '\n')
         scanSeparator();                        Separator*
      currentSpelling =
         new StringBuffer("");
      currentKind = scanToken();                 Token
      return new Token(currentKind,
         currentSpelling.toString());
   }
}
```

The lexical grammar did not distinguish between identifiers and keywords. Nevertheless, the scanner *must* properly classify these tokens. We can conveniently make this happen in the Token constructor, by checking whether the token's spelling matches any of the keywords. The modifications to the Token class definition (originally given in Example 4.2) are italicized below:

```
public class Token {

   public byte kind;
   public String spelling;

   public Token (byte kind, String spelling) {
      this.kind = kind; this.spelling = spelling;
      // If kind is IDENTIFIER and spelling matches one
      // of the keywords, change the token's kind accordingly:
      if (kind == IDENTIFIER)
         for (int k = BEGIN; k <= WHILE; k++)
            if (spelling.equals(spellings[k])) {
               this.kind = k;  break;
            }
   }

   // Constants denoting different kinds of token:
   public final static byte
      IDENTIFIER = 0, INTLITERAL = 1, OPERATOR = 2,
      BEGIN = 3, CONST = 4, DO = 5, ELSE = 6, END = 7,
      IF = 8, IN = 9, LET = 10, THEN = 11, VAR = 12,
      WHILE = 13, SEMICOLON = 14, COLON = 15,
```

```
        BECOMES = 16, IS = 17, LPAREN = 18,
        RPAREN = 19, EOT = 20;

    //  Spellings of different kinds of token (must correspond to the
    //    token kinds above):
    private final static String[] spellings = {
        "<identifier>", "<integer-literal>",
        "<operator>", "begin", "const", "do", "else",
        "end", "if", "in", "let", "then", "var",
        "while", ";", ":", ":=", "~", "(", ")", "<eot>"
    }
  }
```

It is worth reflecting why it made sense to eliminate the nonterminals Identifier, Integer-Literal, Operator, and Comment in Example 4.21. This had the effect of eliminating several methods (scanIdentifier, scanIntegerLiteral, scanOperator, and scanComment) that would otherwise have been developed as part of the scanner. Such a transformation is always possible, because a lexical grammar by definition generates a regular language, so any of its nonterminals can be eliminated by substitution. The transformation was motivated simply by efficiency considerations: measurements have shown that scanning can consume a surprisingly large proportion of compilation time, if not carefully implemented.

Finally, note that since a lexical grammar must generate a regular language, the scanner is always nonrecursive. (By contrast, the context-free grammar of a high-level language invariably exhibits self-embedding, so the parser is always recursive.)

4.6 Case study: syntactic analysis in the Triangle compiler

The Triangle syntactic analyzer consists of a package Triangle.Syntactic-Analyzer, which contains Parser, Scanner, and Token classes. The Parser class depends on the separate package Triangle.AbstractSyntaxTrees, which contains all of the class definitions for ASTs.

4.6.1 Scanning

The Scanner class performs scanning much as described in Section 4.5. The Token class has instance variables kind and spelling as shown in Example 4.21. It also has an additional instance variable, position, which is used to note the token's position in the source program. The spelling and position fields are useful for generating error reports.

The lexical grammar of Triangle expressed in EBNF may be found in Section B.8. Before developing the scanner, the lexical grammar was modified in two respects:

- The production rule for Token was modified to add end-of-text as a distinct token.

- Keywords were grouped with identifiers. (See Exercise 4.18 for an explanation.)

Most nonterminals were eliminated by substitution. The result was a lexical grammar containing only individual characters, nonterminals that represent individual characters (i.e., Letter, Digit, Graphic, and Blank), and the nonterminals Token and Separator:

Token   ::= Letter (Letter | Digit)* | Digit Digit* | (4.24)
           Op-character Op-character* | ' Graphic '
           . | , | ; | : (ε | =) | ~ | (|) | [|] | { | } |
           end-of-text

Separator ::= ! Graphic* end-of-line | Blank   (4.25)

The Triangle scanner was then developed from this lexical grammar, following the procedure described in Section 4.5.

4.6.2 Abstract syntax trees

The package `Triangle.AbstractSyntaxTrees` contains the class definitions for the AST, in a style similar to that of Example 4.19. Each concrete subclass contains a constructor for creating a new AST node, and the parser uses these to construct the complete AST of the whole program.

The package `Triangle.AbstractSyntaxTrees` does not actually hide the AST representation, so other parts of the compiler can directly access the instance variables representing the subtrees of a node. However, the package does define a *design pattern*, known as a *visitor*, for traversing the AST. This design pattern is used by the later phases of the compiler. (Visitors will be explained in Chapter 5.)

In the Triangle compiler, an AST node contains more fields than shown in Example 4.19. One such field, `position`, records the position of the corresponding phrase in the source program. This is derived from the `position` fields of the phrase's constituent tokens, and is useful for generating error reports. Every node in the AST has an associated position, so `position` is declared as an instance variable of the AST class. Some other fields (`decl`, `type`, and `entity`) are specific to certain classes of nodes (principally identifiers, expressions, and declarations, respectively), and are therefore declared as instance variables of the appropriate AST subclasses. These other fields will be used later by the contextual analyzer and code generator to decorate the AST.

4.6.3 Parsing

The `Parser` class contains a recursive-descent parser, as described in Section 4.3. The parser calls the `scan` method of the `Scanner` class to scan the source program, one token at a time. It calls the constructors of the `Triangle.AbstractSyntaxTrees` classes to construct the AST representing the source program.

The grammar of Triangle may be found in Appendix B, in the subsections entitled 'Syntax'. The parser was developed systematically from this grammar, much as described in Section 4.3.4.

The grammar transformations were mostly straightforward, but one transformation required particular care. The Triangle grammar includes the following production rules:

single-Command	::=	V-name **:** **=** Expression	(4.26a)
	|	Identifier **(** Actual-Parameter-Sequence **)**	(4.26b)
	|	...	
primary-Expression	::=	V-name	(4.27a)
	|	Identifier **(** Actual-Parameter-Sequence **)**	(4.27b)
	|	...	
V-name	::=	Identifier	(4.28a)
	|	V-name **.** Identifier	(4.28b)
	|	V-name **[** Expression **]**	(4.28c)

The right-hand sides of both (4.26a) and (4.26b) have identifiers in their starter sets, and so fail to satisfy the LL(1) condition. For the same reason, (4.27a) and (4.27b) fail to satisfy the LL(1) condition.

After left factorization and elimination of left recursion in (4.28a–c), we obtain:

V-name	::=	Identifier (**.** Identifier | **[** Expression **]**)*	(4.29)

Substitution for V-name in (4.26a) and (4.28a), followed by left factorization, yields:

single-Command	::=	Identifier ((**.** Identifier | **[** Expression **]**)*
		: **=** Expression
		| **(** Actual-Parameter-Sequence **)**
		)
	|	...
primary-Expression	::=	Identifier ((**.** Identifier | **[** Expression **]**)*
		| **(** Actual-Parameter-Sequence **)**
		)
	|	...

These production rules do satisfy the LL(1) condition, but they are messy. A nontrivial extended RE has been substituted for V-name in two places. If we proceed to develop a parser from these production rules, a nontrivial section of parsing code will appear in two different places.

Instead, we further transform (4.29) by introducing an auxiliary nonterminal symbol:

V-name	::=	Identifier rest-of-V-name	(4.30)
rest-of-V-name	::=	(**.** Identifier | **[** Expression **]**)*	(4.31)

and *now* substitute for V-name:

single-Command   ::=   Identifier   (rest-of-V-name **:=** Expression   (4.32)
                                         | **(** Actual-Parameter-Sequence **)**
)
                       | ...

primary-Expression   ::=   Identifier   (rest-of-V-name   (4.33)
                                         | **(** Actual-Parameter-Sequence **)**
)
                       | ...

These production rules satisfy the LL(1) condition, since:

$$starters[\![\text{rest-of-V-name := Expression}]\!] \quad = \quad starters[\![\text{rest-of-V-name}]\!] \ \cup \ \{:=\}$$
$$= \quad \{ ., [, := \}$$

$$starters[\![\text{(Actual-Parameter-Sequence)}]\!] = \quad \{ ( ) \}$$

Thus they are suitable for developing into parsing methods.

4.6.4   Error handling

If the syntactic analyzer discovers that the source program is not, in fact, a sentence of the Triangle grammar, it reports a syntactic error. It takes care to compose error reports that are helpful to the programmer. Let us see how this is done.

As already noted, positional information is recorded in tokens and in AST nodes. This information allows error reports generated by the syntactic analyzer (and other modules) to be related to the source program.

Some syntactic errors are detected by method `accept`. Since its argument is the expected token *t*, this method can easily compose a suitable report. For example, the ill-formed Triangle command 'if m > n max := m else max := n' will trigger a report like 'error: "then" expected here', together with positional information.

Other syntactic errors are detected in the situation illustrated by this parsing method:

```
private void parseSingleDeclaration () {
   switch (currentToken.kind) {
   case Token.CONST: {
         acceptIt();
         ...
      }
      break;
   case Token.VAR: {
         acceptIt();
         ...
      }
      break;
```

```
      default:
          report a syntactic error
      }
  }
```

Here too it is easy to compose a suitable report. For example, the ill-formed Triangle declaration 'd ~ 7' will trigger a report like 'error: "d" cannot start a declaration'.

The way in which parsing procedures are written can influence the quality of error handling. Suppose that the above parsing method were written this way instead:

```
  private void parseSingleDeclaration () {
      if (currentToken.kind == Token.CONST) {
          acceptIt(); ...
      } else {
          accept(Token.VAR); ...
      }
  }
```

This method would correctly parse well-formed single-declarations, but its error reporting would be inferior. For example, the ill-formed single-declaration 'd ~ 7' would trigger a misleading report like 'error: "var" expected here'. (The actual error is a missing 'const'.)

The Triangle scanner was made to return a special 'error' token, rather than reporting a lexical error as described in Section 4.5. The error token would then cause the parser to report a syntactic error. This tactic was found to result in better and more consistent error reporting overall.

The Triangle syntactic analyzer simply terminates after detecting and reporting a syntactic error. If it were part of an integrated language processor this would be reasonable behavior, since the Triangle programmer could immediately edit the erroneous part of the source program and recompile.

The Triangle compiler is a self-contained program, however, so the syntactic analyzer really ought to recover and continue parsing, in an attempt to discover and report any further syntactic errors in the source program. Error recovery is an interesting issue that will be discussed further in Section 9.2.1.

4.7 Further reading

A more detailed account of context-free grammars and regular expressions may be found in Chapter 2 of the companion textbook by Watt (1991).

The study of grammars, scanning, and parsing was one of the first major topics in computer science, and a large body of theory and practice has been accumulated. A variety of parsing algorithms have been developed, both top-down (the recursive-descent and backtracking algorithms) and bottom-up (Earley's algorithm, various precedence algorithms, and the LR algorithm). The major triumph of this research has been the discovery of algorithms for generating scanners and parsers *automatically* from lexical grammars and (suitable) context-free grammars, respectively. A comprehensive account of the theory of scanning and parsing may be found in Aho and Ullman (1972).

For practical application in compilers, the recursive-descent and LR algorithms are now generally held to be the best. Both algorithms are described in Chapter 4 of Aho *et al.* (1985), emphasizing practical application rather than theory. Chapter 3 of the same textbook covers scanning, including finite-state scanning (a good alternative to the algorithm described in Section 4.5).

In Section 4.3 we saw how to construct a parser from the source language's context-free grammar, and in Section 4.5 how to construct a scanner from its lexical grammar. It is striking how straightforward the construction algorithms are – almost mechanical. This is also true for other algorithms such as finite-state scanning and LR parsing. A variety of tools have been developed that generate scanners and parsers automatically.

Among the best-known are the UNIX tools Lex and Yacc. Lex (Lesk and Schmidt 1975) accepts the lexical grammar of a source language S, and from it generates a finite-state scanner for S, expressed in C. Analogously, Yacc (Johnson 1975) accepts the context-free grammar of S, and from it generates an LR parser for S, also expressed in C. Both Lex and Yacc are described in Aho *et al.* (1985), which explains how they work and shows how to use them in practical applications. More recently, versions of Lex and Yacc have appeared that generate scanners and parsers in languages other than C.

JavaCC (`www.suntest.com/JavaCC/`) is a powerful tool that can be used to generate a complete syntactic analyzer – scanner, parser, and tree builder – expressed in Java. JavaCC accepts a grammar expressed in EBNF, and the generated parser uses recursive descent.

Exercises

Section 4.1

4.1   Perform syntactic analysis of the Mini-Triangle program:

```
begin while true do putint(1); putint(0) end
```

along the lines of Figures 4.1 through 4.4.

4.2   Modify the class `Token` (Example 4.2) so that the instance variable `spelling` is left empty unless the token is an identifier, literal, or operator.

Section 4.2

4.3 In the following grammar fragment, factorize and eliminate left recursion wherever possible:

Numeral	::=	Digits | Digits . Digits
	|	Digits **e** Sign Digits
	|	Digits . Digits **e** Sign Digits
Digits	::=	Digit | Digits Digit
Digit	::=	**0** | **1** | **2** | **3**

4.4 (a) Compute the starter set of the RE (**P a s c a l** | **C** | **C + +** | **J a v a**).

(b) Compute the starter set of the RE ((**0** | **1** | **2**)* (**a** | **b**) **c**).

(c) Compute the starter sets of Digit, Digits, and Numeral in the grammar fragment of Exercise 4.3.

(d) Compute the starter sets of Subject and Object in the grammar of Example 4.8.

Section 4.3

4.5 Consider the micro-English grammar of Example 4.8.

(a) Perform a bottom-up parse of the micro-English sentence '**I like the mat** .', along the lines of Example 4.9.

(b) Perform a top-down parse of the same sentence, along the lines of Example 4.10.

(c) Show how the micro-English recursive-descent parser (Example 4.11) would parse the same sentence, using a diagram like Figure 4.5.

4.6 Complete the methods `parseObject` and `parseVerb` of the micro-English parser (Example 4.11).

4.7 The micro-English parser (Example 4.11) contains many duplicated checks. Point these out, and show how to eliminate them by using `acceptIt` rather than `accept`.

4.8 The micro-English grammar (Example 4.8) generates some sentences, such as '**I sees the cat** .', that are ungrammatical in English itself.

(a) Modify the grammar to ensure that the subject *agrees* with the verb. '**I**' should agree with '**like**' or '**see**', and other subjects should agree with '**is**' or '**sees**'.

(b) Modify the micro-English parser (Example 4.11) accordingly.

4.9 A calculator accepts commands according to the following EBNF grammar:

$$\text{Command} ::= \text{Expression} =$$

$$\text{Expression} ::= \text{Numeral} ((+ \mid - \mid *) \text{Numeral})*$$

$$\text{Numeral} ::= \text{Digit Digit}*$$

$$\text{Digit} ::= 0 \mid 1 \mid 2 \mid 3 \mid 4 \mid 5 \mid 6 \mid 7 \mid 8 \mid 9$$

(a) Construct a recursive-descent parser for a calculator command. The terminal symbols should be individual characters.

(b) Enhance the parser to display the command's result.

4.10* The following EBNF grammar generates a subset of the UNIX shell command language:

$$\text{Script} ::= \text{Command}*$$

$$\text{Command} ::= \text{Filename Argument}* \text{ eol}$$
$$\mid \text{Variable} = \text{Argument eol}$$
$$\mid \textbf{if } \text{Filename Argument}* \textbf{ then eol}$$
$$\text{Command}*$$
$$\textbf{else } \text{eol}$$
$$\text{Command}*$$
$$\textbf{fi } \text{eol}$$
$$\mid \textbf{for } \text{Variable } \textbf{in } \text{Argument}* \text{ eol}$$
$$\textbf{do } \text{eol}$$
$$\text{Command}*$$
$$\textbf{od } \text{eol}$$

$$\text{Argument} ::= \text{Filename} \mid \text{Literal} \mid \text{Variable}$$

The start symbol is Script. The token eol corresponds to an end-of-line.

Construct a recursive-descent parser for this language. Treat filenames, literals, and variables as single tokens.

4.11* Consider the rules for converting EBNF production rules to parsing methods (Section 4.3.4).

(a) Suggest an alternative refinement rule for 'parse $X \mid Y$', using an if-statement rather than a switch-statement.

(b) In some variants of EBNF, $[X]$ is used as an abbreviation for $X \mid \varepsilon$. Suggest a refinement rule for 'parse $[X]$'.

(c) In some variants of EBNF, X^+ is used as an abbreviation for $X\ X*$. Suggest a refinement rule for 'parse X^+'.

In each case, state any condition that must be satisfied for the refinement rule to be correct.

4.12* Suppose that an if-command with no else-part is added to Mini-Triangle:

single-Command ::=   …
      | **if** Expression **then** single-Command
          else single-Command
      | **if** Expression **then** single-Command

This gives rise to the well-known 'dangling else' ambiguity, illustrated by the if-command:

$$\text{if } E_1 \text{ then if } E_2 \text{ then } C_1 \text{ else } C_2 \qquad (4.34)$$

where C_1 and C_2 are (say) assignment commands. The if-command (4.34) has two possible phrase structures, depending on whether 'else C_2' is associated with 'if E_1 then …' or with 'if E_2 then …'. Demonstrate the ambiguity by showing two different syntax trees for (4.34).

Modify the parsing method `parseSingleCommand` (Example 4.12) to include the new form of if-command. How will your parsing method behave when required to parse (4.34)?

The 'dangling else' ambiguity is also found in Pascal and C. These languages *require* the ambiguity to be resolved by pairing each 'else' with the nearest unmatched 'if'. How does your parser's behavior relate to this requirement?

Section 4.4

4.13 Complete the enhanced Mini-Triangle parser of Example 4.20. Take particular care to construct correct ASTs for expressions. For example, the AST for the expression 'a – b + c' should be the left-branching tree in (a) below. (The right-branching tree (b) is the AST for 'a – (b + c)'.)

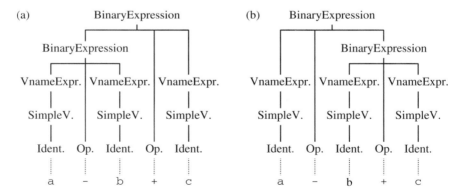

4.14* The grammar of expressions in Mini-Triangle treats all binary operators alike: they all have the same priority, and they all associate to the left. Thus 'a – b * c' is treated as equivalent to '(a – b) * c'.

The following grammar of expressions gives '*' and '/' higher priority than '+' and '−':

Expression	::=	secondary-Expression
	|	Expression add-Operator
		secondary-Expression
secondary-Expression	::=	primary-Expression
	|	secondary-Expression mult-Operator
		primary-Expression
primary-Expression	::=	Numeral
	|	Variable
	|	(Expression)
add-Operator	::=	+ | −
mult-Operator	::=	* | /

In this grammar, 'a − b * c' is treated as equivalent to 'a − (b * c)', but 'a − b + c' is treated as equivalent to '(a − b) + c'.

(a) Construct a recursive-descent parser from this grammar of expressions.

(b) Extend your parser to construct an AST. (Note that the concrete syntactic changes do not affect the abstract syntax.)

4.15 Suppose that a method `display` is to be added to class AST (Example 4.19). Given the Mini-Triangle AST of Figure 4.4, for example, `display` should output something like this:

```
Program
  LetCommand
    VarDeclaration
      Identifier y
      SimpleTypeDenoter
        Identifier Integer
    AssignCommand
      SimpleVname
        Identifier y
      BinaryExpression
        ...
```

Outline an implementation of `display`.

4.16* Consider the following alternative to the representation of ASTs presented in Section 4.4.1. AST nodes are simply classified as nonterminal nodes and terminal nodes. A *nonterminal* node contains a tag and an array of children. The tag distinguishes between different forms of phrases, such as an assignment-command, an if-command, a binary-expression, etc. Each child is just a pointer to another AST node. A *terminal* node contains a tag and a spelling. The tag distinguishes between an identifier, a literal, and an operator.

(a) Reimplement the class `AST` for Mini-Triangle.

(b) Provide this class with a method `display`, as specified in Exercise 4.15.

Section 4.5

4.17 The Mini-Triangle scanner (Example 4.21) stores the spellings of separators, including comments, only to discard them later. Modify the scanner to avoid this inefficiency.

4.18* Suppose that the Mini-Triangle lexical grammar (Example 4.21) were modified as follows, in an attempt to distinguish between identifiers and keywords (such as 'if', 'then', 'else', etc.):

Token	::=	Identifier | Integer-Literal | Operator |
		if | **then** | **else** | ... |
		; | **:** | **:=** | **~** | **(** | **)** | eot
Identifier	::=	Letter (Letter | Digit)*

Point out a serious problem with this lexical grammar. (Remember that the terminal symbols are individual characters.) Can you see any way to remedy this problem?

4.19 (a) Modify the Mini-Triangle lexical grammar (Example 4.21) as follows. Allow identifiers to contain single embedded underscores, e.g., 'set_up' (but not 'set__up', nor 'set_', nor '_up'). Allow real-literals, with a decimal point surrounded by digits, e.g., '3.1416' (but not '4.', nor '.125').

(b) Modify the Mini-Triangle scanner accordingly.

General

4.20* Consider a hypothetical programming language, NewSpeak, with an English-like syntax (expressed in EBNF) as follows:

Program	::=	Command **.**
Command	::=	single-Command single-Command*
single-Command	::=	**do nothing**
	|	**store** Expression **in** Variable
	|	**if** Condition **:** single-Command
		otherwise : single-Command
	|	**do** Expression **times :** single-Command

Expression	::=	Numeral
		Variable
		sum of Expression **and** Expression
		product of Expression **and** Expression
Condition	::=	Expression **is** Expression
		Expression **is less than** Expression
Numeral	::=	Digit Digit*
Variable	::=	Letter Letter*

Consecutive keywords and variables must be separated by blank space; otherwise blank space may be inserted freely between symbols.

Design and implement a syntactic analyzer for Newspeak:

(a) Decide which NewSpeak symbols should be tokens, and how they should be classified. Define the class `Token`. Then implement a NewSpeak scanner.

(b) Name and specify the parsing methods in a recursive-descent parser for NewSpeak. Then implement the NewSpeak parser.

4.21** Design and implement a complete syntactic analyzer for your favorite programming language.

4.22** A *cross-referencer* is a language processor that lists each identifier that occurs in the source program, together with the line numbers where that identifier occurs. Starting with *either* the Mini-Triangle syntactic analyzer *or* the syntactic analyzer you implemented in Exercise 4.21:

(a) Modify the scanner so that every token contains a field for the line number where it occurs.

(b) Develop a simple cross-referencer, reusing appropriate parts of your syntactic analyzer.

(c) Now make your cross-referencer distinguish between defining and applied occurrences of each identifier.

4.23** A *pretty-printer* is a language processor that reproduces the source program with consistent indentation and spacing. Starting with *either* the Mini-Triangle syntactic analyzer *or* the syntactic analyzer you implemented in Exercise 4.21:

(a) Develop a simple pretty-printer, reusing appropriate parts of your syntactic analyzer. At this stage your pretty-printer need not reproduce comments.

(b) Now make your pretty-printer reproduce comments.

CHAPTER FIVE

Contextual Analysis

Given a parsed program, the purpose of contextual analysis is to check that the program conforms to the source language's contextual constraints. For a typical programming language (statically typed and with static bindings), contextual constraints consist of:

- *Scope rules:* These are rules governing declarations and applied occurrences of identifiers.

- *Type rules:* These are rules that allow us to infer the types of expressions, and to decide whether each expression has a valid type.

It follows that contextual analysis consists of two subphases:

- *Identification:* applying the source language's scope rules to relate each applied occurrence of an identifier to its declaration (if any).

- *Type checking:* applying the source language's type rules to infer the type of each expression, and compare that type with the expected type.

In Section 5.1 we study identification, and in Section 5.2 we study type checking. In Section 5.3 we develop a particular contextual analysis algorithm, combining identification and type checking in a single pass, and show how the results of contextual analysis may be recorded. Throughout, we assume that the source language exhibits static bindings and is statically typed.

5.1 Identification

The first task of the contextual analyzer is to relate each applied occurrence of an identifier in the source program to the corresponding declaration. If there is no corresponding declaration, the source program is ill-formed, and the contextual analyzer must generate an error report. This task is called *identification*. Once an applied occurrence of an identifier has been identified, the contextual analyzer will check that the identifier is used in a way consistent with its declaration: that is type checking, to be considered in Section 5.2.

Identification can have a disproportionate effect on the efficiency of the whole compiler. Longer source programs contain more applied occurrences of identifiers, and hence require more identifications to be performed. But also, longer source programs contain more declarations, so each identification is likely to take more time – especially if identification is implemented naively. Some compilers (and assemblers) are indeed very slow, for this reason.

If the source program is represented by an AST, a naive identification algorithm would be to search the AST: starting from a leaf node representing an applied occurrence of an identifier, find the subtree representing the corresponding declaration of that identifier. But such an algorithm would be very cumbersome. (See Exercise 5.5.)

A better method is to employ an *identification table* that associates identifiers with their attributes. The basic operations on the identification table are as follows:

• Make the identification table empty.

• Add an entry associating a given identifier with a given attribute.

• Retrieve the attribute (if any) associated with a given identifier.

An identifier's *attribute* consists of information relevant to contextual analysis, and is obtained from the identifier's declaration. The attribute could be information distilled from the declaration, or just a pointer to the declaration itself. For the moment we need not be specific, since the attributes do not influence the structure of the identification table. We shall return to attributes in Section 5.1.4.

Each declaration in a program has a definite *scope*, which is the portion of the program over which the declaration takes effect. A *block* is any program phrase that delimits the scope of declarations within it. For example, Triangle has a block command, of the form 'let *D* in *C*', in which the scope of each declaration in *D* extends over the subcommand *C*. A Triangle procedure declaration, of the form 'proc *I* (*FPS*) ~ *C*', is also a block, in which the scope of each formal parameter in *FPS* is the procedure body *C*.

The organization of the identification table depends on the source language's *block structure*, which is the textual relationship of blocks in programs. There are three possibilities:

• Monolithic block structure (exemplified by Basic and Cobol).

• Flat block structure (exemplified by Fortran).

• Nested block structure (exemplified by Pascal, Ada, C, and Java).

These block structures are covered in the following subsections.

5.1.1 Monolithic block structure

A programming language exhibits *monolithic block structure* if the only block is the entire program. All declarations are global in scope.

A language with monolithic block structure has very simple scope rules, typically:

(1a) No identifier may be declared more than once.

(1b) For every applied occurrence of an identifier *I*, there must be a corresponding declaration of *I*. (In other words, no identifier may be used unless declared.)

In the case of monolithic block structure, the identification table should contain entries for all declarations in the source program. There will be at most one entry for each identifier. Each entry in the table consists of an identifier *I* and the attribute *A* associated with it.

Example 5.1   Monolithic block structure

Consider a hypothetical programming language in which a program takes the form:

```
program
    D
begin
    C
end
```

D is a sequence of declarations (the only ones in the program). *C* is a command sequence, the executable part of the program. In this example it is not important what kinds of declaration and command are provided. What is important is that the only block is the whole program.

Figure 5.1 shows a program outline, together with a picture of the identification table after all declarations have been processed. The table contains one entry for each declared identifier. The declarations are numbered for cross-referencing, and in the table each identifier's attribute is shown as a cross-reference to the identifier's declaration.

□

Attributes and identification tables can be defined by the Java classes outlined here:

```
public class Attribute {
    ...  //  Attribute details.
}

public class IdentificationTable {

    ...  //  Variables representing the identification table.

    public IdentificationTable ()
    //  Make an empty identification table.
    { ... }

    public void enter (String id, Attribute attr)
    //  Add an entry to the identification table, associating identifier id
    //  with attribute attr.
    { ... }
```

```
public Attribute retrieve (String id)
// Return the attribute associated with identifier id in the identification
// table. If there is no entry for id, return null.
{ ... }
}
```

The contextual analyzer will use these operations as follows:

- To create a new table, the `IdentificationTable` constructor will be called.

- At a declaration of identifier *I*, the method `enter` will be called to add an entry for *I*.

- At an applied occurrence of identifier *I*, the method `retrieve` will be called to find the entry for *I*. If there is no such entry, an error report will be generated.

The identification table should be organized for efficient retrieval. A good implementation would be a standard data structure such as a binary search tree or a hash table. (See Exercise 5.1.)

```
program
(1) integer b = 10
(2) integer n
(3) char c
begin
    ...
    n = n * b
    ...
    write c
    ...
end
```

Ident.	Attr.
b	(1)
n	(2)
c	(3)

Figure 5.1 Identification table: monolithic block structure.

5.1.2   Flat block structure

A programming language exhibits *flat block structure* if a program can be partitioned into several disjoint blocks. There are two scope levels:

- Some declarations are *local* in scope. Applied occurrences of locally declared identifiers are restricted to a particular block.

- Other declarations are *global* in scope. Applied occurrences of locally declared identifiers are allowed anywhere in the program. In effect, the program as a whole is a block, enclosing all the other blocks.

The scope rules for a language with flat block structure might be:

(2a) No globally declared identifier may be redeclared globally. (But the same identifier may also be declared locally.)

(2b) No locally declared identifier may be redeclared in the same block. (But the same identifier may be declared locally in several different blocks.)

(2c) For every applied occurrence of an identifier *I* in a block *B*, there must be a corresponding declaration of *I*. This must be either a global declaration of *I* or a declaration of *I* local to *B*.

In the case of flat block structure, the identification table should contain entries for both global and local declarations. The contents of the table will vary during contextual analysis. During analysis of block *B*, the table should contain entries both for global declarations and for declarations local to *B*. Once analysis of *B* is completed, the entries for local declarations should be discarded. It follows that the entries for local and global declarations must be distinguished in some way.

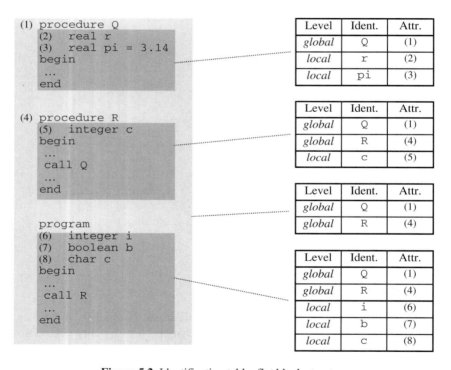

Figure 5.2 Identification table: flat block structure.

Example 5.2   Flat block structure

Consider a hypothetical programming language in which a main program takes the form:

```
program
    D
begin
    C
end
```

The main program's body is a block, and the declarations *D* are local to it. The main program may be preceded by a number of procedure declarations, which take the form:

```
procedure I
    D
begin
    C
end
```

The procedure body is a block, and the declarations *D* are local to it. The procedure declaration itself is global in scope.

Figure 5.2 shows a program outline, with the blocks shaded to distinguish between global and local scopes. It also shows a picture of the identification table as it stands during contextual analysis of each block.

During analysis of procedure Q, the table contains a *global* entry for Q itself, and *local* entries for r and pi. The body of Q may contain applied occurrences of these identifiers only. If the contextual analyzer encounters any other identifier, that identifier will not be found in the table, and the contextual analyzer will generate an error report. After analysis of Q, all the *local* entries are removed from the table. Similar points can be made about the other two blocks.

Note that the program contains two local declarations of identifier c. This causes no confusion, because the two declarations are local to different blocks. Their entries never appear in the identification table at the same time.

□

We still need the `IdentificationTable` constructor and the `enter` and `retrieve` methods specified in Section 5.1.1, but the latter method now has a slightly more complicated specification:

```
public Attribute retrieve (String id)
// Return the attribute associated with identifier id in the identification
// table. If there are both global and local entries for id, return the attribute
// from the local entry. If there is no entry for id, return null.
{ ... }
```

In addition, we need the following new methods:

```
public void openScope ()
// Add a local scope level to the identification table, with no entries yet
// belonging to it.
{ ... }

public void closeScope ()
// Remove the local scope level from the identification table, and all
// entries belonging to it.
{ ... }
```

The contextual analyzer will use the operations as follows:

- To create a new table, the `IdentificationTable` constructor will be called.

- At the start of a block, `openScope` will be called.

- At the end of a block, `closeScope` will be called.

- At a declaration of identifier *I*, `enter` will be called to add an entry for *I*. If open-Scope has been called but not canceled by `closeScope`, the new entry will be marked as *local*; otherwise it will be marked as *global*.

- At an applied occurrence of identifier *I*, `retrieve` will be called to find the entry for *I*. If there is no such entry, an error report will be generated.

It is still easy to implement the identification table. The only minor complication is to distinguish the global and local declaration entries. (See Exercise 5.2.)

5.1.3 Nested block structure

A programming language exhibits ***nested block structure*** if blocks may be nested one within another. Thus there may be many scope levels:

- Declarations in the outermost block are global in scope. We say that the outermost block is at *scope level 1*.

- Declarations inside an inner block are local to that block. Every inner block is completely enclosed by another block. If enclosed by the outermost block, we say that the inner block is at *scope level 2*; if enclosed by a level-2 block, we say that the inner block is at *scope level 3*; and so on.

The scope rules for a language with nested block structure are typically as follows:

(3a) No identifier may be declared more than once in the same block. (But the same identifier may be declared in different blocks, even if they are nested.)

(3b) For every applied occurrence of an identifier *I* in a block *B*, there must be a corresponding declaration of *I*. This declaration must be in *B* itself, or (failing that) in the block *B′* that immediately encloses *B*, or (failing that) in the block *B″* that immediately encloses *B′*, etc. (In other words, the corresponding declaration is in the smallest enclosing block that contains any declaration of *I*.)

In the case of nested block structure, the identification table should contain entries for declarations at all scope levels. Again, the contents of the table will vary during contextual analysis. During analysis of block B, the table should contain entries for declarations in B, entries for declarations in the block B' that encloses B, entries for declarations in the block B'' that encloses B', etc. Once analysis of B is completed, the entries for the declarations in B should be discarded. To make this possible, each entry should contain a scope level number.

Example 5.3   Nested block structure

The language Mini-Triangle introduced in Example 1.3 has block commands of the form 'let D in C'. These may be nested. Mini-Triangle's scope rules are (3a) and (3b) above.

Figure 5.3 shows a program outline, with the blocks shaded to indicate their scope levels. It also shows a picture of the identification table as it stands during contextual analysis of each block.

During analysis of the outermost block, the table contains only entries for identifiers a (declaration (1)) and b (declaration (2)). These entries are marked as level 1.

During analysis of the innermost block, the table contains entries for all the declarations in this block (marked as level 3), the enclosing block (level 2), and the outermost block (level 1). Notice that there are two entries for b (declarations (2) and (3)), but this is legitimate since they are in different blocks, and so their scope levels are different. If the innermost block contains an applied occurrence of b, the table must be searched in such a way as to retrieve attribute (3) – in accordance with scope rule (3b).

□

We still need the `IdentificationTable` constructor, and the `enter`, `retrieve`, `openScope`, and `closeScope` methods, but some of these now have modified specifications:

```
public Attribute retrieve (String id)
// Return  the attribute associated with identifier id in the
// identification table. If there are several entries for id,
// return the attribute from the entry at the highest scope level.
// If there is no entry for id, return null.
{ ... }

public void openScope ()
// Add a new highest scope level to the identification table.
{ ... }

public void closeScope ()
// Remove the highest scope level from the identification table,
// and all entries belonging to it.
{ ... }
```

These are generalizations of the operations specified in Section 5.1.2.

The contextual analyzer will use the operations as follows:

- To create a new, empty table, the `IdentificationTable` constructor will be called.

- At the start of a block, `openScope` will be called.

- At the end of a block, `closeScope` will be called.

- At a declaration of identifier *I*, `enter` will be called to add an entry for *I*. (This entry will contain a scope level number determined by the number of calls of `openScope` not yet canceled by calls of `closeScope`.)

- At an applied occurrence of identifier *I*, `retrieve` will be called to find the correct entry for *I*. If there is more than one entry for *I*, the one with the highest scope level number will be retrieved. If there is no entry for *I*, an error report will be generated.

Nested block structure makes implementation of the identification table a more challenging problem. There may be several entries for each identifier, although there is at most one entry for each (scope level, identifier) combination. The table must be searched in such a way that the highest-level entry is retrieved when there are several entries for the same identifier. And, as usual, retrieval efficiency is important. Some possible implementations are outlined in Section 5.4 and in Exercises 5.4 and 5.5.

5.1.4 Attributes

So far we have been deliberately unspecific about the nature of the attributes associated with identifiers in the identification table. These attributes are stored in the table, and later retrieved, but they have no influence on the *structure* of the table.

Let us now look at these attributes in more detail. At an applied occurrence of an identifier *I*, the attribute associated with *I* is retrieved for use in type checking. If *I* occurs as an operand in an expression, the type checker will need to ensure that *I* has been declared as a constant or variable, and will need to know its type. If *I* occurs as the left-hand side of an assignment command, the type checker will need to ensure that *I* has been declared as a variable (not a constant), and again will need to know its type. If *I* occurs as the first symbol in a procedure call, the type checker will need to ensure that *I* has indeed been declared as a procedure, and will need to know the types of its formal parameters (for comparison with the types of the actual parameters). These examples illustrate the kind of information that must be included in attributes.

One possibility is for the contextual analyzer to extract type information from declarations, and store that information in the identification table. Later that information can be retrieved whenever required.

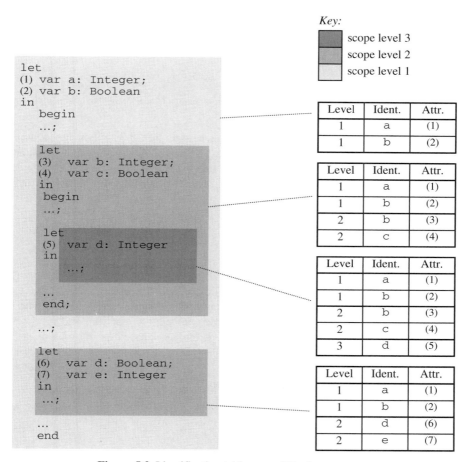

Figure 5.3 Identification table: nested block structure.

Example 5.4 Mini-Triangle attributes

Consider a Mini-Triangle contextual analyzer that extracts type information from a declaration, and uses that information to construct an attribute.

For Mini-Triangle, the relevant information is just whether the declaration is of a constant or a variable, and whether its type is *bool* or *int*. (Other information, such as the actual value of a constant, is irrelevant in contextual analysis of Mini-Triangle.)

Thus the type `Attribute` could be defined as follows:

```
public class Attribute {

    byte kind;          // either CONST or VAR
    byte type;          // either BOOL or INT
```

```
    // Kinds of declaration:
    public static final byte CONST = 0, VAR = 1;

    // Types:
    public static final byte BOOL = 0, INT = 1;

    ...
}
```

Consider the Mini-Triangle program outlined in Figure 5.3. When the contextual analyzer processes declaration (1), it calls `enter` with identifier a and an attribute whose fields are VAR and INT. Whenever it processes an applied occurrence of a, it calls `retrieve` with identifier a, and thus retrieves that attribute. Using the attribute, it determines that a denotes an integer variable. Other declarations are treated similarly.

□

Example 5.5   Triangle attributes

Now imagine a one-pass compiler for Triangle itself. Here the information to be extracted from a declaration is rather complicated, for several reasons. First, there are several kinds of declaration – constant, variable, procedure, function, and type – with different information provided in each case. Secondly, a procedure or function declaration includes a list of formal parameters, and each formal parameter may be a constant, variable, procedural, or functional parameter. Third, the language provides not only primitive types, but also whole families of record and array types.

The classes required to represent types could be defined along the following lines:

```
public abstract class Type { ... }

public class BoolType extends Type { ... }

public class CharType extends Type { ... }

public class IntType extends Type { ... }

public class RecordType extends Type {
   FieldList fields;       // a list of (identifier, type) pairs
}

public class ArrayType extends Type {
   int elementCount;
   Type elementType;
}
```

And the classes required to represent attributes could be defined as follows:

```
public abstract class Attribute { ... }
```

```
public class ConstAttribute extends Attribute {
    Type type;
}

public class VarAttribute extends Attribute {
    Type type;
}

public class ProcAttribute extends Attribute {
    FormalList formals;    // a list of (identifier, attribute) pairs
}

public class FuncAttribute extends Attribute {
    FormalList formals;    // a list of (identifier, attribute) pairs
    Type resultType;
}

public class TypeAttribute extends Attribute {
    Type type;
}
```

For a realistic source language, the information to be stored in the identification table is quite complex, as Example 5.5 illustrates. A lot of tedious programming is required to declare and construct the attributes.

Fortunately, this can be avoided if the source program is represented by an AST. This is because the AST itself contains the information about identifiers that we need to store and retrieve. The information associated with an identifier *I* can be accessed via a pointer to the subtree that represents the declaration of *I*. In other words, we can replace the class `Attribute` with the class `Declaration` throughout the definition of the `IdentificationTable` class (assuming the AST representation described in Section 4.4.1).

Example 5.6   Mini-Triangle attributes represented by declaration ASTs

Consider once more the Mini-Triangle program outlined in Figure 5.3. Figure 5.4 shows part of the AST representing this program, including one of the inner blocks, with the subtree representing each block shaded to indicate its scope level. Figure 5.4 also shows a picture of the identification table as it stands during contextual analysis of each block.

When the contextual analyzer visits the declaration at subtree (1), it calls `enter` with identifier a and a pointer to subtree (1). Whenever it visits an applied occurrence of a, it calls `retrieve` with identifier a, and thus retrieves the pointer to subtree (1). By inspecting this subtree, it determines that a denotes an integer variable. The other declarations are treated similarly.

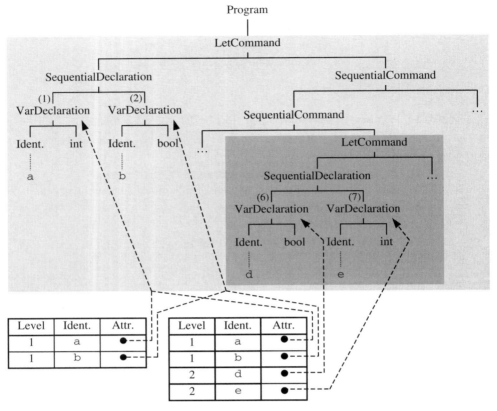

Figure 5.4 Identification table: relationship to AST.

5.1.5 Standard environment

Most programming languages contain a standard collection of predefined constants, variables, types, procedures and functions that the programmer can use without having to introduce them explicitly. For example, there is the package java.lang in Java, the standard prelude in Haskell, and the package Standard in Ada. This collection we call the *standard environment* of the language.

At the start of identification, therefore, the identification table is not empty, but already contains entries corresponding to the declarations of the standard environment. This presents us with a slight problem, as we must construct the corresponding attributes for these identifiers. In the example languages above, this can be achieved by processing the text of the appropriate package before starting on the source program. In other cases, however, the contextual analyzer must contain code that explicitly constructs the corresponding attribute values and enters them into the identification table.

A programming language must also specify the appropriate scope rule for the standard environment. Most programming languages consider the standard environment to be a scope enclosing the whole program, so that the source program may contain a declaration of an identifier present in the standard environment without causing a scope error. Some other programming languages (such as C) introduce the standard environment at the same scope level as the global declarations of the source program.

If the standard environment is to be at a scope enclosing the whole program, the declarations of the standard environment should be entered at scope level 0 in the identification table.

Example 5.7   Standard environment in Mini-Triangle

The standard environment of Mini-Triangle contains the following constant, type, procedure, and operator declarations:

```
type Boolean ~ ...;

const false ~ ...;

const true ~ ...;

func \ (b: Boolean) : Boolean ~ ...;

type Integer ~ ...;

const maxint ~ ...;

func + (i1: Integer, i2: Integer) : Integer ~ ...;

func - (i1: Integer, i2: Integer) : Integer ~ ...;

func * (i1: Integer, i2: Integer) : Integer ~ ...;

func / (i1: Integer, i2: Integer) : Integer ~ ...;

func < (i1: Integer, i2: Integer) : Boolean ~ ...;

func > (i1: Integer, i2: Integer) : Boolean ~ ...;

proc putint (i: Integer) ~ ...;
```

In addition, the following operator is available for every type T (i.e., both `Integer` and `Boolean`):

```
func = (val1: T, val2: T) : Boolean ~ ...;
```

Here, a unary operator declaration is treated like a function declaration with one argument, and a binary operator declaration is treated like a function declaration with two arguments. The operator symbol is treated like a normal identifier. The contextual analyzer only requires information about the types of the arguments and result of an operator, and so these declarations have no corresponding expressions.

The above declarations of the standard environment are not syntactically valid in Mini-Triangle, and so cannot be introduced by processing a normal input file. In fact, these declarations are entered into the identification table using a method called `estab-lishStandardEnvironment`, which the contextual analyzer calls before checking the source program.

Once the standard environment is entered in the identification table, the source program can be checked for any type errors. At every applied occurrence of an identifier, the identification table will be searched in exactly the same way (regardless of whether the identifier turns out to be in the standard environment or the source program), and its corresponding attribute used to determine its type.

□

5.2 Type checking

The second task of the contextual analyzer is to ensure that the source program contains no type errors. The key property of a statically-typed language is that the compiler can detect any type errors without actually running the program. In particular, for every expression E in the language, the compiler can infer *either* that E has some type T *or* that E is ill-typed. If E does have type T, then evaluating E will always yield a value of that type T. If E occurs in a context where a value of type T' is expected, then the compiler can check that T is equivalent to T', without actually evaluating E. This is the task that we call *type checking*.

Here we shall focus on the type checking of expressions. Bear in mind, however, that some phrases other than expressions have types, and therefore also must be type-checked. For example, a variable-name on the left-hand side of an assignment command has a type. Even an operator has a type. We write a unary operator's type in the form $T_1 \rightarrow T_2$, meaning that the operator must be applied to an operand of type T_1, and will yield a result of type T_2. We write a binary operator's type in the form $T_1 \times T_2 \rightarrow T_3$, meaning that the operator must be applied to a left operand of type T_1 and a right operand of type T_2, and will yield a result of type T_3.

For most statically-typed programming languages, type checking is straightforward. The type checker infers the type of each expression bottom-up (i.e., starting with literals and identifiers, and working up through larger and larger subexpressions):

- *Literal:* The type of a literal is immediately known.

- *Identifier:* The type of an applied occurrence of identifier I is obtained from the corresponding declaration of I.

- *Unary operator application:* Consider the expression '$O\ E$', where O is a unary operator of type $T_1 \rightarrow T_2$. The type checker ensures that E's type is equivalent to T_1, and thus infers that the type of '$O\ E$' is T_2. Otherwise there is a type error.

- *Binary operator application*: Consider the expression '$E_1 \, O \, E_2$', where O is a binary operator of type $T_1 \times T_2 \to T_3$. The type checker ensures that E_1's type is equivalent to T_1, and that E_2's type is equivalent to T_2, and thus infers that the type of '$E_1 \, O \, E_2$' is T_3. Otherwise there is a type error.

In general, the type of a nontrivial expression is inferred from the types of its subexpressions, using the appropriate type rule.

In some phrases the type checker must test whether an inferred type is equivalent to an expected type, or test whether two inferred types are equivalent to each other. In a typical language, the type of the expression in an if- or while-command must be equivalent to the type *bool*; and the type of an actual parameter must be equivalent to the type of the corresponding formal parameter. So the type checker must be able to test whether two given types T and T' are ***equivalent***.

Example 5.8   Mini-Triangle type checking

Mini-Triangle has only two types (denoted by `Boolean` and `Integer`), so they can easily be represented as follows:

```
public class Type {
    private byte kind;    // either BOOL or INT

    public static final byte
        BOOL = 0, INT = 1;

    public static Type (byte sort) {
        this.sort = sort;
    }

    public boolean equals (Object other) {
        // Test whether this type is equivalent to other.
        Type otherType = (Type) other;
        return (this.kind == otherType.kind);
    }

}
```

It is a simple matter to infer the type of an applied occurrence of a constant or variable identifier I, provided that a link has already been established to the declaration of I. If I is declared in a constant declaration, whose right-side expression's type has been inferred to be T, then the type of the applied occurrence of I is T:

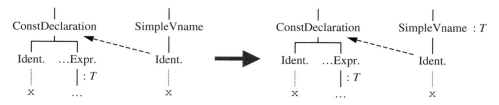

(We show the inferred type T by annotating the AST node with ': T'.)

If I is declared in a variable declaration, whose right side is type T, then the type of the applied occurrence of I is T:

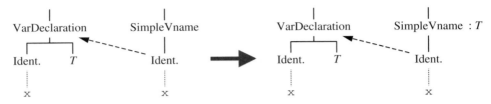

An application of a binary operator such as '<' would be handled as follows:

The operator '<' is of type *int* × *int* → *bool*. Having checked that the type of E_1 is equivalent to *int*, and that the type of E_2 is equivalent to *int*, the type checker infers that the type of '$E_1 < E_2$' is *bool*. Other operators would be handled similarly.

Of course, Mini-Triangle type checking is exceptionally simple: the representation of types is trivial, and testing for type equivalence is also trivial. Type checking is more complicated if the source language has composite types. For example, Triangle array and record types have component types, which are unrestricted. Thus we need to represent types by trees.

Furthermore, there are two possible definitions of type equivalence.

Some programming languages (such as Triangle) adopt **structural equivalence**, whereby two types are equivalent if and only if their structures are the same. If types are represented by trees, structural equivalence can be tested by comparing the structures of these trees. If the implementation language is Java, then this kind of equality is conventionally tested by an `equals` method in the `Type` class.

Other programming languages (such as Pascal and Ada) adopt **name equivalence**. Every occurrence of a type constructor (e.g., `array` or `record`) creates a new and distinct type. In this case type equivalence can be tested simply by comparing pointers to the objects representing the types: distinct objects (created at different times) represent types that are not equivalent, even if they happen to be structurally similar. If the implementation language is Java, then this kind of equality is tested by the '==' operator applied to objects of class `Type`.

In Section 5.4 we shall return to look at a more realistic example of type checking, in the context of the Triangle compiler.

5.3 A contextual analysis algorithm

Contextual analysis consists of identification and type checking. Each applied occurrence of an identifier must be identified before type checking can proceed. Identification could, in principle, be completed before type checking is started, but there would be little advantage in that. Instead, identification and type checking are usually interleaved in a single pass over the source program (or its representation). If the source program is represented by an AST, contextual analysis can be done in a single depth-first traversal.

Throughout this section, we shall assume that the AST is represented as described in Section 4.4.1.

5.3.1 Decoration

The results of contextual analysis can be recorded by ***decorating*** the AST, as explained in Section 3.1.2. The following decorations prove to be useful:

- The results of *identification* can be recorded by making an explicit link from each applied occurrence of an identifier *I* to the corresponding declaration of *I*. This has the advantage of making the decorated AST a self-contained representation of the source program; the identification table may be discarded once identification is complete. In the compiler, we represent this link by a pointer field in each identifier node. In diagrams, we show this link as a dashed arrow.

- The results of *type checking* can be recorded by storing each expression *E*'s inferred type *T* at the root node of *E*. In the compiler, we represent this by a type field in each expression node. In diagrams, we show this inferred type by an annotation ': *T*' to the right of the expression node. The same point applies to the other typed phrases such as value-or-variable-name.

Example 5.9   Representation of decorated ASTs

A class AST suitable for representing Mini-Triangle undecorated ASTs was defined in Example 4.19. Here we extend the definition of AST and its subclasses to make them suitable for Mini-Triangle decorated ASTs, by means of additional instance variables (italicized here for emphasis):

```
public abstract class Expression extends AST {
    // The expression's type:
    public Type type;
    ...
}
```

```
public abstract class Vname extends AST {
    // The value-or-variable-name's type, and an indication of whether
    // it is a variable or a value:
    public Type type;
    public boolean variable;
    ...
}

public class Identifier extends Terminal {
    // A pointer to the identifier's declaration (applied occurrences only):
    public Declaration decl;
    ...
}

public class Operator extends Terminal {
    // A pointer to the operator's declaration:
    public OperatorDeclaration decl;
    ...
}
```

(The decoration of an operator node will be explained later.)

□

5.3.2 Visitor classes and objects

The work to be done by the contextual analyzer depends on the class of phrase to be checked. Checking of a command C will determine simply whether C is well-formed or not. Checking of an expression E will determine whether E is well-formed, but also infer the type of E. Checking of a declaration D will determine whether D is well-formed, but also make entries in the identification table for the identifiers declared in D.

In more detail, the checking of a command depends on the particular form of that command. For example, checking an assignment-command '$V := E$' entails (i) checking V to determine its type and ensure that it is a variable, (ii) checking E to determine its type, and (iii) testing whether the two types are equivalent. Checking a block-command 'let D in C' entails (i) opening an inner scope, (ii) checking D, (iii) checking C, and (iv) closing the inner scope. Similarly, the checking of an expression or declaration depends on the particular form of expression or declaration.

In all cases, checking a particular phrase entails checking its subphrases (if any). If the source program is represented by an AST, contextual analysis therefore entails traversing the AST, visiting the nodes in some suitable order. We shall see in Chapter 7 that code generation also entails traversing the AST, visiting the nodes in some (possibly different) order. Therefore the compiler should be designed such that AST traversals are organized systematically.

The work of the contextual analyzer will be done by a set of ***visitor methods***. There will be exactly one visitor method, `visitA`, for each concrete `AST` subclass *A*. These visitor methods will cooperate to traverse the AST in the desired order.

Example 5.10 Mini-Triangle visitor methods

The visitor methods for Mini-Triangle are summarized by the following Java interface:

```
public interface Visitor {
    // Programs:
    public Object visitProgram
            (Program prog, Object arg);

    // Commands:
    public Object visitAssignCommand
            (AssignCommand com, Object arg);
    public Object visitCallCommand
            (CallCommand com, Object arg);
    public Object visitSequentialCommand
            (SequentialCommand com, Object arg);
    public Object visitIfCommand
            (IfCommand com, Object arg);
    public Object visitWhileCommand
            (WhileCommand com, Object arg);
    public Object visitLetCommand
            (LetCommand com, Object arg);

    // Expressions:
    public Object visitIntegerExpression
            (IntegerExpression expr, Object arg);
    public Object visitVnameExpression
            (VnameExpression expr, Object arg);
    public Object visitUnaryExpression
            (UnaryExpression expr, Object arg);
    public Object visitBinaryExpression
            (BinaryExpression expr, Object arg);

    // Value-or-variable-names:
    public Object visitSimpleVname
            (SimpleVname vname, Object arg);

    // Declarations:
    public Object visitConstDeclaration
            (ConstDeclaration decl, Object arg);
    public Object visitVarDeclaration
            (VarDeclaration decl, Object arg);
    public Object visitSequentialDeclaration
            (SequentialDeclaration decl, Object arg);
```

```
// Type-denoters:
public Object visitSimpleTypeDenoter
        (SimpleTypeDenoter type, Object arg);

// Identifiers:
public Object visitIdentifier
        (Identifier id, Object arg);

// Operators:
public Object visitOperator
        (Operator op, Object arg);

}
```

□

Each visitor method has an argument that is the subtree (phrase) to be visited. It also has an `Object` argument to allow additional data to be passed into the method, where required. Finally, it has an `Object` result to allow data to be passed out of the method, where required.

For example, the result of each `visit…Expression` method in the contextual analyzer will be the expression's type, whereas the result of each `visit…Command` method will be **null**. (Later we shall see why it is worthwhile to provide every visitor method with both an `Object` argument and an `Object` result.)

We will organize AST traversals using the object-oriented *visitor design pattern*. Given a set of node classes, a *visitor class* is one that implements the corresponding set of visitor methods. For example, a Mini-Triangle AST visitor class is one that implements the `Visitor` interface defined in Example 5.10. A *visitor object* (an object of a visitor class) therefore contains a particular set of visitor methods.

Any AST traversal can be implemented as a visitor object. In fact, both the contextual analyzer and the code generator can be implemented as visitor objects. We enhance the `AST` class with an instance method `visit`, which can be used to visit any AST node:

```
public abstract class AST {
    ...
    public abstract Object visit
            (Visitor v, Object arg);
}
```

Like the visitor methods, `visit` has an `Object` argument and an `Object` result. It also has a `Visitor` argument; this tells it which particular visitor object (i.e., which particular set of visitor methods) to apply to the AST node and its descendants.

Each concrete subclass of `AST` must implement the `visit` method, simply by calling the appropriate visitor method. For example, the `AssignCommand` and `IfCommand` classes will implement `visit` as follows:

```
public class AssignCommand extends Command {
   ...
   public Object visit (Visitor v, Object arg) {
      return v.visitAssignCommand(this, arg);
   }
}

public class IfCommand extends Command {
   ...
   public Object visit (Visitor v, Object arg) {
      return v.visitIfCommand(this, arg);
   }
}
```

Each `visit` method 'knows' which particular visitor method to call. For example, `IfCommand`'s `visit` method knows that **this** is an `IfCommand` object, so it calls the `v.visitIfCommand` method, passing **this** (and `arg`) as arguments. In general, the `visit` method in the concrete AST subclass *A* simply calls `v.visitA`:

```
public class A extends ... {
   ...
   public Object visit (Visitor v, Object arg) {
      return v.visitA(this, arg);
   }
}
```

When `visitA` visits an AST node, it may visit any child of that node by calling that child's own `visit` method.

5.3.3   Contextual analysis as a visitor object

The contextual analyzer is a visitor object that performs identification and type checking. Each visitor method `visitA` in the contextual analyzer will check a node of class *A*, generating an error report if it determines that the phrase represented by the node is ill-formed. Visitor methods in the contextual analyzer can conveniently be called *checking methods*.

Example 5.11 Mini-Triangle contextual analysis

The Mini-Triangle contextual analyzer is an implementation of the `Visitor` interface given in Example 5.10.

We shall assume the following representation of Mini-Triangle types, adapted from Example 5.8:

```
public class Type {
   private byte kind;     // either BOOL, INT or ERROR
```

```
public static final byte
    BOOL = 0, INT = 1, ERROR = -1;

public static Type (byte kind) {
    this.kind = kind;
}

public boolean equals (Object other) {
    Type otherType = (Type) other;
    return (this.kind == otherType.kind
            || this.kind == ERROR
            || otherType.kind == ERROR);
}

public static Type bool = new Type(BOOL);
public static Type int = new Type(INT);
public static Type error = new Type(ERROR);
}
```

The Mini-Triangle visitor/checking methods are summarized in Table 5.1. Now we outline how they are implemented.

Table 5.1 Summary of visitor/checking methods for the Mini-Triangle contextual analyzer.

Phrase class	Visitor/checking method(s)	Behavior of visitor/checking method(s)
Program	visitProgram	Check that the program is well-formed, and return **null**.
Command	visit...Command	Check that the command is well-formed and return **null**.
Expression	visit...Expression	Check that the expression is well-formed, decorate it with its type, and return that type.
V-name	visitSimpleVname	Check that the value-or-variable-name is well-formed, decorate it with its type and a flag indicating if it is a variable, and return that type.
Declaration	visit...Declaration	Check that the declaration is well-formed, enter all declared identifiers into the identification table, and return **null**.
Type-Denoter	visit...TypeDenoter	Check that the type-denoter is well-formed, decorate it with its type, and return that type.
Identifier	visitIdentifier	Check that the identifier is declared, link the applied occurrence of the identifier to its declaration, and return that declaration.
Operator	visitOperator	Check that the operator is declared, link the applied occurrence of the operator to its declaration, and return that declaration.

Each of the `visit...Command` visitor/checking methods checks that the given command is well-formed. (The method's result is **null**, and the `arg` object is ignored.) The following are typical:

```
public Object visitAssignCommand
                (AssignCommand com, Object arg) {
    Type vType = (Type) com.V.visit(this, null);
    Type eType = (Type) com.E.visit(this, null);
    if (! com.V.variable)
        ... // Report an error – the left side is not a variable.
    if (! eType.equals(vType))
        ... // Report an error – the left and right sides are not of
            // equivalent type.
    return null;
}

public Object visitSequentialCommand
                (SequentialCommand com, Object arg) {
    com.C1.visit(this, null);
    com.C2.visit(this, null);
    return null;
}

public Object visitIfCommand
                (IfCommand com, Object arg) {
    Type eType = (Type) com.E.visit(this, null);
    if (! eType.equals(Type.bool))
        ... // Report an error – the expression is not boolean.
    com.C1.visit(this, null);
    com.C2.visit(this, null);
    return null;
}

public Object visitLetCommand
                (LetCommand com, Object arg) {
    idTable.openScope();
    com.D.visit(this, null);
    com.C.visit(this, null);
    idTable.closeScope();
    return null;
}
```

These visitor/checking methods are fairly self-explanatory. In the case of the assignment command '$V := E$', `visitAssignCommand` calls V.`visit` to check V and E.`visit` to check E, then ensures that V is indeed a variable and that V's type is equivalent to E's type. In the case of the if-command 'if E then C_1 else C_2', `visitIfCommand` calls E.`visit`, C_1.`visit`, and C_2.`visit`, and ensures that E's type is *bool*.

Here `idTable` is the identification table used during contextual analysis. It is an object of class `IdentificationTable`, as given in Section 5.1.3.

Each of the `visit...Expression` visitor/checking methods checks that the expression is well-formed, and decorates the expression node with its inferred type. The method's result is that type. (The `arg` object is ignored.)

```
public Object visitIntegerExpression
                (IntegerExpression expr, Object arg) {
    expr.type = Type.int;                 // decoration
    return expr.type;
}

public Object visitVnameExpression
                (VnameExpression expr, Object arg) {
    Type vType = (TypeDenoter) expr.V.visit(this, null);
    expr.type = vType;                    // decoration
    return expr.type;
}

public Object visitBinaryExpression
                (BinaryExpression expr, Object arg) {

    Type e1Type = (Type) expr.E1.visit(this, null);
    Type e2Type = (Type) expr.E2.visit(this, null);
    OperatorDeclaration opdecl =
        (OperatorDeclaration) expr.O.visit(this, null);
    if (opdecl == null) {
        ... // Report an error – no such operator.
        expr.type = Type.error;           // decoration
    } else if (opdecl instanceof
            BinaryOperatorDeclaration) {
        BinaryOperatorDeclaration bopdecl =
            (BinaryOperatorDeclaration) opdecl;
        if (! e1Type.equals(bopdecl.operand1Type))
            ... // Report an error – the left subexpression has the wrong  type.
        if (! e2Type.equals(bopdecl.operand2Type))
            ... // Report an error – the right subexpression has the
                // wrong  type.
        expr.type = bopdecl.resultType;  // decoration
    } else {
        ... // Report an error – the operator is not a binary operator.
        expr.type = Type.error;           // decoration
    }
    return expr.type;
}
```

The visitor/checking methods `visitIntegerExpression` and `visitVname-Expression` are self-explanatory. In the case of a binary operator application 'E_1 O E_2', `visitBinaryExpression` assumes that O`.visit` returns a pointer to a 'declaration' of operator O, where the operator's operand and result types may be found. (This declaration will be the attribute value returned by searching the identification table for the operator.) Method `visitUnaryExpression` is similar to `visitBinaryExpression`.

The `visitSimpleVname` visitor/checking method checks that the value-or-variable-name is well-formed, and decorates it with its inferred type together with an indication of whether it is a variable or not. The method's result is the inferred type. (The `arg` object is ignored.) The following are typical:

```
public Object visitSimpleVname
                   (SimpleVname vname, Object arg) {
   Declaration decl =
        (Declaration) vname.I.visit (this, null);
   if (decl == null) {
      ... // Report an error – this identifier is not declared.
      vname.type = Type.error;
      vname.variable = true;                  // decoration
   } else if (decl instanceof ConstDeclaration) {
      vname.type = ((ConstDeclaration) decl).E.type;
      vname.variable = false;                 // decoration
   } else if (decl instanceof VarDeclaration) {
      vname.type = ((VarDeclaration) decl).T.type;
      vname.variable = true;                  // decoration
   }
   return vname.type;
}
```

Each of the `visit...Declaration` visitor/checking methods checks that the declaration is well-formed, and enters all declared identifiers into the identification table. (The method's result is **null**, and the `arg` object is ignored.)

```
public Object visitConstDeclaration
                   (ConstDeclaration decl, Object arg) {
   decl.E.visit(this, null);                // result is ignored
   idTable.enter(decl.I.spelling, decl);
   return null;
}

public Object visitVarDeclaration
                   (VarDeclaration decl, Object arg) {
   decl.T.visit(this, null);                // result is ignored
   idTable.enter(decl.I.spelling, decl);
   return null;
}
```

```
public Object visitSequentialDeclaration
            (SequentialDeclaration decl, Object arg) {
    decl.D1.visit(this, null);
    decl.D2.visit(this, null);
    return null;
}
```

Each of the `visitConstDeclaration` and `visitVarDeclaration` visitor/checking methods makes an entry in the identification table for the declared identifier. This entry consists of the identifier's spelling and a pointer to the declaration itself. Also, in both of these visitor/checking methods, a subtree is visited only for the side-effect of decorating that subtree with type information; the type information returned by the visitor/checking method is ignored.

The visitor/checking method `visitSimpleTypeDenoter` (not shown) checks whether the given type-denoter is the identifier 'Boolean' or 'Integer', decorates the node with the corresponding type (`Type` object), and returns that type.

The `visitIdentifier` visitor/checking method links an applied occurrence of an identifier to the corresponding declaration (if any). Its result is a pointer to that declaration. (The `arg` object is ignored.).

```
public Object visitIdentifier
                (Identifier id, Object arg) {
    id.decl = idTable.retrieve        // decoration,
                (id.spelling);        // possibly null
    return id.decl;
}
```

Finally, the contextual analyzer must define a method that checks an entire program. The completed contextual analyzer becomes:

```
public final class Checker implements Visitor {

    private IdentificationTable idTable;

    ... // Visitor/checking methods, as above.

    public void check (Program prog) {
        idTable = new IdentificationTable();
        idTable.enter("false", ...);
        idTable.enter("true", ...);
        ...
        idTable.enter("putint", ...);
        prog.visit(this, null);
    }
}
```

Method `check` illustrates how the source language's standard environment can be handled. It initializes the identification table with entries for all standard constants, types, procedures, and so on. These entries will then be retrieved in the usual way at applied occurrences of the corresponding identifiers.

Making the contextual analyzer a visitor object has important advantages:

- It brings all of the contextual analyzer code together in a single class, `Checker`. This makes the contextual analyzer easier to study and modify. (The principal alternative, whereby each `AST` subclass contains its own visitor/checking method, would result in the contextual analyzer code being spread over a large number of class definitions, and thus harder to understand and harder to modify.)

- It ensures that the AST traversal is complete, i.e., that the contextual analyzer includes the code to visit every class of node in the AST. (The alternative, whereby the contextual analyzer traverses the AST in an *ad hoc* manner, would risk accidental omission of code for some classes of node.)

- The same structure can later be used for the code generator, and indeed for any other process that needs to traverse the AST.

5.4   Case study: contextual analysis in the Triangle compiler

The Triangle contextual analyzer consists of a package `Triangle.Contextual-Analyzer` that contains the `Checker` and `IdentificationTable` classes. The `Checker` class depends on the package `Triangle.AbstractSyntaxTrees`, which contains all of the class definitions for ASTs.

Triangle has static bindings and is statically-typed. The Triangle contextual analyzer works in much the same way as described in Section 5.3, interleaving identification and type checking in a single traversal of the AST. It is structured as a visitor object.

5.4.1   Identification

Triangle exhibits nested block structure, so identification is performed with the aid of a multilevel identification table as described in Section 5.1.3. The attribute stored in each table entry is a pointer to a declaration in the AST. At each applied occurrence of an identifier *I*, the table is used to find the corresponding declaration of *I*, and the applied occurrence is linked to this declaration. Once contextual analysis of the source program is completed, the identification table is no longer required and is discarded.

The current implementation of the identification table is naive. It is a stack in which each entry contains a scope level, an identifier, and a declaration. Method `enter` pushes a new entry on to the stack. Method `retrieve` searches the stack from the top down, i.e., it uses linear search. Method `openScope` simply increments the current scope level. Method `closeScope` pops entries belonging to the current scope level, which it then decrements.

Two rather better implementations of the identification table are suggested by Exercises 5.4 and 5.5.

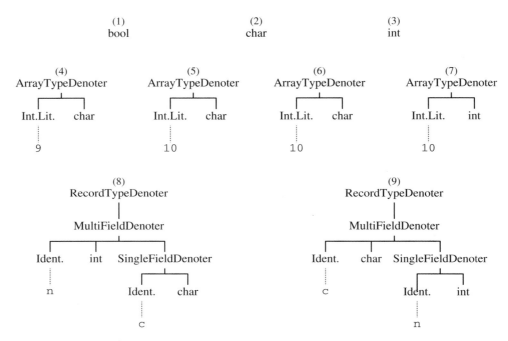

Figure 5.5 Representation of Triangle types by small ASTs.

5.4.2 Type checking

Triangle has not only primitive types (denoted by `Boolean`, `Char`, and `Integer`) but also array types and record types. An array type is characterized by the number and type of the elements. A record type is characterized by the identifiers, types, and order of its fields. These types are conveniently represented by small ASTs. So there is no need for the class `Type` used in Section 5.3; it is replaced by the class `TypeDenoter`. The ASTs used to represent the following Triangle types are shown in Figure 5.5:

   (1) `Boolean`
   (2) `Char`
   (3) `Integer`
   (4) `array 9 of Char`

```
(5)  array 10 of Char
(6)  array 10 of Char
(7)  array 10 of Integer
(8)  record n: Integer, c: Char end
(9)  record c: Char, n: Integer end
```

In Triangle type equivalence is structural. Of the types shown in Figure 5.5, only (5) and (6) are equivalent to each other. To test whether two types are equivalent, the type checker just compares their ASTs structurally. This test is performed by defining an `equals` method in each subclass of `TypeDenoter`. Class `TypeDenoter` itself is enhanced as follows:

```
public abstract class TypeDenoter extends AST {
    public abstract boolean equals (Object other);
    ...
}
```

Type *identifiers* in the AST would complicate the type equivalence test. To remove this complication, the visitor/checking methods for type-denoters are made to eliminate all type identifiers. This is achieved by replacing each type identifier by the type it denotes.

Figure 5.6 shows the ASTs representing the following Triangle declarations:

```
type Word ~ array 8 of Char;
var w1: Word;
var w2: array 8 of Char
```

Initially the type subtrees (1) and (2) in the two variable declarations are different. After these subtrees have been checked, however, the type identifiers 'Char' and 'Word' have been eliminated. The resulting subtrees (3) and (4) are structurally similar. The elimination of type identifiers makes it clear that the types of variables w1 and w2 are equivalent.

A consequence of this transformation is to make each type 'subtree' (and hence the whole AST) into a *directed acyclic graph*. Fortunately, this causes no serious complication in the Triangle compiler. (But recursive types – as found in Pascal, Ada, and ML – would cause a complication: see Exercise 5.9.)

The Triangle type checker infers and checks the types of expressions and value-or-variable-names in much the same way as in Example 5.8. Types are tested for structural equivalence by using the `equals` method of the `TypeDenoter` class. (Instead, comparing types by means of '==' would implement name equivalence.)

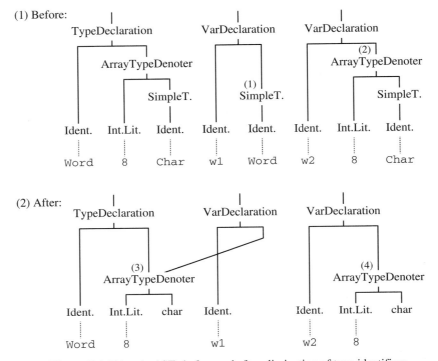

Figure 5.6 Triangle ASTs before and after elimination of type identifiers.

5.4.3 Standard environment

Like all programming languages, Triangle has a standard environment (described in Section B.9). This is represented by a collection of small ASTs, representing the 'declarations' of the standard identifiers. Some of these 'declarations' are:

```
(1) type Boolean ~ ...;
(2) const false ~ ...;
(3) const true ~ ...;
(4) func eof () : Boolean  ...;
(5) proc get (var c: Char ...;
(6) proc put (c: Char) ~ ...;
(7) func \   (b: Boolean) : Boolean ~ ...;
(8) func <   (i1: Integer, i2: Integer) : Boolean ~ ...;
```

The ASTs corresponding to these 'declarations' are shown in Figure 5.7. There are 'type declarations' for standard types, such as Boolean (1); 'constant declarations' for standard constants, such as false (2) and true (3); 'function declarations' for standard functions, such as eof (4); and 'procedure declarations' for standard procedures, such as put (5) and get (6).

Before analyzing a source program, the contextual analyzer initializes the identification table with entries for the standard identifiers, at scope level 0, as shown in Figure 5.8. The attribute stored in each of these entries is a pointer to the appropriate 'declaration'. Thus standard identifiers are treated in exactly the same way as identifiers declared in the source program.

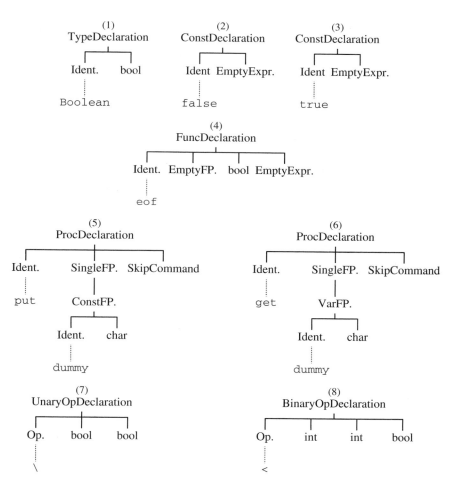

Figure 5.7 Small ASTs representing the Triangle standard environment (abridged).

Level	Ident.	Attr.
0	Boolean	(1)
0	false	(2)
0	true	(3)
0	eof	(4)
0	put	(5)
0	get	(6)
0	\	(7)
0	<	(8)
...	...	...

Figure 5.8 Identification table for the Triangle standard environment (abridged).

The Triangle standard environment also includes a collection of unary and binary operators. It is convenient to treat operators in much the same way as identifiers, as shown in Figures 5.7 and 5.8.[1]

The representation of the Triangle standard environment therefore includes small ASTs representing 'operator declarations', such as one for the unary operator '\' (7), and one for the binary operator '<' (8). (See Figure 5.7.) An 'operator declaration' merely defines the types of the operator's operand(s) and result. Entries are also made for operators in the identification table. (See Figure 5.8.) At an application of operator O, the identification table is used to retrieve the 'operator declaration' of O, and thus to find the operand and result types for type checking.

5.5 Further reading

For a more detailed discussion of declarations, scope, and block structure, see Chapter 4 of the companion textbook by Watt (1990). Section 2.5 of the same textbook discusses simple type systems (of the kind found in Triangle, Pascal, and indeed most programming languages). Chapter 7 goes on to explore more advanced type systems. *Coercions* (found in most languages) are implicit conversions from one type to another. *Overloading* (found in Ada and Java) allows several functions/procedures/methods with different bodies and different types to have a common identifier, even in the same scope. In a function/procedure/method call with this common identifier, a technique called *overload resolution* is needed to identify which of several functions/procedures/methods is being called. *Parametric polymorphism* (found in ML) allows a single function to operate

---

[1] Indeed, some programming languages, such as ML and Ada, actually allow operators to be declared like functions in the source program. This emphasizes the analogy between operators and function identifiers.

uniformly on arguments of a family of types (e.g., the list types). Moreover, the types of functions, parameters, etc., need not be declared explicitly. *Polymorphic type inference* is a technique that allows the types in a source program to be inferred in the context of a polymorphic type system.

For a comprehensive account of type checking, see Chapter 6 of Aho *et al.* (1985). As well as elementary techniques, the authors discuss techniques required by the more advanced type systems: type checking of coercions, overload resolution, and polymorphic type inference. For some reason, however, Aho *et al.* defer discussion of identification to Chapter 7 (run-time organization).

A classic paper on polymorphic type inference by Milner (1978) was the genesis of the type system that was adopted by ML, and borrowed by later functional languages.

For a good short account of contextual analysis in a one-pass compiler for a Pascal subset, see Chapter 2 of Welsh and McKeag (1980). The authors clearly explain ways of representing the identification table, attributes, and types. They also present a simple error recovery technique that enables the contextual analyzer to generate sensible error reports when an identifier is declared twice in the same scope, or not declared at all.

The visitor pattern used to structure the Triangle compiler is not the only possible object-oriented design. One alternative design, explained in Appel (1997), is to associate the checking methods (and the encoding methods in the code generator) for a particular AST object with the AST object itself. This design is initially easier to understand than the visitor design pattern, but it has the disadvantage that the checking methods (and encoding methods) are spread all over the AST subclass definitions instead of being grouped together in one place.

You should be aware of a lack of standard terminology in the area of contextual analysis. Identification tables are often called 'symbol tables' or 'declaration tables'. Contextual analysis itself is often misnamed 'semantic analysis'.

Exercises

Section 5.1

5.1   Consider a source language with monolithic block structure, as in Section 5.1.1, and consider the following ways of implementing the identification table:

(a)   an ordered list;
(b)   a binary search tree;
(c)   a hash table.

In each case implement the IdentificationTable class, including the methods enter and retrieve.

In efficiency terms, how do these implementations compare with one another?

5.2   Consider a source language with flat block structure, as in Section 5.1.2. Devise an efficient way of implementing the identification table. Implement the `IdentificationTable` class, including the methods `enter`, `retrieve`, `openScope`, and `closeScope`.

5.3*   For a source language with nested block structure, as in Section 5.1.3, we could implement the identification table by a stack of binary search trees (BSTs). Each BST would contain entries for declarations at one scope level. Consider the innermost block of Figure 5.3, for example. At the stack top there would be a BST containing the level-3 entries; below that there would be a BST containing the level-2 entries; and at the stack bottom there would be a BST containing the level-1 entries.

Implement the `IdentificationTable` class, including the methods `enter`, `retrieve`, `openScope`, and `closeScope`.

In efficiency terms, how does this implementation compare with that used in the Triangle compiler (Section 5.4.1)?

5.4*   For a source language with nested block structure, we can alternatively implement the identification table by a sparse matrix, with columns indexed by scope levels and rows indexed by identifiers. Each column links the entries at a particular scope level. Each row links the entries for a particular identifier, in order from innermost scope to outermost scope. In the innermost block of Figure 5.3, for example, the table would look like Figure 5.9.

Implement the `IdentificationTable` class, including the methods `enter`, `retrieve`, `openScope`, and `closeScope`.

In efficiency terms, how does this implementation compare with that used in the Triangle compiler (Section 5.4.1), and with a stack of binary search trees (Exercise 5.3)?

5.5*   Outline an identification algorithm that does not use an identification table, but instead searches the AST. For simplicity, assume monolithic block structure.

In efficiency terms, how does this algorithm compare with one based on an identification table?

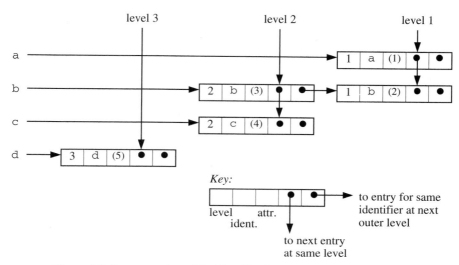

Figure 5.9 Representation of the identification table by a sparse matrix.

Section 5.2

5.6 Draw (undecorated) ASTs representing the following type declarations.

(a) Triangle type declarations:

```
type Age      = Integer;
type Letter   = Char;
type Alphanum = Char;
type Name     = array 20 of Letter;
type Address  = array 20 of Char;
type City     = array 10 of Letter;
type ZipCode  = array 10 of Alphanum
```

Eliminate the type identifiers (as in Figure 5.6). Which of the types are structurally equivalent to one another?

(b) Repeat with the corresponding type definitions in Pascal. (*Note:* Pascal adopts name equivalence of types, rather than structural equivalence.)

5.7 Suppose that name equivalence were to be adopted in Triangle. How would the Triangle contextual analyzer be modified?

5.8* Consider the following Triangle record types:

```
type T1 = record i: Integer; c: Char end;
type T2 = record j: Integer; h: Char end;
type T3 = record c: Char; i: Integer end
```

No two of these types are equivalent, since a Triangle record type is characterized by the identifiers, types, and order of its fields. The `TypeDenoter` class's `equals` method tests whether the two type ASTs are structurally identical.

Suppose, hypothetically, that two alternative ways of characterizing a Triangle record type are being considered. In each case, describe how the `equals` method would be modified.

(a) A record type is to be characterized only by the types and order of its fields (ignoring their identifiers). Thus types `T1` and `T2` (but not `T3`) are to be equivalent.

(b) A record type is to be characterized only by the identifiers and types of its fields (ignoring their order). Thus types `T1` and `T3` (but not `T2`) are to be equivalent.

5.9 In Pascal, type definitions may be mutually recursive, e.g.:

```
type IntList  = ^ IntNode;
     IntNode  = record
                    head: Integer;
                    tail: IntList
                end
```

These definitions introduce two new types: `IntList` is a pointer to an `IntNode` record, and `IntNode` is a record that contains an integer and an `IntList` pointer.

Draw (undecorated) ASTs representing these type definitions. Then eliminate the type identifiers (as in Figure 5.6). What do you observe about the transformed ASTs? Why would this complicate type checking if Pascal adopted structural equivalence for types?

5.10 Suppose that Mini-Triangle were to be extended with single-parameter function declarations:

```
single-Declaration  ::=  ...
                    |  func Identifier ( Identifier : Type-denoter )
                           : Type-denoter ~
                       Expression
```

and function calls:

```
primary-Expression ::=  ...
                    |  Identifier ( Expression )
```

Describe how function calls would be type-checked.

CHAPTER SIX

Run-Time Organization

A programming language supports high-level concepts such as types and values, expressions, variables, procedures, functions, and parameters. The target machine typically supports low-level concepts such as bits, bytes, words, registers, stacks, addresses, and (sub)routines. The gap between the higher and lower levels is often called the *semantic gap*. Bridging this gap is the task of the code generator.

Before writing a code generator, however, we must decide how to marshal the resources of the target machine (instructions, storage, and system software) in order to implement the source language. This is called ***run-time organization***, and is the subject of this chapter.

The following are key issues in run-time organization:

- ***Data representation****:* How should we represent the values of each source-language type in the target machine?

- ***Expression evaluation****:* How should we organize the evaluation of expressions, taking care of intermediate results?

- ***Storage allocation****:* How should we organize storage for variables, taking into account the different lifetimes of global, local, and heap variables?

- ***Routines****:* How should we implement procedures, functions, and parameters, in terms of low-level routines?

We shall study all these topics in this chapter, together with another topic of ever-increasing interest:

- ***Run-time organization for object-oriented languages****:* How should we represent objects and methods?

A thorough knowledge of run-time organization is essential for implementors of language processors, but a basic knowledge is useful to any serious programmer. In order to make rational programming decisions, the application programmer should have a feel for the efficiency of various high-level language constructs. An example is the choice of data structures: as we shall see, records and static arrays can be represented very efficiently, but the representations of dynamic arrays and recursive types carry overheads (indirect addressing, garbage collection) that might be unacceptable in some applications. This chapter covers all of these topics, for the sake of completeness, although not all of them are essential to understand the Triangle language processor.

6.1 Data representation

Programming languages provide high-level data types such as truth values, integers, characters, records, and arrays, together with operations over these types. Target machines provide only machine 'types' such as bits, bytes, words, and double-words, together with low-level arithmetic and logical operations. To bridge the semantic gap between the source language and the target machine, the implementor must decide how to *represent* the source language's types and operations in terms of the target machine's types and operations.

In the following subsections we shall survey representations of various types. As we study these representations, we should bear in mind the following fundamental principles of data representation:

• *Nonconfusion:* Different values of a given type should have different representations.

• *Uniqueness:* Each value should always have the same representation.

The *nonconfusion* requirement should be self-evident. If two different values are confused, i.e., have the same representation, then comparison of these values will incorrectly treat the values as equal.

Nevertheless, confusion does arise in practice. A well-known example is the approximate representation of real numbers: real numbers that are slightly different mathematically might have the same approximate representation. This confusion is inevitable, however, given the design of our digital computers. So language designers must formulate the semantics of real-number operations with care; and programmers on their part must learn to live with the problem, by avoiding naive comparisons of real numbers.

On the other hand, confusion can and *must* be avoided in the representations of discrete types, such as truth values, characters, and integers.

If the source language is statically typed, the nonconfusion requirement refers only to values of the same type; values of distinct types need not have distinct representations. Thus the word $00...00_2$ may represent the truth value *false*, the integer 0, the real number 0.0, and so on. Compile-time type checks will ensure that values of different types cannot be used interchangeably at run-time, and therefore cannot be confused. Thus we can be sure that if $00...00_2$ turns up as an operand of a logical operation, it represents *false*, whereas if it turns up as an operand of an arithmetic operation, it represents the integer 0.

The *uniqueness* requirement is likewise self-evident. Comparison of values would be complicated by the possibility of any value having more than one representation. Correct comparison is possible, however, so uniqueness is desirable rather than essential.

An example of nonuniqueness is the ones-complement representation of integers, in which zero is represented both by $00...00_2$ and by $11...11_2$. (These are +0 and –0!) A simple bit-string comparison would incorrectly treat these values as unequal, so a more specialized integer comparison must be used. The alternative twos-complement representation does give us unique representations of integers.

As well as these fundamental principles, we should bear in mind the following pragmatic issues in data representation:

- **Constant-size representation:** The representations of all values of a given type should occupy the same amount of space.

- **Direct representation** or **indirect representation:** Should the values of a given type be represented directly, or indirectly through pointers?

Constant-size representation makes it possible for a compiler to plan the allocation of storage. Knowing the type of a variable, but not its actual value, the compiler will know exactly how much storage space the variable will occupy.

The *direct representation* of a value x is just the binary representation of x itself, which consists of one or more bits, bytes, or words. This is illustrated in Figure 6.1(a).

The *indirect representation* of x is a **handle**, which points to a storage area (usually in the heap) that contains the binary representation of x. See Figure 6.1(b).

To understand the distinction, it is helpful to visualize what happens when the value x is copied (e.g., passed as an argument). With the direct representation, it is the binary representation of x that is copied. With the indirect representation, it is only the handle to x that is copied. The direct representation is so called because x can be accessed using direct addressing; the indirect representation is so called because x must be accessed using indirect addressing.

The choice of direct or indirect representation is a key design decision in run-time organization. Implementations of imperative languages like Pascal and C adopt the direct representation wherever possible, because values can be accessed more efficiently by direct addressing, and because the overheads of heap storage management are avoided. Implementations of functional languages like ML and Haskell usually adopt the indirect representation, because it simplifies the implementation of polymorphic functions. Implementations of object-oriented languages like Java adopt the direct representation for primitive types and the indirect representation for objects (see Section 6.7).

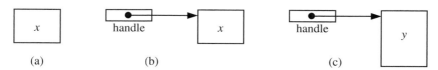

Figure 6.1 (a) Direct representation of a value x; (b) indirect representation of a value x; (c) indirect representation of a value y, of the same type as x but requiring more space.

Indirect representation is essential for types whose values vary greatly in size. For example, a list or dynamic array may have any number of elements, and clearly the total amount of space depends on the number of elements. For types such as this, indirect representation is the only way to satisfy the constant-size requirement. This is illustrated in Figure 6.1(b) and (c) where, although the values x and y occupy different amounts of space, the handles to x and y occupy the same amount of space.

We now survey representations of the more common types found in programming languages. We shall assume direct representation wherever possible, i.e., for primitive types, records, disjoint unions, and static arrays. But we shall see that indirect representation is necessary for dynamic arrays and recursive types.

We shall use the following notation:

- $\#T$ stands for the cardinality of type T, i.e., the number of distinct values of type T. For example, $\#[\![\texttt{Boolean}]\!] = 2$.

- *size* T stands for the amount of space (in bits, bytes, or words) occupied by each value of type T. If indirect representation is used, only the handle is counted.

We use emphatic brackets to enclose a specific type-denoter, as in $\#[\![\texttt{Boolean}]\!]$ or *size*$[\![\texttt{Boolean}]\!]$ or *size*$[\![\texttt{array 8 of Char}]\!]$.

If a direct representation is chosen for values of type T, we can assert the inequality:

$$size\ T \geq \log_2 (\#T), \quad \text{or equivalently} \quad 2^{(size\ T)} \geq \#T \qquad (6.1)$$

where *size* T is expressed in bits. This follows from the nonconfusion requirement: in n bits we can represent at most 2^n distinct values if we are to avoid confusion.

6.1.1 Primitive types

The *primitive types* of a programming language are those whose values are primitive, i.e., cannot be decomposed into simpler values. Examples of primitive types are `Boolean`, `Char`, and `Integer`. Most programming languages provide these types, equipped with the elementary logical and arithmetic operations.

Machines typically support such types and operations directly, so the choice of representation is straightforward.

The values of the type `Boolean` are the truth values *false* and *true*. We can represent a truth value by one word, one byte, or even a single bit. (Since $\#[\![\texttt{Boolean}]\!] = 2$, clearly *size*$[\![\texttt{Boolean}]\!] \geq 1$ bit.)

Using a single bit, the conventional representations are 0 for *false* and 1 for *true*. Using a byte or word, the conventional representations are $00...00_2$ for *false*, and either $00...01_2$ or $11...11_2$ for *true*. The operations on truth values – negation, conjunction, and disjunction – can be implemented by the machine's logical NOT, AND, and OR operations. (See also Exercise 6.2.)

The values of the type Char are the elements of a character set. Sometimes the source language specifies a particular character set. For example, Ada specifies the ISO-Latin1 character set, which consists of 2^8 distinct characters, and Java specifies the Unicode character set, which consists of 2^{16} distinct characters. Most programming languages, however, are deliberately unspecific about the character set. This allows the compiler writer to choose the target machine's 'native' character set. Typically this consists of 2^7 or 2^8 distinct characters. In any case, the choice of character set determines the representation of individual characters. For example, ISO defines the representation of character 'A' to be 01000001_2. We can represent a character by one byte or one word.

The values of the type Integer are integer numbers. Obviously we cannot represent an unbounded range of integers within a fixed amount of space. All major programming languages take account of this in their semantics: Integer denotes an implementation-defined[1] bounded range of integers. The binary representation of integers is determined by the target machine's arithmetic unit, and almost always occupies one word. The source language's integer operations can then, for the most part, be implemented by the corresponding machine operations.

In Pascal and Triangle, Integer denotes the range *–maxint*, ..., –1, 0, +1, ..., *+maxint*, where the constant *maxint* is implementation-defined. In this case we have #⟦Integer⟧ $= 2 \times maxint + 1$, and therefore we can specialize (6.1) as follows:

$$2^{size⟦\text{Integer}⟧} \geq 2 \times maxint + 1 \qquad (6.2)$$

If the word size is w bits, then $size⟦\text{Integer}⟧ = w$. To ensure that (6.2) is satisfied, the implementation should define $maxint = 2^{w-1} - 1$.

In Java, **int** denotes the range -2^{31}, ..., –1, 0, +1, ..., $+2^{31}-1$. In this case we have #⟦**int**⟧ $= 2^{32}$.

Example 6.1 *Primitive data representations in TAM*

TAM is the target machine of the Triangle compiler. Storage is organized in 16-bit words. There are no smaller storage units, but multi-word objects are addressable. The Triangle primitive types are represented as follows:

Type	Representation	Size
Boolean	$00...00_2$ for false; $00...01_2$ for true	1 word
Char	Unicode representation	1 word
Integer	twos-complement representation	1 word

Thus $maxint = 2^{15} - 1 = 32767$.

□

---

[1] An attribute of a programming language L is implementation-defined if it is not defined by the specification of L, but must be defined by each individual L language processor.

Example 6.2   Primitive data representations in the Intel Pentium

The Intel Pentium processor is ubiquitous. Storage is organized in 8-bit bytes, 16-bit half-words, 32-bit words, and 64-bit double-words. Primitive types could be represented as follows:

Type	Representation	Size
`Boolean`	00000000_2 for false; 11111111_2 for true	1 byte
`Char`	ASCII representation	1 byte
`Integer`	twos-complement representation	1 half-word or 1 word

Thus *maxint* = $2^{15} - 1$ = 32767, *or maxint* = $2^{31} - 1$ = 2147483647.

□

Some programming languages allow the programmer to define new primitive types. An example is the ***enumeration type*** of Pascal. The values of such a type are called *enumerands*. Enumerands can be represented by small integers.

Example 6.3   Enumerand representation

Consider the following Pascal type definition:

```
type Color = (red, orange, yellow, green, blue)
```

This creates a new enumeration type consisting of five enumerands, which we shall write as *red*, *orange*, *yellow*, *green*, and *blue*. It also binds the identifiers `red`, `orange`, etc., to these enumerands.[2]

The enumerands will be represented by $00...000_2$ for *red*, $00...001_2$ for *orange*, $00...010_2$ for *yellow*, $00...011_2$ for *green*, and $00...100_2$ for *blue*. Since #[[Color]] = 5, clearly *size*[[Color]] ≥ 3 bits. In practice we would use one byte or one word.

□

To generalize, consider the enumeration type defined by:

```
type T = (I₀, I₁, ..., Iₙ₋₁)
```

We can represent each I_i by (the binary equivalent of) i. Since #$T = n$, *size* $T \geq \log_2 n$ bits.

The enumeration type is equipped with operations such as `succ` (which returns the successor of the given enumerand) and `ord` (which returns the integer representation of the given enumerand). The representation chosen allows `succ` to be implemented by the target machine's INC operation (if available). The `ord` operation becomes a NOP.

---

[2] We must distinguish between the identifiers and the enumerands they denote, because the identifiers could be redeclared.

6.1.2   Records

Now we proceed to examine the representation of *composite types*. These are types whose values are composed from simpler values.

A ***record*** consists of several *fields*, each of which has an identifier. A record type designates the identifiers and types of its fields, and all the records of a particular type have fields with the same identifiers and types. The fundamental operation on records is *field selection*, whereby we use one of the field identifiers to access the corresponding field.

Records occur obviously in Pascal, Ada, and Triangle, and as **struct**s in C.

There is an obvious and good direct representation for records: we simply juxtapose the fields, i.e., make them occupy consecutive positions in storage. This representation is compact, and makes it easy to implement field selection very efficiently.

Example 6.4   *Triangle record representation*

Consider the record types and variables introduced by the following Triangle declarations:

```
type Date    = record
                   y: Integer,
                   m: Integer,
                   d: Integer
               end;

type Details = record
                   female: Boolean,
                   dob:    Date,
                   status: Char
               end;

var today: Date;
var her:   Details
```

Assume for simplicity that each primitive value occupies one word. Then the variables today and her (after initialization) would look like this:

Each box in the diagram is a word. A variable of type Date (such as today) occupies three consecutive words, one for each of its fields. A variable of type Details (such as her) occupies five consecutive words, one for its field female, three for its field dob, and one for its field status.

We can predict not only the total size of each record variable, but also the position of each field relative to the base of the record. If `today` is located at address 100 (i.e., it occupies the words at addresses 100 through 102), then `today.y` is located at address 100, `today.m` is located at address 101, and `today.d` is located at address 102. In other words, the fields `y`, `m`, and `d` have *offsets* of 0, 1, and 2, respectively, within any record of type `Date`. Likewise, the fields `female`, `dob`, and `status` have offsets of 0, 1, and 4, respectively, within any record of type `Details`.

Summarizing:

$$size[\![\texttt{Date}]\!] \qquad\qquad = 3 \text{ words}$$

$$address[\![\texttt{today.y}]\!] \quad = address[\![\texttt{today}]\!] + 0$$
$$address[\![\texttt{today.m}]\!] \quad = address[\![\texttt{today}]\!] + 1$$
$$address[\![\texttt{today.d}]\!] \quad = address[\![\texttt{today}]\!] + 2$$

$$size[\![\texttt{Details}]\!] \qquad\quad = 5 \text{ words}$$

$$address[\![\texttt{her.female}]\!] \quad = address[\![\texttt{her}]\!] + 0$$
$$address[\![\texttt{her.dob}]\!] \quad\;\; = address[\![\texttt{her}]\!] + 1$$
$$address[\![\texttt{her.dob.y}]\!] \quad = address[\![\texttt{her.dob}]\!] + 0 \quad = address[\![\texttt{her}]\!] + 1$$
$$address[\![\texttt{her.dob.m}]\!] \quad = address[\![\texttt{her.dob}]\!] + 1 \quad = address[\![\texttt{her}]\!] + 2$$
$$address[\![\texttt{her.dob.d}]\!] \quad = address[\![\texttt{her.dob}]\!] + 2 \quad = address[\![\texttt{her}]\!] + 3$$
$$address[\![\texttt{her.status}]\!] \quad = address[\![\texttt{her}]\!] + 4$$

We shall use the notation *address v* to stand for the address of variable *v*. If the variable occupies several words, this means the address of the first word. We use emphatic brackets $[\![\ldots]\!]$ to enclose a specific variable-name, as in *address*$[\![\texttt{her.dob}]\!]$.

Let us now generalize from this example. Consider a record type *T* and variable *r*:

$$\texttt{type } T = \texttt{record } I_1\colon T_1, \;\; \ldots, \;\; I_n\colon T_n \texttt{ end;} \tag{6.3}$$

$$\texttt{var } r\colon T$$

We represent each record of type *T* by juxtaposing its *n* fields, as shown in Figure 6.2. It is clear that:

$$size\ T = size\ T_1 + \ldots + size\ T_n \tag{6.4}$$

This satisfies the constant-size requirement. If $size\ T_1$, ..., and $size\ T_n$ are all constant, then $size\ T$ is also constant.

The implementation of field selection is simple and efficient. To access field I_i of the record *r*, we use the following address computation:

$$address[\![r.I_i]\!] = address\ r + (size\ T_1 + \ldots + size\ T_{i-1}) \tag{6.5}$$

Since $size\ T_1$, ..., and $size\ T_{i-1}$ are all constant, the address of the field $r.I_i$ is just a constant offset from the base address of *r* itself. Thus, if the compiler knows the address of the record, it can determine the exact address of any field, and can generate code to access the field directly. In these circumstances, field selection is a zero-cost operation!

However, note that some machines have *alignment restrictions*, which may force unused space to be left between record fields. Such alignment restrictions invalidate equations (6.4) and (6.5). (See Exercise 6.9.)

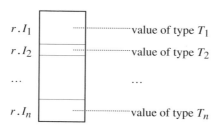

Figure 6.2 Representation of a record r.

6.1.3 Disjoint unions

A **disjoint union** consists of a *tag* and a *variant part*, in which the *value* of the tag determines the *type* of the variant part. Mathematically we can describe a disjoint union type as follows:

$$T = T_1 + \ldots + T_n \tag{6.6}$$

In each value of type T, the variant part is a value chosen from one of the types T_1, …, or T_n; the tag indicates which one. The fundamental operations on disjoint unions are: (a) *tag testing*; and (b) for each component type T_i, *projection* of the variant part to give an ordinary value of type T_i. (The projection operation must be designed with care to avoid any loophole in the type rules of a statically-typed language.)

Disjoint unions occur as *variant records* in Pascal and Ada, as *unions* in Algol-68, and as so-called *datatypes* in Haskell and ML. In a variant record, the tag is just a field, and each possible variant is a distinct field (or tuple of fields); projection is then similar to field selection from an ordinary record. In the other languages mentioned, projection is done by pattern matching.

A suitable representation for a disjoint union is juxtaposition of the tag and variant part. But there is a complication: the variant part may have several possible types, and therefore several possible sizes. Therefore, we must be careful to satisfy the constant-size requirement. Fortunately, this is not difficult.

Example 6.5   Pascal variant record representation

Consider the following Pascal variant record type:

```
type Number = record
                case acc: Boolean of
                   true:  ( i: Integer );
                   false: ( r: Real )
             end;

var num: Number
```

Every value of type `Number` has a tag field, named `acc`, and a variant part. The value of the tag determines the form of the variant part. If the tag is *true*, the variant part is an integer field named `i`. If the tag is *false*, the variant part is a real field named `r`.

Assume that a truth value or integer occupies one word, but a real number occupies two words. Then the variable num would look like this:

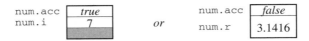

Some values of type `Number` occupy two words; others occupy three words. This apparently contradicts the constant-size requirement, which we wish to avoid at all costs. We want the compiler to allocate a fixed amount of space to each variable of type `Number`, and let it change form within this space. To be safe we must allocate three words: one word for the tag field, and two words for the variant part. The fields `i` and `r` can be overlaid within the latter two words. When the tag is *true*, one word is unused (shaded gray in the diagram), but this is a small price to pay for satisfying the constant-size requirement. Thus:

$$size[\![Number]\!] \quad = 3 \text{ words}$$

$$address[\![num.acc]\!] = address[\![num]\!] + 0$$
$$address[\![num.i]\!] = address[\![num]\!] + 1$$
$$address[\![num.r]\!] = address[\![num]\!] + 1$$

Now consider the following variant record type, which illustrates an empty variant and a variant with more than one field:

```
type Shape  = (point, circle, box);
     Figure = record
                case s: Shape of
                   point:  ( );
                   circle: ( r: Integer );
                   box:    ( h, w: Integer )
             end;

var fig: Figure
```

Every value of type `Figure` has a tag field, named `s`, and a variant part. The value of the tag (*point*, *circle*, or *box*) determines the form of the variant part. If the tag is *point*, the variant part is empty. If the tag is *circle*, the variant part is an integer field named `r`. If the tag is *box*, the variant part is a pair of integer fields named `h` and `w`.

Assume that each primitive value occupies one word. Then the variable `fig` would look like this:

```
fig.s   ┌─────────┐          fig.s   ┌─────────┐          fig.s   ┌─────────┐
        │  point  │          fig.r   │ circle  │          fig.h   │   box   │
        ├─────────┤    or            ├─────────┤    or            ├─────────┤
        │░░░░░░░░░│                  │    5    │                  │    3    │
        └─────────┘                  │░░░░░░░░░│                  ├─────────┤
                                     └─────────┘                  │    4    │
                                                                  └─────────┘
```

(The enumerands *point*, *circle*, and *box* would be represented by small integers, as discussed in Section 6.1.1.)

It is easy to see that:

$size[\![\texttt{Figure}]\!]$ = 3 words

$address[\![\texttt{fig.s}]\!]$ = $address[\![\texttt{fig}]\!] + 0$

$address[\![\texttt{fig.r}]\!]$ = $address[\![\texttt{fig}]\!] + 1$

$address[\![\texttt{fig.h}]\!]$ = $address[\![\texttt{fig}]\!] + 1$

$address[\![\texttt{fig.w}]\!]$ = $address[\![\texttt{fig}]\!] + 2$

□

Let us now generalize. Consider a Pascal variant record type T and variable u:

```
type T = record                                          (6.7)
             case Itag: Ttag of
                 v1:  (I1:  T1);
                 ...;
                 vn:  (In:  Tn)
         end;
var u: T
```

where each variant is labeled by one possible value of the type $T_{tag} = \{v_1, ..., v_n\}$. We represent each record of type T by juxtaposing its tag field and variant part. Within the variant part we overlay the different variants, which are of types $T_1, T_2, ...,$ and T_n. This representation is shown in Figure 6.3. It is clear that:

$$size\ T = size\ T_{tag} + max\ (size\ T_1, ..., size\ T_n) \qquad (6.8)$$

This satisfies the constant-size requirement. If $size\ T_{tag}$, $size\ T_1$, ..., and $size\ T_n$ are all constant, then $size\ T$ is also constant.

The operations on variant records are easily implemented. To access the tag and variant fields of the variant record u, we use the following address computations:

$$address[\![u.I_{tag}]\!] = address\ u + 0 \qquad (6.9)$$

$$address[\![u.I_i]\!] = address\ u + size\ T_{tag} \qquad (6.10)$$

– both being constant offsets from the base address of u.

This analysis can easily be generalized to variants with no fields or many fields, as in Example 6.5.

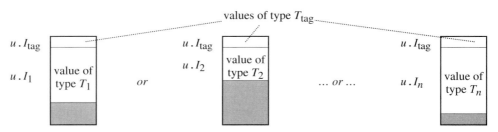

Figure 6.3 Representation of a disjoint union (variant record) *u*.

6.1.4 Static arrays

An ***array*** consists of several *elements*, which are all of the same type. The array has a bounded range of *indices* (which are usually integers), and for each index it has exactly one element. The fundamental operation on arrays is *indexing*, whereby we access an individual element by giving its index; in general, this index is evaluated at run-time.

A ***static array*** is an array whose index bounds are known at compile-time. A suitable direct representation for a static array is to juxtapose the array elements, in order of increasing indices. The indexing operation is implemented by a run-time address computation.

For the moment we make the simplifying assumption that the lower index bound is zero. This is the case in the programming languages Triangle, C, and Java. (Later we shall relax this assumption.)

Example 6.6   Triangle array representation

Consider the array types and variables introduced by these Triangle declarations:

```
type Name   = array 6 of Char;
type Coding = record
                 c: Char, n: Integer
              end;

var me:   Name;
var us:   array 2 of Name;
var code: array 3 of Coding
```

The variable me is just an array of six characters (indexed from 0 through 5). The variable us is an array of two elements, each of which is itself an array of six characters. The variable code is an array of three elements, each of which is a record with two fields.

Assume again that each primitive value occupies one word. Then the variables me, us, and code would be represented as follows:

me[0]	'W'		us[0][0]	'W'
me[1]	'a'		us[0][1]	'a'
me[2]	't'		us[0][2]	't'
me[3]	't'	us[0] {	us[0][3]	't'
me[4]	' '		us[0][4]	' '
me[5]	' '		us[0][5]	' '

code[0] {	code[0].c	'I'		us[1][0]	'B'
	code[0].n	1		us[1][1]	'r'
code[1] {	code[1].c	'V'	us[1] {	us[1][2]	'o'
	code[1].n	5		us[1][3]	'w'
code[2] {	code[2].c	'X'		us[1][4]	'n'
	code[2].n	10		us[1][5]	' '

It is easy to see that:

$size[\![Name]\!]$ $= 6 \times size[\![Char]\!]$ $= 6$ words
$size[\![array\ 2\ of\ Name]\!]$ $= 2 \times size[\![Name]\!]$ $= 12$ words
$size[\![array\ 3\ of\ Coding]\!]$ $= 3 \times size[\![Coding]\!]$ $= 6$ words

$address[\![me[0]]\!]$ $= address[\![me]\!] + 0$
$address[\![me[3]]\!]$ $= address[\![me]\!] + 3$
$address[\![me[i]]\!]$ $= address[\![me]\!] + i$
$address[\![code[2]]\!]$ $= address[\![code]\!] + 4$
$address[\![code[i]]\!]$ $= address[\![code]\!] + 2i$
$address[\![code[i].n]\!]$ $= address[\![code[i]]\!] + 1 = address[\![code]\!] + 2i + 1$
$address[\![us[i]]\!]$ $= address[\![us]\!] + 6i$
$address[\![us[i][j]]\!]$ $= address[\![us[i]]\!] + j = address[\![us]\!] + 6i + j$

□

Let us now generalize from this example. Consider a Triangle array type T and array variable a:

type T = array n of T_{elem}; $\qquad$ (6.11)

var a: T

Each array of type T has n elements, indexed from 0 through $n-1$. We represent each array by juxtaposing its elements, as shown in Figure 6.4. It is clear that:

$$size\ T = n \times size\ T_{elem} \qquad (6.12)$$

This satisfies the constant-size requirement. The number of elements n is constant, so if $size\ T_{elem}$ is constant, then $size\ T$ is also constant.

Since the elements of the array a are positioned in order of increasing index, and since the first element has index 0, the element with index i is addressed as follows:

$$address[\![a[i]]\!] = address\ a + (i \times size\ T_{elem}) \qquad (6.13)$$

Here $size\ T_{elem}$ is known at compile-time, but (in general) the value of i is known only at run-time. Thus array indexing implies a run-time address computation.

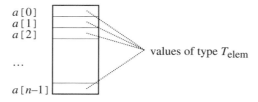

Figure 6.4 Representation of a zero-based static array

Now let us consider static arrays where the programmer may choose both the lower and upper index bounds, as in Pascal.

Example 6.7   Pascal array representation

Consider the array variables introduced by the following Pascal declarations:

```
var grade: array [-2..3] of Char;
    gnp:   array [2000..2004] of Integer
```

This declares two arrays: grade is an array of six elements of type Char, and gnp is an array of five elements of type Integer.

Assume that each primitive value occupies one word. Then the arrays would be represented as follows:

grade[-2]	'G'
grade[-1]	'F'
grade[0]	'N'
grade[1]	'C'
grade[2]	'B'
grade[3]	'A'

gnp[2000]	13500
gnp[2001]	14200
gnp[2002]	15000
gnp[2003]	15200
gnp[2004]	15100

It is easy to see that:

$$size[\![\texttt{array [-2..3] of Integer}]\!] = 6 \text{ words}$$

$$
\begin{aligned}
address[\![\texttt{grade[-2]}]\!] &= address[\![\texttt{grade}]\!] + 0 \\
address[\![\texttt{grade[0]}]\!] &= address[\![\texttt{grade}]\!] + 2 \\
address[\![\texttt{grade[2]}]\!] &= address[\![\texttt{grade}]\!] + 4 \\
address[\![\texttt{grade[}i\texttt{]}]\!] &= address[\![\texttt{grade}]\!] - (-2) + i
\end{aligned}
$$

$$size[\![\texttt{array [2000..2004] of Integer}]\!] = 5 \text{ words}$$

$$
\begin{aligned}
address[\![\texttt{gnp[2003]}]\!] &= address[\![\texttt{gnp}]\!] + 3 \\
address[\![\texttt{gnp[}i\texttt{]}]\!] &= address[\![\texttt{gnp}]\!] - 2000 + i
\end{aligned}
$$

To be concrete, suppose that $address[\![\texttt{grade}]\!] = 100$ (i.e., grade occupies the words at addresses 100 through 105). Then $address[\![\texttt{grade[}i\texttt{]}]\!] = 100 - (-2) + i = 102 + i$. So we can compute the address of any element of this array with a single run-time addition (rather than a subtraction and an addition).

But what is the significance of this number 102? It is just *address*⟦grade[0]⟧. We call this address the ***origin*** of the array grade. An array's origin coincides with its base address only if its lower bound is zero.

Similarly, *address*⟦gnp[i]⟧ = *address*⟦gnp[0]⟧ + i, where the origin of the array gnp is *address*⟦gnp[0]⟧ = *address*⟦gnp⟧ − 2000. Of course, this particular array has no element with index 0, but that does not prevent us from using its origin (which is just a number!) to compute the addresses of its elements at run-time.

□

Let us now generalize. Consider a Pascal array type *T* and array variable *a*:

$$\texttt{type } T = \texttt{array } [l..u] \texttt{ of } T_{\text{elem}}; \tag{6.14}$$

$$\texttt{var } a: T$$

The constants *l* and *u* are the lower and upper index bounds, respectively, of the array type. Each array of type *T* has $(u - l + 1)$ elements, indexed from *l* through *u*. As before, we represent each array by juxtaposing its elements, as shown in Figure 6.5. It is clear that:

$$size\ T = (u - l + 1) \times size\ T_{\text{elem}} \tag{6.15}$$

Again, this satisfies the constant-size requirement, since *l* and *u* are constant.

The element of array *a* with index *i* is addressed as follows:

$$address⟦a[i]⟧ \quad = \ address\ a + (i - l) \times size\ T_{\text{elem}}$$
$$= \ address\ a - (l \times size\ T_{\text{elem}}) + (i \times size\ T_{\text{elem}})$$

From this we can determine the origin *address*⟦a[0]⟧, and use it to simplify the formula:

$$address⟦a[0]⟧ \quad = \ address\ a - (l \times size\ T_{\text{elem}}) \tag{6.16}$$

$$address⟦a[i]⟧ \quad = \ address⟦a[0]⟧ + (i \times size\ T_{\text{elem}}) \tag{6.17}$$

Equation (6.17) has the same form as (6.13). The only difference is that *a*[0] no longer need be the first element of the array *a*. Indeed, *a*[0] might not even exist! But that does not matter, as we saw in Example 6.7, because *address*⟦a[0]⟧ is just a number.

There is more to array indexing than an address computation. An *index check* is also needed, to ensure that the evaluated index lies within the array's index bounds. When an array of the type *T* of (6.14) is indexed by *i*, the index check must ensure that:

$$l \leq i \leq u \tag{6.18}$$

Since the index bounds *l* and *u* are known at compile-time, the compiler can easily generate such an index check.

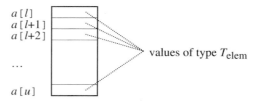

Figure 6.5 Representation of a static array *a*.

6.1.5 Dynamic arrays

A *dynamic array* is an array whose index bounds are not known until run-time. Dynamic arrays are found in Algol and Ada. In such languages, different dynamic arrays of the same type may have different index bounds, and therefore different numbers of elements. How then can we make dynamic arrays satisfy the constant-size requirement?

We are forced to adopt an indirect representation, in which the dynamic array's handle (also called an *array descriptor*) contains not only a pointer to the array's elements but also the array's index bounds. The handle has a constant size.

Example 6.8   Ada dynamic array representation

Consider the array type and variables introduced by the following Ada declarations:

```
type String is array (Integer range <>) of Character;
d: String(1 .. k);
s: String(m .. n - 1);
```

This declares a new array type `String`, and two variables of type `String`. The first variable, `d`, contains elements indexed from 1 to the value of `k`, and the second variable, `s`, contains elements indexed from the value of `m` to the value of `n-1`.

The values of type `String` are arrays of characters, indexed by integers. Different arrays of type `String` may have different index bounds; moreover, these index bounds may be evaluated at run-time. Operations such as concatenation and lexicographic comparison are applicable to any arrays of type `String`, even if they have different numbers of elements. But any attempt to assign one array of type `String` to another will fail at run-time unless they happen to have the same number of elements.

A suitable representation for arrays of type `String` is as follows. Each array's handle contains the array's origin, i.e., the address of the (possibly notional) element with index 0. The handle also contains the array's lower and upper index bounds. The array's elements are stored separately.

Suppose that the variables `k`, `m`, and `n` turn out to have values 7, 0, and 4, respectively. Then the array `d` will have index bounds 1 and 7, and the array `s` will have index bounds 0 and 3. The arrays will look like this:

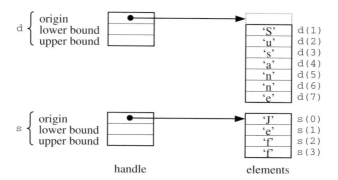

handle   elements

Each array's handle occupies 3 words exactly (assuming that integers and addresses occupy one word each). The elements of d occupy 7 words, whereas the elements of s occupy 4 words (assuming that characters occupy one word each). Since the elements are stored separately, we take $size[\![\text{String}]\!]$ to be the size of the handle:

$$size[\![\text{String}]\!] = 3 \text{ words}$$

Likewise, we shall take $address[\![\text{d}]\!]$ to be the address of d's handle. The address of element d(0) is stored at offset 0 within the handle. Thus the address of an arbitrary element can be computed as follows:

$$\begin{aligned} address[\![\text{d}(i)]\!] &= address[\![\text{d}(0)]\!] + i \\ &= content(address[\![\text{d}]\!]) + i \end{aligned}$$

where $content(x)$ stands for the content of the word at address x.

□

Let us now generalize. Consider an Ada array type T and array variable a:

$$\text{type } T \text{ is array (Integer range <>) of } T_{\text{elem}}; \tag{6.19}$$

$$a\text{: } T \text{ } (E_1 \text{ .. } E_2);$$

We represent each array of type T by a handle, consisting of an address and two integers, as shown in Figure 6.6. Thus:

$$size\ T = address\text{-}size + 2 \times size[\![\text{Integer}]\!] \tag{6.20}$$

where $address\text{-}size$ is the amount of space required to store an address – usually one word. Equation (6.20) clearly satisfies the constant-size requirement.

The declaration of array variable a is elaborated as follows. First the expressions E_1 and E_2 are evaluated to yield a's index bounds. Suppose that their values turn out to be l and u, respectively. Space is then allocated for $(u - l + 1)$ elements, juxtaposed in the usual way, but located separately from a's handle. The array's origin is computed as follows:

$$address[\![a(0)]\!] = address[\![a(l)]\!] - (l \times size\ T_{\text{elem}}) \tag{6.21}$$

The values $address[\![a(0)]\!]$, l, and u are stored in a's handle, as shown in Figure 6.6. As usual, $a(0)$ might not actually exist; but that does not matter, because $address[\![a(0)]\!]$ is just a number.

The element with index i will be addressed as follows:

$$\begin{aligned} address[\![a(i)]\!] &= address[\![a(0)]\!] + (i \times size\ T_{elem}) \\ &= content(address[\![a]\!]) + (i \times size\ T_{elem}) \end{aligned} \tag{6.22}$$

The index bounds of a are stored at constant offsets within a's handle. Using these, the above address computation should be preceded by the following index check:

$$l \le i \le u \tag{6.23}$$

where
$$\begin{aligned} l &= content(address[\![a]\!] + address\text{-}size) \\ u &= content(address[\![a]\!] + address\text{-}size + size[\![\texttt{Integer}]\!]) \end{aligned}$$

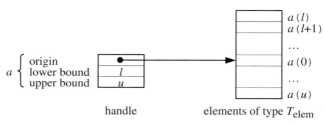

handle   elements of type T_{elem}

Figure 6.6 Representation of a dynamic array a.

6.1.6   Recursive types

A ***recursive type*** is one defined in terms of itself. Values of a recursive type T have components that are themselves of type T. Typical examples are lists (the tail of a list being itself a list) and trees (the subtrees being themselves trees).

In Pascal recursive types are defined by means of pointers. A record cannot contain a record of the same type, but a record may contain a pointer to a record of the same type.

Example 6.9   Pascal linked list representation

In Pascal we define linked lists of integers by means of a pair of mutually recursive type definitions:

```
type IntList = ^IntNode;
     IntNode = record
                   head: Integer;
                   tail: IntList
               end;
var primes: IntList
```

Here, `IntList` is a pointer to an `IntNode` record, which contains an `Integer` and a further `IntList` pointer. A nonempty list is represented by a pointer to a record, whose fields contain the list's head and tail. An empty list is represented by the special pointer value *nil*, which points to nothing.

A list consisting of the integers 2, 3, 5, and 7 would be represented as follows:

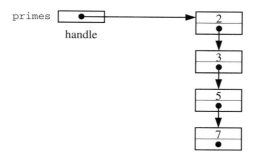

A value of type `IntList` is represented by a pointer, so typically:

$size[\![IntList]\!]$ = 1 word

Each node of the list will occupy two words (assuming that integers also occupy one word). There may be any number of nodes, of course, so the total amount of space occupied by the list is unbounded. However, the size of its handle is constant.

□

In general, the amount of storage occupied by a pointer will be:

$$size[\![^T]\!] = \textit{address-size} \tag{6.24}$$

The value *address-size* is implementation-defined. It is, however, the same for all pointer types in a given implementation.

The same indirect representation can be adopted for lists in other programming languages, whether the list type is built-in or programmer-defined. Even if the language supports recursive type definitions (without pointers), pointers must still be used to *represent* values of the recursive type. For example, in ML:

```
datatype intlist = nil | cons of (int * intlist);

val primes = cons(2, cons(3, cons(5, cons(7, nil))))
```

Here, `intlist` is a datatype with two constructors. The first, `nil`, represents an empty `intlist`, and the second, `cons`, combines an `int` and an `intlist` to produce an `intlist`. The constructors, `nil` and `cons`, as well as being used to create values of type `intlist` (such as `primes`), are also used as the tags in pattern matching. The representation illustrated in Example 6.9 would still be suitable. Thus:

$size[\![intlist]\!] = \textit{address-size}$

Similar principles apply to the representation of other recursive types such as trees.

6.2 Expression evaluation

Historically, one of the first distinguishing characteristics of high-level programming languages was that they allowed the programmer to write algebraic expressions, such as the following Triangle expressions:

```
2 * (h + w)
(0 < i) /\ (i <= n)
a * b + (1 - (c * 2))
```

Such expressions are concise, and the notation is familiar from mathematics.

The implementation problem is the need to keep intermediate results somewhere, during evaluation of the more complicated expressions. For example, during evaluation of the expression 'a * b + (1 - (c * 2))', the subexpressions 'a * b', 'c * 2', and '1 - (c * 2)' will give rise to intermediate results.

The problem can be seen in a more general setting if we consider the semantics of such expressions (1.21d). To evaluate an expression of the form 'E_1 O E_2', we must evaluate both the subexpressions E_1 and E_2, then apply the binary operator O to the two intermediate results. If we evaluate E_1 first, then its result must be kept somewhere safe during the evaluation of E_2.

Many machines provide *registers* that can be used to store intermediate results. Such a machine typically provides registers named R0, R1, R2, and so on, and instructions like those listed in Table 6.1. (Depending on the details of the instruction set, x could be the address of a storage cell, a literal, another register, etc.)

Example 6.10 Expression evaluation in a register machine

To evaluate the expression '(a * b) + (1 - (c * 2))' on our register machine, we could use the following sequence of instructions:

```
LOAD  R1  a    – now R1 contains the value of a
MULT  R1  b    – now R1 contains the value of a*b
LOAD  R2  #1   – now R2 contains the literal value 1
LOAD  R3  c    – now R3 contains the value of c
MULT  R3  #2   – now R3 contains the value of c*2
SUB   R2  R3   – now R2 contains the value of 1-(c*2)
ADD   R1  R2   – now R1 contains the value of a*b+(1-(c*2))
```

Of course, if *address*⟦a⟧ = 100 (say), the first instruction would really be 'LOAD R1 100', and the other instructions likewise. In order to make our examples of object code readable, we will adopt the convention that *a* stands for *address*⟦a⟧, *b* for *address*⟦b⟧, and so on.

□

Table 6.1 Typical instructions in a register machine

Instruction	Meaning
STORE R*i* *a*	Store the value in register *i* at address *a*.
LOAD R*i* *x*	Fetch the value of *x* and place it in register *i*.
ADD R*i* *x*	Fetch the value of *x* and add it to the value in register *i*.
SUB R*i* *x*	Fetch the value of *x* and subtract it from the value in register *i*.
MULT R*i* *x*	Fetch the value of *x* and multiply it into the value in register *i*.

The object code for expression evaluation in registers is efficient but rather complicated. A compiler generating such code must assign a specific register to each intermediate result. It is important to do this well, but quite tricky. In particular, a problem arises when there are not enough registers for all the intermediate results. (See Exercise 6.11.)

A very different kind of machine is one that provides a **stack** for holding intermediate results. This allows us to evaluate expressions in a very natural way. Such a machine typically provides instructions like those listed in Table 6.2.

Example 6.11 Expression evaluation in a stack machine

To evaluate the expression '(a * b) + (1 − (c * 2))' on our stack machine, we could use the sequence of instructions shown below left. Note the one-to-one correspondence with the same expression's *postfix* representation, shown below right.

```
LOAD   a      a
LOAD   b      b
MULT          *
LOADL  1      1
LOAD   c      c
LOADL  2      2
MULT          *
SUB           −
ADD           +
```

Figure 6.7 shows the effect of each instruction on the stack, assuming that the stack is initially empty.[3]

---

[3] In Figure 6.7 and throughout this book, the stack is shown growing downwards, with the stack top nearest the bottom of the diagram. If this convention seems perverse, recall the convention for drawing trees in computer science textbooks! Shading indicates the unused space beyond the stack top.

Table 6.2 Typical instructions in a stack machine

Instruction	Meaning
STORE a	Pop the top value off the stack and store it at address a.
LOAD a	Fetch a value from address a and push it on to the stack.
LOADL n	Push the literal value n on to the stack.
ADD	Replace the top two values on the stack by their sum.
SUB	Replace the top two values on the stack by their difference.
MULT	Replace the top two values on the stack by their product.

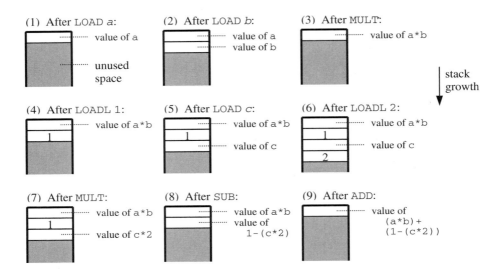

Figure 6.7 Evaluation of $(a*b)+(1-(c*2))$ on a stack.

The stack machine requires more instructions than a register machine to evaluate an expression, but the individual instructions are simpler. There is one instruction for each operator, and one for each operand. In fact, as we noted in Example 6.11, the instruction sequence is in one-to-one correspondence with the expression's postfix representation. Because the problem of register assignment is removed, code generation for a stack machine is much simpler than code generation for a register machine.

The *net effect* of evaluating a (sub)expression on the stack is to leave its result at the stack top, on top of whatever was there already. For example, consider the evaluation of the subexpression 'c * 2' – steps (5) through (7) in Figure 6.7. The net effect is to push the value of 'c * 2' on to the stack top, and meanwhile the two values already on the stack remain undisturbed.

These desirable and simple properties of evaluation on the stack hold true regardless of how complicated the expression is. An expression involving function calls can be evaluated in just the same way. Likewise, an expression involving operands of different types (and therefore different sizes) can be evaluated in just the same way.

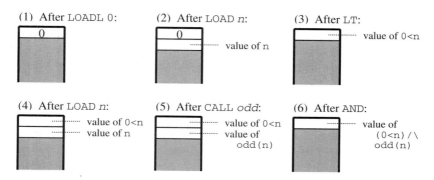

Figure 6.8 Evaluation of '(0 < n) /\ odd(n)' on a stack.

Example 6.12 Evaluation of function calls in a stack machine

To evaluate the expression '(0 < n) /\ odd(n)' on our stack machine, we could use the following sequence of instructions:

```
LOADL  0
LOAD   n
LT
LOAD   n
CALL   odd
AND
```

Figure 6.8 shows the effect of each instruction on the stack, assuming that the stack is initially empty. The instructions 'LT' and 'AND' are analogous to 'ADD', 'SUB', etc., in that each replaces two values at the stack top by a single value, but some of the values involved are truth values rather than integers.

Note the analogy between 'CALL odd' and instructions like 'ADD', 'LT', etc. – each takes its argument(s) from the stack top, and replaces them by its result.

6.3 Static storage allocation

We now study the allocation of storage to variables. In this section we consider only global variables. In Section 6.4 we shall consider local variables, and in Section 6.6 heap variables.

Each variable in the source program requires enough storage to contain any value that might be assigned to it. The compiler cannot know, in general, which particular values will be assigned to the variable. But if the source language is statically typed, the compiler will know the variable's type, *T*. Thus, as a consequence of constant-size representation, the compiler will know how much storage needs to be allocated to the variable, namely *size T*.

The simplest case is storage allocation for *global variables*. These are variables that exist (and therefore occupy storage) throughout the program's run-time. The compiler can simply locate these variables at some fixed positions in storage. In this way it can decide each global variable's exact address. (More precisely, the compiler decides each global variable's address relative to the base of the storage region in which global variables are located.) This is called **static storage allocation**.

Example 6.13 Static storage allocation

Consider the following Triangle program outline:

```
let
    type Date = record
                     y: Integer,
                     m: Integer,
                     d: Integer
                end;
    var a: array 3 of Integer;
    var b: Boolean;
    var c: Char;
    var t: Date
in
    ...
```

Assuming that each primitive value occupies one word, the global variables a, b, c, and t would be laid out as shown in Figure 6.9. Thus:

$$address[\![a]\!] \;\; = 0$$
$$address[\![b]\!] \;\; = 3$$
$$address[\![c]\!] \;\; = 4$$
$$address[\![t]\!] \;\; = 5$$

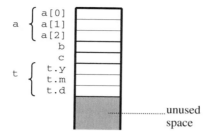

Figure 6.9 Layout of global variables for the program of Example 6.13.

6.4 Stack storage allocation

Let us now take into account *local variables*. A local variable *v* is one that is declared inside a procedure (or function). The variable *v* exists (i.e., occupies storage) only during an activation of that procedure. This time interval is called a *lifetime* of *v*. If the same procedure is activated several times, then *v* will have several lifetimes. (Each activation creates a distinct variable.)

Example 6.14 Stack storage allocation

Consider the following outline of a Triangle program, containing parameterless procedures Y and Z:

```
let
    var a: array 3 of Integer;
    var b: Boolean;
    var c: Char;

    proc Y () ~
        let
            var d: Integer;
            var e: record c: Char, n: Integer end
        in
            ...;

    proc Z () ~
        let
            var f: Integer
        in
            begin ...; Y(); ... end

in
    begin ...; Y(); ...; Z(); ... end
```

The variables a, b, and c are global. The variables d and e are local to procedure Y. The variable f is local to procedure Z.

The main program calls Y directly. Later it calls Z, which itself calls Y.

The lifetimes of the global and local variables are summarized in Figure 6.10. The lifetime of each local variable corresponds to an activation of the procedure in which it is declared. Since there are two activations of Y, its local variables have two lifetimes.

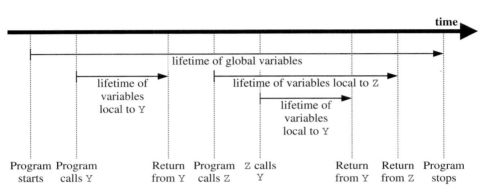

Figure 6.10 Lifetimes of global and local variables in the program of Example 6.14.

There are two important observations that we can make about programs with global and local variables:

- The global variables are the only ones that exist throughout the program's run-time.

- The lifetimes of local variables are properly nested. That is to say, the later a local variable is created, the sooner it must be deleted. The reason why variables' lifetimes are nested is simply that the procedure activations themselves are nested.

The first observation suggests that we should use static allocation for global variables only. The second observation suggests that for local variables we should use a *stack*. On entry to a procedure, we expand the stack to make space at the stack top for that procedure's local variables. On return, we release that space by contracting the stack. This is *stack storage allocation*.

6.4.1 Accessing local and global variables

For the moment, we assume that a procedure may access global variables and its own local variables only. (This is the case in languages such as Fortran and C.)

The stack allocation method, in detail, works as follows. The global variables are always at the base of the stack (and therefore in fixed locations). At each point during run-time, the stack also contains a number of *frames* – one frame for each currently active procedure. Each procedure's frame contains space for its own local variables. Whenever a procedure is called, a new frame is pushed on to the stack. Whenever a procedure returns, its frame is popped off the stack.

Example 6.15 Stack frames

Consider again the Triangle program of Example 6.14. Successive snapshots of the stack are shown in Figure 6.11. (SB, ST, and LB are registers. The roles of these registers and of the dynamic links will be explained shortly.)

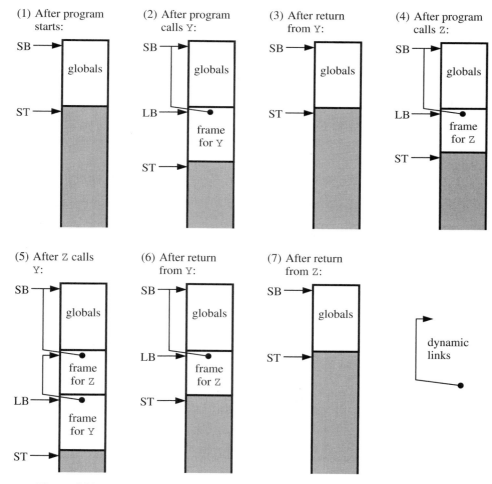

Figure 6.11 Stack snapshots in the program of Example 6.14 (showing dynamic links).

Initially, when the main program is running, only the global variables are occupying storage – snapshot (1). When the program calls procedure Y, a frame with space for Y's local variables is pushed on to the stack – snapshot (2). When Y returns, this frame is popped, leaving only the global variables – snapshot (3). Later, when the program calls procedure Z, a frame for Z is pushed on to the stack – snapshot (4). When Z in turn calls Y, a frame for Y is pushed on top of that one – snapshot (5). And so on.

Compare Figure 6.11 in detail with Figure 6.10. This shows that the period during which the frame for Z is on the stack coincides with the lifetime of Z's local variables, i.e., the activation of Z. Similarly, each period during which the frame for Y is on the stack coincides with a lifetime of Y's local variables, i.e., an activation of Y.

□

The stack of course varies in size. Furthermore, the position of a particular frame within the stack cannot always be predicted in advance. For example, during the two activations of procedure Y in Example 6.15, the frames that provide space for Y's local variables are in two different positions. So that variables can be addressed within the frames, registers must be dedicated to point to the frames. These dedicated registers, named SB, ST, and LB, are shown in Figure 6.11.

Register *SB* (Stack Base) is fixed, pointing to the base of the stack. This is where the global variables are located. So the global variables can be addressed relative to SB:

LOAD d[SB]   – fetch the value of the global variable at address d.
STORE d[SB]   – store a value in the global variable at address d.

Register *LB* (Local Base) points to the base of the topmost frame in the stack. This frame always contains the local variables of the currently running procedure. So these local variables can be addressed relative to LB.

LOAD d[LB]   – fetch the value of the local variable at address d relative to
                                  the frame base.
STORE d[LB]   – store a value in the local variable at address d relative to
                                  the frame base.

Register *ST* (Stack Top) points to the very top of the stack, i.e., the top of the topmost frame. If the currently running procedure evaluates an expression on the stack, the topmost frame expands and contracts, and ST keeps track of the frame boundary.

What about the frames that lie below the topmost one? Each such frame contains the local variables of a procedure that is active but not currently running. That frame is temporarily fixed in size. In the absence of a register pointing to the frame, the variables it contains cannot (currently) be accessed. Therefore only the global variables and the currently running procedure's local variables can be accessed.

As well as space for local variables, a frame contains certain housekeeping information, known collectively as ***link data***:

- The **return address** is the code address to which control will be returned at the end of the procedure activation. It is the address of the instruction following the call instruction that activated the procedure in the first place.

- The **dynamic link** is a pointer to the base of the underlying frame in the stack. It is the old content of LB, which will be restored at the end of the procedure activation.

The dynamic links are shown in Figure 6.11. Notice that they link together all the frames on the stack, in reverse order of creation.

A frame typically has the layout shown in Figure 6.12. The part shown as 'local data' contains space for local variables. It may be expanded to make space for anonymous data, such as the intermediate results of expression evaluation – but only when the frame is topmost in the stack. Since there are two words of link data, the local variables start at address displacement 2 within each frame.

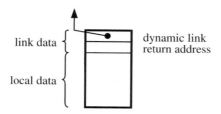

Figure 6.12 Layout of a frame (with dynamic but not static link).

Example 6.16 Accessing global and local variables

Consider again the Triangle program of Example 6.14. The layout of the globals and of the two procedures' frames would be as shown in Figure 6.13.

Here are some examples of instructions to access global and local variables:

LOAD 0[SB]	– for any part of the program to fetch the value of global variable a[0]
LOAD 4[SB]	– for any part of the program to fetch the value of global variable c
LOAD 2[LB]	– for procedure Y to fetch the value of its local variable d
LOAD 4[LB]	– for procedure Y to fetch the value of its local variable e.n
LOAD 2[LB]	– for procedure Z to fetch the value of its local variable f

It might appear that the local variables d and f have the same address, 2[LB]. But remember that d can be accessed only by procedure Y, and while that procedure is running LB is pointing to the base of a frame containing Y's local variables. Similarly, f can be accessed only by procedure Z, and while that procedure is running LB is pointing to the base of a frame containing Z's local variables.

□

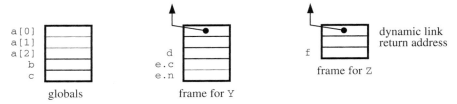

Figure 6.13 Layout of globals and frames for the program of Example 6.14.

The compiler cannot determine the *absolute* address of a local variable; but it can determine its address displacement *relative to the base of the frame* containing it. In order that the local variable can be accessed at run-time, we need only arrange that a particular register (such as LB) points to the base of the frame.

Stack allocation is economical of storage. If static allocation were used on the program of Example 6.14, every variable would occupy storage space throughout the program's run-time. With stack allocation, however, only some of the local variables occupy storage at any particular time. This is illustrated by Figure 6.11. (At snapshot (5), all the local variables are occupying storage at the same time; but this rarely happens in real programs with many procedures.)

Even more importantly, stack storage allocation works well in the presence of recursive procedures, whereas static allocation would not work at all. The effect of recursion will be discussed in Section 6.5.4.

6.4.2   Accessing nonlocal variables

So far we have assumed that a procedure can access only global variables and its own local variables. Now we remove this restriction. Procedures are allowed to be nested. Moreover, a procedure P may directly access any *nonlocal* variable, i.e., a variable that is not local to P but is local to an enclosing procedure. (This is the case in languages such as Pascal and Ada.)

As we have already observed, the compiler cannot determine the absolute address of any variable (other than a global), but only its address displacement within a frame. To access the variable at run-time, we must arrange for a particular register to point to the base of that frame. We use SB to point to the global variables, and LB to point to the frame containing variables local to the running procedure. Now we also need registers pointing to any frames that contain accessible nonlocal variables. We introduce registers L1, L2, etc., for this purpose.

Example 6.17 Accessing nonlocal variables

Figure 6.14 shows an outline of a Triangle program with nested procedures. The levels of nesting are indicated by shades of gray. As a consequence of Triangle's scope rules:

- Procedure P can access global variables and its own local variables.

- Procedure Q can access global variables, its own local variables, and variables local to the enclosing procedure P.

- Procedure R can access global variables, its own local variables, and variables local to the enclosing procedures P and Q.

- Procedure S can access global variables, its own local variables, and variables local to the enclosing procedure P.

Figure 6.15 shows a possible sequence of stack snapshots as this program runs.

```
let
    var g1: Integer;
    var g2: array 3 of Boolean;

    proc P () ~
        let
            var p1: Boolean;
            var p2: Integer;

            proc Q () ~
                let
                    var q: array 3 of Char;

                    proc R () ~
                        let
                            var r: Boolean
                        in
                            begin ... end !R!

                in
                    begin ... end; !Q!

            proc S () ~
                let
                    var s: array 4 of Char
                in
                    begin ... end !S!

        in
            begin ... end !P!

in
    begin ... end
```

Key:
- routine level 3
- routine level 2
- routine level 1
- routine level 0

Figure 6.14 A Triangle program with global and local variables.

Consider snapshot (2), taken when procedure P has called procedure Q. At this time, register LB points to the frame that contains Q's local variables, and register L1 points to the underlying frame that contains P's local variables. This is necessary because Q can access P's local variables. Q might contain instructions like the following:

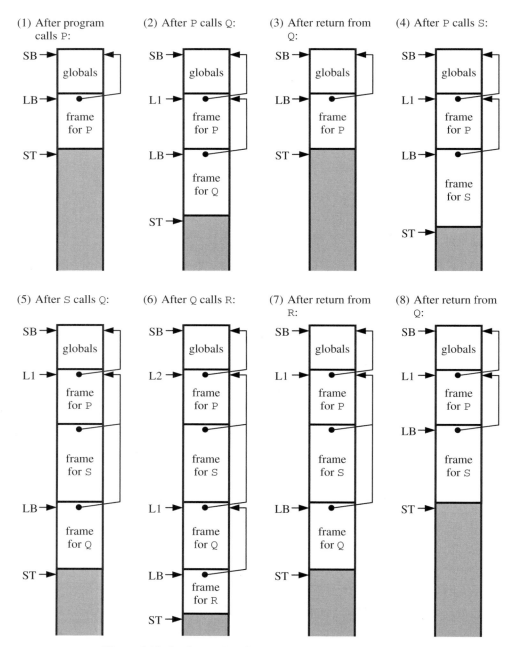

Figure 6.15 Stack snapshots in Example 6.17 (showing static links).

```
LOAD  d[SB]      – for procedure Q to fetch the value of a global variable
LOAD  d[LB]      – for procedure Q to fetch the value of a variable local to itself
LOAD  d[L1]      – for procedure Q to fetch the value of a variable local to P
```

where in each case d is the appropriate address displacement.

Now consider snapshot (5), also taken when procedure P has called procedure Q, but this time indirectly through S. At this time also, LB points to the frame that contains Q's local variables, and L1 points to the underlying frame that contains P's local variables. So the above instructions will still work correctly. No register points to the frame that contains S's local variables. This is correct, because Q may not directly access these variables.

The following snapshot (6) illustrates a situation where R, the most deeply-nested procedure, has been activated by Q. Now register LB points to R's frame, register L1 points to the frame belonging to Q (the procedure immediately enclosing R), and register L2 points to the frame belonging to P (the procedure immediately enclosing Q). This allows R to access not only its own local variables, but also variables local to Q and P:

```
LOAD  d[SB]      – for procedure R to fetch the value of a global variable
LOAD  d[LB]      – for procedure R to fetch a variable local to itself
LOAD  d[L1]      – for procedure R to fetch a variable local to Q
LOAD  d[L2]      – for procedure R to fetch a variable local to P
```

But no register points to the frame containing S's local variables, since R may not directly access these variables.

□

By arranging for registers L1, L2, etc., to point to the correct frames, we allow each procedure to access nonlocal variables. To achieve this, we need to add a third item to the link data in each frame. Consider a routine (procedure or function) R that is enclosed by routine R' in the source program. In a frame that contains variables local to routine R:

• The *static link* is a pointer to the base of an underlying frame that contains variables local to R'. The static link is set up when R is called. (This will be demonstrated in Section 6.5.1.)

The static links were shown in Figure 6.15. Notice that the static link in a frame for Q always points to a frame for P, since it is P that immediately encloses Q in the source program. Similarly, the static link in a frame for R always points to a frame for Q, and the static link in a frame for S always points to a frame for P. (The static link in a frame for P always points to the globals, but that static link is actually redundant.)

The layout of a stack frame is now as shown in Figure 6.16. Since there are now three words of link data, the local variables now start at address displacement 3. Figure 6.17 shows the layout of frames for the procedures in Figure 6.14.

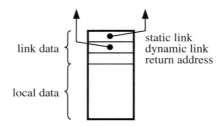

Figure 6.16 Layout of a frame (with dynamic and static links).

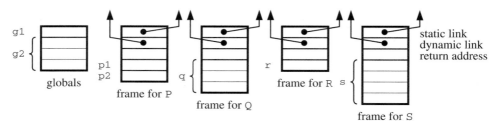

Figure 6.17 Layout of globals and frames for the program of Figure 6.14 (with static links).

The static links allow us to set up the registers L1, L2, etc. LB points to the first word of the topmost frame, which is the static link and points to a frame for the enclosing routine. Therefore:

$$\text{L1} = \textit{content}(\text{LB}) \tag{6.25}$$

where *content*(r) stands for the content of the word to which register r points. In turn, L1 points to the next static link. Therefore:

$$\text{L2} = \textit{content}(\text{L1}) = \textit{content}(\textit{content}(\text{LB})) \tag{6.26}$$
$$\text{L3} = \textit{content}(\text{L2}) = \textit{content}(\textit{content}(\textit{content}(\text{LB}))) \tag{6.27}$$
...

These equations are invariants: L1, L2, etc., automatically change whenever LB changes, i.e., on a routine call or return.

At any moment during run-time:

• Register SB points to the global variables.

• Register LB points to the topmost frame, which always belongs to the routine R that is currently running.

• Register L1 points to a frame belonging to the routine R' that encloses R in the source program.

• Register L2 points to a frame belonging to the routine R'' that encloses R' in the source program.

And so on.

The collection of registers LB, L1, L2, ..., and SB is often called the **display**. The display allows access to local, nonlocal, and global variables. The display changes whenever a routine is called or returns.

The critical property of the display is that the *compiler* can always determine which register to use to access any variable. A global variable is always addressed relative to SB. A local variable is always addressed relative to LB. A nonlocal variable is addressed relative to one of the registers L1, L2, ... The appropriate register is determined entirely by the nesting levels of the routines in the source program.

We assign routine levels as follows: the main program is at *routine level 0*; the body of each routine declared at level 0 is at *routine level 1*; the body of each routine declared at level 1 is at *routine level 2*; and so on.

Let v be a variable declared at routine level l, and let v's address displacement be d. Then the current value of v is fetched by various parts of the code as follows:

If $l = 0$ (i.e., v is a global variable):
>   LOAD d[SB]   – for any code to fetch the value of v

If $l > 0$ (i.e., v is a local variable):
>   LOAD d[LB]   – for code at level l to fetch the value of v
>   LOAD d[L1]   – for code at level l+1 to fetch the value of v
>   LOAD d[L2]   – for code at level l+2 to fetch the value of v
>   ...

Storing to variable v is analogous.

6.5 Routines

A **routine** (or *subroutine*) is the machine-code equivalent of a procedure or function in a high-level language. Control is transferred to a routine by means of a **call** instruction (or instruction sequence). Control is transferred back to the caller by means of a **return** instruction in the routine.

When a routine is called, some **arguments** may be passed to it. An argument could be, for example, a value or an address. There may be zero, one, or many arguments. A routine may also return a **result** – that is if it corresponds to a function in the high-level language.

We have already studied one aspect of routines, namely allocation of storage for local variables. In this section we study other important aspects:

• protocols for passing arguments to routines and returning their results

• how static links are determined

- the arguments themselves

- the implementation of recursive routines.

6.5.1   Routine protocols

When a routine is called, the arguments are computed by the caller, and used by the called routine. Thus we need a suitable ***routine protocol***, a convention to ensure that the caller deposits the arguments in the place where the called routine expects to find them. Conversely, the routine's result (if any) is computed by the routine, and used by the caller. Thus the routine protocol must also ensure that, on return, the called routine deposits its result in the place where the caller expects to find it.

There are numerous possible routine protocols. Sometimes the implementor has to design a protocol from scratch. More often, the operating system dictates a standard protocol to which all compilers must conform. In every case, the choice of protocol is influenced by the target machine, such as whether the latter is a register machine or a stack machine.

Example 6.18 Routine protocol for a register machine

In a register machine, the routine protocol might be:

- Pass the first argument in R1, the second argument in R2, etc.

- Return the result (if any) in R0.

Such a simple protocol works only if there are fewer arguments than registers, and if every argument and result is small enough to fit into a register. In practice, a more elaborate protocol is needed. (See Exercise 6.20.)

□

Example 6.19 Routine protocol for a stack machine

In a stack machine, the routine protocol might be:

- Pass the arguments at the stack top.

- Return the result (if any) at the stack top, in place of the arguments.

This protocol places no limits on the number of arguments, nor on the sizes of the arguments or result.

□

The stack-based routine protocol of Example 6.19 is simple and general. For that reason it is adopted by the abstract machine TAM. Variants of this protocol are also adopted by machines equipped with both registers and stacks (such as the Pentium). Due to the popularity of this protocol, we shall study the TAM routine protocol in detail.

Some routines (functions) have results, whereas others (procedures) do not. For the sake of simplicity, we shall discuss the protocol in terms of the more general case, namely a routine with a result. We can treat a procedure as a routine with a 0-word 'result'. (Compare the use of a **void** function in C or Java, or a `unit` function in ML, to achieve the effect of a procedure.)

Before calling a routine, the caller is responsible for evaluating the arguments and pushing them on to the stack top. (Since expression evaluation is done on the stack, as in Section 6.2, the stack top is where the arguments will be evaluated anyway.) After return, the caller can expect to find the result at the stack top, in the place formerly occupied by the arguments. This is shown in Figure 6.18. The net effect of calling the routine (ignoring any side effects) will be to replace the arguments by the result at the stack top.

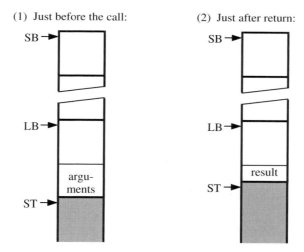

Figure 6.18 The TAM routine protocol.

The called routine itself is responsible for evaluating its result and depositing it in the correct place. Let us examine a call to some routine R, from the point of view of the routine itself (see Figure 6.19):

(1) Immediately before the call, the arguments to be passed to R must be at the stack top.

(2) The call instruction pushes a new frame, on top of the arguments. Initially, the new frame contains only link data. Its return address is the address of the code following the call instruction. Its dynamic link is the old content of LB. Its static link is supplied by the call instruction. Now LB is made to point to the base of the new frame, and control is transferred to the first instruction of R.

(3) The instructions within R may expand the new frame, to make space for local variables and to perform expression evaluation. These instructions can access the arguments relative to LB. Immediately before return, R evaluates its result and leaves it at the stack top.

(4) The return instruction pops the frame and the arguments, and deposits the result in the place formerly occupied by the arguments. LB is reset using the dynamic link, and control is transferred to the instruction at the return address.

TAM has a single call instruction that does all the work described in step (2). Some other machines have a less powerful call instruction, and we need a *sequence* of instructions to do the same work. TAM also has a single return instruction that does all the work described in step (4).

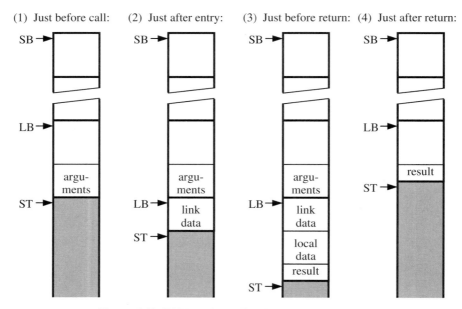

Figure 6.19 TAM routine call and return (in detail).

Example 6.20 Passing arguments

Consider the following Triangle program, containing a function F with two parameters, and a procedure W with one parameter:

```
let var g: Integer;
    func F (m: Integer, n: Integer) : Integer ~
        m * n;
```

```
proc W (i: Integer) ~
    let const s ~ i * i
    in
        begin
        putint(F(i, s));
        putint(F(s, s))
        end

in
    begin
    getint(var g);
    W(g+1)
    end
```

This (artificial) program reads an integer, and writes the cube and fourth power of its successor.

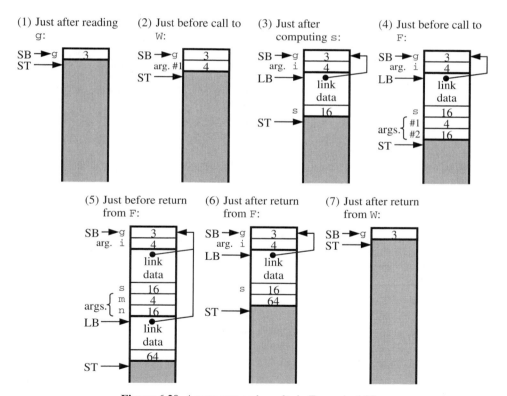

Figure 6.20 Arguments and results in Example 6.20.

Figure 6.20 shows a sequence of stack snapshots. The main program first reads an integer, say 3, into the global variable g – snapshot (1). Then it evaluates 'g+1', which yields 4, and leaves that value at the stack top as the argument to be passed to procedure W – snapshot (2).

On entry to procedure W, a new frame is pushed on to the stack top, and the argument becomes known to the procedure as i. The constant s is defined by evaluating 'i*i', which yields 16 – snapshot (3). Next, the procedure prepares to evaluate 'F(i, s)' by pushing the two arguments, 4 and 16, on to the stack top – snapshot (4).

On entry to function F, a new frame is pushed on to the stack, and the arguments become known to the function as m and n, respectively. F immediately evaluates 'm*n' to determine its result, 64, and leaves that value on the stack top – snapshot (5). On return from F, the topmost frame and the arguments are popped, and the result is deposited in place of the arguments – snapshot (6). This value is used immediately as an argument to putint, which writes it out.

Similarly, W evaluates 'F(s, s)', yielding 256, and passes the result as an argument to putint. Finally, on return from W, the topmost frame and the argument are popped; this time there is no result to replace the arguments – snapshot (7).

It is instructive to study the corresponding object code. It would look something like this (using symbolic names for routines, and omitting some minor details):

```
       PUSH        1            – expand globals to make space for g
       LOADA       0[SB]        – push the address of g
       CALL        getint       – read an integer into g
       LOAD        0[SB]        – push the value of g
       CALL        succ         – add 1
       CALL(SB)    W            – call W (using SB as static link)
       POP         1            – contract globals
       HALT
  W:   LOAD        -1[LB]       – push the value of i
       LOAD        -1[LB]       – push the value of i
       CALL        mult         – multiply; the result will be the value of s
       LOAD        -1[LB]       – push the value of i
       LOAD        3[LB]        – push the value of s
       CALL(SB)    F            – call F (using SB as static link)
       CALL        putint       – write the value of F(i,s)
       LOAD        3[LB]        – push the value of s
       LOAD        3[LB]        – push the value of s
       CALL(SB)    F            – call F (using SB as static link)
       CALL        putint       – write the value of F(s,s)
       RETURN(0)   1            – return, replacing the 1-word argument
                                  by a 0-word 'result'
```

```
F:  LOAD       -2[LB]    – push the value of m
    LOAD       -1[LB]    – push the value of n
    CALL       mult      – multiply
    RETURN(1)  2         – return, replacing the 2-word argument pair
                           by a 1-word result
```

Here the instruction 'LOADA $d[r]$' (load address) pushes the address d + register r on to the stack, and 'RETURN (n) d' returns from the current routine with an n-word result, removing d words of argument data. (*Note:* In TAM, operations like addition, subtraction, logical negation, etc., are performed by calling primitive routines – *add*, *sub*, *not*, etc. This avoids the need to provide many individual instructions – ADD, SUB, NOT, etc.)

□

6.5.2   Static links

One loose end in our description of the routine protocol is how the static link is determined. Recall that the static link is needed only for a source language with nested block structure (such as Pascal, Ada, or Triangle). The scope rules of such a language guarantee that, at the time of call, the correct static link is in one or other of the display registers. The caller need only copy it into the newly-created frame.

Example 6.21 Static links

Consider the outline Triangle program of Figure 6.14. Some stack snapshots were shown in Figure 6.15.

When P calls Q, the required static link is a pointer to a frame for P itself, since P encloses Q in the source program, and the caller can find that pointer in LB – snapshots (1) and (2). Similarly, when P calls S, the required static link is a pointer to a frame for P itself, since P encloses S, and the caller can find that pointer in LB – snapshots (3) and (4).

When S calls Q, the required static link is a pointer to a frame for P, since P encloses Q, and the caller can find that pointer in L1 – snapshots (4) and (5).

If R were to call Q or S, the required static link would be a pointer to a frame for P, since P encloses Q and S, and the caller could find that pointer in L2 – snapshot (6).

Here is a summary of all the possible calls in this program:

```
CALL(SB)  P     – for any call to P

CALL(LB)  Q     – for P to call Q
CALL(L1)  Q     – for Q to call Q (recursively)
CALL(L2)  Q     – for R to call Q
CALL(L1)  Q     – for S to call Q
```

```
CALL(LB)  R       – for Q to call R
CALL(L1)  R       – for R to call R (recursively)

CALL(LB)  S       – for P to call S
CALL(L1)  S       – for Q to call S
CALL(L2)  S       – for R to call S
CALL(L1)  S       – for S to call S (recursively)
```

(In the TAM call instruction, the field in parentheses nominates the register whose content is to be used as the static link.)

☐

In general, the *compiler* can always determine which register to use as the static link in any call instruction. A call to a global routine (i.e., one declared at the outermost level of the source program) always uses SB. A call to a local routine (i.e., one declared inside the currently running routine) always uses LB. A call to any other routine uses one of the registers L1, L2, …. The appropriate register is determined entirely by the nesting levels of the routines in the source program.

Let R be a routine declared at routine level l (thus the *body* of R is at level $l+1$). Then R is called as follows:

If $l = 0$ (i.e., R is a global routine):
```
CALL(SB)  R       – for any call to R
```

If $l > 0$ (i.e., R is enclosed by another routine):
```
CALL(LB)  R       – for code at level l to call R
CALL(L1)  R       – for code at level l+1 to call R
CALL(L2)  R       – for code at level l+2 to call R
…
```

(Compare this with the code used for addressing variables, at the end of Section 6.4.2.)

6.5.3 Arguments

We have already seen some examples of argument passing. We now examine two other aspects of arguments: how the called routine accesses its own arguments, and how arguments are represented under different parameter mechanisms.

According to the routine protocol studied in the previous subsection, the arguments to be passed to a routine are deposited at the top of the *caller*'s frame (or at the top of the globals, if the caller is the main program). Since the latter frame is just under the *called* routine's frame, the called routine can find its arguments just under its own frame. In other words, the arguments have small negative addresses relative to the base of the called routine's frame. In all other respects, they can be accessed just like variables local to the called routine.

Example 6.22 Accessing arguments

In the Triangle program of Example 6.17, the two routines accessed their arguments as follows:

```
LOAD  -1[LB]     – for procedure W to fetch its argument i

LOAD  -2[LB]     – for function F to fetch its argument m
LOAD  -1[LB]     – for function F to fetch its argument n
```

We can easily implement a variety of parameter mechanisms:

- *Constant parameter* (as in Triangle and ML) or *value parameter* (as in Pascal, C, and Java): The argument is an ordinary value (such as an integer or record). The caller evaluates an expression to compute the argument value, and leaves it on the stack.

- *Variable parameter* (as in Triangle and Pascal) or *reference parameter* (as in C++): The argument is the address of a variable. The caller simply pushes this address on to the stack.

- *Procedural/functional parameter* (as in Triangle, Pascal, and ML): The argument is a (static link, code address) pair representing a routine. This pair, known as a ***closure***, contains just the information that will be needed to call the argument routine.

Constant parameters have already been illustrated, in Example 6.20. Value parameters differ in only one respect: the formal parameter is treated as a local *variable*, and thus may be updated. If procedure W had a *value* parameter i, the procedure body could contain assignments to i, implemented by 'STORE -1[LB]'. Note, however, that the word corresponding to i will be popped on return from P, so any such updating would have no effect outside the procedure. This conforms to the intended semantics of value parameters.

Example 6.23 Variable parameter

Consider the following outline Triangle program, containing a procedure S with a variable parameter n as well as a constant parameter i:

```
let
    proc S (var n: Integer, i: Integer) ~
        n := n + i;
    var b: record y: Integer, m: Integer, d: Integer end
in
    begin
    b := {y ~ 1978, m ~ 5, d ~ 5};
    S(var b.m, 6);
    end
```

Figure 6.21 shows some snapshots of the stack as this program runs.

The procedure call 'S(var b.m, 6)' works by first pushing the *address* of the variable b.m, along with the value 6, and then calling S.

The procedure S itself works as follows. Its first argument is the address of some variable. S can access the variable by indirect addressing. It can fetch the variable's value by an indirect load instruction, and update it by an indirect store instruction.

We can see this by studying the TAM code corresponding to the above program:

```
        ...
        LOADL       1978
        LOADL       5
        LOADL       5
        STORE(3)    0[SB]      – store a record value in b
        LOADA       1[SB]      – push the address of b.m
        LOADL       6          – push the value 6
        CALL(SB)    S          – call S
        ...

S:      LOAD        -2[LB]     – push the argument address n
        LOADI                  – push the value contained at that address
        LOAD        -1[LB]     – push the argument value i
        CALL        add        – add (giving the value of n+i)
        LOAD        -2[LB]     – push the argument address n
        STOREI                 – store the value of n+i at that address
        RETURN(0)   2          – return, replacing the 2-word argument
                                 pair by a 0-word 'result'
```

Here the instruction LOADI (load indirect) pops an address off the stack, and then fetches a value from that address. STOREI (store indirect) pops an address and a value, and then stores that value at that address.

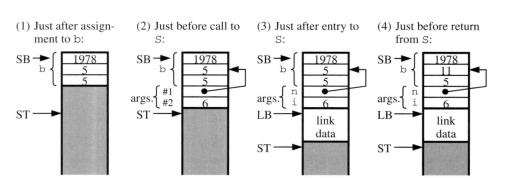

(1) Just after assignment to b:

(2) Just before call to S:

(3) Just after entry to S:

(4) Just before return from S:

Figure 6.21 Variable and constant parameters in Example 6.23.

6.5.4   Recursion

We have already noted that stack allocation is more economical of storage than static allocation. As a bonus, stack allocation supports the implementation of *recursive* routines. In fact, there is nothing to add to the techniques introduced in Section 6.4; we need only illustrate how stack allocation works in the presence of recursive routines.

Example 6.24 Recursion

Consider the following Triangle program. It includes a recursive procedure, P, that writes a given nonnegative integer, i, to a given base, b, in the range 2–10:

```
let
    proc P (i: Integer, b: Integer) ~
        let const d ~ chr(i//b + ord('0'))
        in
            if i < b then
                put(d)
            else
                begin P(i//b, b); put(d) end;
    var n: Integer
in
    begin
    getint(var n); P(n, 8)
    end
```

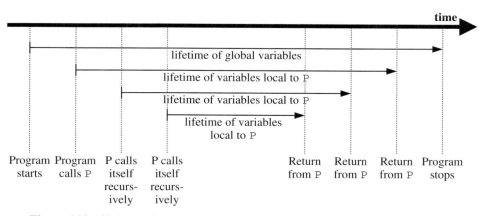

Figure 6.22 Lifetimes of variables local to the recursive procedure of Example 6.24.

Figure 6.22 shows the lifetimes of the variables in this program (and also formal parameters such as i and b, and declared constants such as d, because they too occupy storage). Note that each recursive activation of P creates a new set of local variables, which coexist with the local variables of continuing activations. In Figure 6.22, like Figure 6.10, all the variable's lifetimes are nested. This suggests that stack allocation will cope with recursion.

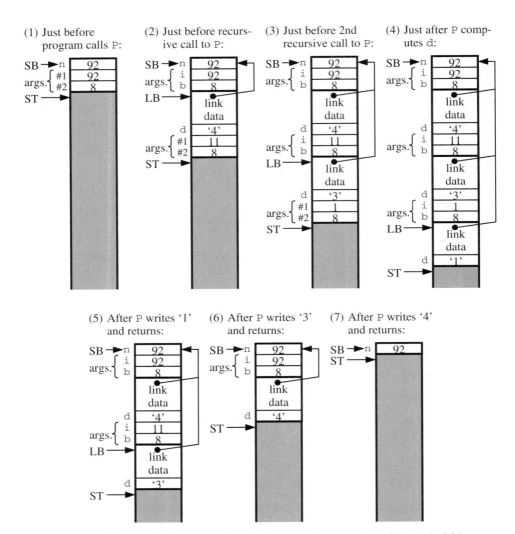

Figure 6.23 Stack snapshots for the recursive procedure of Example 6.24.

Figure 6.23 shows some stack snapshots as this program runs. Having read a value into n, say 92, the main program pushes a pair of arguments, here 92 and 8, in preparation for calling P – snapshot (1). Inside P these arguments are known as i and b, respectively. In the constant definition, d is defined to be '4'. Now, since the value of 'i < b' is *false*, P pushes a pair of arguments, here 11 and 8, in preparation for calling itself recursively – snapshot (2). Inside P these arguments are known as i and b. At this point there are two activations of P, the original one and the recursive one, and each activation has its own arguments i and b. In the constant definition, using the *current* activation's i and b, d is defined to be '3'. Now, since the value of 'i < b' is again *false*, P pushes a pair of arguments, here 1 and 8, in preparation for calling itself recursively – snapshot (3). In this third activation of P, d is defined to be '1', but the value of 'i < b' turns out to be *true* – snapshot (4). So P merely writes '1', then returns to the second activation of itself – snapshot (5). This activation writes '3', and then returns to the original activation of P – snapshot (6). This activation writes '4', and then returns to the main program – snapshot (7).

□

6.6 Heap storage allocation

In Section 6.4 we saw how local variables are allocated storage. A lifetime of a local variable corresponds exactly to an activation of the procedure, function, or block within which the local variable was declared. Since their lifetimes are always nested, local variables can be allocated storage on a stack.

On the other hand, a **heap variable** is allocated (created) by executing an **allocator** (such as new in Pascal, malloc in C, or **new** in Java). The allocator returns a pointer through which the heap variable can be accessed. Later the heap variable may be deallocated, either explicitly by executing a **deallocator** (such as dispose in Pascal or free in C), or automatically (as in Java). The heap variable's lifetime extends from the time it is allocated until the time it is deallocated.

Thus heap variables behave quite differently from local variables. Consequently they demand a different method of storage allocation, called **heap storage allocation**.

Example 6.25 Heap storage allocation

Consider the following outline of a Pascal program, which manipulates linked lists:

```
type IntList = ...;    {linked list of integers}
     Symbol  = array [1..2] of Char;
     SymList = ...;     {linked list of symbols}

var ns: IntList; ps: SymList;

procedure insertI (i: Integer; var l: IntList);
    ...;      {Insert a node containing i at the front of list l.}
```

```
procedure deleteI (i: Integer; var l: IntList);
   ...;      {Delete the first node containing i from list l.}

procedure insertS (s: Symbol; var l: SymList);
   ...;      {Insert a node containing s at the front of list l.}

procedure deleteS (s: Symbol; var l: SymList);
   ...;      {Delete the first node containing s from list l.}

...
ns := nil;        ps := nil;                    (1)
insertI(6, ns);   insertS('Cu', ps);
insertI(9, ns);   insertS('Ag', ps);
insertI(10, ns);  insertS('Au', ps);           (2)
deleteI(10, ns);  deleteS('Cu', ps);           (3)
insertI(12, ns);  insertS('Pt', ps);           (4)
```

Here, the heap variables are nodes of linked lists. Procedures insertI and insertS allocate nodes, and procedures deleteI and deleteS deallocate nodes.

Figure 6.24 shows the lifetimes of the heap variables. Observe that there is no particular pattern to their lifetimes: the program allocates and deallocates them whenever it chooses. Those not deallocated by the program cease to exist when the program stops.

□

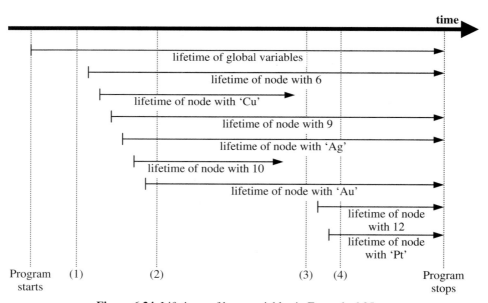

Figure 6.24 Lifetimes of heap variables in Example 6.25.

6.6.1   Heap management

Since heap variables can be allocated and deallocated at any time, their lifetimes bear no particular relationship to one another. So these variables are allocated on a **heap**, a storage region managed differently from a stack.

The heap will expand and (occasionally) contract as the program runs. Let us assume that registers HB (Heap Base) and HT (Heap Top) point to the boundaries of the heap. (Note the analogy with SB and ST, which point to the boundaries of the stack.)

Since the stack and the heap both expand and contract, it is a good idea to place them at opposite ends of the available storage space. Contraction of the stack leaves more space for the heap to expand, and *vice versa*. It is only when the stack and heap collide that the program must fail due to storage exhaustion.

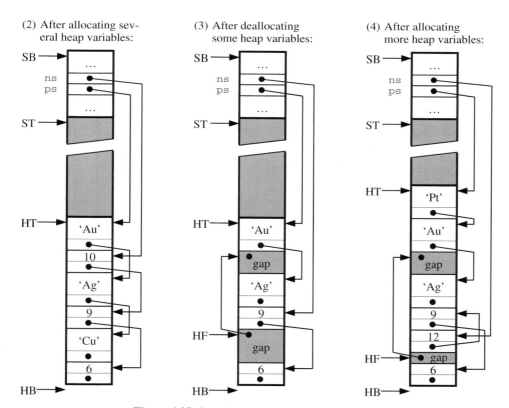

Figure 6.25 Snapshots of the heap in Example 6.25.

Figure 6.25 shows several snapshots of the heap as the program of Example 6.25 runs. The heap is initially empty, but expands as nodes are allocated – snapshot (2).

When nodes are deallocated, gaps appear – snapshot (3). Some of these gaps may be partly or wholly refilled as further nodes are allocated – snapshot (4).

Deallocation of a heap variable at the heap top causes the heap to contract. But deallocation elsewhere in the heap leaves a **gap**, i.e., a piece of unused storage surrounded by used storage. (This never happens in the stack, where deallocation always takes place at the stack top.) Gaps may appear in the heap at any time, and they have to be managed. Thus the object program must be supported by a run-time module called the **heap manager**.

The heap manager privately maintains a **free list**, which is a linked list of gaps within the heap. Each gap contains a size field, and a link to the next gap. The size fields are necessary because the gaps are of differing sizes. The heap manager needs a pointer to the first gap in the free list; we shall call this HF (Heap Free-list pointer). In Figure 6.25, the free list is initially empty – snapshot (2), but later accumulates some gaps – snapshots (3) and (4).

A simple heap manager works as follows. To *allocate* a heap variable of size s, the heap manager searches the free list for a gap of size at least s:

- If it finds a gap whose size is s exactly, it removes that gap from the free list.

- If it finds a gap whose size is greater than s, it replaces that gap in the free list by the residual gap.

- If there is no gap big enough, it expands the heap by the amount s.

- If there is no room to expand the heap, storage is exhausted and the program fails.

To *deallocate* a heap variable, the heap manager simply adds it to the free list.

All this seems very straightforward, but in practice such a simple heap manager does not work very well. One major problem is **fragmentation**. As many allocations and deallocations take place, gaps tend to become smaller and more numerous. (This can already be seen in snapshot (4) of Figure 6.25.) When the heap manager tries to allocate a heap variable, there might be no *single* gap big enough, although the *total* amount of free space is sufficient.

There are several techniques for reducing fragmentation:

- When allocating a heap variable, the heap manager could choose the *smallest* gap that is big enough (rather than choosing just any gap). This technique implies an increased time overhead on allocation, because the entire free list must be searched – unless the heap manager keeps the gaps sorted by size, which implies an increased time overhead on deallocation. This technique helps to preserve large gaps for when they are really needed, but also tends to make many very small gaps.[4]

---

[4] This is a *best-fit* allocation algorithm. A *worst-fit* allocation algorithm is also worth considering. It makes very small gaps less frequent, but also tends to split up large gaps.

- When deallocating a heap variable, the heap manager could *coalesce* the heap variable with any adjacent gap(s). In a naive implementation, this technique implies an increased time overhead on deallocation, because the entire free list must be searched. (See Example 6.26 and Exercise 6.22.) A more sophisticated algorithm is possible that uses additional space to allow adjacent regions to be coalesced without the need to search the free list (Standish 1998).

- The heap manager could occasionally *compact* the heap by shifting heap variables together. This technique is quite complicated to manage: to shift a heap variable, the heap manager must find and redirect all pointers to that heap variable. The technique implies a large time overhead whenever the heap is compacted, because the whole heap is affected. (See Example 6.27 and Exercise 6.23.)

Example 6.26 Coalescence in the heap

Figure 6.26 illustrates coalescence of gaps in the heap. Deallocating heap variable *c* allows the space it occupied to be coalesced with an adjacent gap. Deallocating heap variable *b* is even more effective, since the space it occupied can be coalesced with two adjacent gaps. (What would the free list look like without coalescence of gaps?)

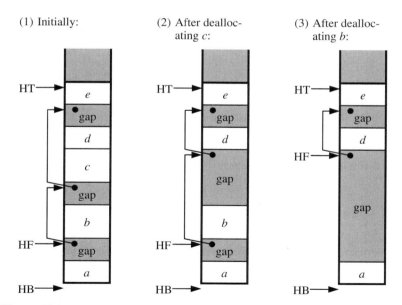

Figure 6.26 Coalescing deallocated heap variables with adjacent gaps in the heap.

Example 6.27 Heap compaction

Figure 6.27 illustrates heap compaction. To understand this, start by convincing yourself that the states of the heap before and after compaction are equivalent.

Since a pointer is represented by the address of the heap variable it points to, moving a heap variable to a different address implies that every pointer to it must be adjusted. There are two pointers to heap variable c: one in the stack, a second in another heap variable, b. Indeed, b and c point to each other. All these pointers have to be adjusted consistently.

□

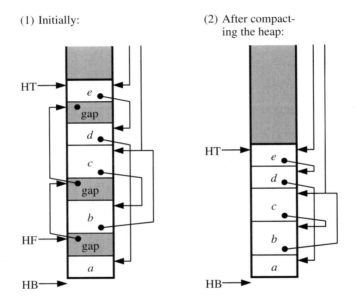

Figure 6.27 Compacting the heap.

Example 6.27 illustrates the complications that can arise in heap compaction. There may be several pointers to the same heap variable. Pointers may be located both in the stack and in other heap variables. *All* such pointers must be found and adjusted.

To implement heap compaction, the heap manager must create a table containing the old address and new address of each heap variable. Then, for every pointer in the stack or heap, it must use the table to replace the old address by the new address. Finally it can actually copy the heap variables to their new addresses.

Compaction is usually combined with garbage collection, so we defer a more detailed explanation until Section 6.6.3.

6.6.2 Explicit storage deallocation

Programming languages differ in how they allow heap variables to be deallocated. In this subsection we study *explicit storage deallocation*. A program may explicitly deallocate a heap variable by, for example, calling `dispose` in Pascal, or `free` in C.

Example 6.28 Explicit storage deallocation

The procedure `deleteI` of Example 6.25 might be implemented as follows:

```
procedure deleteI (i: Integer; var l: IntList);
    {Delete the first node containing i from list l.}
    var p, q: IntList;
    begin
    ...;      {Make q point to the first node containing i in list l,
              and make p point to the preceding node (if any).}
    if q = l then
        {If q is at the start of the list, then delete it by making
         the head of the list point to q's successor. }
        l := q^.tail
    else
        {Otherwise remove node q by making the previous node p
         point to q's successor. }
        p^.tail := q^.tail;
    {Node q^ is now no longer part of the list and the space associated
     with it can be deallocated.}
    dispose(q)
    end {deleteI}
```

□

Explicit storage deallocation is efficient, and allows the programmer fine control over heap storage allocation.

In Examples 6.25 and 6.28 explicit storage deallocation was used in a controlled manner. In practice, however, explicit storage deallocation is notoriously error-prone. Two problems arise frequently in practice: garbage accumulation and dangling pointers.

A heap variable is *inaccessible*, or *garbage*, if there exists no pointer to it. If such a heap variable has not been deallocated, the space it occupies is wasted.

Example 6.29 Garbage in the heap

Figure 6.28 illustrates how garbage can appear. At first p and q point to different heap variables, *a* and *b*, respectively – snapshot (1). After the assignment 'p := q', both p and q point to *b* – snapshot (2). Now there exists no pointer to *a*, so the latter is garbage. Worse still, there is no way to retrieve this situation; without a pointer to *a*, it cannot be explicitly deallocated.

This situation could have been averted by greater care on the programmer's part: *a* should have been deallocated *before* the assignment 'p : = q'.

□

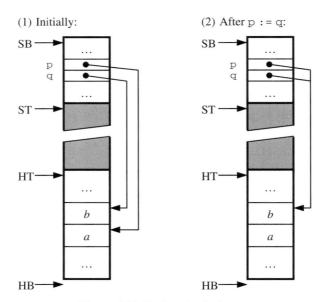

(1) Initially:

(2) After p : = q:

Figure 6.28 Garbage in the heap.

Since pointers can be copied, several pointers to the same heap variable might exist at the same time. When one of these pointers is used to deallocate the heap variable, the other pointers are left pointing to a gap. They are called ***dangling pointers***.

The program might accidentally use a dangling pointer to update a heap variable that no longer exists. The effect will be to corrupt the gap left by deallocation, or perhaps to corrupt a new heap variable subsequently allocated (by chance) in that gap.

Example 6.30 Dangling pointer

The following Pascal program fragment illustrates a possible effect of a dangling pointer:

```
var p, q: ^T1; r: ^T2;
...
new(p);   p^ : = value of type T1;
q := p;                                           (1)
```

```
...;
dispose(p);                                                    (2)
...;
new(r);    r^ := value of type T2;                             (3)
...;
q^ := value of type T1;                                        (4)
```

Figure 6.29 shows the effect. At first, both p and q point to the same heap variable, which contains a value of type T1 – snapshot (1). Now the program uses dispose(p) to deallocate p^, which adds this heap variable to the free list, and which (in a typical implementation) changes p to *nil*. But of course dispose knows nothing about q. (How could it?) So q still contains the same address, which is a dangling pointer – snapshot (2). Any assignment to q^ now would corrupt the gap.

Later the program executes 'new(r)', and then stores a value of type T2 in the newly allocated heap variable – snapshot (3). This new heap variable might (purely by chance) be located at the same address as the old one, as shown in snapshot (3).

This is a situation in which a disaster is just waiting to happen. The program might attempt to inspect q^, expecting to find a value of type T1. Worse still, it might attempt to store a value of type T1 in q^, which would corrupt the value already there.

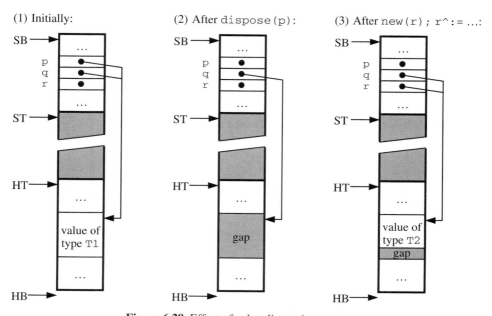

Figure 6.29 Effect of a dangling pointer.

The situation illustrated in Figure 6.29 is no less than a violation of Pascal's type rules, which are supposed to guarantee that every pointer of type $^\wedge T$ is either *nil* or points to a heap variable of type T. To restore the guarantee, a Pascal implementation would have to take extreme measures. One measure would be never to allocate a heap variable in space released by deallocation. But this would prevent the heap from ever contracting. An alternative measure would be to make dispose find, and change to *nil*, *all* pointers to the deallocated heap variable. But this would imply a large time overhead, negating the main advantage of explicit storage deallocation.

6.6.3 Automatic storage deallocation and garbage collection

In a programming language that supports explicit storage deallocation, the appearance of garbage is usually a consequence of a programming error. In a language that does not support explicit storage deallocation, garbage must inevitably appear. A heap variable becomes inaccessible when the last pointer to it is overwritten (as in Example 6.29) or otherwise ceases to exist.

Fortunately, *automatic storage deallocation* of inaccessible heap variables is possible. The space they occupied can then be recycled by being added to the free list. The recycling process is called *garbage collection*, and is performed by a heap manager routine called the *garbage collector*.

Garbage collection is a feature of the run-time support for some imperative languages (such as Ada), most object-oriented languages (including Java), and all functional languages (such as Lisp and ML). It is generally not provided for languages (such as Pascal and C) that have explicit storage deallocation.

Many garbage collection algorithms have been invented. *Mark–sweep garbage collection* is a simple and commonly-used algorithm. The idea is to mark as accessible every heap variable that can be reached (directly or indirectly) by pointers from the stack. All other heap variables are inaccessible and may be deallocated.

Example 6.31 Mark–sweep garbage collection

Figure 6.30 illustrates mark–sweep garbage collection. The initial state of the heap shows typical patterns. The stack contains pointers to some of the heap variables (b and j). These heap variables in turn contain pointers to other heap variables (f and h), and so on (d). But there are also some inaccessible heap variables to which no pointers exist (c, e, g, and i), and others to which the only pointers are themselves in inaccessible heap variables (a).

The garbage collector starts by marking *all* heap variables as inaccessible (shown by ×).

Next, the garbage collector follows all chains of pointers from the stack, marking each heap variable it reaches as accessible (shown by √). By following the first pointer from the stack it reaches b. It marks b as accessible. By following the second pointer from the stack it reaches j; by following the pointers in j it reaches f and h; and by following the pointer in f it reaches d. It marks all these heap variables as accessible. By following the third pointer from the stack it reaches j; but it has already marked j as accessible, so it need take no further action there.

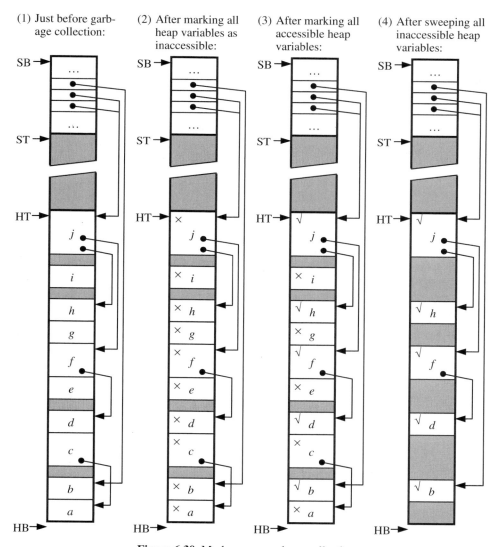

Figure 6.30 Mark–sweep garbage collection.

The garbage collector finishes by scanning the heap for heap variables still marked as inaccessible: a, c, e, g, and i. These really *are* inaccessible, so the garbage collector deallocates them.

□

Mark–sweep garbage collection may be seen to be a simple graph algorithm. The heap variables and the stack are the nodes of a directed graph, and the pointers are the edges. Our aim is to determine the largest subgraph in which all nodes can be reached from the stack node. The *mark–sweep garbage collection algorithm* can be expressed recursively as follows:

> Procedure to collect garbage:
> > mark all heap variables as inaccessible;
> > scan all frames in the stack;
> > add all heap variable*s* still marked as inaccessible to the free list.

> Procedure to scan the storage region R:
> > for each pointer p in R:
> > > if p points to a heap variable v that is marked as inaccessible:
> > > > mark v as accessible;
> > > > scan v.

For this algorithm to work, it must be able to visit all heap variables, it must know the size of each, and it must be able to mark each as accessible or inaccessible. One way to meet these requirements is to extend each heap variable with the following hidden fields: a size field; a link field (used to connect all heap variables into a single linked list, to permit them all to be visited); and a 1-bit accessibility field. These hidden fields are used by the garbage collector but invisible to the programmer.

Another requirement is that pointers must be distinguishable from other data in the store. (This is a requirement not only for garbage collection, but also for heap compaction as described in Section 6.6.2.) This is an awkward problem: pointers are represented by addresses, which typically have exactly the same form as integers. Some clever techniques have been devised to solve this problem – see Wilson (1992).

6.7 Run-time organization for object-oriented languages

Object-oriented (OO) languages give rise to interesting and special problems in run-time organization. An object is a special kind of record. Attached to each object are some methods, each method being a kind of procedure or function that is able to operate on that object. Objects are grouped into classes, such that all objects of the same class have identical structure and identical methods.

We shall assume the following more precise definitions:

- An **object** is a group of instance variables, to which a group of instance methods are attached.

- An **instance variable** is a named component of a particular object.

- An **instance method** is a named operation, which is attached to a particular object and is able to access that object's instance variables.

- An **object class** (or just *class*) is a family of objects with similar instance variables and identical methods.

In a pure OO language, all instance variables would be private, leaving the instance methods as the *only* way to operate on the objects. In practice, most OO languages (such as Java and C++) allow the programmer to decide which of the instance variables are public and which are private. Anyway, this issue does not affect their representation.

An instance-method call explicitly identifies a particular object, called the *receiver object*, and a particular instance method attached to that object. In Java, such a method call has the form:

$$E_0.I(E_1, \ldots, E_n)$$

The expression E_0 is evaluated to yield the receiver object. The identifier I names an instance method attached to that object. The expressions $E_1, \ldots, E_n$ are evaluated to yield the arguments passed to the method.

Although an object is somewhat similar to a record, the representation of an object must reflect the close association between the object and its instance methods. From an object we must be able to locate the attached instance methods. In turn, each instance method must somehow 'know' which object it is attached to.

Example 6.32 *Java object representation (single class)*

Consider the following Java class:

```
class Point {
    // A Point object represents a geometric point located at (x, y).

    protected int x, y;

(1) public Point (int x, int y) {
        this.x = x; this.y = y;
    }

(2) public void move (int dx, int dy) {.
        this.x += dx; this.y += dy;
    }

(3) public float area () {
        return 0.0;
    }
```

```
(4) public float dist (Point that) {.
        int dx = this.x - that.x;
        int dy = this.y - that.y;
        return Math.sqrt(dx*dx + dy*dy);
    }
}
```

Associated with class Point is a unique *class-object* that looks like this:

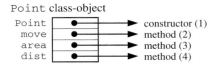

Point class-object

Point	•	→ constructor (1)
move	•	→ method (2)
area	•	→ method (3)
dist	•	→ method (4)

The Point class-object contains the addresses of the class's instance methods named move, area, and dist, as well as its constructor.

An object of class Point looks like this:[5]

class [•] → Point class-object
x [ ]
y [ ]

A Point object consists of the instance variables named x and y, together with a *class-tag*. The class-tag is just a pointer to the Point class-object. Class-tags serve to distinguish objects of different classes. (Later we shall see why this is necessary.) They also serve to link each object to the methods of that object's class.

Objects are created by the allocator new. (They are heap variables in the terminology of Section 6.6.) Each variable declared with class Point may be assigned a pointer to a Point object:

```
Point p = new Point(2, 3);
Point q = new Point(0, 0);
p.move(1, 1);
```

p [•]
q [•]

class [•]
x [3]
y [4]   → Point class-object

class [•]
x [0]
y [0]

Now the method call 'q.dist(p)' would return 5.0.

Object assignment copies only the pointer (not the object itself[6]):

---

[5] Note that throughout this section, we assume that a class only has a single constructor.

[6] The Java clone method can be used to copy an object.

```
q = p;
```

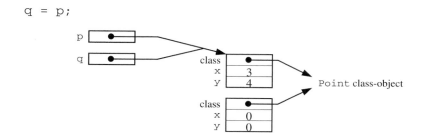

Now p and q point to the same object. The method call 'q.dist(p)' returns 0.0. The method call 'p.move(1, 1)' would update the object that both p and q point to.

The method call 'p.move(1, 1)' works as follows. The receiver object is the object that p points to. The address of the called method is found by following the pointer from the receiver object to the corresponding class-object, where the address of the instance method named move is found. As well as the explicit arguments (both 1 in this case), the receiver object is passed as an implicit argument, and bound to the keyword this. In this way the instance method 'knows' which object it is attached to.

Note that a side effect of the assignment 'q = p;' above was to leave one of the objects inaccessible. A garbage collector is needed to deallocate inaccessible objects.

☐

A *subclass* of class *C*, say *S*, is a family of objects similar to objects of class *C*, but possibly with extra instance variables, extra methods, and/or overridden methods. *C* is known as the *superclass* of S.

Any object of subclass *S* can be treated like an object of class *C*, simply by ignoring its extra instance variables and methods.

By default, each instance method of class *C* is *inherited* by subclass *S*. In other words, the same method code is attached to objects of class *C* and to objects of class *S*. (The language's scope rules must ensure that the body of the inherited method accesses only the instance variables of *C*, not those of *S*.)

Alternatively, an instance method of class *C* can be *overridden* by a method of the same name in class *S*. In other words, different method code is attached to objects of class *C* and to objects of class *S*. (The overriding method may access the instance variables of *S*, not just those of *C*.)

Here we shall assume that the OO language enforces *single inheritance*, i.e., each class has at most one superclass. This is (more or less) the case in Java.[7]

---

[7] C++ supports *multiple inheritance*, whereby a class may have several superclasses. Java actually supports a limited form of multiple inheritance, *via* interfaces.

The superclass of `Point` in Example 6.32 is `Object`, by default. A consequence of this is that `Point` inherits the methods of class `Object` (but for simplicity we have omitted these inherited methods in the `Point` class-object).

Example 6.33 *Java object representation (class and subclasses)*

Consider the following Java classes, both of which are subclasses of `Point`:

```
class Circle extends Point {
    // A Circle object represents a circle of radius r, centered at (x, y).

    protected int r;

(5) public Circle (int x, int y, int r) {
        this.x = x; this.y = y;  this.r = r;
    }

(6) public int radius () {
        return this.r;
    }

(7) public double area () {
        double pi = 3.1416;
        return pi * this.r * this.r;
    }
}

class Box extends Point {
    // A Box object represents a rectangle of width w and depth d,
    // centered at (x, y).

    protected int w, d;

(8) public Box (int x, int y, int w, int d) {
        this.x = x; this.y = y; this.w = w; this.d = d;
    }

(9) public int width () {
        return this.w;
    }

(10) public int depth () {
        return this.d;
    }

(11) public double area () {
        return (double) (this.w * this.d);
    }
}
```

The `Circle` and `Box` class-objects look like these:

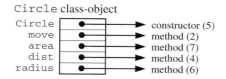

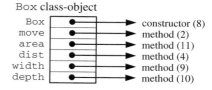

The `Circle` class-object is an extension of the `Point` class-object in Example 6.32. It starts with the instance methods named `move` (which is inherited from the `Point` class), `area` (which is overridden), and `dist` (which is inherited); these are followed by the extra method named `radius`. The `Box` class-object is likewise an extension of the `Point` class-object, but its extra instance methods are named `width` and `depth`.

Objects of classes `Circle` and `Box` look like these:

Each `Circle` object starts with a class-tag and the instance variables `x` and `y`; these are followed by the extra instance variable named `r`. Its class-tag is a pointer to the `Circle` class-object. A `Box` object is similar, but its extra instance variables are named `w` and `d`. Its class-tag is a pointer to the `Box` class-object.

The following code illustrates the behavior of `Circle` and `Box` objects:

```
int s     = 4;
Point p   = null;
Circle c  = new Circle(0, 3*s, s);
Box b     = new Box(0, s, 2*s, 2*s);
```

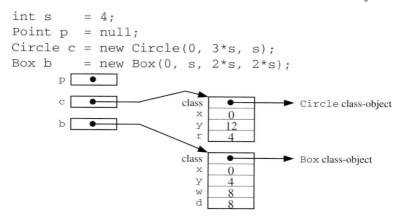

Now the method call '`c.dist(b)`' would return 8.0, since `dist` is inherited by class `Circle` (and by class `Box`); the answer is in fact the distance between the *centers* of c and b.

```
p = c;
p.move(20, 20);
```

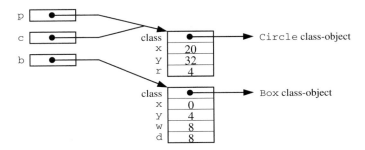

Now the `Point` variable `p` points to an object of class `Circle`, which is legal. The program can still access `p.x` and `p.y`, but any attempt to access `p.r` would be a type error. In this context the object pointed to by `p` is treated like a `Point` object. However, the method call 'p.area()' would return 50.3, not 0.0, because it is actually the overriding method (7) that is called.

In detail, the method call 'p.area()' works as follows. The receiver object is the object that `p` points to. The address of the called method is found by following the pointer from the receiver object to the corresponding class-object, which in this example is the `Circle` class-object, and there the instance method named `move` is (7) rather than (3). Thus method overriding works as required.

This example illustrates several important points:

- Each instance variable has a fixed offset relative to the base of every object that contains it. Assuming that class-tags and integers occupy one word each, the instance variables `x` and `y` have offsets 1 and 2, respectively, not only in `Point` objects but also in `Circle` and `Box` objects (and indeed in objects of any subclass of `Point`). A variable such as `p` can point to any `Point`, `Circle`, or `Box` object, but the addressing formula for `p.x` (or `p.y`) does not depend on the class of object that `p` currently points to.

- Likewise, every instance method has a fixed offset relative to the base of every class-object that 'contains' it. Assuming that code pointers occupy one word each, the instance methods `move`, `area`, and `dist` have offsets 1, 2, and 3, respectively, not only in the `Point` class-object but also in the `Circle` and `Box` class-objects (and indeed in the class-object of any subclass of `Point`). Thus a method call such as 'p.area ()' can be implemented efficiently using the known offset of `area`. (Relative to the cost of an ordinary procedure call, an instance-method call carries an overhead of two indirections. This is the price we must pay for dynamic method selection.)

- Method inheritance and overriding work as required. All objects of the same class have class-tags that point to the same class-object. But each subclass has a distinct class-object, in which some methods are the same as those of the superclass-object (the inherited methods), some methods are different (the overridden methods), and some methods are extra.

So far we have neglected class variables and methods. A *class variable* is a variable associated with a class, but not a component of a particular object. A *class method* is an operation associated with a class, but not attached to a particular object.

Class variables are global in terms of their lifetime, so static storage allocation is sufficient. Class methods are like ordinary procedures, so they also need no special treatment. It may be convenient to make class variables and class methods part of the corresponding class-object.

6.8   Case study: the abstract machine TAM

TAM (the Triangle Abstract Machine) was designed specifically to support the implementation of high-level programming languages, and in particular the run-time organization techniques described in Sections 6.1 through 6.6. Thus:

- The low-address end of the data store is reserved as a stack. This is used both for stack storage allocation and for expression evaluation. Operations are provided for pushing and popping values at the stack top.

- The high-address end of the data store is reserved as a heap. Operations are provided for allocating and deallocating heap variables.

- The call and return instructions handle frames automatically. The call instruction pushes a new frame, with all its link data. The return instruction pops a frame, and also replaces the routine's arguments by its result (if any).

- There are no general-purpose registers that could be used for storing data. All registers are dedicated to specific purposes: registers SB and ST delimit the stack; registers HB and HT delimit the heap; register LB points to the topmost frame on the stack; and so on. Updating of registers is always implicit: LB is updated by call and return instructions; ST is updated by load, store, and many other instructions; and so on.

In these respects TAM is quite similar to some other real and abstract stack machines (such as the JVM, see Section 2.4). But a detailed look at TAM reveals a number of interesting design features, some of which are discussed below. A complete description of TAM may be found in Appendix C.

TAM is implemented by an interpreter. This interpreter is described in Section 8.3, and is available from our Web site.

Addressing and registers

Most instructions have address operands. An address operand is always of the form '$d[r]$', where r names a register that points to the base of a store segment or frame, and d is a displacement:

address denoted by $d[r]$ = d + register r

This method of addressing is used uniformly for accessing global variables within the global segment, local and nonlocal variables within stack frames, and instructions within the code segment.

The registers SB, LB, L1, L2, etc., together form a display: SB allows access to global variables; LB allows access to local variables; and L1, L2, etc., allow access to nonlocal variables.

An interesting implementation decision is how exactly to maintain the registers L1, L2, etc. They are related to LB by the invariants:

$$L1 = content(LB)$$
$$L2 = content(content(LB))$$
$$\ldots$$

Thus registers L1, L2, etc., change whenever LB changes, i.e., on a routine call or return. But it turns out that these registers are rarely needed in practice.[8] So, rather than updating these registers on every routine call or return, it is more efficient to compute L1 or L2 or whichever only when and if needed. In fact, the interpreter can compute the address of any variable as follows:

$$
\begin{aligned}
\text{address denoted by } d[\text{SB}] &= d + \text{SB} \\
\text{address denoted by } d[\text{LB}] &= d + \text{LB} \\
\text{address denoted by } d[\text{L1}] &= d + \text{L1} = d + content(\text{LB}) \\
\text{address denoted by } d[\text{L2}] &= d + \text{L2} = d + content(content(\text{LB}))
\end{aligned}
$$

and so on. Thus L1, L2, etc., are redundant! Although they can be named in the address operands of instructions, they need not exist as actual registers.

Primitive routines

The machine's primitive operations are provided by a set of *primitive routines*, such as `add`, `mult`, `lt`, and `not`. A primitive routine behaves like an ordinary routine, as far as the caller is concerned. That is to say, the caller must evaluate and push its arguments before calling the primitive routine, and on return the caller can expect to find the result at the stack top in place of the arguments. This design avoids the need for a large number of distinct instructions (such as ADD, MULT, LT, and NOT). It has the further advantage of allowing a primitive to be treated exactly like an ordinary routine, e.g., we can pass it as an argument represented by a closure (see Section 6.5.2).

Each primitive routine has a dedicated address in the code store. Thus a call to a primitive routine can be trapped by the interpreter and treated appropriately.

---

[8] One study of a collection of Pascal programs suggested that, in practice, accesses to global variables (49%) and to local variables (49%) are far more common than accesses to nonlocal variables (2%).

Data representation

TAM storage is organized in words. However, the instruction set provides consistent support for composite values of any size from 1 word to 255 words. In the LOAD, STORE, and some other instructions there is an 8-bit size field, n, that indicates how many words are to be loaded, stored, or whatever. For example, the following instruction sequence:

```
LOAD(6)   4[LB]        – push 6 words from address 4 in the local frame
STORE(6) 21[SB]        – store them to address 21 in the global segment
```

copies a 6-word value (perhaps a record or an array) from one place to another in the store. As well as copying multi-word values, we can pass them as arguments to routines, return them as results, and so on.

In practice, most load and store instructions work on single-word values. By convention, therefore, we abbreviate 'LOAD(1)' to 'LOAD', 'STORE(1)' to 'STORE', etc., when writing instructions in mnemonic form.

6.9 Further reading

The essential background to the material presented in this chapter is a knowledge of basic programming language concepts. See the companion textbook by Watt (1990), and in particular Chapter 2 (primitive and composite types), Chapter 3 (variables and storage), and Chapter 5 (procedures, functions, and parameters).

The main topics of this chapter are covered in any good compiler textbook. See, for example, Chapter 7 of Aho et al. (1985).

Data representation has long been part of compiler writers' folklore. A classic treatment of the topic may be found in a pair of illuminating papers by Hoare (1972, 1975). A more theoretical view of data representation issues – in the context of algebraic specification of data types – may be found in Chapter 6 of the companion textbook by Watt (1991).

Static storage allocation was used in implementations of the earliest programming languages (Fortran and Cobol). These languages deliberately rejected recursion in order to make static allocation feasible. When the Algol-like languages (Algol-60 and its successors) introduced recursion and nested block structure, stack storage allocation was developed to implement them, along with the use of display registers to access nonlocal variables. A classic account of this method may be found in Dijkstra (1960).

Heap storage allocation and garbage collection were first developed when Lisp introduced recursive data structures. Most object-oriented and all functional languages rely heavily on garbage collection. This topic is both fascinating and difficult, and remains an active research area. For a more detailed account, see Wilson (1992) or Jones and Lins (1996). For an alternative introduction to heap management, see Chapter

7 of Standish (1998).

In functional programming languages, functions are first-class values, i.e., they can be passed as arguments, returned as function results, incorporated in data structures, and so on. In such a language local variables have lifetimes that are not strictly nested, so stack storage allocation as described in Section 6.4 is unsuitable. See Cardelli (1984) for an account of a run-time organization suitable for ML, a typical example of this kind of language. (The run-time organization described in this chapter is, however, perfectly suitable for languages – such as Triangle, Pascal, and even Fortran – that allow functions and procedures to be passed as arguments.)

Exercises

Section 6.1

6.1 Consider the following Pascal types:

```
type
   Player = (white, black);

   Piece  = (pawn, knight, bishop,
             rook, queen, king);

   Square = record
               case empty: Boolean of
                  true:  ( );
                  false: ( occupant: Piece;
                           owner: Player   )
            end;

   Board  = array [1..8] of
               array [1..8] of Square;

   State  = record
               pos:   Board;
               next:  Player;
               moves: Integer
            end
```

Or consider the following C types:

```
typedef enum {white, black} Player;

typedef enum {pawn, knight, bishop,
              rook, queen, king} Piece;
```

```
typedef struct {
                    int     empty;  /*  1 if square is empty,
                                            otherwise 0  */
                    Piece   occupant;
                    Player  owner;
            } Square;

typedef Square Board[8][8];

typedef struct {
                    Board   pos;
                    Player  next;
                    int     moves;
            } State;
```

(a)   Show how these types would be represented, and state the size of each
      type. Assume that the target machine is TAM, in which every primitive
      value occupies one word.

(b)   Repeat, but now assume that the target machine has byte addressing, with
      1 word = 4 bytes = 32 bits.

6.2   In Pascal, the type `Boolean` behaves like an enumeration type:

```
type Boolean = (false, true)
```

and is therefore equipped with operations such as `succ`, `pred`, and `ord` as
well as the logical operations. How does this influence the choice of representation for Pascal truth values?

6.3   Many real machines have a choice of integer representations (word or double-
word), and a corresponding choice of machine operations (ADD or DADD,
MULT or DMULT, etc.).

Assuming that the source language has a single type `Integer`, the compiler
writer has to make a choice between the two representations. List the
arguments in favor of each. How does your favorite compiler make this choice?

6.4   Consider the record type T of (6.3). Express #T in terms of #T_1, ..., and #T_n.
Check that your #T, together with *size* T (6.4), satisfies (6.1).

6.5   In Pascal, the programmer can choose not only the index *bounds* but also the
index *type* of a static array.

(a)   Show how the following arrays would be represented:

```
var freq:  array ['a'..'z'] of Integer;
    pixel: array [Color] of 0..15
```

where `Color` is defined as in Example 6.3.

(b) Generalize (6.15), (6.16), and (6.17) to cater for the general case:

type T = array [T_{index}] of T_{elem}

where T_{index} may be any primitive discrete type, i.e., Boolean, Char, Integer, an enumeration type, or a subrange thereof.

6.6 In Triangle (or Pascal), the effect of a multi-dimensional array may be obtained by an array of arrays: see array us in Example 6.6. Generalize (6.12) and (6.13) to cater for the two-dimensional case:

type T = array m of array n of T_{elem}

6.7 In Ada, the programmer can choose the index type of a dynamic array.

(a) Show how the array freq would be represented:

```
type Profile is
        array (Character range <>) of Integer;

first: Character := 'a';
last:  Character := 'z';
freq:  Profile (first .. last);
```

(b) Generalize (6.20), (6.21), and (6.22) to cater for the general case:

type T is array (T_{index} range <>) of T_{elem};

a: $T(E_1 \ .. \ E_2)$;

where T_{index} may be any primitive discrete type, i.e., Boolean, Character, Integer, or an enumeration type, and where E_1 and E_2 are expressions of type T_{index}.

6.8* Suggest a representation for two-dimensional dynamic arrays, as in Ada:

type T is
        array (T_1 range <>, T_2 range <>) of T_{elem};

a: $T(E_1..E_2, \ E_3..E_4)$;

6.9 Suppose that a machine's storage is organized as follows. A word is 4 bytes or 32 bits. Byte addressing is used. Every single-word and multi-word variable must be located on a word boundary, i.e., its byte address must be a multiple of 4. (This is an example of an *alignment restriction*.)

Assuming that the types Boolean, Char, 1..12, and 1..31 occupy one byte each, show how the following Pascal variables would be represented in storage:

```
type Date    = record
                    d: 1..31;
                    m: 1..12;
                    y: Integer
               end;

     Name    = array [1..10] of Char;

     Person = record
                    surname, forename: Name;
                    dob: Date;
                    female: Boolean
               end;

var  today: Date;
     us: array [1..2] of Person
```

Section 6.2

6.10 Consider the Triangle expression '(0 < n) /\ odd(n)' whose evaluation on a stack machine was illustrated in Example 6.12. Illustrate the same expression's evaluation on a different stack machine with byte addressing. Assume that stack elements may differ in size, that a truth value occupies 1 byte, and that an integer occupies 4 bytes.

6.11 In most programming languages, the semantics of the expression 'E_1 O E_2' (where O is a binary operator) are such that the subexpressions E_1 and E_2 may be evaluated in any order.

(a) Consider the expression '(a * b) + (1 - (c * 2))' and the corresponding instruction sequence in Example 6.10. Find a shorter instruction sequence that evaluates this expression using only two registers.

(b) Now consider a machine with a single register (the accumulator). How could this expression be evaluated on such a machine?

Section 6.3

6.12 Consider a Pascal program with the type definitions of Exercise 6.1 and the following global variable declarations:

```
var computer, human: Player;
    initial: Board;
    current: State
```

or the corresponding C extern declarations.

Show how the global variables would be located in storage, assuming a target machine with 1 word = 4 bytes = 32 bits. Write down the address of each variable, assuming that the first variable is located at address 0.

6.13 Suppose that a Triangle program has the following global variable declarations:

$$\text{var } v_1\colon T_1; \quad \ldots; \quad \text{var } v_n\colon T_n$$

Write down a formula for *address* v_i. Assume that *address* $v_1 = 0$.

Observe that each variable's address depends on the order of the variable declarations. But the semantics of Triangle places no significance on the order of variable declarations. Discuss this paradox.

Section 6.4

6.14 Consider the Triangle program of Example 6.20. Suppose that the main program calls procedure Y, which in turn calls procedure Z. Draw a stack snapshot at each point during this sequence. Show frames and dynamic links as in Figure 6.11; also show individual global and local variables.

6.15 Consider the Triangle program of Figure 6.14. Suppose that the main program calls procedure P, which in turn calls procedure Q, which in turn calls procedure R, which in turn calls procedure S.

(a) Draw a stack snapshot at each point during this sequence. Show frames and static links as in Figure 6.15; also show individual global, local, and nonlocal variables.

(b) According to Example 6.17, procedure R can fetch a variable local to Q by an instruction of the form 'LOAD *d*[L1]'. Write down the instruction that R would use to fetch the value of q. Verify that this instruction will work correctly at the point when R is running during the above sequence.

(c) Which nonlocal variables may procedure S access? Verify that these nonlocal variables, and no others, are indeed accessible at the point when S is running during the above sequence. Write down instructions for S to fetch the values of these nonlocal variables.

6.16* Algol is a programming language with nested block structure. (In this respect it is much like Triangle, with procedures and block (let-) commands.) It has a few primitive types, namely Boolean, integer, and real. Its only composite type is the (dynamic) array. Arrays are indexed by integers, and their elements are always primitive – arrays of arrays are not supported. An example of an array declaration is:

```
real array v [1 : n]
```

where n must have been declared in an enclosing scope.

Design a run-time organization suitable for Algol. In particular, decide where the handle and elements of a dynamic array such as v should be located.

6.17** In this chapter, SB, LB, L1, L2, etc., are classified as display registers. SB always points to the globals; LB points to the topmost frame, which belongs to the currently running routine R; L1 points to a frame belonging to the routine R' immediately enclosing R; L2 points to a frame belonging to the routine R'' immediately enclosing R'; etc.

An alternative form of display consists of registers D0, D1, D2, etc. D0 always points to the globals; D1 points to a frame belonging to a routine whose body is at level 1; D2 points to a frame belonging to a routine whose body is at level 2; etc. If the currently running routine R has its body at level n, Dn points to the topmost frame (which belongs to R); and D(n+1), D(n+2), etc., are undefined. This is illustrated in Figure 6.31, which corresponds to part of Figure 6.15.

How should D0, D1, D2, etc., be updated:

(a) when code at level m calls a routine S whose body is at level n ($\leq m+1$)?

(b) when S returns?

Discuss the advantages and disadvantages of this form of display.

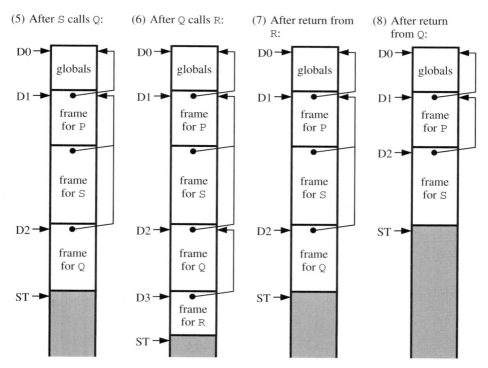

Figure 6.31 An alternative form of display (cf. Figure 6.15).

Section 6.5

6.18* Consider the following Triangle program:

```
let
   func sqr (i: Integer): Integer ~
      i * i;

   func even (i: Integer): Boolean ~
      ((i // 2) = 0);

   func power (x: Integer, n: Integer): Integer ~
      if n = 0 then
         1
      else if even(n) then
         sqr(power(x, n / 2))
      else
         sqr(power(x, n / 2)) * x
in
   ...
```

Draw stack snapshots, showing arguments and results, at relevant points as this program evaluates:

(a) `power(2, 1)`
(b) `power(2, 6)`

6.19 Consider the routine protocols of Examples 6.18 and 6.19. Compare the code that would be used to evaluate the following function calls:

(a) `f(a, b, c)`
(b) `f(g(a), h(b, c), d)`

Assume the instruction sets of Tables 6.1 and 6.2, augmented by suitable CALL instructions.

6.20* Consider a target machine that has just eight general-purpose single-word registers, R0 through R7. Design a routine protocol that uses these registers as much as possible, but also allows for multi-word arguments and for a large number of arguments.

Section 6.6

6.21 Consider the following outline Pascal program:

```
type IntList = ...;     {linked list of integers}
var p: Integer;
    ps, ns: IntList;
```

```
function cons (n: Integer; ns: IntList)
                    : IntList;
    ...;       {Return the list obtained by inserting n
                at the front of ns.}

procedure removeMultiples (n: Integer;
                                var ns: IntList);
    ...;       {Remove n and all its multiples from ns.}
begin
ps := nil;
ns := cons(3, cons(5, cons(7, cons(9, cons(11,
        cons(13, cons(15, cons(17, cons(19,
            cons(21, cons(23, cons(25, cons(27,
                cons(29, cons(31, cons(33, cons(35,
                    cons(37, nil)))))))))))))))));
repeat
    p := ns^.head;
    removeMultiples(p, ns);
    ps := cons(p, ps)
until ns = nil
end
```

Function cons allocates a new node, and procedure removeMultiples deallocates one or more nodes. Draw snapshots of the heap after the first five iterations of the loop. Do this for each of the following heap managers:

Version 1: On allocation, the heap manager just uses the first gap in the free list. On deallocation, the new gap is just added to the front of the free list.

Version 2: On allocation, the heap manager uses the smallest gap that is big enough. On deallocation, the new gap is coalesced with any adjacent gap(s).

6.22* Design an algorithm that coalesces adjacent gaps in the heap whenever a heap variable is deallocated, as illustrated by Figure 6.26.

6.23* Design an algorithm that compacts the heap, as illustrated by Figure 6.27. When should heap compaction be done?

Section 6.7

6.24 Consider the following Java class:

```
class Date {
    short day, month;  int year;

    public Date (short day, short month,
                    int year) { ... }
```

```
public short getDay () { ... }
public short getMonth () { ... }
public int   getYear () { ... }

public int difference (Date today) {
    // Return the difference between this date and today
    // in whole years.
    ...
}
}
```

Draw the representations of the Date class-object and a Date object as illustrated in Example 6.32.

6.25 Consider the following Java classes (which use the Date class from Exercise 6.24):

```
class Person {
  String name;  Date dob;

  public Person (name, dob) { ... }

  public int age (Date today) { ... }
}

class Staff extends Person {
  String staffId;
  int salary;

  public Staff (String name, Date dob,
                String staffId, int salary)
  { ... }

  public String getStaffId () { ... }
  public int    getSalary () { ... }
  public void   setSalary (int salary) { ... }

}

class Faculty extends Staff {
  Course[] teaches;

  public Faculty (String name, Date dob,
                  String staffId,
                  int salary) { ... }

  public void assign (Course course) { ... }
}

class Student extends Person {
  String studentId;
  Course[] studies;
```

```
        public Student (String name, Date dob,
                        String studentId) { ... }

        public void enrol (Course course) { ... }
    }
```

Draw the representations of the `Person`, `Staff`, `Faculty` and `Student` class-objects and an example object of each class, as illustrated in Example 6.33.

6.26* Using the class definitions from Exercise 6.25, consider the following hypothetical class definition:

```
    class TeachingAssistant extends Staff, Student
    { ... }
```

This would be an example of *multiple inheritance* (which is not supported in Java). Consider how an object in the class `TeachingAssistant` could be represented. Note that such an object would contain only a single occurrence of the instance variables of `Person`, which would be inherited from both `Staff` and `Student`.

CHAPTER SEVEN

Code Generation

Syntactic and contextual analysis are concerned with analysis of the source program; thus they are dependent only on the source language. Code generation is concerned with translation of the source program to object code, and so is dependent on both the source language and the target machine (whether real or abstract). It is possible to expound general principles of syntactic or contextual analysis, as in Chapters 4 and 5. But the influence of the target machine makes it much harder to expound general principles of code generation.

The main problem is that target machines are extremely varied. Some machines provide registers for storage of intermediate results; others provide a stack; still others provide both. Some machines provide instructions with zero, one, two, or three operands, or a mixture of these. Some machines provide a single addressing mode; others provide many. The structure of a code generator is heavily influenced by such aspects of the target machine architecture. A code generation algorithm suitable for one target machine might be difficult or impossible to adapt to a dissimilar target machine.

The major subproblems of code generation are the following:

- *Code selection*. This is the problem of deciding which sequence of target machine instructions will be the object code of each phrase in the source program. For this purpose we write *code templates*. A code template is a general rule specifying the object code of all phrases of a particular form (e.g., all assignment commands, or all function calls). In practice, code selection is often complicated by special cases.

- *Storage allocation*. This is the problem of deciding the storage address of each variable in the source program. The code generator can decide the address of each global variable exactly (*static storage allocation*), but it can decide the address of each local variable only relatively (*stack storage allocation*).

- *Register allocation*. If the target machine has registers, they should be used to hold intermediate results during expression evaluation. The code generator, knowing that a particular register contains the current value of variable v, should take advantage of that to save a memory cycle when the value of v is needed. Many complications arise in practice: there might not be enough registers to evaluate a complex expression; or some registers might be reserved for particular purposes (such as indexing).

Code generation for a stack machine is significantly easier than code generation for a register machine. As we saw in Chapter 6, we need a stack anyway to implement procedures and local variables. A stack is also convenient for expression evaluation. The problem of register allocation simply disappears. In this book, therefore, we consider only code generation for a stack machine, and concentrate on the subproblems of code selection and storage allocation. We use the abstract machine TAM as an illustrative target machine. (TAM was introduced in Chapter 6, and is fully described in Appendix C.)

7.1   Code selection

The function of the code generator is to translate source programs to semantically equivalent object programs. When we design a code generator, therefore, we must be guided by the semantics of the source language. Now a semantic specification is generally structured in terms of the semantics of phrases such as expressions, commands, and declarations. In code generation we should follow the same structure: we should specify the translation of source programs to object programs inductively, by specifying the translation of individual phrases to object code.

Usually there are many correct translations of a given program or phrase. There may be several sequences of instructions that correctly perform a given source-language operation. So a basic task of the code generator is to decide which sequence of instructions to generate in each case. This is called *code selection*.

7.1.1   Code templates

In general, we specify code selection inductively over the phrases of the source language, using *code functions* and *code templates*. The following example introduces the basic idea.

Example 7.1   Code functions and code templates

Consider translation of some hypothetical source language to object code. We can specify the translation of commands to object code by introducing the following code function:

> *execute* : Command $\rightarrow$ Instruction*

This function will translate each command C to a sequence of target-machine instructions that achieves the effect of executing C. We must define this function over all the commands in the source language. This we do by means of code templates.

Consider a sequential command, typically of the form 'C_1 ; C_2'. Its semantics was specified by (1.20c):

> The sequential command 'C_1 ; C_2' is executed as follows. First C_1 is executed; then C_2 is executed.

We can easily specify the translation of 'C_1 ; C_2' to object code by means of the following code template:

execute $[\![C_1 ; C_2]\!]$ =
 execute C_1
 execute C_2

This code template may be read as follows: the code to execute 'C_1 ; C_2' consists of the code to execute C_1, followed by the code to execute C_2.

Most code templates contain specific instructions. For example, the code template for a simple assignment command '$I := E$', where I is a variable identifier, might look like this:

execute $[\![I := E]\!]$ =
 evaluate E
 STORE a where a = address of variable named I

This code template may be read as follows: the code to execute '$I := E$' consists of the code to evaluate E, followed by a STORE instruction whose operand field is the address of the variable I.

For instance, here is a possible translation of a sequential command containing two assignment commands:[1]

$$
execute\ [\![\texttt{f := f*n;}\ \texttt{n := n-1}]\!]
\begin{cases}
execute\ [\![\texttt{f := f*n}]\!] & \begin{cases} \texttt{LOAD} & f \\ \texttt{LOAD} & n \\ \texttt{CALL} & mult \\ \texttt{STORE} & f \end{cases} \\
execute\ [\![\texttt{n := n-1}]\!] & \begin{cases} \texttt{LOAD} & n \\ \texttt{CALL} & pred \\ \texttt{STORE} & n \end{cases}
\end{cases}
$$

☐

Each code template specifies the object code to which a phrase is translated, in terms of the object code to which its subphrases are translated. If a phrase is primitive (i.e., contains no subphrases), then its code template should specify its object code directly. A complete set of code functions and code templates specifies the translation of the entire source language to object code. More precisely:

- The **object code** of each source-language phrase is the sequence of instructions to which it will be translated. The object code is in Instruction*.

---

[1] The actual machine instructions will contain numerical addresses. Here we write f and n to stand for the addresses of variables f and n, and *mult* and *pred* for the addresses of the respective primitive routines. We will use this convention freely, to make the examples readable.

- For each phrase class **P** in the source language's abstract syntax, we introduce a **code function**, f_P, that translates each phrase in class **P** to object code:

$$f_P : P \rightarrow \text{Instruction*}$$

- We define the code function f_P by a number of **code templates**, with (at least) one code template for each distinct form of phrase in class **P**. If some form of phrase in **P** has subphrases Q and R, then the corresponding code template will look something like this:

$$f_P [\![\dots Q \dots R \dots]\!] = $$
$$\dots$$
$$f_Q\, Q$$
$$\dots$$
$$f_R\, R$$
$$\dots$$

where f_Q and f_R are code functions appropriate for subphrases Q and R. (The order shown above is not fixed: Q's object code may precede or follow R's object code.)

A **code specification** is a collection of code functions and code templates. It must cover the entire source language, i.e., it must specify the translation of every well-formed source program to object code. Let us now examine a complete code specification.

Example 7.2   Code specification for Mini-Triangle to TAM code

Consider the language Mini-Triangle, whose syntax and semantics were given in Examples 1.3 and 1.8. We will present a code specification for the translation from Mini-Triangle to TAM code.

The relevant phrase classes in this language are Program, Command, Expression, Operator, V-name, and Declaration. We first introduce code functions for these phrase classes:

run	: Program	$\rightarrow$ Instruction*	(7.1)
execute	: Command	$\rightarrow$ Instruction*	(7.2)
evaluate	: Expression	$\rightarrow$ Instruction*	(7.3)
fetch	: V-name	$\rightarrow$ Instruction*	(7.4)
assign	: V-name	$\rightarrow$ Instruction*	(7.5)
elaborate	: Declaration	$\rightarrow$ Instruction*	(7.6)

The object code of each phrase is a sequence of instructions that will behave as shown in Table 7.1.

(Mini-Triangle has other phrase classes, but these will not have corresponding code functions. There are two code functions for V-name, which will be used in different contexts.)

Table 7.1 Summary of code functions for Mini-Triangle.

Phrase class	Code function	Effect of generated object code
Program	*run P*	Run the program P and then halt, starting and finishing with an empty stack.
Command	*execute C*	Execute the command C, possibly updating variables, but neither expanding nor contracting the stack.
Expression	*evaluate E*	Evaluate the expression E, pushing its result on to the stack top, but having no other effect.
V-name	*fetch V*	Push the value of the constant or variable named V on to the stack top.
V-name	*assign V*	Pop a value from the stack top, and store it in the variable named V.
Declaration	*elaborate D*	Elaborate the declaration D, expanding the stack to make space for any constants and variables declared therein.

A Mini-Triangle program is simply a command C. The program is run simply by executing C and then halting. The code template for a program is therefore as follows:

$$run \ [\![C]\!] \ = \hfill (7.7)$$
$$\qquad execute \ C$$
$$\qquad \texttt{HALT}$$

The code templates for commands are as follows:

$$execute \ [\![V := E]\!] \ = \hfill (7.8a)$$
$$\qquad evaluate \ E$$
$$\qquad assign \ V$$

This is easy to understand: '*evaluate E*' will have the net effect of pushing the value yielded by E on to the stack, and '*assign V*' will pop that value and store it in the variable V.

$$execute \ [\![I \ (\ E \ )]\!] \ = \hfill (7.8b)$$
$$\qquad evaluate \ E$$
$$\qquad \texttt{CALL} \ p \qquad \text{where } p = \text{address of primitive routine } I$$

This is the code template for a procedure call. Since there are no procedure declarations in Mini-Triangle, I must be the identifier of a predefined procedure such as `putint`. The above `CALL` instruction calls the corresponding primitive routine in TAM.

$$execute \ [\![C_1 \ ; \ C_2]\!] \ = \hfill (7.8c)$$
$$\qquad execute \ C_1$$
$$\qquad execute \ C_2$$

This was explained in Example 7.1.

execute $[\![\text{if } E \text{ then } C_1 \text{ else } C_2]\!]$ = (7.8d)
    evaluate E
    JUMPIF(0) *g*
    execute C_1
    JUMP *h*
  g : *execute* C_2
  h :

Here the code '*evaluate E*' will have the net effect of pushing a truth-value on to the stack. The JUMPIF instruction will pop and test this value. If it is 0 (representing *false*), control will be transferred to *g* where the code '*execute* C_2' will be selected; otherwise the code '*execute* C_1' will be selected. (The labels *g* and *h* stand for the addresses of the following instructions.)

execute $[\![\text{while } E \text{ do } C]\!]$ = (7.8e)
    JUMP *h*
  g : *execute C*
  h : *evaluate E*
    JUMPIF(1) *g*

Here again, the code '*evaluate E*' will have the net effect of pushing a truth-value on to the stack. The JUMPIF instruction will pop and test this value. If it is 1 (representing *true*), the code '*execute C*' will be iterated; otherwise iteration will cease. The initial JUMP instruction ensures that the code '*evaluate E*' will be executed first; this is in accordance with the semantics of the while-command. (See Exercise 7.1 for discussion of an alternative code template.)

execute $[\![\text{let } D \text{ in } C]\!]$ = (7.8f)
    elaborate D
    execute C
    POP(0) *s*   if $s > 0$
                      where s = amount of storage allocated by D

This code template shows how storage allocation and deallocation comes in. The code '*elaborate D*' will expand the stack, as a consequence of allocating storage for constants and variables declared in D. The code '*execute C*' will be able to access these variables. The POP instruction contracts the stack to its original size – in effect, deallocating these constants and variables.

The code templates for expressions are as follows. In each case the object code must have the net effect of pushing a value on to the stack.

evaluate $[\![IL]\!]$ = (7.9a)
    LOADL *v*   where *v = value of IL*

The LOADL instruction will simply push the integer-literal's value v on to the stack top.

evaluate $[\![V]\!]$ = (7.9b)
    fetch V

This is self-explanatory.

$$evaluate \ [\![O\ E]\!] \ = \tag{7.9c}$$
$$\quad evaluate\ E$$
$$\quad \text{CALL}\ \ p \qquad\qquad \text{where } p = \text{address of primitive routine}$$
$$\qquad\qquad\qquad\qquad\qquad\qquad \text{corresponding to } O$$

$$evaluate\ [\![E_1\ O\ E_2]\!] \ = \tag{7.9d}$$
$$\quad evaluate\ E_1$$
$$\quad evaluate\ E_2$$
$$\quad \text{CALL}\ \ p \qquad\qquad \text{where } p = \text{address of primitive routine}$$
$$\qquad\qquad\qquad\qquad\qquad\qquad \text{corresponding to } O$$

The above two code templates show how applications of unary and binary operators will be translated. Note how expression evaluation exploits the stack: the object code will first evaluate the operand(s), and then apply the operation corresponding to O. The latter is achieved by calling an appropriate primitive routine, e.g., not for '\', add for '+', or lt for '<'.

In Mini-Triangle, a value-or-variable-name is just an identifier that has been declared as a constant or variable. Being global, that constant or variable will be addressed relative to register SB. Here (anticipating Section 7.3) we assume that its address has already been determined:

$$fetch\ [\![I]\!] \ = \tag{7.10}$$
$$\quad \text{LOAD}\ \ d[\text{SB}] \qquad \text{where } d = \text{address bound to } I \text{ (relative to SB)}$$

$$assign\ [\![I]\!] \ = \tag{7.11}$$
$$\quad \text{STORE}\ \ d[\text{SB}] \qquad \text{where } d = \text{address bound to } I \text{ (relative to SB)}$$

The code templates for declarations are as follows. In each case the object code must expand the stack to make space for the declared constants and variables.

$$elaborate\ [\![\text{const } I \sim E]\!] \ = \tag{7.12a}$$
$$\quad evaluate\ E$$

The constant declaration's object code must expand the stack by enough space to contain the constant's value. The code '*evaluate E*' will do that, simply by depositing the value at the stack top. (In addition, the constant's address must be bound to I for future reference – this address will be needed whenever (7.10) is applied. We will see in Section 7.3 how this is done.)

$$elaborate\ [\![\text{var } I : T]\!] \ = \tag{7.12b}$$
$$\quad \text{PUSH}\ 1$$

This PUSH instruction will expand the stack by one word, enough space to accommodate the newly allocated variable. (The only types in Mini-Triangle are truth values and integers, and these occupy one word each in TAM.) The newly allocated variable is not initialized. (The variable's address must be bound to I for future reference – this address will be needed whenever (7.10) or (7.11) is applied.)

$$elaborate \; [\![D_1 \; ; \; D_2]\!] \; =$$
$$elaborate \; D_1$$
$$elaborate \; D_2$$

(7.12c)

Note that in code templates (7.12a–c) it is a simple matter to predict the total amount of storage allocated by the declaration. This information is required in (7.8f).

Example 7.3   Translation of a while-command

The following translation illustrates code templates (7.8a) and (7.8e), among others:

```
execute [[while i > 0 do      execute [[i := i-2]]    30:  JUMP    35
           i := i-2]]                                 31:  LOAD    i
                                                      32:  LOADL   2
                                                      33:  CALL    sub
                                                      34:  STORE   i
                              evaluate [[i > 0]]      35:  LOAD    i
                                                      36:  LOADL   0
                                                      37:  CALL    gt
                                                      38:  JUMPIF(1) 31
```

Here we are assuming that the while-command's object code starts at address 30. The numbers to the left of the instructions are their addresses.[2]

Example 7.4   Translation of a let-command

The following translation of a let-command illustrates code templates (7.8f) and (7.12b), among others:

```
execute [[let              elaborate [[var i:Integer]]     PUSH    1
          var i:Integer                                    LOAD    i
          in i := i+2]]         execute [[i := i+2]]        LOADL   2
                                                            CALL    add
                                                            STORE   i
                                                            POP(0)  1
```

The code generated from this let-command expands the stack by one word to allocate storage for the local variable i, and later contracts the stack by one word to deallocate it. The address of this word, say i, is used to access the variable within the let-command.

---

[2] Usually we omit instruction addresses, but we show them in instruction sequences that include jump instructions.

Example 7.5   Code templates for Triangle values and variables

Code templates (7.10), (7.11), and (7.12b) assume that every Mini-Triangle value occupies one word exactly. This is justified because Mini-Triangle supports only truth values and integers, which occupy one word each in TAM.

The full Triangle language, on the other hand, supports a variety of types including arrays and records. A value or variable of type T will occupy a number of words given by *size T*. (See Section 6.1.) For Triangle we must generalize the code templates to take this into account:

fetch $[\![I]\!]$ = ⠀⠀⠀⠀⠀⠀⠀⠀⠀⠀⠀⠀⠀⠀⠀⠀⠀⠀⠀⠀⠀⠀⠀⠀⠀⠀⠀⠀⠀⠀⠀⠀⠀⠀⠀⠀(7.13)
⠀⠀⠀⠀LOAD(s) d[SB]⠀⠀⠀where s = *size*(type of I),
⠀⠀⠀⠀⠀⠀⠀⠀⠀⠀⠀⠀⠀⠀⠀⠀⠀⠀⠀⠀d = address bound to I (relative to SB)

assign $[\![I]\!]$ = ⠀⠀⠀⠀⠀⠀⠀⠀⠀⠀⠀⠀⠀⠀⠀⠀⠀⠀⠀⠀⠀⠀⠀⠀⠀⠀⠀⠀⠀⠀⠀⠀⠀⠀⠀(7.14)
⠀⠀⠀⠀STORE(s) d[SB]⠀⠀where s = *size*(type of I),
⠀⠀⠀⠀⠀⠀⠀⠀⠀⠀⠀⠀⠀⠀⠀⠀⠀⠀⠀⠀d = address bound to I (relative to SB)

elaborate $[\![\text{var } I : T]\!]$ = ⠀⠀⠀⠀⠀⠀⠀⠀⠀⠀⠀⠀⠀⠀⠀⠀⠀⠀⠀⠀⠀⠀⠀⠀⠀(7.15)
⠀⠀⠀⠀PUSH s⠀⠀⠀⠀⠀⠀⠀⠀where s = *size T*

We shall use these more general code templates from now on. They are still valid for Mini-Triangle, in which *size T* is always 1.

☐

7.1.2   Special-case code templates

There are often several ways to translate a given source-language phrase to object code, some more efficient than others. For example, the TAM code to evaluate the expression 'n + 1' could be:

⠀⠀⠀(a)⠀LOAD⠀⠀*n*⠀⠀⠀⠀⠀*or* (b)⠀LOAD *n*
⠀⠀⠀⠀⠀⠀LOADL 1⠀⠀⠀⠀⠀⠀⠀⠀⠀⠀CALL *succ*
⠀⠀⠀⠀⠀⠀CALL⠀⠀*add*

Object code (a) follows code template (7.9d). That code template is always applicable, being valid for any binary operator and for any subexpressions. Object code (b) is correct only in the special case of the binary operator '+' being applied to the literal value 1. When applicable, this special case gives rise to more efficient object code. It could be specified as follows:

evaluate $[\![E_1 + 1]\!]$ =
⠀⠀⠀*evaluate* E_1
⠀⠀⠀CALL *succ*

A **special-case code template** is one that is applicable only to phrases of a special form. Invariably such phrases are also covered by a more general code template. A special-case code template is worth having if phrases of the special form occur frequently, and if they allow translation into particularly efficient object code. The following example illustrates another common special case.

Example 7.6 Mini-Triangle constant declarations

The right side of a constant declaration is frequently a literal, as in:

```
let
    ...
    const n ~ 7
    ...
in
    ... n ... n ...
```

Code template (7.12a) specifies that the code '*elaborate* [[const n ~ 7]]' will deposit the value 7 in a suitable cell (at the current stack top). Whenever n is used, code template (7.10) specifies that the value will be loaded from that cell. The following translation illustrates these code templates:

$$
\textit{execute } [[\texttt{let const n} \sim \texttt{7;} \atop \texttt{var i: Integer} \atop \texttt{in i := n*n}]]
\left\{
\begin{array}{l}
\textit{elaborate } [[\texttt{const n} \sim \texttt{7}]] \left\{ \begin{array}{ll} \texttt{LOADL} & \texttt{7} \end{array} \right. \\
\textit{elaborate } [[\texttt{var i: Integer}]] \left\{ \begin{array}{ll} \texttt{PUSH} & \texttt{1} \end{array} \right. \\
\\
\textit{execute } [[\texttt{i := n*n}]] \left\{ \begin{array}{ll} \texttt{LOAD} & n \\ \texttt{LOAD} & n \\ \texttt{CALL} & \textit{mult} \\ \texttt{STORE} & i \end{array} \right. \\
\quad\quad\quad\quad\quad\quad \texttt{POP(0)2}
\end{array}
\right.
$$

The first instruction 'LOADL 7' makes space for the constant n on the stack top. Instructions of the form 'LOAD n' fetch the constant's value, wherever required. The final instruction 'POP(0) 2' pops the constant and variable off the stack.

A much better translation is possible: simply use the literal value 7 wherever n is fetched. This special treatment is possible whenever an identifier is bound to a *known value* in a constant declaration. This is expressed by the following special-case code templates:

fetch [[I]] =   (7.16)
    LOADL v where v = value bound to *I* (if known)

elaborate [[const *I* ~ *IL*]] =   (7.17)
                    (i.e., no code)

In (7.17) no code is required to elaborate the constant declaration. It is sufficient that the value of the integer-literal *IL* is bound to *I* for future reference. In (7.16) that value is incorporated into a LOADL instruction. Thus the object code is more efficient in both places. The following alternative translation illustrates these special-case code templates:

$$execute \; \llbracket \texttt{let const n} \sim \texttt{7;} \atop \quad\quad \texttt{var i: Integer} \atop \quad\quad\quad \texttt{in i := n*n} \rrbracket \Bigg\{ \begin{array}{l} elaborate \; \llbracket \texttt{const n} \sim \texttt{7} \rrbracket \Big\{ \\ \quad elaborate \; \llbracket \texttt{var i: Integer} \rrbracket \Big\{ \quad \texttt{PUSH} \quad \texttt{1} \\ \quad\quad\quad\quad\quad\quad\quad\quad\quad\quad\quad\quad \texttt{LOADL} \quad \texttt{7} \\ \quad\quad\quad execute \; \llbracket \texttt{i := n*n} \rrbracket \quad \texttt{LOADL} \quad \texttt{7} \\ \quad\quad\quad\quad\quad\quad\quad\quad\quad\quad\quad\quad \texttt{CALL} \quad\;\; mult \\ \quad\quad\quad\quad\quad\quad\quad\quad\quad\quad\quad\quad \texttt{STORE} \quad i \\ \quad\quad\quad\quad\quad\quad\quad\quad\quad\quad\quad\quad \texttt{POP(0)} \quad \texttt{1} \end{array}$$

In this object code, each applied occurrence of n has been translated to the literal value 7, and the instruction to elaborate the declaration of n has been eliminated.

□

7.2   A code generation algorithm

A code specification does more than specify a translation from the source language to object code. It also suggests an algorithm for performing this translation. This algorithm traverses the decorated AST representing the source program, emitting target-machine instructions one by one. Both the order of traversal and the instructions to be emitted are determined straightforwardly by the code templates.

In this section we see how to develop a code generator from a code specification. We illustrate this with the Mini-Triangle code specification of Example 7.2.

7.2.1   Representation of the object program

Since its basic function is to generate an object program consisting of target-machine instructions, the code generator must obviously define representations of instructions and instruction sequences. This is easy, as the following example illustrates.

Example 7.7   Representing TAM instructions

A code generator that generates TAM object code must represent TAM instructions and their fields (see Section C.2):

```
public class Instruction {
    public byte    op;        // op-code (0 .. 15)
    public byte    r;         // register field (0 .. 15)
    public byte    n;         // length field (0 .. 255)
    public short   d;         // operand field (−32767 .. +32767)

    public static final byte    // op-codes (Table C.2)
            LOADop  =  0,  LOADAop =  1,
            LOADIop =  2,  LOADLop =  3,
            STOREop =  4,  STOREIop = 5,
```

```
            CALLop    =  6,   CALLIop   =  7,
            RETURNop  =  8,
            PUSHop    = 10,   POPop     = 11,
            JUMPop    = 12,   JUMPIop   = 13,
            JUMPIFop  = 14,   HALTop    = 15;
    public static final byte   // register numbers (Table C.1)
            CBr =   0,   CTr =   1,   PBr =   2,   PTr =   3,
            SBr =   4,   STr =   5,   HBr =   6,   HTr =   7,
            LBr =   8,   L1r =   9,   L2r =  10,   L3r =  11,
            L4r =  12,   L5r =  13,   L6r =  14,   CPr =  15;

    public Instruction (byte op, byte r, byte n,
                    short d)
    { ... }

}
```

Now the object program can be represented as follows:

```
private Instruction[] code = new Instruction[1024];
private short nextInstrAddr = 0;     // address of next instruction
                                     // to be stored in code
```

The code generator will append instructions in the correct order by successive calls to the following method:

```
private void emit (byte op, byte n, byte r, short d) {
    // Append an instruction with fields op, n, r, d to the object program.
    code[nextInstrAddr++] =
        new Instruction(op, n, r, d);
}
```

□

7.2.2   Systematic development of a code generator

A code specification determines the action of a code generator. The code generator will consist of a set of *encoding methods*, which cooperate to traverse the decorated AST representing the source program. There will be one encoding method for each ordinary code template, and its task will be to emit object code according to that code template.

In Section 5.3.2 we showed how to design a contextual analyzer as a visitor object. This consisted of a set of visitor methods, visit$A$, one for each concrete subclass A of AST. These visitor methods performed tasks appropriate to contextual analysis (identification and type checking).

Here we will show how to design a code generator likewise as a visitor object. In this case the visitor methods visit$A$ will perform tasks appropriate to code generation.

Many of these visitor methods will simply be encoding methods. For example, the visitor/encoding methods for commands will be `visitAssignCommand`, `visit-CallCommand`, etc., and their implementations will be determined by the code templates for '*execute* $[\![V := E]\!]$', '*execute* $[\![I (E)]\!]$', etc.

Table 7.2 Summary of visitor/encoding methods for the Mini-Triangle code generator.

Phrase class	Visitor/encoding method	Behavior of visitor/encoding method
Program	`visitProgram`	Generate code as specified by '*run P*'.
Command	`visit...Command`	Generate code as specified by '*execute C*'.
Expression	`visit...Expression`	Generate code as specified by '*evaluate E*'.
V-name	`visit...Vname`	Return an entity description for the given value-or-variable-name (explained in Section 7.3.)
Declaration	`visit...Declaration`	Generate code as specified by '*elaborate D*'.
Type-denoter	`visit...TypeDenoter`	Return the size of the given type.

Example 7.8   Mini-Triangle-to-TAM code generator

Let us design a code generator that translates Mini-Triangle to TAM object code. We shall assume the code specification of Example 7.2, and the definition of `AST` and its subclasses in Example 4.19.

The code generator will include visitor/encoding methods for commands, expressions, and declarations:

```
public Object visit...Command
                (...Command com, Object arg);
     // Generate code as specified by 'execute com'.

public Object visit...Expression
                (...Expression expr, Object arg);
     // Generate code as specified by 'evaluate expr'.

public Object visit...Declaration
                (...Declaration decl, Object arg);
     // Generate code as specified by 'elaborate decl'.
```

There will be one visitor/encoding method for each form of command (`visit-AssignmentCommand`, `visitIfCommand`, `visitWhileCommand`, etc.). Each such method will have an argument `com` of the appropriate concrete subclass of `Command` (`AssignmentCommand`, `IfCommand`, `WhileCommand`, etc.). Each such method will also have an `Object` argument and an `Object` result, but for the moment these will not actually be needed.

Likewise there will be one visitor/encoding method for each form of expression, and one visitor/encoding method for each form of declaration.

Value-or-variable-names cannot be mapped so simply on to the visitor pattern. There are two code functions for value-or-variable-names, *fetch* and *assign*, each with its own code template. So we need distinct visitor and encoding methods. The encoding methods will be:

```
private void encodeFetch (Vname vname);
    // Generate code as specified by 'fetch vname'.

private void encodeAssign (Vname vname);
    // Generate code as specified by 'assign vname'.
```

Each of these encoding methods will call the visitor method (visit...Vname) to find out information about the run-time representation of vname. However, they will use this information differently: one to generate a LOAD instruction, the other to generate a STORE instruction.

There is a single encoding method for a program, visitProgram, that will generate code for the entire program:

```
public Object visitProgram (Program prog, Object arg);
    // Generate code as specified by 'run prog'.
```

The visitor/encoding methods of the Mini-Triangle code generator are summarized in Table 7.2.

Now that we have designed the code generator, let us implement some of the encoding methods. The following method generates code for a complete program, using code template (7.7):

```
public Object visitProgram                    run [[C]] =
            (Program prog,
             Object arg) {
    prog.C.visit(this, arg);                  execute C
    emit(Instruction.HALTop, 0, 0, 0);        HALT
}
```

(For ease of comparison, we show each code template alongside the corresponding code generator steps.)

Now let us implement the visitor/encoding methods for commands. Each such method translates one form of command to object code, according to the corresponding code template (7.8a–f):

```
public Object visitAssignCommand              execute [[V := E]] =
            (AssignCommand com,
             Object arg) {
```

```
        com.E.visit(this, arg);                    evaluate E
        encodeAssign(com.V);                        assign V
        return null;
}

public Object visitCallCommand              execute [[I ( E ) ]] =
            (CallCommand com,
             Object arg) {
    com.E.visit(this, arg);                         evaluate E
    short p = address of primitive routine
                named com.I;
    emit(Instruction.CALLop,                        CALL p
        Instruction.SBr,
        Instruction.PBr, p);
    return null;
}

public Object visitSequentialCommand        execute [[C_1 ; C_2]] =
            (SequentialCommand com,
             Object arg) {
    com.C1.visit(this, arg);                        execute C_1
    com.C2.visit(this, arg);                        execute C_2
    return null;
}

public Object visitLetCommand               execute [[let D
            (LetCommand com,                               in C]] =
             Object arg) {
    com.D.visit(this, arg);                         elaborate D
    com.C.visit(this, arg);                         execute C
    short s = amount of storage allocated by D;
    if (s > 0)                                      if s > 0
        emit(Instruction.POPop, 0, 0, s);           POP(0) s
    return null;
}
```

The visitIfCommand and visitWhileCommand methods, omitted here, will be implemented in Example 7.9. The visitLetCommand method will be completed in Example 7.13.

In visitCallCommand, the address of a primitive routine I relative to PB is determined from information associated with the declaration of that routine. The various primitive routines and their addresses are given in Table C.3.

Now let us implement the visitor/encoding methods for expressions. Each such method translates one form of expression to object code, according to the corresponding code template (7.9a–d):

```
public Object visitIntegerExpression          evaluate ⟦IL⟧ =
            (IntegerExpression expr,
             Object arg) {
    short v = valuation(expr.IL.spelling);
    emit(Instruction.LOADLop, 0, 0, v);         LOADL v
    return null;
}

public Object visitVnameExpression            evaluate ⟦V⟧ =
            (VnameExpression expr,
             Object arg) {
    encodeFetch(expr.V);                        fetch V
    return null;
}

public Object visitUnaryExpression            evaluate ⟦O E⟧ =
            (UnaryExpression expr,
             Object arg) {
    expr.E.visit(this, arg);                    evaluate E
    short p = address of primitive routine
                named expr.O;
    emit(Instruction.CALLop,                    CALL p
         Instruction.SBr,
         Instruction.PBr, p);
    return null;
}

public Object visitBinaryExpression           evaluate ⟦E₁ O
            (BinaryExpression expr,                       E₂⟧ =
             Object arg) {
    expr.E1.visit(this, arg);                   evaluate E₁
    expr.E2.visit(this, arg);                   evaluate E₂
    short p = address of primitive routine
                named expr.O;
    emit(Instruction.CALLop,                    CALL p
         Instruction.SBr,
         Instruction.PBr, p);
    return null;
}
```

In `visitIntegerExpression`, we used the following auxiliary function:

```
private static short valuation (String intLit)
    // Return the value of the integer-literal spelled intLit.
```

The visitor/encoding methods for declarations, and the encoding methods `encode-Fetch` and `encodeAssign`, will be implemented in Example 7.13.

Finally, the code generator must define a method that initiates the AST traversal. The completed code generator becomes:

```
public final class Encoder implements Visitor {
    ... // Auxiliary methods, as above.
    ... // Visitor/encoding methods, as above.
    public void encode (Program prog) {
        prog.visit(this, null);
    }
}
```

□

Compare the code generator developed in Example 7.8 with the code specification of Example 7.2. For the most part, it is easy to see how the code generator was developed:

- For each AST concrete subclass *A* there is an encoding method, visit*A*. This method has an argument that represents a phrase of class *A*. The implementation of visit*A* is developed from the corresponding code template.

- Wherever a code template applies a code function to a subphrase, visit is applied to that subphrase to generate the corresponding object code. Where the subphrase is a value-or-variable-name, however, the auxiliary method encodeFetch or encodeAssign is applied to the subphrase.

- Wherever a code template contains a target machine instruction, the auxiliary method emit is called to append that instruction to the object program.

The encoding methods developed in this way cooperate to traverse the AST, generating the object program one instruction at a time.

In a code template, the order of the object code most commonly follows the order of the subphrases. But sometimes the order is different, as in code templates (7.8a) and (7.8e). This causes no difficulty to our code generator: it simply traverses the AST in the order specified by the code templates.[3]

A special-case code template does not turn into a distinct encoding method. Instead, it influences the behavior of the encoding method that deals with the more general case. For example, the special-case code templates (7.16) and (7.17) influence the behavior of the encoding methods encodeFetch and visitConstDeclaration, as we shall see in Example 7.13.

Now we have outlined a code generator, but a number of particular problems require particular solutions. The following subsection deals with the problem of generating code

---

[3] On the other hand, out-of-order code generation cannot easily be achieved by a one-pass compiler, since such a compiler generates object code 'on the fly' as it parses the source program.

for control structures. Thereafter Sections 7.3 and 7.4 deal with the problems of generating code for declared constants and variables, procedures, functions, and parameters.

7.2.3 Control structures

The code generator appends one instruction at a time to the object program. It can easily determine the address of each instruction, simply by counting the instructions as they are generated.

Source-language control structures, such as if-commands and while-commands, are implemented using unconditional and conditional jump instructions. The *destination address* (i.e., the address of the instruction to which the jump is directed) is the operand field of the jump instruction. A *backward* jump causes no problem, because the jump instruction is generated *after* the instruction at the destination address, so the destination address is already known. But a *forward* jump is awkward, because the jump instruction must be generated *before* the instruction at the destination address, and the destination address cannot generally be predicted at the time the jump instruction is generated.

Fortunately, there is a simple solution to the problem of forward jumps, a technique known as ***backpatching***. When the code generator has to generate a forward jump, it generates an incomplete jump instruction, whose destination address is temporarily set to (say) zero. At the same time the code generator records the address of the jump instruction in a local variable. Later, when the destination address becomes known, the code generator goes back and patches it into the jump instruction.[4]

The following example illustrates the method. Recall that the code generator maintains a variable, `nextInstrAddr`, that contains the address of the next instruction to be generated, and is incremented whenever an instruction is appended to the object program. (See Example 7.7.)

Example 7.9 Backpatching

Recall code template (7.8e):

$$execute \; [\![\text{while } E \text{ do } C]\!] \; =$$
```
        JUMP  h
    g:  execute C
    h:  evaluate E
        JUMPIF(1)  g
```

Here g stands for the address of the first instruction of the object code '*execute C*', and h stands for the address of the first instruction of the object code '*evaluate E*'. Let us see how `visitWhileCommand` should implement this code template.

---

[4] A similar solution to a similar problem is also used in one-pass assemblers.

The backward jump instruction 'JUMPIF(1) *g*' is easily generated as follows. Immediately before code is generated for '*execute C*', the next instruction address is saved in a variable, say g, local to visitWhileCommand. When the backward jump instruction is later generated, the address in g is used as its destination address.

When the forward jump instruction 'JUMP *h*' is to be generated, on the other hand, its destination address is not yet known. Instead, an incomplete JUMP instruction is generated, with a zero address field. The address of this incomplete instruction is saved in another local variable, say j. Later, just before code is generated for '*evaluate E*', the next instruction address is noted, and patched into the instruction at address j.

For instance, in Example 7.3 we saw the translation of 'while i > 0 do i := i - 2'. Here we show in detail how visitWhileCommand generates this object code:

(1)   It saves the next instruction address (say 30) in j.

(2)   It generates a JUMP instruction with a zero address field:

        30:   JUMP   0

(3)   It saves the next instruction address (namely 31) in g.

(4)   It translates the subcommand 'i := i - 2' to object code:

        31:   LOAD   *i*
        32:   LOADL   2
        33:   CALL   *sub*
        34:   STORE   *i*

(5)   It takes the next instruction address (namely 35), and patches it into the address field of the instruction whose address was saved in j (namely 30):

        30:   JUMP   **35**

(6)   It translates the expression 'i > 0' to object code:

        35:   LOAD   *i*
        36:   LOADL   0
        37:   CALL   *gt*

(7)   It generates a JUMPIF instruction whose address field contains the address that was saved in g (namely 31):

        38:   JUMPIF(1) 31

The following encoding methods illustrate how backpatching is implemented:

```
public Object visitWhileCommand (          execute ⟦while E
            (WhileCommand com,                      do C⟧ =
                Object arg) {
    short j = nextInstrAddr;                    j:
    emit(Instruction.JUMPop, 0,                 JUMP h
        Instruction.CBr, 0);
```

```
        short g = nextInstrAddr;              g:
        com.C.visit(this, arg);               execute C
        short h = nextInstrAddr;              h:
        patch(j, h);
        com.E.visit(this, arg);               evaluate E
        emit(Instruction.JUMPIFop, 1,         JUMPIF(1) g
                Instruction.CBr, g);
        return null;
    }

    public Object visitIfCommand             execute ⟦if E
                    (IfCommand com,                 then C₁
                    Object arg) {                   else C₂⟧ =
        com.E.visit(this, arg);              evaluate E
        short i = nextInstrAddr;              i:
        emit(Instruction.JUMPIFop, 0,         JUMPIF(0) g
                Instruction.CBr, 0);
        com.C1.visit(this, arg);              execute C₁
        short j = nextInstrAddr;              j:
        emit(Instruction.JUMPop, 0,           JUMP h
                Instruction.CBr, 0);
        short g = nextInstrAddr;              g:
        patch(i, g);
        com.C2.visit(this, arg);              execute C₂
        short h = nextInstrAddr;              h:
        patch(j, nextInstrAddr);
        return null;
    }
```

Here we have used the following auxiliary method for patching instructions:

```
    private void patch (short addr, short d) {
        // Store d in the operand field of the instruction at address addr.
        code[addr].d = d;
    }
```

☐

7.3 Constants and variables

In a source program, the role of each declaration is to bind an identifier I to some **entity**, such as a value, variable, or procedure. Within the scope of its declaration, there may be many applied occurrences of I in expressions, commands, and so on. Each applied occurrence of I denotes the entity to which I was bound.

In an object program, each entity will have a suitable representation, which is decided by the code generator. Identifiers will not themselves occur in the object program. Instead, the code generator translates each applied occurrence of an identifier to (the representation of) the corresponding entity.

How the code generator handles identifiers and declarations is the topic of this section and Section 7.4. Here we concentrate on declarations and applied occurrences of constants and variables, and the closely related topic of storage allocation. In Section 7.4 we go on to consider procedures, functions, and parameters.

7.3.1   Constant and variable declarations

A constant declaration binds an identifier to an ordinary value (such as a truth-value, integer, or record). We studied the representation of values of various types in Section 6.1.

A variable declaration allocates a variable and binds an identifier to it. A variable will be represented by one or more consecutive storage cells, based at a particular data address.

The code generator, when it visits a constant or variable declaration, must decide how to represent the declared entity (as a value or address). It should create an ***entity description***, containing details of how the declared entity will be represented, and bind the identifier to that entity description for future reference. The following example illustrates the idea, and also suggests a simple method by which the code generator can represent the binding of identifiers to entity descriptions.

Example 7.10 Accessing a known value and known address

Consider the following Mini-Triangle command:

```
let
    const b ~ 10;
    var i: Integer
in
    i := i * b
```

Figure 7.1(a) shows the decorated AST representing this command. The sub-AST (1) represents the declaration of b, and the applied occurrence of b at (5) has been linked to (1). The sub-AST (2) represents the declaration of i, and the applied occurrences of i at (3) and (4) have been linked to (2).

The constant declaration binds the identifier b to the integer value 10. The variable declaration binds the identifier i to a newly allocated integer variable, whose address must be decided by the code generator. To be concrete, let us suppose that this address is 4 (relative to SB).

Each applied occurrence of b should be translated to the value 10 (more precisely, to the target-machine representation of 10), and each applied occurrence of i should be translated to the address 4. So the subcommand 'i := i * b' should be translated to the following object code:

```
LOAD   4[SB]   – fetch from the address bound to i
LOADL 10       – fetch the value bound to b
CALL   mult    – multiply
STORE 4[SB]   – store to the address bound to i
```

Now let us see how this treatment of identifiers can be achieved. The code generator first visits the declarations. It creates an entity description for the known value 10, and attaches that entity description to the declaration of b at (1). It creates an entity description for the known address 4, and attaches that entity description to the declaration of i at (2). Figure 7.1(b) shows the AST at this point.

Thereafter, when the code generator encounters an applied occurrence of b, it follows the link to the declaration (1). From the entity description attached to (1) it determines that b denotes the known value 10. Likewise, when the code generator encounters an applied occurrence of i, it follows the link to the declaration (2). From the entity description attached to (2) it determines that i denotes the known address 4.

□

Example 7.11 Accessing an unknown value

Consider the following Mini-Triangle command:

```
let var x: Integer
in
    let const y ~ 365 + x
    in
        putint(y)
```

Figure 7.2 shows the decorated AST representing this command. The applied occurrences of x and y at (3) and (4) have been linked to the corresponding declarations at (1) and (2), respectively.

The variable declaration binds the identifier x to a newly allocated integer variable. To be concrete, let us suppose that its address is 5 (relative to SB).

The constant declaration binds the identifier y to an integer value that is *unknown* at compile-time. So the code generator cannot simply translate an applied occurrence of y to the value that it denotes. (Contrast the constant declaration of Example 7.10.)

Fortunately, there is a simple solution to this problem. The code generator translates the constant declaration to object code that evaluates the unknown value and stores it *at a known address*. Suppose that the value of y is to be stored at address 6 (relative to SB). Then the applied occurrence of y in 'putint(y)' should be translated to an instruction to fetch the value contained at address 6:

(a) Decorated AST:

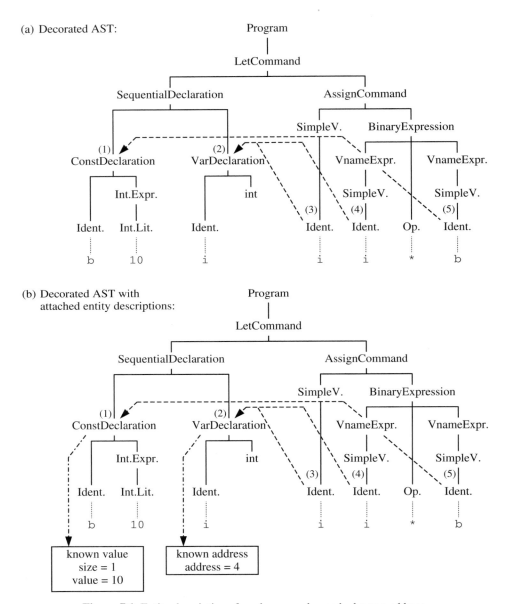

(b) Decorated AST with attached entity descriptions:

Figure 7.1 Entity descriptions for a known value and a known address.

```
LOAD   6[SB]      – fetch the value bound to y
CALL   putint     – write it
```

The code generator first visits the declarations. It creates an entity description for the known address 5, and attaches that entity description to the declaration of x at (1). It creates an entity description for an unknown value at address 6, and attaches that entity description to the declaration of y at (2). These entity descriptions are shown in Figure 7.2.

Thereafter, whenever the code generator encounters an applied occurrence of y, it follows the link to the declaration (2). From the entity description attached to (2) it determines that y denotes the unknown value contained at address 6.

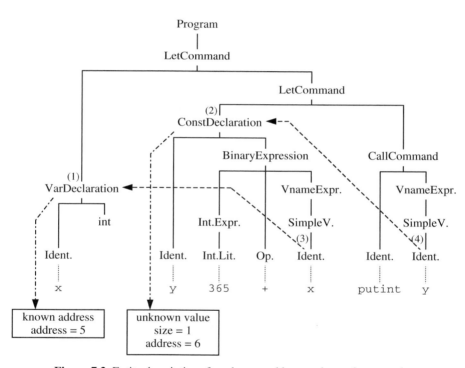

Figure 7.2 Entity descriptions for a known address and an unknown value.

In summary, the code generator handles declarations and applied occurrences of identifiers as follows:

• When it encounters a declaration of identifier *I*, the code generator binds *I* to a newly created entity description. This entity description contains details of the entity bound to *I*.

- When it encounters an applied occurrence of identifier *I*, the code generator consults the entity description bound to *I*, and translates the applied occurrence of *I* to the described entity.

If the source program is represented by a decorated AST, there is a particularly simple way to bind an identifier *I* to an entity description: simply attach the entity description to the sub-AST that represents the declaration of *I*. Every applied occurrence of *I* has already been linked to the corresponding declaration of *I*. So, whenever the code generator encounters an applied occurrence of *I*, it follows the link to the declaration of *I*, and there it finds the attached entity description.

In declarations, identifiers may be bound to entities such as *values* and *addresses*. Each entity may be either *known* or *unknown* (at compile-time). All combinations are possible, and all actually occur in some languages:

- **Known value:** This describes a value bound in a constant declaration whose right side is a literal.

- **Unknown value:** This describes a value bound in a constant declaration whose right side must be evaluated at run-time, or an argument value bound to a constant parameter.

- **Known address:** This describes an address allocated and bound in a variable declaration.

- **Unknown address:** This describes an argument address bound to a variable parameter.

(Constant and variable parameters will be discussed in Section 7.4.3.)

We can systematically deal with both known and unknown entities by the techniques illustrated in Examples 7.10 and 7.11. In general:

- If an identifier *I* is bound to a *known* entity, the code generator creates an entity description containing that known entity, and attaches that entity description to the declaration of *I*. It translates each applied occurrence of *I* to that known entity.

- If an identifier *I* is bound to an *unknown* entity, the code generator generates code to evaluate the unknown entity and store it at a known address, creates an entity description containing that known address, and attaches that entity description to the declaration of *I*. At each applied occurrence of *I*, the code generator generates code to fetch the unknown entity from the known address.

An important task for the code generator is to allocate addresses for variables (and unknown values). We study this topic in the following subsections. We shall take advantage of the constant-size requirement explained in Section 6.1: given the type of a variable, the code generator knows exactly how much storage must be allocated for it.

7.3.2 Static storage allocation

Consider a source language with only global variables. As explained in Section 6.3, static storage allocation is appropriate for such a language. The code generator can determine the exact address of every variable in the source program.

Example 7.12 Addressing global variables

Consider the following Mini-Triangle program:

```
let
    var a: Integer;
    var b: Boolean;
    var c: Integer;
    var d: Integer
in
    begin
    ...
    end
```

If the target machine is TAM, each variable of type `Boolean` or `Integer` will occupy one word. If instead the target machine is the x86, each variable of type `Boolean` will occupy one byte, and each variable of type `Integer` will occupy one half-word (= 2 bytes). The following table summarizes the allocated addresses in each case:

Variable	TAM address (words)	x86 address (bytes)
a	0	0
b	1	2
c	2	3
d	3	5

Now consider the following Mini-Triangle program with nested blocks:

```
let var a: Integer
in
    begin
    ...;
    let var b: Boolean;
        var c: Integer
    in
        begin ... end;
    ...;
    let var d: Integer
    in
        begin ... end;
    ...
    end
```

Now the variables b and c can safely occupy the same storage as the variable d, since they can never coexist. The following table summarizes the allocated addresses when the target machine is TAM or the x86:

Variable	TAM address (words)	x86 address (bytes)
a	0	0
b	1	2
c	2	3
d	1	2

The code generator must keep track of how much storage has been allocated at each point in the source program. We can arrange this by using the additional Object argument of each visitor/encoding method to indicate how much storage is already in use. Since elaborating a declaration may allocate extra storage, we use the Object result of a declaration's visitor/encoding method to pass back the amount of extra storage it has allocated. We also use the Object result of an expression's visitor/encoding method to pass back the size of the expression's result. In both cases, the result will be of class Short.

Example 7.13 Static storage allocation in the Mini-Triangle code generator

We define entity descriptions as follows:

```
public abstract class RuntimeEntity {
    public short size;
    ...
}

public class KnownValue extends RuntimeEntity {
    public short value;    // the known value itself
    ...
}

public class UnknownValue extends RuntimeEntity {
    public short address;  // the address where the
                           //  unknown value is stored
    ...
}

public class KnownAddress extends RuntimeEntity {
    public short address;  // the known address itself
    ...
}
```

Each of these classes should be equipped with a suitable constructor.

In addition, to each nonterminal node of the AST we add a field `entity`, which is initially **null** but can later be updated to point to an entity description:

```
public abstract class AST {
    ...
    public RuntimeEntity
            entity;   // used in declaration nodes,  mainly
}
```

In the Mini-Triangle code generator, we enhance the visitor/encoding methods as follows:

```
public Object visit...Command
                (...Command com, Object arg) {
    short gs = shortValueOf(arg);
    ...       // Generate code as specified by 'execute com'.
              // gs is the amount of global storage already in use.
    return null;
}

public Object visit...Expression
                (...Expression expr, Object arg) {
    short gs = shortValueOf(arg);
    ...       // Generate code as specified by 'evaluate expr'.
              // gs is the amount of global storage already in use.
    return new Short(size of expr's result) ;
}

public Object visit...Declaration
                (...Declaration decl, Object arg) {
    short gs = shortValueOf(arg);
    ...       // Generate code as specified by 'elaborate decl'.
              // gs is the amount of global storage already in use.
    return new Short(amount of extra storage allocated by decl) ;
}
```

Here and elsewhere, the following auxiliary method proves useful:

```
private static short shortValueOf (Object obj) {
    return ((Short) obj).shortValue();
}
```

Recall the code templates for declarations (7.12a), (7.17), (7.15), and (7.12c):

elaborate [[const *I* ~ *E*]] =
    evaluate E

elaborate [[const *I* ~ *IL*]] =   (special case)
                (i.e., no code)

$$\begin{aligned} &\textit{elaborate} \; [\![\text{var } I : T]\!] = \\ &\qquad \text{PUSH } s \qquad\qquad \textbf{where } s = \textit{size } T \end{aligned}$$

$$\begin{aligned} &\textit{elaborate} \; [\![D_1 \; ; \; D_2]\!] = \\ &\qquad \textit{elaborate } D_1 \\ &\qquad \textit{elaborate } D_2 \end{aligned}$$

These are implemented by the following visitor/encoding methods:

```
public Object visitConstDeclaration
               (ConstDeclaration decl,
                Object arg) {
   short gs = shortValueOf(arg);
   if (decl.E instanceof
       IntegerExpression) {
      IntegerLiteral IL =
        ((IntegerExpression) decl.E).IL;
      decl.entity = new KnownValue
           (1, valuation(IL.spelling));
      return new Short(0);
   } else {
      short s = shortValueOf(
           decl.E.visit(this, arg));
      decl.entity = new UnknownValue
           (s, gs);
      return new Short(s);
   }
}

public Object visitVarDeclaration
               (VarDeclaration decl,
                Object arg) {
   short gs = shortValueOf(arg);
   short s = shortValueOf(decl.T.visit
        (this, null));
   emit(Instruction.PUSHop, 0, 0, s);
   decl.entity = new KnownAddress
        (1, gs);
   return new Short(s);
}

public Object visitSequentialDeclaration
            (SequentialDeclaration decl,
             Object arg) {
   short gs = shortValueOf(arg);
   short s1 = shortValueOf(
        decl.D1.visit(this, arg));
```

elaborate $[\![$const
$I \sim IL]\!] =$
(no code)

elaborate $[\![$const
$I \sim E]\!] =$
evaluate E

elaborate $[\![$var
$I : T]\!] =$

$s = \textit{size } T$
PUSH s

elaborate $[\![D_1 ;$
$D_2]\!] =$

elaborate D_1

```
    short s2 = shortValueOf(
            decl.D2.visit(this,                          elaborate D₂
                new Short (gs + s1)));
    return new Short(s1 + s2);
}
```

The statement 'decl.entity = **new** KnownAddress(...);' creates an entity description for a known address and attaches it to the declaration node in the AST. Entity descriptions for known and unknown values are created and attached to the AST in an analogous way.

Recall the code template for a let-command (7.8f):

$execute$ [[let D in C]] =
    $elaborate$ D
    $execute$ C
    POP(0) s if $s > 0$
                           where s = amount of storage allocated by D

The corresponding visitor/encoding method in Example 7.8 omitted one important detail: how does it determine the amount of storage allocated by D? We can now see that this information is supplied by the visitor/encoding method for a declaration:

```
public Object visitLetCommand                    execute [[let D
                (LetCommand com,                          in C]] =
                Object arg) {
    short gs = shortValueOf(arg);
    short s = shortValueOf(
            com.D.visit(this, arg));                 elaborate D
    com.C.visit(this, new Short (gs + s));       execute C
    if (s > 0)                                        if s > 0
        emit(Instruction.POPop, 0, 0, s);            POP(0) s
    return null;
}
```

Now recall the code templates for value-or-variable-names, namely (7.14), (7.16), and (7.13):

$assign$ [[I]] =
    STORE(s) d[SB]   where s = $size$(type of I),
                              d = address bound to I (relative to SB)

$fetch$ [[I]] =   (special case)
    LOADL v where v = value bound to I (if known)

$fetch$ [[I]] =
    LOAD(s) d[SB]   where s = $size$(type of I),
                              d = address bound to I (relative to SB)

These are implemented by the following encoding methods:

```
private void encodeAssign (Vname vname, short s) {
    RuntimeEntity entity =
            (RuntimeEntity) vname.visit(this, null);
    short d = ((KnownAddress) entity).address;
    emit(Instruction.STOREop, s, Instruction.SBr, d);
}

private void encodeFetch (Vname vname, short s) {
    RuntimeEntity entity =
            (RuntimeEntity) vname.visit(this, null);
    if (entity instanceof KnownValue) {
        short v = ((KnownValue) entity).value
        emit(Instruction.LOADLop, 0, 0, v);
    } else {
        short d = (entity instanceof UnknownValue) ?
                ((UnknownValue) entity).address :
                ((KnownAddress) entity).address;
        emit(Instruction.LOADop, s, Instruction.SBr, d);
    }
}
```

In encodeAssign we can safely assume that entity is an instance of Known-Address. (The contextual analyzer will already have checked that *I* is a variable identifier.) In encodeFetch, however, entity could be an instance of KnownValue, UnknownValue, or KnownAddress.

Both encodeFetch and encodeAssign visit vname. The corresponding visitor method simply returns the corresponding entity description:

```
public Object visitSimpleVname
                    (SimpleVname vname, Object arg) {
    return vname.I.decl.entity;
}
```

(Recall that the contextual analyzer has linked each applied occurrence of identifier *I* to the corresponding declaration of *I*. The field decl represents this link. Therefore, I.decl.entity points to the entity description bound to *I*.)

Finally, method encode starts off code generation with no storage allocated:

```
public void encode (Program prog) {
    prog.visit(this, new Short(0));
}
```

7.3.3 Stack storage allocation

Consider now a source language with procedures and local variables. As explained in Section 6.4, stack storage allocation is appropriate for such a language. The code generator cannot predict a local variable's absolute address, but it can predict the variable's address displacement relative to the base of a frame – a frame belonging to the procedure within which the variable was declared. At run-time, a display register will point to the base of that frame, and the variable can be addressed relative to that register. The appropriate register is determined entirely by a pair of routine levels known to the code generator: the routine level of the variable's declaration, and the routine level of the code that is addressing the variable. (See Section 6.4.2 for details.)

To make the code generator implement stack storage allocation, we must modify the form of addresses in entity descriptions. The address of a variable will now be held as a pair (l, d), where l is the routine level of the variable's declaration, and d is the variable's address displacement relative to its frame base. As in Section 6.4.2, we assign a routine level of 0 to the main program, a routine level of 1 to the body of each procedure or function declared at level 0, a routine level of 2 to the body of each procedure or function declared at level 1, and so on.

Example 7.14 Storage allocation for global and local variables

Recall the Triangle program of Figure 6.14. The same program is outlined in Figure 7.3, with each procedure body shaded to indicate its routine level.

Entity descriptions are shown attached to the variable declarations in the source program. (This is for clarity. In reality, of course, the entity descriptions would be attached to the sub-ASTs that represent these declarations, as in Figures 7.1 and 7.2.)

The addresses of the global variables $g1$ and $g2$ are shown as $(0, 0)$ and $(0, 1)$, meaning displacements of 0 and 1, respectively, relative to the base of the level-0 frame (i.e., the globals).

The addresses of the local variables $p1$ and $p2$ are shown as $(1, 3)$ and $(1, 4)$, meaning displacements of 3 and 4, respectively, relative to the base of a level-1 frame. The address of the local variable q is shown as $(2, 3)$, meaning a displacement of 3 relative to the base of a level-2 frame. And so on.

Notice that the address displacements of local variables start at 3. The reason is that the first three words of a frame contain link data, as shown in Figure 6.16.

□

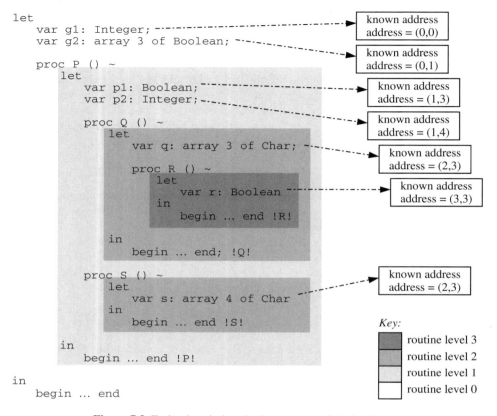

Figure 7.3 Entity descriptions in the presence of stack allocation.

The code templates (7.13) and (7.14) assumed static storage allocation. They must be modified to take account of stack storage allocation.

Example 7.15 Code templates for global and local variables

Although Mini-Triangle has no procedures, let us anticipate their introduction – just in order to study the code generator's treatment of local variables.

The code templates for *fetch* (7.13) and *assign* (7.14) would be generalized as follows:

fetch $[\![I]\!]$ =   (7.18)

       LOAD(s) $d[r]$ where $s = size$(type of I),

                               (l, d) = address bound to I,

                               cl = current routine level,

                               $r = display\text{-}register(cl, l)$

assign $[\![I]\!]$ =   (7.19)
      STORE (s) $d[r]$ where $s = size$(type of I),
                            (l, d) = address bound to I,
                            cl = current routine level,
                            $r = display\text{-}register(cl, l)$

The current routine level, cl, is the routine level of the code that is addressing the variable.

The auxiliary function $display\text{-}register(cl, l)$ selects the display register that will enable code at routine level cl to address a variable declared at routine level l:

$$display\text{-}register(cl, l) \;=\; \begin{cases} \text{SB} & \text{if } l = 0 & (7.20\text{a}) \\ \text{LB} & \text{if } l > 0 \text{ and } cl = l & (7.20\text{b}) \\ \text{L1} & \text{if } l > 0 \text{ and } cl = l + 1 & (7.20\text{c}) \\ \text{L2} & \text{if } l > 0 \text{ and } cl = l + 2 & (7.20\text{d}) \\ \ldots \end{cases}$$

Note that the special-case code template (7.16) is unaffected.

In order to implement (7.18) and (7.19), the code generator must know the routine level of each command, expression, and so on. Previously, all variables were allocated at level 0, and the argument passed to each encoding method was simply the size of the global frame. Now the argument must include both the level and the size of the current frame. For this purpose let us introduce a `Frame` class with appropriate instance variables:

```
public class Frame {
    public byte   level;
    public short size;
    ...
}
```

Example 7.16 Stack storage allocation in the Mini-Triangle code generator

We generalize entity descriptions as follows:

```
public abstract class RuntimeEntity {
    public short size;
    ...
}

public class KnownValue extends RuntimeEntity {
    public short value;                    //  the known value itself
    ...
}
```

```java
public class UnknownValue extends RuntimeEntity {
    public EntityAddress address;      // the address where the
    ...                                // unknown value is stored
}

public class KnownAddress extends RuntimeEntity {
    public EntityAddress address;      // the known address itself
    ...
}

public class EntityAddress {
    public byte  level;
    public short displacement;
    ...
}
```

In the Mini-Triangle code generator, we enhance the visitor/encoding methods as follows:

```java
public Object visit...Command
                (...Command com, Object arg) {
    Frame frame = (Frame) arg;
    ...       // Generate code as specified by 'execute com'.
              // frame.level is the routine level of com.
              // frame.size is the amount of frame storage already in use.
    return null;
}

public Object visit...Expression
                (...Expression expr, Object arg) {
    Frame frame = (Frame) arg;
    ...       // Generate code as specified by 'evaluate expr'.
              // frame.level is the routine level of expr.
              // frame.size is the amount of frame storage already in use.
    return new Short(size of expr's result);
}

public Object visit...Declaration
                (...Declaration decl, Object arg) {
    Frame frame = (Frame) arg;
    ...       // Generate code as specified by 'elaborate decl'.
              // frame.level is the routine level of decl.
              // frame.size is the amount of frame storage already in use.
    return new Short(amount of extra storage allocated by decl);
}
```

We can provide encodeAssign and encodeFetch with explicit Frame arguments:

```
private void encodeAssign
            (Vname vname, Frame frame, short s) {
...     // Generate code as specified by 'assign vname'.
        // frame.level is the routine level of vname.
        // s is the size of the value to be assigned.
}

private void encodeFetch
            (Vname vname, Frame frame, short s) {
...     // Generate code as specified by 'fetch vname'.
        // frame.level is the routine level of vname.
        // s is the size of the value to be assigned.
}
```

The following method implements code template (7.19):

```
private void encodeAssign
            (Vname vname, Frame frame, short s) {
    RuntimeEntity entity =
        (RuntimeEntity) vname.visit(this, null);
    EntityAddress address =
      ((KnownAddress) entity).address;
    emit(Instruction.STOREop, s,
        displayRegister(frame.level, address.level),
        address.displacement);
}
```

The following method implements code templates (7.16) and (7.18):

```
private void encodeFetch (Vname vname,
                Frame frame, short s) {
    RuntimeEntity entity =
        (RuntimeEntity) vname.visit(this, null);
    if (entity instanceof KnownValue) {
      short v = ((KnownValue) entity).value;
      emit(Instruction.LOADLop, 0, 0, v);
    } else {
      EntityAddress address =
            (entity instanceof UnknownValue) ?
            ((UnknownValue) entity).address :
            ((KnownAddress) entity).address;
      emit(Instruction.LOADop, s,
            displayRegister(frame.level,
              address.level), address.displacement);
    }
}
```

The following auxiliary method `displayRegister` implements equations (7.20):

```
private byte displayRegister
                (byte currentLevel, byte entityLevel)
{ ... }
```

The following methods show how the entity descriptions are now set up:

```
public Object visitConstDeclaration
                (ConstDeclaration decl, Object arg) {
   Frame frame = (Frame) arg;
   if (decl.E instanceof IntegerExpression) {
      IntegerLiteral IL =
         ((IntegerExpression) decl.E).IL;
      decl.entity = new KnownValue
         (1, valuation(IL.spelling));
      return new Short(0);
   } else {
      short s =
         shortValueOf(decl.E.visit(this, frame));
      decl.entity = new UnknownValue
            (s, frame.level, frame.size);
      return new Short(s);
   }
}

public Object visitVarDeclaration
                (VarDeclaration decl, Object arg) {
   Frame frame = (Frame) arg;
   short s = shortValueOf(decl.T.visit(this, null));
   emit(Instruction.PUSHop, 0, 0, s);
   decl.entity = new KnownAddress
            (1, frame.level, frame.size);
   return new Short(s);
}
```

When the appropriate visitor/encoding method is called to translate a procedure body, the frame level must be incremented by one and the frame size set to 3, leaving just enough space for the link data:

```
Frame outerFrame = ...;
Frame localFrame = new Frame(outerFrame.level + 1, 3);
```

Finally, method encode starts off with a frame at level 0 and with no storage allocated:

```
public void encode (Program prog) {
   Frame globalFrame = new Frame(0, 0);
   prog.visit(this, globalFrame);
}
```

□

7.4 Procedures and functions

In this section we study how the code generator handles procedure and function declarations, procedure and function calls, and the association between actual and formal
parameters. We start by looking at global procedures and functions. Then we consider
nested procedures and functions. Finally we examine the implementation of parameter
mechanisms.

A procedure declaration binds an identifier to a procedure, and a function declaration
binds an identifier to a function. The run-time representation of a procedure or function
is a *routine*. At its simplest, a routine is just a sequence of instructions with a designated
entry address.

7.4.1 Global procedures and functions

Consider a programming language in which all procedures are declared globally. In the
implementation of such a language, a routine is completely characterized by its *entry
address* (i.e., the address of its first instruction). The routine is called by a call
instruction that designates the entry address. This instruction will pass control to the
routine, where control will remain until a return instruction is executed.

From the above, we see that the code generator should treat a procedure declaration
as follows. It should create an entity description for a known routine, containing the
routine's entry address, and bind that entity description to the procedure identifier. At an
applied occurrence of this identifier, in a procedure call, the code generator should
retrieve the corresponding routine's entry address, and generate a call instruction
designating that entry address.

Example 7.17 Code templates for Mini-Triangle plus global procedures

Consider again the language Mini-Triangle, for which code templates were given in
Example 7.2. Let us now extend Mini-Triangle with parameterless procedures. The
syntactic changes, for procedure declarations and procedure calls, are as follows:

Declaration	::=	...	
	|	**proc** Identifier ( ) ~ Command	(7.21)
Command	::=	...	
	|	Identifier ( )	(7.22)

We shall assume that all procedure declarations are global, not nested.

The code template specifying translation of a procedure declaration to TAM code
would be:

$$\textit{elaborate } [\![\text{proc } I \text{ ( ) } \sim C]\!] = \qquad\qquad (7.23)$$

```
        JUMP  g
  e:    execute C
        RETURN(0)  0
  g:
```

The generated routine body consists simply of the object code '*execute C*' followed by a RETURN instruction. The two zeros in the RETURN instruction indicate that the routine has no result and no arguments. Since we do not want the routine body to be executed at the point where the procedure is *declared*, only where the procedure is *called*, we must generate a jump round the routine body. The routine's entry address, *e*, must be bound to *I* for future reference.

The code template specifying translation of a procedure call would be:

$$\textit{execute } [\![I \text{ ( ) }]\!] = \qquad\qquad (7.24)$$

```
        CALL(SB)  e          where e = entry address of routine bound to I
```

This is straightforward. The net effect of executing this CALL instruction will be simply to execute the body of the routine bound to *I*.

□

Example 7.18 Object code for Mini-Triangle plus global procedures

The following extended Mini-Triangle program illustrates a procedure declaration and call:

```
let
    var n: Integer;
    proc p () ~
        n := n * 2
in
    begin
    n := 9;
    p()
    end
```

The corresponding object program illustrates code templates (7.23) and (7.24):

```
elaborate [[var n:
            Integer]]
                                                    0:  PUSH      1
                                                    1:  JUMP      7
                                                    2:  LOAD      0[SB]
elaborate [[proc p () ~    execute [[n := n*2]]     3:  LOADL     2
            n := n*2]]                              4:  CALL      mult
                                                    5:  STORE     0[SB]
                                                    6:  RETURN(0) 0
```

$$\textit{execute } [\![\text{begin n} := 9;\ \text{p() end}]\!] \left\{ \begin{array}{l} \textit{execute } [\![\text{n} := 9]\!] \left\{ \begin{array}{llll} 7: & \text{LOADL} & & 9 \\ 8: & \text{STORE} & & 0\,[\text{SB}] \end{array} \right. \\ \textit{execute } [\![\text{p()}]\!] \left\{ \begin{array}{llll} 9: & \text{CALL(SB)} & & 2 \\ 10: & \text{POP(0)} & & 1 \\ 11: & \text{HALT} & & \end{array} \right. \end{array} \right.$$

The corresponding decorated AST and entity descriptions are shown in Figure 7.4.

A function is translated in much the same way as a procedure. The only essential difference is in the code that returns the function result.

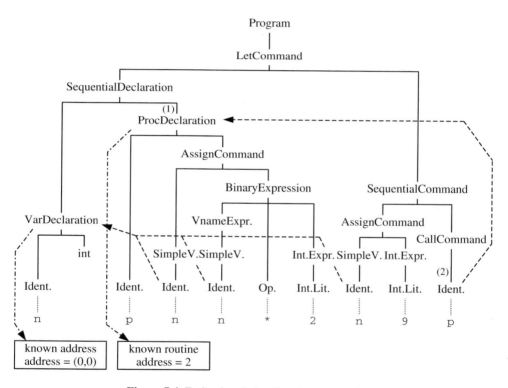

Figure 7.4 Entity description for a known routine.

Example 7.19 Code templates for Mini-Triangle plus global functions

Suppose that Mini-Triangle is to be extended with parameterless functions. The syntactic changes are as follows:

Declaration   ::=   ...

                    | **func** Identifier **( )** **:** Type-denoter ~ Expression   (7.25)

Expression   ::=   ...

                    | Identifier **( )**   (7.26)

As in Example 7.17, we shall assume that all function declarations are global.

The code template specifying translation of a function declaration to TAM code would be:

$$
\begin{aligned}
&elaborate \; [\![\texttt{func} \; I \; (\;) \; \texttt{:} \; T \sim E]\!] = \\
&\qquad \texttt{JUMP} \; g \\
&e\texttt{:} \quad evaluate \; E \\
&\qquad \texttt{RETURN}(s) \quad 0 \qquad \text{where } s = size \; T \\
&g\texttt{:}
\end{aligned}
\qquad (7.27)
$$

This RETURN instruction returns a result of size s, that result being the value of E. The function has no arguments, so the RETURN instruction removes 0 words of arguments from the stack.

The code template specifying translation of a function call to TAM code would be:

$$
\begin{aligned}
&evaluate \; [\![I \; (\;)]\!] = \\
&\qquad \texttt{CALL(SB)} \quad e \qquad \text{where } e = \text{entry address of routine bound to } I
\end{aligned}
\qquad (7.28)
$$

which is similar to (7.24).

$\square$

7.4.2   Nested procedures and functions

Now consider a source language that allows procedures and functions to be nested, and allows them to access nonlocal variables. In this case the implementation needs static links, as explained in Section 6.4.2. The call instruction (or instruction sequence) must designate not only the entry address of the called routine but also an appropriate static link.

Suppose that a procedure is represented by a routine R in the object code. R's entry address is known to the code generator, as we have already seen. The appropriate static link for a call to R will be the base address of a frame somewhere in the stack. This base address is not known to the code generator. But the code generator can determine which display register will contain that static link, at the time when R is called. The appropriate register is determined entirely by a pair of routine levels known to the code generator: the routine level of R's declaration and the routine level of the code that calls R.

The address of routine *R* must, therefore, be held as a pair (*l*, *e*), where *l* is the routine level of *R*'s declaration (with global routines at level 0), and *e* is *R*'s entry address.

Example 7.20 Nested procedures

The Triangle program outline of Figure 7.3 is reproduced in Figure 7.5, with entity descriptions shown attached to the procedure declarations.

The entity description for procedure P describes it as a known routine with address (0, 3), signifying that P was declared at level 0, and its entry address is 3. The entity description for procedure Q describes it as a known routine with address (1, 6), signifying that Q was declared at level 1, and its entry address is 6. And so on.

The code template (7.24) in Example 7.17 assumed global procedures only. It must be modified to take account of nested procedures.

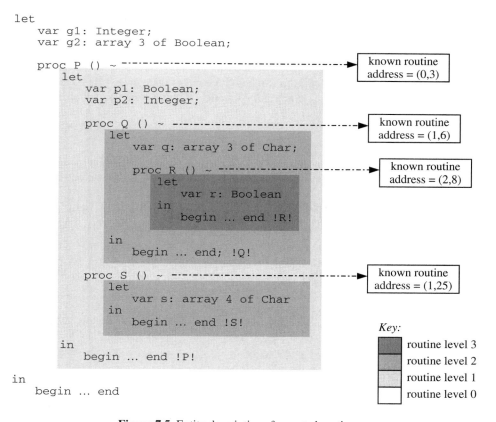

Figure 7.5 Entity descriptions for nested routines.

Example 7.21 Code templates for Mini-Triangle plus nested procedures

Consider again the language Mini-Triangle extended with parameterless procedures. The syntax is unchanged from Example 7.17, but now we shall allow nested procedure declarations.

The code template for a procedure declaration is unchanged:

$$
\textit{elaborate } [\![\mathrm{proc}\ I\ (\ )\ \sim\ C]\!] = \tag{7.29}
$$
```
          JUMP  g
    e:    execute C
          RETURN(0)  0
    g:
```

but now the entity description bound to I must include the address pair (l, e), where l is the current routine level, and e is the entry address.

The code template for a procedure call becomes:

$$
\textit{execute } [\![I\ (\ )\ ]\!] = \tag{7.30}
$$
```
          CALL(r)  e          where (l, e) = address of routine bound to I,
                                  cl = current routine level,
                                   r = display-register(cl, l)
```

The net effect of executing this CALL instruction will be to execute the command C that is the body of the procedure bound to I, using the content of register r as the static link. The latter is determined using the auxiliary function *display-register*, which is defined by equations (7.20).

□

Example 7.22 Code generation for Mini-Triangle plus nested procedures

Code template (7.29) would be implemented by the following new visitor/encoding method:

```
public Object visitProcDeclaration              elaborate [[proc I
            (ProcDeclaration decl,                      ( ) ~ C]] =
            Object arg) {
    Frame outerFrame = (Frame) arg;
    short j = nextInstrAddr;                    j:
    emit(Instruction.JUMPop, 0,                    JUMP g
        Instruction.CBr, 0);
    short e = nextInstrAddr;                    e:
    decl.entity = new KnownRoutine
        (2, outerFrame.level, e);
    Frame localFrame = new Frame
        (outerFrame.level + 1, 3);
    decl.C.visit(this, localFrame);             execute C
```

```
        emit(Instruction.RETURNop, 0, 0, 0);        RETURN(0)  0
        short g = nextInstrAddr;                     g:
        patch(j, g);
        return new Short(0);
    }
```

This assumes a new kind of entity description:

```
    public class KnownRoutine extends RuntimeEntity {
        public EntityAddress address;
        ...
    }
```

where `address.level` is the level of the routine and `address.displacement` is its entry address.

Code template (7.30) would be implemented by the following visitor/encoding method:

```
    public Object visitCallCommand          execute [[I ( )]] =
                  (CallCommand com,
                   Object arg) {
      Frame frame = (Frame) arg;
      EntityAddress address =
          ((KnownRoutine)
             com.I.decl.entity).address;
      emit(Instruction.CALLop,                CALL(r)  e
          displayRegister(
              frame.level,
              address.level),
          Instruction.CBr,
          address.displacement);
      return null;
    }
```

☐

7.4.3 Parameters

Now let us consider how the code generator implements parameter passing. Every source language has one or more ***parameter mechanisms***, the means by which arguments are associated with the corresponding formal parameters.

As explained in Section 6.5.1, a routine protocol is needed to ensure that the calling code deposits the arguments in a place where the called routine expects to find them. If the operating system does not impose a routine protocol, the language implementor must design one, taking account of the source language's parameter mechanisms and the target machine architecture.

The routine protocol adopted in TAM is for the calling code to deposit the arguments at the stack top immediately before the call. Thus the called routine can address its own arguments using negative displacements relative to its own frame base. The code generator can represent the address of each argument in the usual way by a pair (l, d), where l is the routine level of the routine's body and d is the negative displacement.

Example 7.23 Addressing parameters

Recall the Triangle program of Example 6.23, whose run-time behavior was shown in Figure 6.21. The same program is reproduced in Figure 7.6, with appropriate entity descriptions attached to the declarations and formal parameters.

The constant parameter i will be bound to an argument *value* whenever procedure S is called. Therefore its entity description is that of an unknown value, stored at address $(1, -1)$.

The variable parameter n, on the other hand, will be bound to an argument *address*. Therefore its entity description is that of an unknown address, which is itself stored at address $(1, -2)$. This entity description implies that each applied occurrence of n must be implemented by indirect addressing.

In TAM, indirect addressing is supported by the instructions LOADI (load indirect) and STOREI (store indirect). These were illustrated in Example 6.23.

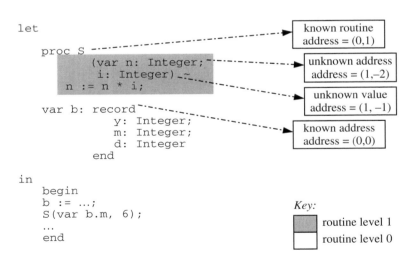

Figure 7.6 Entity descriptions for constant and variable parameters.

Now we have encountered all combinations of known and unknown values, and known and unknown addresses, in entity descriptions. We must therefore generalize our code templates for value-or-variable-names accordingly.

Example 7.24 Code templates for procedures with parameters

Consider Mini-Triangle extended with procedures, and constant and variable parameters. For simplicity we shall assume that each procedure has a single formal parameter. The syntactic changes, for procedure declarations and procedure calls, are as follows:

Declaration	::= ...		
	| **proc** Identifier (Formal-Parameter) ~ Command	(7.31)
Formal-Parameter	::= Identifier **:** Type-denoter	(7.32a)
	| **var** Identifier **:** Type-denoter	(7.32b)
Command	::= ...		
	| Identifier (Actual-Parameter)	(7.33)
Actual-Parameter	::= Expression	(7.34a)
	| **var** V-name	(7.34b)

Production rules (7.32a) and (7.34a) are concerned with constant parameters; production rules (7.32b) and (7.34b) are concerned with variable parameters.

The code template for a procedure declaration is now:

$$elaborate \; [\![\texttt{proc} \; I \; (\; FP \;) \; \sim \; C]\!] = \qquad\qquad\qquad (7.35)$$

```
        JUMP  g
   e:   execute C
        RETURN(0)  d        where d = size of formal parameter FP
   g:
```

Since the TAM routine protocol requires the *caller* to push the argument on to the stack, the routine body itself contains no code corresponding to the formal parameter *FP*.

The code template specifying translation of a procedure call to TAM code is now:

$$execute \; [\![I \; (\; AP \;) \;]\!] = \qquad\qquad\qquad\qquad\qquad (7.36)$$

```
        pass-argument AP
        CALL(r)  e          where (l, e) = address of routine bound to I,
                                  cl = current routine level,
                                  r = display-register(cl, l)
```

The code templates for actual parameters are:

$$pass\text{-}argument \; [\![E]\!] = \qquad\qquad\qquad\qquad\qquad (7.37a)$$
        evaluate E

$$pass\text{-}argument \; [\![\texttt{var} \; V]\!] = \qquad\qquad\qquad\qquad (7.37b)$$
        fetch-address V

Code template (7.37b) uses a new code function for value-or-variable-names:

$$fetch\text{-}address \; : \; \text{V-name} \; \rightarrow \; \text{Instruction*} \qquad\qquad (7.38)$$

where '*fetch-address V*' is code that will push the address of the variable *V* on to the stack top.

The code templates for value-or-variable-names are generalized as follows:

fetch $\llbracket I \rrbracket$ =   (7.39)

    (i)   if *I* is bound to a known value:

           LOADL *v*   where *v* = value bound to *I*

    (ii) if *I* is bound to an unknown value or known address:

           LOAD(*s*) *d*[*r*]   where *s* = *size*(type of *I*),

                                      (l, d) = address bound to *I*,

                                      cl = current routine level,

                                      r = *display-register*(*cl*, *l*)

    (iii) if *I* is bound to an unknown address:

           LOAD(1) *d*[*r*]

           LOADI(*s*)   where *s* = *size*(type of *I*),

                                          (l, d) = address bound to *I*,

                                      cl = current routine level,

                                      r = *display-register*(*cl*, *l*)

assign $\llbracket I \rrbracket$ =   (7.40)

    (i)   if *I* is bound to a known address:

           STORE(*s*) *d*[*r*]   where *s* = *size*(type of *I*),

                                        (l, d) = address bound to *I*,

                                      cl = current routine level,

                                      r = *display-register*(*cl*, *l*)

    (ii) if *I* is bound to an unknown address:

           LOAD(1) *d*[*r*]

           STOREI(*s*)   where *s* = *size*(type of *I*),

                                        (l, d) = address bound to *I*,

                                      cl = current routine level,

                                      r = *display-register*(*cl*, *l*)

fetch-address $\llbracket I \rrbracket$ =   (7.41)

    (i)   if *I* is bound to a known address:

           LOADA *d*[*r*]   where (l, d) = address bound to *I*,

                                        cl = current routine level,

                                      r = *display-register*(*cl*, *l*)

    (ii) if *I* is bound to an unknown address:

           LOAD(1) *d*[*r*]   where (l, d) = address bound to *I*,

                                        cl = current routine level,

                                      r = *display-register*(*cl*, *l*)

□

7.5   Case study: code generation in the Triangle compiler

The Triangle code generator consists of a package `Triangle.CodeGenerator` that contains the `Encoder`, and the classes for the various kinds of run-time entity. The `Encoder` class depends on the package `Triangle.AbstractSyntaxTrees`, which contains all of the class definitions for ASTs, and on the package `TAM`, which contains the definition of the Triangle abstract machine.

The Triangle code generator was designed and implemented using techniques similar to those described in this chapter. Some extensions were necessary to deal with particular features of Triangle. Here we briefly discuss some of these extensions.

7.5.1   Entity descriptions

The Triangle code generator deals with a wide variety of entities and entity descriptions, some of which we have not yet met. The following kinds of entity description are used:

- *Known value:* This describes a value bound in a constant declaration whose right side is a literal, e.g.:

```
const daysPerWeek ~ 7;
const currency    ~ '$'
```

- *Unknown value:* This describes a value bound in a constant declaration, if obtained by evaluating an expression at run-time, e.g.:[5]

```
const area ~ length * breadth;
const nul  ~ chr(0)
```

It also describes an argument value bound to a constant parameter, e.g., the value bound to n in:

```
func odd (n: Integer) : Boolean ~ ...
```

- *Known address:* This describes an address allocated and bound in a variable declaration. The code generator represents each address by a (level, displacement) pair, as described in Section 7.3.3.

- *Unknown address:* This describes an argument address bound to a variable parameter, e.g., the address bound to n in:

```
proc inc (var n: Integer) ~ ...
```

---

[5] In principle, `nul` in this example could be treated as bound to a known value. However, the code generator would have to be enhanced to evaluate the expression 'chr(0)' itself, using a technique called *constant folding*.

- *Known routine:* This describes a routine bound in a procedure or function declaration, e.g., the routines bound to `inc` and `odd` in the above examples.

- *Unknown routine:* This describes an argument routine bound to a procedural or functional parameter, e.g., the routine bound to `p` in:

```
proc filter (func p (x: Integer): Boolean;
             var l: IntegerList) ~ ...
```

- *Primitive routine:* This describes a primitive routine provided by the abstract machine. Primitive routines are bound in the standard environment to operators and identifiers, e.g., to '+', '<', `eof`, and `get`.

- *Equality routine:* This describes one of the primitive routines provided by the abstract machine for testing (in)equality of two values. Equality routines are generic, in that the values can be of any size. Equality routines are bound to the operators '=' and '\='.

- *Field:* This describes a field of a record type. Every record field has a known offset relative to the base of the record (see Section 6.1.2), and the field's entity description includes this offset.

- *Type representation:* This describes a type. Every type has a known size, which is constant for all values of the type (see Section 6.1), and the type's entity description includes that size.

7.5.2   Constants and variables

A value-or-variable-name in the Triangle program identifies a constant or variable. Either a constant or a variable may be used as an expression operand, but only a variable may be used on the left side of an assignment command. These two usages give rise to two different code functions on value-or-variable-names:

> *fetch*   : V-name → Instruction*
> *assign* : V-name → Instruction*

In the little language Mini-Triangle used as a running example in this chapter, a value-or-variable-name was just an identifier (declared in a constant or variable declaration). Accordingly, *fetch* was defined by a single code template (plus a special-case code template), and *assign* by a single code template.

More realistic programming languages have composite types, and operations to select components of composite values and variables. In Triangle, a record value-or-variable-name can be subjected to field selection, and an array value-or-variable-name can be indexed.

Example 7.25 Addressing composite variables

Consider the following Triangle declarations:

```
type   Name       = array 15 of Char;
       TelNumber  = array 10 of Char;
       Entry      = record
                        name: Name;
                        num:  TelNumber
                    end;
       Directory  = record
                        count: Integer;
                        entry: array 100 of Entry
                    end;

var    dir: Directory
```

Now, the following are all value-or-variable-names:

```
dir
dir.count
dir.entry
dir.entry[i]
dir.entry[i].num
dir.entry[i].name
dir.entry[i].name[j]
```

The code generator will compute the following type sizes:

$$
\begin{aligned}
size[\![\texttt{Name}]\!] &= 15 \times 1 &= 15 \text{ words} \\
size[\![\texttt{TelNumber}]\!] &= 10 \times 1 &= 10 \text{ words} \\
size[\![\texttt{Entry}]\!] &= 15 + 10 &= 25 \text{ words} \\
size[\![\texttt{array 100 of Entry}]\!] &= 100 \times 25 &= 2500 \text{ words} \\
size[\![\texttt{Directory}]\!] &= 1 + 2500 &= 2501 \text{ words}
\end{aligned}
$$

It will also compute the offsets of the fields of record type `Entry`:

$$
\begin{aligned}
offset[\![\texttt{name}]\!] &= 0 \text{ words} \\
offset[\![\texttt{num}]\!] &= 15 \text{ words}
\end{aligned}
$$

and those of record type `Directory`:

$$
\begin{aligned}
offset[\![\texttt{count}]\!] &= 0 \text{ words} \\
offset[\![\texttt{entry}]\!] &= 1 \text{ word}
\end{aligned}
$$

As in Section 6.1, we use the notation *address* v for the address of variable (or constant) v. For the various components of `dir` we find:

$$
\begin{aligned}
address[\![\texttt{dir.count}]\!] &= address[\![\texttt{dir}]\!] + 0 \\
address[\![\texttt{dir.entry}]\!] &= address[\![\texttt{dir}]\!] + 1 \\
address[\![\texttt{dir.entry[i]}]\!] &= address[\![\texttt{dir}]\!] + 1 + 25i
\end{aligned}
$$

$$address[\![\text{dir.entry[i].num}]\!] \quad = address[\![\text{dir}]\!] + 1 + 25i + 15$$
$$= address[\![\text{dir}]\!] + 16 + 25i$$

$$address[\![\text{dir.entry[i].name}]\!] \quad = address[\![\text{dir}]\!] + 1 + 25i + 0$$
$$= address[\![\text{dir}]\!] + 1 + 25i$$

$$address[\![\text{dir.entry[i].name[j]}]\!] = address[\![\text{dir}]\!] + 1 + 25i + j$$
$$= address[\![\text{dir}]\!] + 1 + (25i + j)$$

where i and j are the values of i and j.

In each case the address formula contains some constant terms. These constant terms are accumulated by the code generator, simplifying the address formula to the sum of (at most) three terms: the address of the entire variable (or constant), plus a known offset, plus an unknown value. The known offset is obtained by adding together the offsets of any record fields. The unknown value is determined by evaluating array indices at run-time.

The following instruction sequences illustrate how the Triangle code generator uses this information. To be concrete, assume that $address[\![\text{dir}]\!] = (0, 100)$:

```
fetch [dir.count]  {                            LOAD(1)      100[SB]

                          evaluate [i]  {  LOAD(1)      i
                                           LOADL        25
fetch [dir.entry[i]]                       CALL         mult
                                           LOADA        101[SB]
                                           CALL         add
                                           LOADI(25)

                          evaluate [i]  {  LOAD(1)      i
                                           LOADL        25
fetch [dir.entry[i].num]                   CALL         mult
                                           LOADA        116[SB]
                                           CALL         add
                                           LOADI(10)
```

In each case, the known offset is added into the displacement part of $address[\![\text{dir}]\!]$. Thus the address arithmetic implied by field selection can be done entirely at compile-time. Only indexing must be deferred until run-time.

□

7.6 Further reading

The target machine architecture strongly influences the structure of a code generator. Once upon a time, machines were designed by engineers with no knowledge of code generation. Such machines often had cunning features that skilled assembly language programmers could exploit, but were very difficult for code generators to exploit. But now nearly all programs – even operating systems – are written in high-level languages. So it makes more sense for the machine to support the code generator by, for example, providing a simple regular instruction set. A lucid discussion of the interaction between code generation and machine design may be found in Wirth (1986).

Almost all real machines have general-purpose and/or special-purpose registers; some have a stack as well. The number of registers is usually small and always limited. It is quite hard to generate object code that makes effective use of registers. Code generation for register machines is therefore beyond the scope of this introductory textbook. For a thorough treatment, see Chapter 9 of Aho *et al.* (1985).

The code generator described in this chapter works in the context of a multi-pass compiler: it traverses an AST that represents the entire source program. In the context of a one-pass compiler, the code generator would be structured rather differently: it would be a collection of methods, which can be called by the syntactic analyzer to generate code 'on the fly' as the source program is parsed. For a clear account of how to organize code generation in a one-pass compiler, see Welsh and McKeag (1980).

The sheer diversity of machine architectures is a problem for implementors. A common practice among software vendors is to construct a family of compilers, translating a single source language to several different target machine languages. These compilers will have a common syntactic analyzer and contextual analyzer, but a distinct code generator will be needed for each target machine. Unfortunately, a code generator suitable for one target machine might be difficult or impossible to adapt to a dissimilar target machine. *Code generation by pattern matching* is an attractive way to reduce the amount of work to be done. In this method the semantics of each machine instruction is expressed in terms of low-level operations. Each source-program command is translated to a combination of these low-level operations; code generation then consists of finding an instruction sequence that corresponds to the same combination of operations. A survey of code generation by pattern matching may be found in Ganapathi *et al.* (1982).

Fraser and Hansen (1995) describe in detail a C compiler with three alternative target machines. This gives a clear insight into the problems of code generation for dissimilar register machines.

Exercises

Section 7.1

7.1   The Triangle compiler uses code template (7.8e) for while-commands, but many compilers use the following alternative code template:

$$execute \; [\![\texttt{while} \; E \; \texttt{do} \; C]\!] \; =$$

```
  g:   evaluate E
       JUMPIF(0)  h
       execute C
       JUMP  g
  h:
```

Convince yourself that the alternative code template is semantically equivalent to (7.8e).

Apply the alternative code template to determine the object code of:

$$execute \; [\![\texttt{while} \; \texttt{n} > 0 \; \texttt{do} \; \texttt{n} := \texttt{n} - 2]\!]$$

Compare with Example 7.3, and show that the object code is less efficient.

Why, do you think, is the alternative code template commonly used?

7.2* Suppose that Mini-Triangle is to be extended with the following commands:

(a) $V_1 , V_2 := E_1 , E_2$

This is a simultaneous assignment: both E_1 and E_2 are to be evaluated, and then their values assigned to the variables V_1 and V_2, respectively.

(b) C_1 , C_2

This is a collateral command: the subcommands C_1 and C_2 are to be executed in any order chosen by the implementor.

(c) if E then C

This is a conditional command: if E evaluates to *true*, C is executed, otherwise nothing.

(d) repeat C until E

This is a loop command: E is evaluated at the end of each iteration (after executing C), and the loop terminates if its value is *true*.

(e) repeat C_1 while E do C_2

This is a loop command: E is evaluated in the middle of each iteration (after executing C_1 but before executing C_2), and the loop terminates if its value is *false*.

Write code templates for all these commands.

7.3* Suppose that Mini-Triangle is to be extended with the following expressions:

(a) if E_1 then E_2 else E_3

This is a conditional expression: if E evaluates to *true*, E_2 is evaluated, otherwise E_3 is evaluated. (E_2 and E_3 must be of the same type.)

(b) `let D in E`

This is a block expression: the declaration D is elaborated, and the resultant bindings are used in the evaluation of E.

(c) `begin C ; yield E end`

Here the command C is executed (making side effects), and then E is evaluated.

Write code templates for all these expressions.

Section 7.2

7.4* Implement the visitor/encoding methods `visit...Expression` (along the lines of Example 7.8) for the expressions of Exercise 7.3.

7.5* Implement the visitor/encoding methods `visit...Command` (along the lines of Example 7.8) for the commands of Exercise 7.2. Use the technique illustrated in Example 7.9 for generating jump instructions.

Section 7.3

7.6 Classify the following declarations according to whether they bind identifiers to known or unknown values, variables, or routines.

(a) Pascal constant, variable, and procedure declarations, and Pascal value, variable, and procedural parameters.

(b) ML value and function declarations, and ML parameters.

(c) Java local variable declarations, and Java parameters.

7.7* Suppose that Mini-Triangle is to be extended with a for-command of the form 'for I `from` E_1 `to` E_2 `do` C', with the following semantics. First, the expressions E_1 and E_2 are evaluated, yielding the integers m and n, respectively. Then the subcommand C is executed repeatedly, with I bound to the integers m, $m+1$, ..., n in successive iterations. If $m > n$, C is not executed at all. The scope of I is C, which may fetch I but may not assign to it.

(a) Write a code template for the for-command.

(b) Use it to implement a visitor/encoding method `visitForCommand` (along the lines of Example 7.13).

7.8* Suppose that Mini-Triangle is to be extended with array types, as found in Triangle itself. The relevant extensions to the Mini-Triangle grammar are:

```
V-name        ::=   ...
              |     V-name [ Expression ]
```

```
Type-denoter   ::=   ...
             |   array Integer-Literal of Type-denoter
```

(a)   Modify the Mini-Triangle code specification accordingly.

(b)   Modify the Mini-Triangle code generator accordingly.

Section 7.4

7.9*   Modify the Mini-Triangle code generator to deal with parameterized procedures, using the code templates of Example 7.24.

7.10*   A hypothetical programming language's function declaration has the form 'func *I* (*FP*) : *T* ~ *C*', i.e., its body is a command. A function body may contain one or more commands of the form 'result *E*'. This command evaluates expression *E*, and stores its value in an anonymous variable associated with the function. On return from the function, the *latest* value stored in this way is returned as the function's result.

(a)   Modify the Mini-Triangle code specification as if Mini-Triangle were extended with functions of this form.

(b)   Modify the Mini-Triangle code generator accordingly.

CHAPTER EIGHT

Interpretation

An interpreter takes a source program and executes it immediately. Immediacy is the key characteristic of interpretation; there is no prior time-consuming translation of the source program into a low-level representation.

In an interactive environment, immediacy is highly advantageous. For example, the user of a command language expects an immediate response from each command; it would be absurd to expect the user to enter an entire sequence of commands before seeing the response from the first one. Similarly, the user of a database query language expects an immediate answer to each query. In this mode of working, the 'program' is entered once and then discarded.

The user of a programming language, on the other hand, is much more likely to retain the program for further use, and possibly further development. Even so, translation from the programming language to an intermediate language followed by interpretation of the intermediate language (i.e., interpretive compilation) is a good alternative to full compilation, especially during the early stages of program development.

In this chapter we study two kinds of interpretation:

- *iterative interpretation*

- *recursive interpretation.*

Iterative interpretation is suitable when the source language's instructions are all primitive. The instructions of the source program are fetched, analyzed, and executed, one after another. Iterative interpretation is suitable for real and abstract machine codes, for some very simple programming languages, and for command languages.

Recursive interpretation is necessary if the source language has composite instructions. (In this context, 'instructions' could be statements, expressions, and/or declarations.) Interpretation of an instruction may trigger interpretation of its component instructions. An interpreter for a high-level programming language or query language must be recursive. However, recursive interpretation is slower and more complex than iterative interpretation, so we usually prefer to compile high-level languages, or at least translate them to lower-level intermediate languages that are suitable for iterative interpretation.

8.1 Iterative interpretation

Conventional interpreters are iterative: they work in a fetch–analyze–execute cycle. This is captured by the following *iterative interpretation scheme*:

```
    initialize
    do {
        fetch the next instruction
        analyze this instruction
        execute this instruction
    } while (still running);
```

First, an instruction is fetched from storage, or in some cases entered directly by the user. Second, the instruction is analyzed into its component parts. Third, the instruction is executed. The whole cycle is then repeated.

Typically the source language has several forms of instruction, so execution of an instruction decomposes into several cases, one case for each form of instruction.

In the following subsections we apply this scheme to the interpretation of machine code, the interpretation of simple command languages, and the interpretation of simple programming languages.

8.1.1 Iterative interpretation of machine code

An interpreter of machine code is often called an *emulator*. It is worth recalling here that a real machine *M* is functionally equivalent to an emulator of *M*'s machine code. The only difference is that a real machine uses electronic (and perhaps parallel) hardware to fetch, analyze, and execute instructions, and is therefore much faster than an emulator. (Refer back to Section 2.3 for a fuller discussion of this point.)

A machine-code instruction is essentially a record, consisting of an operation field (usually called the *op-code*) and some operand fields. Instruction analysis (or *decoding*) is simply unpacking these fields. Instruction execution is controlled by the op-code.

To implement an emulator, we employ the following simple techniques:

- Represent the machine's storage by an array. If storage is partitioned, for example into separate stores for code and data, then represent each store by a separate array.

- Represent the machine's registers by variables. This applies equally to visible and hidden registers.[1] One register, the *code pointer* or *program counter*, will contain the address of the next instruction to be executed. Another, the *status register*, will be used to control program termination.

---

[1] Hidden registers are those that cannot be accessed explicitly, even by a machine-code program.

- Fetch each instruction from the (code) store.

- Analyze each instruction by isolating its op-code and operand field(s).

- Execute each instruction by means of a switch-statement, with one case for each possible value of the op-code. In each case, emulate the instruction by updating storage and/or registers.

Example 8.1   Interpreter for Hypo

Consider the hypothetical machine, *Hypo*, summarized in Table 8.1.

Hypo has a 4096-word code store that contains the instructions of the program. An instruction consists of a 4-bit op-code *op* and a 12-bit operand field *d*. Details of the instructions are given in Table 8.1. The program counter, PC, contains the address of the next instruction to be executed. The instruction located at address 0 will be executed first.

Hypo also has a 4096-word data store and a 1-word accumulator, ACC. Each word consists of 16 bits. Data may be placed anywhere in the data store.

Figure 8.1 illustrates the Hypo code store and data store. The illustrative program in the code store takes two integers (already stored at addresses 0 and 1) and computes their product (at address 2). (For greater readability, the program is also shown with mnemonic op-codes.)

Figure 8.2 illustrates how the machine's state – data store, accumulator, and program counter – would change during the first few execution steps of the stored program.

The following class represents Hypo instructions:

```
public class HypoInstruction {
    public byte op;                         // op-code field (0 .. 7)
    public short d;                         // operand field (0 .. 4095)

    public static final byte                // op-codes, as in Table 8.1
        STOREop = 0, LOADop  = 1,
        LOADLop = 2, ADDop   = 3,
        SUBop   = 4, JUMPop  = 5,
        JUMPZop = 6, HALTop  = 7;
}
```

The following class represents the machine's state:

```
public class HypoState {

    public static final short CODESIZE = 4096;
    public static final short DATASIZE = 4096;

    // Code store ...
    public HypoInstruction[] code =
        new HypoInstruction[CODESIZE];
```

```
    // Data store ...
    public short[] data = new short[DATASIZE];

    // Registers ...
    public short PC;
    public short ACC;
    public byte status;

    public static final byte   // status values
        RUNNING = 0, HALTED = 1, FAILED = 2;
}
```

Here the code store is represented by an array of instructions, code; the data store is represented by an array of words, data; and the registers are represented by variables PC, ACC, and status.

The following class will implement the Hypo loader and emulator:

```
public class HypoInterpreter extends HypoState {

    public void load () {
        ...  // Load the program into the code store,
             // starting at address 0.
    }

    public void emulate () {
        ...  // Run the program contained in the code store,
             // starting at address 0.
    }

}
```

The following method is the emulator proper. Its control structure is a switch-statement within a loop, preceded by initialization of the registers. Each case of the switch-statement follows directly from Table 8.1.

```
public void emulate () {
    // Initialize ...
    PC = 0;   ACC = 0;   status = RUNNING;

    do {

        // Fetch the next instruction ...
        HypoInstruction instr = code[PC++];

        // Analyze this instruction ...
        byte op = instr.op;
        short d = instr.d;

        // Execute this instruction ...
        switch (op) {
```

```
        case STOREop:   data[d] = ACC; break;
        case LOADop:    ACC = data[d]; break;
        case LOADLop:   ACC = d; break;
        case ADDop:     ACC += data[d]; break;
        case SUBop:     ACC -= data[d]; break;
        case JUMPop:    PC = d; break;
        case JUMPZop:   if (ACC == 0) PC = d; break;
        case HALTop:    status = HALTED; break;

        default:        status = FAILED;

    }

  } while (status == RUNNING);
}
```

This emulator has been kept as simple as possible, for clarity. But it might behave unexpectedly if, for example, an ADD or SUB instruction overflows. A more robust version would set status to FAILED in such circumstances. (See Exercise 8.1.)

□

When we write an interpreter like that of Example 8.1, it makes no difference whether we are interpreting a real machine code or an abstract machine code. For an abstract machine code, the interpreter will be the only implementation. For a real machine code, a hardware interpreter (processor) will be available as well as a software interpreter (emulator). Of these, the processor will be much faster. But an emulator is much more flexible than a processor: it can be adapted cheaply for a variety of purposes. An emulator can be used for experimentation before the processor is ever constructed. An emulator can also easily be extended for diagnostic purposes. (Exercises 8.2 and 8.3 suggest some of the possibilities.) So, even when a processor is available, an emulator for the same machine code complements it nicely.

Table 8.1 Instruction set of the hypothetical machine Hypo.

Op-code	Instruction	Meaning
0	STORE d	word at address $d \leftarrow$ ACC
1	LOAD d	ACC $\leftarrow$ word at address d
2	LOADL d	ACC $\leftarrow d$
3	ADD d	ACC $\leftarrow$ ACC + word at address d
4	SUB d	ACC $\leftarrow$ ACC – word at address d
5	JUMP d	PC $\leftarrow d$
6	JUMPZ d	PC $\leftarrow d$, if ACC = 0
7	HALT	stop execution

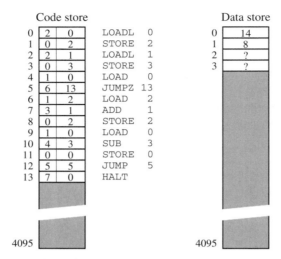

Figure 8.1 Hypo: code store and data store.

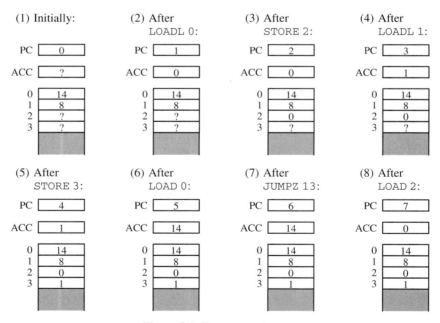

Figure 8.2 Hypo: state changes.

8.1.2   Iterative interpretation of command languages

Command languages (such as the UNIX *shell* language) are relatively simple languages. In normal usage, the user enters a sequence of commands, and expects an immediate response to each command. Each command will be executed just once. These factors suggest interpretation of each command as soon as it is entered. In fact, command languages are specifically designed to be interpreted. Below we illustrate interpretation of a simple command language.

Example 8.2   Interpreter for Mini-Shell

Consider a simple command language, *Mini-Shell*, that allows us to enter commands such as:

```
delete a b c
create f
list
edit f
/bin/sort f
print f 2
quit
```

The above is an example of a *script*, which is just a sequence of commands. Each command is to be executed as soon as it is entered.

Mini-Shell provides several built-in commands. In addition, any executable program (such as `/bin/sort`) can be run simply by giving the name of the file containing it. A command can be passed any number of arguments, which may be filenames or literals. The commands and their meanings are given in Table 8.2.

Table 8.2 Commands in Mini-Shell.

Command	Argument(s)	Meaning
`create`	filename	Create an empty file with the given name.
`delete`	$filename_1$ ... $filename_n$	Delete all the named files.
`edit`	filename	Edit the named file.
`list`	none	List the names of all files owned by the current user.
`print`	filename number	Print the given number of copies of the named file.
Run executable program	filename arg_1 ... arg_n	Run the executable program contained in the named file, with the given arguments.

The syntax of a script is as follows:

Script	::=	Command*	(8.1)
Command	::=	Command-Name Argument* end-of-line	(8.2)
Argument	::=	Filename	(8.3a)
	|	Literal	(8.3b)
Command-Name	::=	**create**	(8.4a)
	|	**delete**	(8.4b)
	|	**edit**	(8.4c)
	|	**list**	(8.4d)
	|	**print**	(8.4e)
	|	**quit**	(8.4f)
	|	Filename	(8.4g)

Production rules for Filename and Literal have been omitted here.

In the Mini-Shell interpreter, we can represent commands as follows:

```java
public class MiniShellCommand {
    public String   name;
    public String[] args;
}
```

The following class represents the Mini-Shell state:

```java
public class MiniShellState {

    // File store ...
    public ...;

    // Registers ...
    public byte status;   // RUNNING or HALTED or FAILED

    public static final byte   // status values
        RUNNING = 0, HALTED = 1, FAILED = 2;
}
```

There is no need for either a code store or a code pointer, since each command will be executed only once, as soon as it is entered.

The following class will implement the Mini-Shell interpreter:

```java
public class MiniShell extends MiniShellState {

    public void interpret () {
        ... // Execute the commands entered by the user,
            // terminating on command quit.
    }
```

```
public MiniShellCommand readAnalyze () {
    ...  // Read, analyze, and return the next command entered by the user.
}

public void create (String fname) {
    ...  // Create an empty file with the given name.
}

public void delete (String[] fnames) {
    ...  // Delete all the named files.
}

public void edit (String fname) {
    ...  // Edit the named file.
}

public void list (){
    ...  // List names of all files owned by the current user.
}

public void print (String fname, String copies) {
    ...  // Print the given number of copies of the named file.
}

public void exec (String fname, String[] args) {
    ...  // Run the executable program contained in the named file, with
        //  the given arguments.
}

}
```

It will be convenient to combine fetching and analysis of commands. This is done by method readAnalyze.

The following method is the interpreter proper. It just reads, analyzes, and executes the commands, one after another:

```
public void interpret () {

    // Initialize ...
    status = RUNNING;

    do {
        // Fetch and analyze the next instruction ...
        MiniShellCommand com = readAnalyze();

        // Execute this instruction ...
        if (com.name.equals("create"))
            create(com.args[0]);

        else if (com.name.equals("delete"))
            delete(com.args);
```

```
        else if (com.name.equals("edit"))
            edit(com.args[0]);

        else if (com.name.equals("list"))
            list();

        else if (com.name.equals("print"))
            print(com.args[0], com.args[1]);

        else if (com.name.equals("quit"))
            status = HALTED;

        else   // executable program
            exec(com.name, com.args);

    } while (status == RUNNING);
}
```

□

8.1.3 Iterative interpretation of simple programming languages

Iterative interpretation is also possible for certain programming languages, provided that a source program is just a sequence of primitive commands. The programming language must not include any composite commands, i.e., commands that contain subcommands.

In the iterative interpretation scheme, the 'instructions' are taken to be the commands of the programming language. Analysis of a command consists of syntactic and perhaps contextual analysis. This makes analysis far slower and more complex than decoding a machine-code instruction. Execution is controlled by the form of command, as determined by syntactic analysis.

Example 8.3   Interpreter for Mini-Basic

Consider a simple programming language, *Mini-Basic*, with the following syntax (expressed in EBNF):

Program	::=	Command*	(8.5)
Command	::=	Variable **=** Expression	(8.6a)
	|	**read** Variable	(8.6b)
	|	**write** Variable	(8.6c)
	|	**go** Label	(8.6d)
	|	**if** Expression Relational-Op Expression	(8.6e)
		go Label	
	|	**stop**	(8.6f)
Expression	::=	primary-Expression	(8.7a)
	|	Expression Arithmetic-Op primary-Expression	(8.7b)

primary-Expression	::=	Numeral	(8.8a)
	|	Variable	(8.8b)
	|	(Expression)	(8.8c)
Arithmetic-Op	::=	+ | – | * | /	(8.9a–d)
Relational-Op	::=	= | \= | < | =< | >= | >	(8.10a–f)
Variable	::=	a | b | c | … | z	(8.11a–z)
Label	::=	Digit Digit*	(8.12)

A Mini-Basic program is just a sequence of commands. The commands are implicitly labeled 0, 1, 2, etc., and these labels may be referenced in go and if commands. The program may use up to twenty-six variables, which are predeclared.

The semantics of Mini-Basic programs should be intuitively clear. All values are real numbers. The program shown in Figure 8.3 reads a number (into variable a), computes its square root accurate to two decimal places (in variable b), and writes the square root.

It is easy to imagine a *Mini-Basic abstract machine*. The Mini-Basic program is loaded into a code store, with successive commands at addresses 0, 1, 2, etc. The code pointer, CP, contains the address of the command due to be executed next.

The program's data are held in a data store of 26 cells, one cell for each variable. Figure 8.3 illustrates the code store and data store. Figure 8.4 shows how the abstract machine's state would change during the first few execution steps of the square-root program, assuming that the number read is 10.0.

We must decide how to represent Mini-Basic commands in the code store. The choices, and their consequences, are as follows:

(a) *Source text:* Each command must be scanned and parsed at run-time (i.e., every time the command is fetched from the code store).

(b) *Token sequence:* Each command must be scanned at load-time, and parsed at run-time.

(c) *AST:* All commands must be scanned and parsed at load-time.

Choice (a), illustrated in Figure 8.3, would slow the interpreter drastically. Choice (c) is better but would slow the loader somewhat. Choice (b) is a reasonable compromise, so let us adopt it here:

```
class Token {
    byte kind;
    String spelling;
}
class ScannedCommand {
    Token[] tokens;
}
```

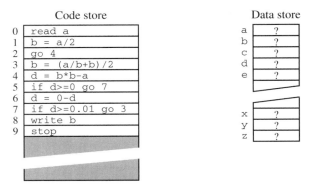

Figure 8.3 Mini-Basic abstract machine: code store and data store.

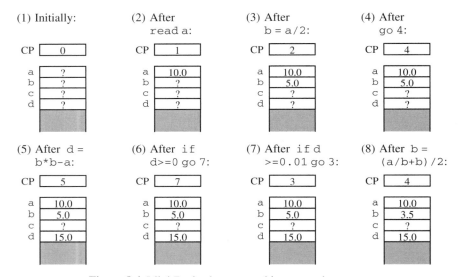

Figure 8.4 Mini-Basic abstract machine: state changes.

Although a sequence of tokens is a convenient way of representing a command in storage, it would be inconvenient for execution. Analysis of a scanned command should parse it and translate it to an internal form suitable for execution. In Mini-Basic all variables are predeclared, so there is no need to check for undeclared variables; and there is only one data type, so there is no need for type checking.

For this internal form let us adopt the command's AST. Note that only a single AST will exist at any one time, representing the current command to be executed. We introduce an abstract class for command ASTs, equipped with a method to execute a command AST:

```
public abstract class Command {
    // A Command object is an AST representing a Mini-Basic command.

    public void execute (MiniBasicState state);
    // Execute the command, using state.
}
```

And similarly for expression ASTs:

```
public abstract class Expression {
    // An Expression object is an AST representing a Mini-Basic
    //   expression.

    public float evaluate (MiniBasicState state);
    // Evaluate the expression, using state, and return its result.
}
```

Later we shall define concrete subclasses for particular forms of commands and expressions. These will implement the methods `execute` and `evaluate`, which we shall call *interpreting methods*.

Note that we must allow the interpreting methods to access the state of the Mini-Basic abstract machine, hence their argument `state`. The following class will represent the abstract machine state:

```
public class MiniBasicState {

    public static final short CODESIZE = 4096;
    public static final short DATASIZE = 26;

    // Code store ...
    public ScannedCommand[] code =
            ScannedCommand[CODESIZE];

    // Data store ...
    public float[] data = new float[DATASIZE];

    // Registers ...
    public short CP;
    public byte status;

    public static final byte   // status values
            RUNNING = 0, HALTED = 1, FAILED = 2;
}
```

Here the code store is represented by an array of scanned commands, `code`. The data store is represented by an array of real numbers, `data`, indexed by variable addresses (using 0 for a, 1 for b, ..., 25 for z). The registers are represented by variables `CP` and `status`.

The following class will define the Mini-Basic interpreter:

```
public class MiniBasicInterpreter
                extends MiniBasicState {

  public void load () {
    ...  // Load the program into the code store, starting at address 0.
  }

  public void run () {
    ...  // Run the program in the code store, starting at address 0.
  }

  public static Command parse
                (ScannedCommand scannedCom) {
    ...  // Parse scannedCom, and return the corresponding
         // command AST.
  }
}
```

Note that we need a method, here called parse, to parse a scanned command and translate it to an AST.

The following method is the interpreter proper. It just fetches, analyzes, and executes the commands, one after another:

```
public void run () {

  // Initialize ...
  CP = 0; status = RUNNING;

  do {
    // Fetch the next instruction ...
    ScannedCommand scannedCom = code[CP++];

    // Analyze this instruction ...
    Command analyzedCom = parse(scannedCom);

    // Execute this instruction ...
    analyzedCom.execute((MiniBasicState) this);

  } while (status == RUNNING);
}
```

Now we must define how to represent and execute analyzed commands. We introduce a subclass of Command for each form of command in Mini-Basic:

```
public class AssignCommand extends Command {
  byte V;              // left-side variable address
  Expression E;        // right-side expression
```

```
    public void execute (MiniBasicState state) {
        state.data[V] = E.evaluate(state);
    }
}

public class GoCommand extends Command {
    short L;                      // destination label

    public void execute (MiniBasicState state) {
        state.CP = L;
    }
}

public class IfCommand extends Command {
    Token R;                      // relational-op
    Expression E1, E2;            // subexpressions
    short L;                      // destination label

    public void execute (MiniBasicState state) {
        float num1 = E1.evaluate(state);
        float num2 = E2.evaluate(state);
        if compare(R, num1, num2)
            state.CP = L;
    }

    private static boolean compare
                (Token relop, float num1, float num2) {
        ... // Return the result of applying relational operator
            // relop to num1 and num2.
    }
}

public class StopCommand extends Command {

    public void execute (MiniBasicState state) {
        state.status = state.HALTED;
    }
}
```

(The Command subclasses ReadCommand and WriteCommand, and the various Expression subclasses, are omitted here. See Exercise 8.5.)

Study the object-oriented design of this interpreter. Once we decided to represent each command by an AST, we had to introduce the abstract class Command, and its subclasses AssignCommand, GoCommand, etc. We then found it convenient to equip each subclass of Command with an interpreting method, execute, allowing the interpreter to use dynamic method selection to select the right code to execute a particular command. However, these interpreting methods were outside the MiniBasic-Interpreter class, so we had to pass the abstract machine state to them *via* their argument state.

The alternative to dynamic method selection would have been to make the interpreter test the subclass of each command before executing it, along the following lines:

```
// Execute this instruction …

if (analyzedCom instanceof AssignCommand) {
    AssignCommand com = (AssignCommand) analyzedCom;
    data[com.V] = evaluate(com.E);
}

else if (analyzedCom instanceof GoCommand) {
    GoCommand com = (GoCommand) analyzedCom;
    CP = com.L;
}

else …
```

But this would not be in the true spirit of object-oriented design!

8.2 Recursive interpretation

Modern programming languages are higher-level than the simple programming language of Example 8.3. In particular, commands may be composite: they may contain subcommands, subsubcommands, and so on.

It is possible to interpret higher-level programming languages. However, the iterative interpretation scheme is inadequate for such languages. Analysis of each command in the source program entails analysis of its subcommands, recursively. Likewise, execution of each command entails execution of its subcommands, recursively. Thus we are driven inexorably to a two-stage process, whereby the entire source program is analyzed before interpretation proper can begin. This gives rise to the ***recursive interpretation scheme***:

> fetch and analyze the program
> execute the program

where both analysis and execution are recursive.

We must decide how the program will be represented at each stage. If it is supplied in source form, 'fetch and analyze the program' must perform syntactic and contextual analysis of the program. A decorated AST is therefore a suitable representation for the result of the analysis stage. Therefore 'execute the program' will operate on the program's decorated AST.

Example 8.4   Interpreter for Mini-Triangle

Consider a recursive interpreter for the programming language Mini-Triangle of

Examples 1.3 and 1.8. Assume that the analyzed program is to be represented by a decorated AST. The source program will be subjected to syntactic and contextual analysis, and also storage allocation, before execution commences.

We must choose a representation of Mini-Triangle values. These include not only truth values and integers, but also *undefined* (which is the initial value of a variable). The following classes represent all these types of values:

```
public abstract class Value { }

public class IntValue extends Value {
    public short i;
}

public class BoolValue extends Value {
    public boolean b;
}

public class UndefinedValue extends Value {
}
```

We assume that each of these classes is equipped with a suitable constructor.

The following class will define the abstract machine state:

```
public class MiniTriangleState {

    public static final short DATASIZE = ...;

    // Code store ...
    Program program;   // decorated AST

    // Data store ...
    Value[] data = new Value[DATASIZE];

    // Register ...
    byte status;

    public static final byte   // status values
            RUNNING = 0, HALTED = 1, FAILED = 2;
}
```

Here we represent the data store, as usual, by an array. The 'code store' is just the decorated AST representing the Mini-Triangle program. We assume the class AST, and its subclasses Program, Command, Expression, Declaration, etc., defined in Example 4.19.

The following class will implement the Mini-Triangle interpreter. In particular, methods fetchAnalyze and run will implement the two stages of the recursive interpretation scheme.

```
public class MiniTriangleProcessor
        extends MiniTriangleState implements Visitor {
```

```
public void fetchAnalyze () {
    ... // Load the program into the code store, after
        // subjecting it to syntactic and contextual analysis.
}

public void run () {
    ... // Run the program contained in the code store.
}

// Visitor/interpreting methods ...

public Object visit...Command
                (...Command com, Object arg);
    // Execute com, returning null (and ignoring arg).

public Object visit...Expression
                (...Expression expr, Object arg);
    // Evaluate expr, returning its result (and ignoring arg).

public Object visit...Declaration
                (...Declaration decl, Object arg);
    // Elaborate decl, returning null (and ignoring arg).

// Other interpreting methods ...

private Value fetch (Vname vname);
    // Return the value of the constant or variable vname.

private void assign (Vname vname, Value val);
    // Assign val to the variable vname.

// Auxiliary methods ...

private static short valuation
                (IntegerLiteral intLit);
    // Return the value of intLit.

private static Value applyUnary
                (Operator op, Value val);
    // Return the result of applying unary operator op to val.

private static Value applyBinary
                (Operator op, Value val1, Value val2);
    // Return the result of applying binary operator op to val1 and val2.

private static void callStandardProc
                (Identifier id, Value val);
    // Call the standard procedure named id, passing val as its argument.

}
```

This Mini-Triangle processor is a visitor object (see Section 5.3.2), in which the visitor methods act as interpreting methods.

The visitor/interpreting methods for commands are implemented as follows:

```
public Object visitAssignCommand
                (AssignCommand com, Object arg) {
   Value val = (Value) com.E.visit(this, null);
   assign(com.V, val);
   return null;
}

public Object visitCallCommand
                (CallCommand com, Object arg) {
   Value val = (Value) com.E.visit(this, null);
   callStandardProc(com.I, val);
   return null;
}

public Object visitSequentialCommand
                (SequentialCommand com, Object arg) {
   com.C1.visit(this, null);
   com.C2.visit(this, null);
   return null;
}

public Object visitIfCommand
                (IfCommand com, Object arg) {
   BoolValue val = (BoolValue) com.E.visit(this, null);
   if (val.b) com.C1.visit(this, null);
   else       com.C2.visit(this, null);
   return null;
}

public Object visitWhileCommand
                (WhileCommand com, Object arg) {
   for (;;) {
      BoolValue val = (BoolValue)
            com.E.visit(this, null);
      if (! val.b) break;
      com.C.visit(this, null);
   }
   return null;
}

public Object visitLetCommand
                (LetCommand com, Object arg) {
   com.D.visit(this, null);
   com.C.visit(this, null);
   return null;
}
```

The visitor/interpreting methods for expressions are implemented as follows:

```java
public Object visitIntegerExpression
                (IntegerExpression expr, Object arg) {
    return new IntValue(valuation(expr.IL));
}

public Object visitVnameExpression
                (VnameExpression expr, Object arg) {
    return fetch(expr.V);
}

public Object visitUnaryExpression
                (UnaryExpression expr, Object arg) {
    Value val = (Value) expr.E.visit(this, null);
    return applyUnary(expr.O, val);
}

public Object visitBinaryExpression
                (BinaryExpresion expr, Object arg) {
    Value val1 = (Value) expr.E1.visit(this, null);
    Value val2 = (Value) expr.E2.visit(this, null);
    return applyBinary(expr.O, val1, val2);
}
```

The visitor/interpreting methods for declarations are implemented as follows:

```java
public Object visitConstDeclaration
                (ConstDeclaration decl, Object arg) {
    KnownAddress entity = (KnownAddress) decl.entity;
    Value val = (Value) decl.E.visit(this, null);
    data[entity.address] = val;
    return null;
}

public Object visitVarDeclaration
                (VarDeclaration decl, Object arg) {
    KnownAddress entity = (KnownAddress) decl.entity;
    data[entity.address] = new UndefinedValue();
    return null;
}

public Object visitSequentialDeclaration
                (SequentialDeclaration decl,
                 Object arg) {
    decl.D1.visit(this, null);
    decl.D2.visit(this, null);
    return null;
}
```

Finally, the auxiliary methods for value-or-variable-names are implemented as follows:

```
private Value fetch (Vname vname) {
    KnownAddress entity =
            (KnownAddress) vname.visit(this, null);
    return data[entity.address];
}

private void assign (Vname vname, Value val) {
    KnownAddress entity =
            (KnownAddress) vname.visit(this, null);
    data[entity.address] = val;
}
```

To fetch and analyze a Mini-Triangle program, we need the following:

- A *parser*. The class `Parser` of Example 4.12 exports a method `parse`, which parses a Mini-Triangle source program and returns the corresponding AST.

- A *contextual analyzer*. The class `Checker` of Example 5.11 exports a method `check`, which performs identification and type checking on a given AST and decorates it accordingly.

- A *static storage allocator*. Let us assume a class `StorageAllocator` that exports a method `allocateAddresses`. This method visits each constant and variable declaration in a given AST, allocates a suitable address to the declared constant or variable, and records that address in a `KnownAddress` entity description attached to the declaration. (See Example 7.13.)

```
public void fetchAnalyze () {
    Parser parser = new Parser(...);
    Checker checker = new Checker(...);
    StorageAllocator allocator = new StorageAllocator();
    program = parser.parse();
    checker.check(program);
    allocator.allocateAddresses(program);
}
```

To run the program, we simply visit the program command:

```
public void run () {
    program.C.visit(this, null);
}
```

This design for a Mini-Triangle recursive interpreter reuses the visitor design pattern already exploited in our Mini-Triangle contextual analyzer (Example 5.11) and code generator (Example 7.8). This design allows the interpreting methods to be located in the `MiniTriangleInterpreter` class, where they have direct access to the abstract machine state.

A design similar to that of Example 8.3 would be a reasonable alternative. That would entail equipping each `Command` subclass with an `execute` method, each `Expression` subclass with an `evaluate` method, each `Declaration` subclass with an `elaborate` method, and so on. Each of these interpreting methods would be passed the abstract machine state as an argument.

□

The kind of interpreter we have just illustrated analyzes the entire source program before execution commences. Thus it forgoes one of the usual advantages of interpretation, that is immediacy. This explains why recursive interpretation is not generally used for higher-level programming languages. For such languages, a better alternative is compilation of source programs to a simple intermediate language, followed by iterative interpretation of the intermediate language, as outlined in Section 2.4.

Some notable exceptions to the general rule, namely Lisp and Prolog, will be discussed in Section 8.4.

8.3 Case study: the TAM interpreter

The abstract machine TAM was outlined in Section 6.8, and is fully described in Appendix C. It is the target machine of the Triangle compiler.

TAM is implemented by an interpreter that is in most respects similar to other machine-code interpreters, such as that of Example 8.1. But of course it is more sophisticated, since TAM directly supports many features of high-level languages.

The `TAM` package includes the classes `Instruction`, `State`, and `Interpreter` outlined here.

The following class represents TAM instructions (Figure C.5):

```
public class Instruction {
    public byte   op;      // op-code (0 .. 15), from Table C.2
    public byte   r;       // register field (0 .. 15), from Table C.1
    public byte   n;       // length field (0 .. 255)
    public short  d;       // operand field (–32767 .. +32767)
    ...
}
```

The following class represents the TAM state. The code and data stores are represented as usual by arrays. The registers are represented by variables (with read-only registers declared as **final**).

```
public class State {

    public static final short CODESIZE = ...;
    public static final short DATASIZE = ...;
```

```
    //  Code store ...
    public Instruction[] code =
           new Instruction[CODESIZE];

    //  Data store ...
    public short[] data = new short[DATASIZE];

    //  Registers ...
    public short final    CB = 0;
    public short          CT;
    public short final    PB = CODESIZE;
    public short final    PT = CODESIZE + 28;
    public short final    SB = 0;
    public short          ST;
    public short final    HB = DATASIZE;
    public short          HT;
    public short          LB;
    public short          CP;
    public byte           status;

    public static final byte   //  status values
           RUNNING = 0, HALTED = 1, FAILED = 2;
}
```

The following class implements the TAM interpreter proper:

```
public class Interpreter extends State {

    public void loadProgram () {
        ...  //  Load the program into the code store, starting at address 0.
        ...  //  Set CT to the address of the last instruction + 1.
    }

    public void runProgram () {
        ...  //  Run the program contained in the code store,
             //  starting at address 0.
    }

}
```

The interpreter proper is as follows. Its main control structure is a switch-statement within a loop. There is one case for each of the fifteen valid op-codes, and a default case for invalid op-codes:

```
public void runProgram () {
    //  Initialize ...
    ST = SB;   HT = HB;   LB = SB;   CP = CB;
    status = RUNNING;
```

```
do {
    // Fetch the next instruction ...
    Instruction instr = code[CP++];

    // Analyze this instruction ...
    byte  op = instr.op;
    byte  r  = instr.r;
    byte  n  = instr.n;
    short d  = instr.d;

    // Execute this instruction ...
    switch (op) {

        case LOADop:    ...
        case LOADAop:   ...
        case LOADIop:   ...
        case LOADLop:   ...
        case STOREop:   ...
        case STOREIop:  ...
        case CALLop:    ...
        case CALLIop:   ...
        case RETURNop:  ...
        case PUSHop:    ...
        case POPop:     ...
        case JUMPop:    ...
        case JUMPIFop:  ...

        case HALTop:    status = HALTED;  break;

        default:        status = FAILED;
    }

} while (status == RUNNING);
}
```

The fact that TAM is a stack machine gives rise to many differences in detail from an interpreter for a register machine. Load instructions push values on to the stack, and store instructions pop values off the stack. For example, the TAM LOADL instruction is interpreted as follows:

```
case LOADLop:
    data[ST++] = d;
    break;
```

(Register ST points to the word immediately *above* the stack top, as shown in Figure C.1.)

Further differences arise from the special design features of TAM (outlined in Section 6.8).

Addressing and registers

The operand of a LOAD, LOADA, or STORE instruction is of the form '*d* [*r*] ', where *r* is usually a display register, and *d* is a constant displacement. The displacement *d* is added to the current content of register *r*.

The display registers allow addressing of global variables (using SB), local variables (using LB), and nonlocal variables (using L1, L2, …). The latter registers are related to LB by the invariants L1 = *content*(LB), L2 = *content*(*content*(LB)), and so on – see (6.25–27) in Section 6.4.2.

As explained in Section 6.8, it is not really worthwhile to have separate registers for access to nonlocal variables. The cost of updating them (on every routine call and return) outweighs the benefit of having them immediately available to compute the addresses of nonlocal variables. In the TAM interpreter, therefore, L1, L2, etc., are only *pseudo-registers*: their values are computed only when needed, using the above invariants. This is captured by the following auxiliary method in the interpreter:

```
private static short relative (short d, byte r) {
    // Return the address defined by displacement d relative to register r.
    switch (r) {
        ...
        case SBr:    return d + SB;
        case LBr:    return d + LB;
        case L1r:    return d + data[LB];
        case L2r:    return d + data[data[LB]];
        ...
    }
}
```

For example, the LOAD and STORE instructions (on the simplifying assumption that the length field n is 1) would be interpreted as follows:

```
case LOADop: {
    short addr = relative(d, r);
    data[ST++] = data[addr];
    break;
}

case STOREop: {
    short addr = relative(d, r);
    data[addr] = data[--ST];
    break;
}
```

The operand of a CALL, JUMP, or JUMPIF instruction is also of the form '*d* [*r*] ', where *r* is generally CB or PB, and *d* is a constant displacement. As usual, the displacement *d* is added to the content of register *r*. The auxiliary method relative also handles these cases.

Primitive routines

Each primitive routine (such as *mult*, *lt*, or *not*) has a designated address within the code store's primitives segment, which is delimited by registers PB and PT. (See Figure C.1.) Thus the interpreter traps any call to an address within the primitives segment:

```
case CALLop: {
    short addr = relative(d, r);
    if (addr >= PB)
        ...  // Execute the primitive operation at address addr.
    else
        ...  // Call the code routine at address addr.
    break;
}
```

The interpreter performs the appropriate primitive operation itself. For example, *mult*, *lt*, and *not* are interpreted as follows:

```
case mult: {
    --ST;
    data[ST-1] *= data[ST];
    break;
}

case lt: {
    --ST;
    data[ST-1] = (data[ST-1] < data[ST]) ? 1 : 0;
    break;
}

case not: {
    data[ST-1] = 1 - data[ST-1];   // replacing 0 by 1, or 1 by 0
    break;
}
```

8.4 Further reading

Interpretation is still popular despite the obvious performance problems. Indeed, since an interpreter is easier to implement than a compiler, many programming languages rely on an interpreter for their first implementation (see Section 9.1.3).

The original Basic was one of the few 'high-level' programming languages for which interpretation was normal. A typical Basic language processor allowed programs to be entered, edited, and executed incrementally. Such a language processor could run on a microcomputer with very limited storage, hence its popularity in the early days of microcomputers. But this was possible only because the language was very primitive indeed. Its control structures were more typical of a low-level language, making it unattractive for serious programmers. More recently, 'structured' dialects of Basic have become more popular, and compilation has become an alternative to interpretation.

Recursive interpretation is less common. However, this form of interpretation has long been associated with Lisp (McCarthy *et al.* 1965). A Lisp program is not just represented by a tree: it *is* a tree! Several features of the language – dynamic binding, dynamic typing, and the possibility of manufacturing extra program code at run-time – make interpretation of Lisp much more suitable than compilation. A description of a Lisp interpreter may be found in McCarthy *et al.* (1965). Lisp has always had a devoted band of followers, but not all are prepared to tolerate slow execution. A more recent successful dialect, Scheme (Kelsey *et al.* 1998), has discarded Lisp's problematic features in order to make compilation feasible.

It is noteworthy that two popular programming languages, Basic and Lisp, both suitable for interpretation but otherwise utterly different, have evolved along somewhat parallel lines, spawning structured dialects suitable for compilation!

Another example of a high-level language suitable for interpretation is Prolog. This language has a very simple syntax, a program being a flat collection of clauses, and it has no scope rules and few type rules to worry about. Interpretation is almost forced by the ability of a program to modify itself by adding and deleting clauses at run-time.

Exercises

8.1 Make the Hypo interpreter of Example 8.1 detect the following exceptional conditions, and set the status register accordingly:

(a) overflow;
(b) invalid instruction address;
(c) invalid data address.

(Assume that Hypo may have less than 4096 words of code store and less than 4096 words of data store, thus making conditions (b) and (c) possible.)

8.2 Make the Hypo interpreter of Example 8.1 display a summary of the machine state after executing each instruction. Display the contents of ACC and CP, the instruction just executed, and a selected portion of the data store.

8.3* Make the Hypo interpreter of Example 8.1 into an interactive debugger. Provide the following facilities: (a) execute the next instruction only (*single-step*); (b) set or remove a breakpoint at a given instruction; (c) execute instructions until the next breakpoint; (d) display the contents of ACC and CP; (e) display a selected portion of the data store; (f) terminate execution.

8.4** Write an emulator for a real machine with which you are familiar.

8.5   Fill in the missing details of the Mini-Basic interpreter of Example 8.3.

8.6   The Mini-Basic interpreter of Example 8.3 represents each stored command as a token sequence.

(a)   Discuss in detail the advantages and disadvantages of this choice of representation, and of the other possible representations. Assume a typical Basic-style language processor, in which the user may interactively enter, edit, or delete any command.

(b)   How does the choice of representation influence the method `analyze`, the method that loads a command into the code store, and the method that edits a stored command?

8.7*   Extend the Mini-Basic interpreter of Example 8.3 to deal with the following extensions:

> Command ::=   ...
> | **perform** Label **to** Label
> | **while** Expression Relational-Op Expression
>   **do** Command

The effect of 'perform L_1 to L_2' is to execute the commands labeled L_1 through L_2 (where L_1 must not follow L_2). This is a kind of parameterless procedure call.

The effect of 'while E_1 R E_2 do C' is to repeat the subcommand C as long as the comparison 'E_1 R E_2' yields *true*. C is restricted to be a primitive command (i.e., it may not itself be a while-command).

Do these extensions lead you to reconsider the choice of representation for a stored command (Exercise 8.6)?

8.8*   Extend the Mini-Shell interpreter of Example 8.2 to deal with a new command, `call`. This takes a single argument, a filename. The named file is expected to contain a Mini-Shell script, whose commands are to be executed one after another.

8.9*   Suppose that Mini-Basic (Example 8.3) is to be replaced by a structured dialect with similar expressive power. The syntax of commands is to become:

> Command ::=   Variable **=** Expression
> | **read** Variable
> | **write** Variable
> | **if** Expression Relational-Op Expression
>   **then** Command* **else** Command* **end**
> | **while** Expression Relational-Op Expression
>   **do** Command* **end**
> | **stop**

Expressions, operators, and variables are unchanged, but labels are removed. Write a recursive interpreter for this structured dialect.

8.10** The TAM interpreter (Section 8.3) sacrifices efficiency for clarity. For example, the fetch/analyze/execute cycle could be combined and replaced by a single switch-statement of the form:

```
switch ((instr = code[CP++]).op) {
   case LOADop:    ...

   ...
}
```

Another efficiency gain could be achieved by holding the top one or two stack elements in simple variables, and possibly avoiding the unnecessary updating of the stack pointer during a long sequence of arithmetic operations. (This is effectively turning TAM into a register machine!)

Consider these and other possible improvements to the TAM interpreter, and develop a more efficient implementation. Compare your version with the original TAM interpreter, and measure the performance gain.

CHAPTER NINE

Conclusion

The subject of this book is programming language implementation. As we study this subject, we should remember that implementation is only part of the *programming language life cycle*, where it takes its place along with programming language design and specification. In Section 9.1 we discuss the programming language life cycle, emphasizing the interactions among design, specification, and implementation. We also distinguish between cheap, low-quality implementations (*prototypes*) and high-quality implementations.

This naturally leads to a discussion of quality issues in implementation. In previous chapters we have concentrated on introducing the basic methods of compilation and interpretation, and relating these to the source language's specification. Correctness of the implementation, with respect to the language specification, has been our primary consideration. Quality of the implementation is a secondary consideration, although still very important. The key quality issues are *error reporting* and *efficiency*. Sections 9.2 and 9.3 discuss these issues, as they arise both at compile-time and at run-time.

9.1   The programming language life cycle

Every programming language has a life cycle, which has some similarities to the well-known software life cycle. The language is *designed* to meet some requirement. A formal or informal *specification* of the language is written in order to communicate the design to other people. The language is then implemented by means of language processors. Initially, a *prototype* implementation might be developed so that programmers can try out the language quickly. Later, high-quality (industrial-strength) *compilers* will be developed so that realistic application programming can be undertaken.

As the term suggests, the programming language life cycle is an iterative process. Language design is a highly creative and challenging endeavor, and no designer makes a perfect job at the first attempt. The experience of specifying or implementing a new language tends to expose irregularities in the design. Implementors and programmers might discover flaws in the specification, such as ambiguity, incompleteness, or inconsistency. They might also discover unpleasant features of the language itself, features that make the language unduly hard to implement efficiently, or unsatisfactory for programming.

334

In any case, the language might have to be redesigned, respecified, and reimplemented, perhaps several times. This is bound to be costly, i.e., time-consuming and expensive. It is necessary, therefore, to plan the life cycle in order to minimize costs.

Figure 9.1 illustrates a life cycle model that has much to recommend it. Design is immediately followed by specification. (This is needed to communicate the design to implementors and programmers.) Development of a prototype follows, and development of compilers follows that. Specification, prototyping, and compiler development are successively more costly, so it makes sense to order them in this way. The designer gets the fastest possible feedback, and costly compiler development is deferred until the language design has more or less stabilized.

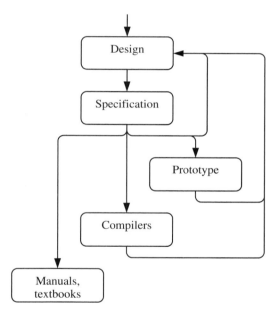

Figure 9.1 A programming language life cycle model.

9.1.1 Design

The essence of programming language design is that the designer selects concepts and decides how to combine them. This selection is, of course, determined largely by the intended use of the language. A variety of concepts have found their way into programming languages: basic concepts such as values and types, storage, bindings, and abstraction; and more advanced concepts such as encapsulation, polymorphism, exceptions, and concurrency. A single language that supports all these concepts is likely to be very large and complex indeed (and its implementations will be large, complex, and costly). Therefore a judicious selection of concepts is necessary.

The designer should strive for simplicity and regularity. Simplicity implies that the language should support only the concepts essential to the applications for which the language is intended. Regularity implies that the language should combine these concepts in a systematic way, avoiding restrictions that might surprise programmers or make their task more difficult. (Language irregularities also tend to make implementation more difficult.)

A number of principles have been discovered that provide useful guidance to the designer:

- The *type completeness principle* suggests that no operation should be arbitrarily restricted in the types of its operands. For instance, operations like assignment and parameter passing should, ideally, be applicable to all types in the language.

- The *abstraction principle* suggests that, for each program phrase that specifies some kind of computation, there should be a way of abstracting that phrase and parameterizing it with respect to the entities on which it operates. For instance, it should be possible to abstract any expression to make a function, or (in an imperative language) to abstract any command to make a procedure.

- The *correspondence principle* suggests that, for each form of declaration, there should be a corresponding parameter mechanism. For instance, it should be possible to take a block with a constant definition and transform it into a procedure (or function) with a constant parameter.

These are principles, not dogma. Designers often have to make compromises (for example to avoid constructions that would be unduly difficult to implement). But at least the principles help the designer to make the hard design decisions rationally and fully conscious of their consequences.

The main purpose of this brief discussion has been to give an insight into why language design is so difficult. Pointers to more extensive discussions of language design may be found in Section 9.4.

9.1.2 Specification

A new language design exists only in the mind of the designer until it is communicated to other people. For this purpose a precise specification of the language's syntax and semantics must be written. The specification may be informal, formal, or (most commonly) a hybrid.

Nearly all language designers specify their syntax formally, using BNF, EBNF or syntax diagrams. These formalisms are widely understood and easy to use. Some older languages, such as Fortran and Cobol, did not have their syntax formalized, and it is noteworthy that their syntax is clumsy and irregular. Formal specification of syntax tends to encourage syntactic simplicity and regularity, as illustrated by Algol (the language for which BNF was invented) and its many successors. For example, the earlier versions of Fortran had several different classes of expression, permissible in different contexts (assignment, array indexing, loop parameters); whereas Algol from the start had just one class of expression, permissible in all contexts.

Similarly, formal specification of semantics tends to encourage semantic simplicity and regularity. Unfortunately, few language designers yet attempt this. Semantic formalisms are much more difficult to master than BNF. Even then, writing a semantic specification of a real programming language (as opposed to a toy language) is a substantial task. Worst of all, the designer has to specify, not a stable well-understood language, but one that is gradually being designed and redesigned. Most semantic formalisms are ill-suited to meet the language designer's requirements, so it is not surprising that almost all designers content themselves with writing informal semantic specifications.

The advantages of formality and the disadvantages of informality should not be underestimated, however. Informal specifications have a strong tendency to be inconsistent or incomplete or both. Such specification errors lead to confusion when the language designer seeks feedback from colleagues, when the new language is implemented, and when programmers try to learn the new language. Of course, with sufficient investment of effort, most specification errors can be detected and corrected, but an informal specification will probably never be completely error-free. The same amount of effort could well produce a formal specification that is at least guaranteed to be precise.

The very act of writing a specification tends to focus the designer's mind on aspects of the design that are incomplete or inconsistent. Thus the specification exercise provides valuable and timely feedback to the designer. Once the design is completed, the specification (whether formal or informal) will be used to guide subsequent implementations of the new language.

9.1.3 Prototypes

A prototype is a cheap low-quality implementation of a new programming language. Development of a prototype helps to highlight any features of the language that are hard to implement. The prototype also gives programmers an early opportunity to try out the language. Thus the language designer gains further valuable feedback. Moreover, since a prototype can be developed relatively quickly, the feedback is timely enough to make a language revision feasible. A prototype might lack speed and good error reporting; but these qualities are deliberately sacrificed for the sake of rapid implementation.

For a suitable programming language, an interpreter might well be a useful prototype. An interpreter is very much easier and quicker to implement than a compiler for the same language. The drawback of an interpreter is that an interpreted program will run perhaps 100 times more slowly than an equivalent machine-code program. Programmers will quickly tire of this enormous inefficiency, once they pass the stage of trying out the language and start to use it to build real applications.

A more durable form of prototype is an interpretive compiler. This consists of a translator from the programming language to some suitable abstract machine code, together with an interpreter for the abstract machine. The interpreted object program will run 'only' about 10 times more slowly than a machine-code object program. Developing the compiler and interpreter together is still much less costly than developing a compiler that translates the programming language to real machine code. Indeed, a suitable abstract machine might be available 'off the shelf', saving the cost of writing the interpreter.

Another method of developing the prototype implementation is to implement a translator from the new language into an existing high-level language. Such a translation is usually straightforward (as long as the target language is chosen with care). Clearly the existing target language must already be supported by a suitable implementation. This was precisely the method chosen for the first implementation of C++, which used the `cfront` translator to convert the source program into C.

Development of the prototype must be guided by the language specification, whether the specification is formal or informal. The specification tells the implementor which programs are well-formed (i.e., conform to the language's syntax and contextual constraints) and what these programs should do when run.

9.1.4 Compilers

A prototype is not suitable for use over an extended period by a large number of programmers building real applications. When it has served its purpose of allowing programmers to try out the new language and provide feedback to the language designer, the prototype should be superseded by a higher-quality implementation. This is invariably a compiler – or, more likely, a family of compilers, generating object code for a number of target machines. Such a high-quality implementation is referred as an *industrial-strength* compiler.

The work that went into developing a prototype need not go to waste. If the prototype was an interpretive compiler, for example, we can bootstrap it to make a compiler that generates real machine code (see Section 2.6).

Development of compilers must be guided by the language specification. A syntactic analyzer can be developed systematically from the source language's syntactic specification (see Chapter 4). A specification of the source language's scope rules and type rules should guide the development of a contextual analyzer (see Chapter 5). Finally, a specification of the source language's semantics should guide the development of a code specification, which should in turn be used to develop a code generator systematically (see Chapter 7).

In practice, contextual constraints and semantics are rarely specified formally. If we compare separately-developed compilers for the same language, we often find that they are consistent with respect to syntax, but inconsistent with respect to contextual constraints and semantics. This is no accident, because syntax is usually specified formally, and therefore precisely, and everything else informally, leading inevitably to misunderstanding.

9.2   Error reporting

All programmers make errors – frequently. A high-quality language processor assists the programmer to locate and correct these errors. Here we examine detection and reporting of both compile-time and run-time errors.

9.2.1   Compile-time error reporting

The language specification defines a set of well-formed programs. A minimalist view of a compiler's function is that it simply rejects any ill-formed program. But a good-quality compiler should be more helpful.

As well as rejecting an ill-formed program, the compiler should report the location of each error, together with some explanation. It should at least distinguish between the major categories of compile-time error:

• *Syntactic error:* missing or unexpected characters or tokens. The error report might indicate what characters or tokens *were* expected.

• *Scope error:* a violation of the language's scope rules. The error report should indicate which identifier was declared twice, or used without declaration.

• *Type error:* a violation of the language's type rules. The error report should indicate which type rule was violated, and/or what type was expected.

Ideally the error report should be self-explanatory. If this is not feasible, it should at least refer to the appropriate section of the language specification.

If the compiler forms part of an integrated language processor, and thus the programmer can switch very easily between editing and compiling, it is acceptable for the compiler to halt on detecting the first error. The compiler should highlight the erroneous phrase and pass control immediately to the editor. The programmer can then correct the error and reinvoke the compiler.

On the other hand, a 'batch' or 'software tool' compiler – one intended to compile the entire source program without interaction with the programmer – should detect and report as many errors as it can find. This allows the programmer to correct several errors after each compilation. This requirement has a significant impact on the compiler's internal organization. After detecting and reporting an error, the compiler should attempt *error recovery*. This means that the compiler should try to get itself into a state where analysis of the source program can continue as normally as possible. Unfortunately, effective error recovery is difficult.

Example 9.1   Reporting syntactic errors

The following Triangle program fragment contains some common syntactic errors:

```
      let
          var score: Integer;
          var grade: Char
(1)       var pass:  Boolean
      in
          begin
          ...;
(2)       if 50 <= score /\ score < 60 then
(3)           grade := 'C';
(4)           pass = true
(5)       else
              ...
          end
```

These errors should be detected during parsing.

At (1), the token 'var' is encountered unexpectedly. Clearly, the error is a missing semicolon between the declarations, and the best error recovery is to continue parsing as if the semicolon had been there.

After the assignment command at (3), a semicolon is encountered where 'else' was expected. Here error recovery is more difficult. (Recall that the parser works in a single pass through the source program, and has not yet seen the tokens after the semicolon.) There are two reasonable ways in which the parser might attempt to recover at this point:

(a) The parser might assume that the else-part of the if-command is missing, and continue as if the if-command had been completely parsed. Given the above source program, this error recovery would turn out badly: the parser would later and unexpectedly encounter the token 'else' at (5), and would spuriously report a syntactic error at that point.

(b) Alternatively, the parser might skip tokens in the hope of finding the expected 'else'. Given the above source program, this error recovery would turn out reasonably well: the parser would find the token 'else' at (5), and would then resume parsing the if-command. The only drawback is that the parser would skip the tokens 'pass = true', and thus would overlook the syntactic error there.

In contrast, given a different program where the 'else' really was missing, error recovery (a) would turn out well, but (b) would turn out badly.

The expression at (2) illustrates another problem with error reporting. This expression is syntactically well-formed, but the Triangle parser will treat this expression as equivalent to '((50 <= score) /\ score) < 60' – not at all what the programmer intended! Consequently, contextual analysis will report type errors in connection with the operators '/\' and '<'. The programmer's actual mistake, however, was the syntactic mistake of failing to parenthesize the expression properly.

Example 9.2 *Reporting contextual errors*

The following Triangle program fragment contains scope and type errors:

```
    let
        var phonenum: Integer;
        var local: Boolean
    in
        begin
        ...;
(1)     if phonenum[0] = '0' then
(2)         locale := false
        else
            ...
        end
```

These errors should be detected during contextual analysis.

Consider the expression at (1). The phrase 'phonenum[0]' clearly violates the indexing operation's type rule, since phonenum is not of array type. But what error recovery is appropriate? It is not at all obvious what type should be ascribed to 'phonenum[0]', to allow type checking to continue. If the type checker ascribes the type *int*, for example, then at the next step it will find that the operands of '=' appear to violate that operator's type rule (one operand being *int* and the other *char*), and it will generate a second error report, which is actually spurious. Fortunately, the result type of '=' does not depend on the types of its operands, so the type checker should obviously ascribe the type *bool* to the expression 'phonenum[0] = '0''. At the next step the type checker will find that this expression satisfies the if-command's type rule.

At (2), there is an applied occurrence of an identifier, locale, that has not been declared, in violation of a scope rule. Again, what error recovery is appropriate? Suppose that the type checker arbitrarily chooses *int* as the type of locale. Subsequently the type checker will find that the assignment command's type rule appears to be violated (one side being *int* and the other *bool*), and again it will generate a spurious error report.

□

To facilitate error recovery during type checking, it is useful for the type checker to ascribe a special improper type, *error-type*, to any ill-typed expression. The type checker can then ignore *error-type* whenever it is subsequently encountered. This technique would avoid both the spurious error reports mentioned in Example 9.2.

As these examples illustrate, it is easy for a compiler to discover that the source program is ill-formed, and to generate error reports; but it is difficult to ensure that the compiler never generates misleading error reports. There is a genuine tension between the task of compiling well-formed source programs and the need to make some sense of ill-formed programs. A compiler is structured primarily to deal with well-formed source programs, so it must be enhanced with special error recovery algorithms to make it deal reasonably with ill-formed programs.

Syntactic error recovery is particularly difficult. At one extreme, an over-ambitious error recovery algorithm might induce an avalanche of spurious error reports. At the opposite extreme, an over-cautious error recovery algorithm might skip a large part of the source program and fail to detect genuine syntactic errors.

9.2.2   Run-time error reporting

Run-time error reporting is a completely different but equally important problem. Among the more common run-time errors are:

• arithmetic overflow

• division by zero

• out-of-range array indexing

These errors can be detected only at run-time, because they depend on values computed at run-time.[1]

Some run-time errors are detected by the target machine. For example, overflow may result in a machine interrupt. But in some machines the only effect of overflow is to set a bit in the condition code register, and the object program must explicitly test this bit whenever there is a risk of overflow.

Other run-time errors are not detected by the machine at all, but instead must be detected by tests in the object program. For example, out-of-range array indexing might result in computing the address of a word that is not actually part of the array. This is usually not detected by the machine unless the computed address is outside the program's address space.

These examples illustrate only typical machine behavior. Real machines range from one extreme, where *no* run-time errors are detected automatically, to the opposite extreme, where all the more common run-time errors are detected automatically. The typical situation is that some run-time errors are detected by hardware, leaving others to be detected by software.

Where a particular run-time error is *not* detected by hardware, the compiler should generate code to test for the error explicitly. In array indexing, for example, the compiler should generate code not only to evaluate the index but also to check whether it lies within the array's index range.

---

[1] If the language is dynamically typed, i.e., a variable can take values of different types at different times, then type errors also are run-time errors. However, we do not consider dynamically-typed languages here.

Example 9.3   Detecting array indexing errors

The following Triangle program fragment illustrates array indexing:

```
let
    var name: array 4 of Char;
    var i: Integer
in
    begin
        ...;
(1)     name[i] := ' ';
        ...
    end
```

Assume that characters and integers occupy one word each, and that the addresses of global variables name and i are 200 and 204, respectively. Thus name occupies words 200 through 203; and the address of name[i] is $200 + i$, provided that $0 \le i \le 3$.

The Triangle compiler does not currently generate index checks. The assignment command at (1) will be translated to object code like this (omitting some minor details):

```
LOADL  48        – fetch the blank character
LOAD   204       – fetch the value of i
LOADL  200       – fetch the address of name[0]
CALL   add       – compute the address of name[i]
STOREI           – store the blank character at that address
```

This code is dangerous. If the value of i is out of range, the blank character will be stored, not in an element of name, but in some other variable – possibly of a different type. (If the value of i happens to be 4, then i itself will be corrupted in this way.)

We could correct this deficiency by making the compiler generate object code with index checks, like this:

```
LOADL  48            – fetch the blank character
LOAD   204           – fetch the value of i
LOADL  0             – fetch the lower bound of name
LOADL  3             – fetch the upper bound of name
CALL   rangecheck    – check that the index is within range
LOADL  200           – fetch the address of name[0]
CALL   add           – compute the address of name[i]
STOREI               – store the blank character at that address
```

The index check is italicized for emphasis. The auxiliary routine *rangecheck*, when called with arguments *i*, *m*, and *n*, is supposed to return *i* if $m \le i \le n$, or to fail otherwise. The space cost of the index check is three instructions, and the time cost is three instructions plus the time taken by *rangecheck* itself.

□

Software run-time checks are expensive in terms of object-program size and speed. Without them, however, the object program might overlook a run-time error, eventually failing somewhere else, or terminating with meaningless results. And, let it be emphasized, if a compiler generates object programs whose behavior differs from the language specification, it is simply incorrect. The compiler should, at the very least, allow the programmer the option of including or suppressing run-time checks. Then a program's unpredictable behavior would be the responsibility of the programmer who opts to suppress run-time checks.

Whether the run-time check is performed by hardware or software, there remains the problem of generating a suitable error report. This should not only describe the nature of the error (e.g., 'arithmetic overflow' or 'index out of range'), but should also locate it in the source program. An error report stating that overflow occurred at instruction address 1234 (say) would be unhelpful to a programmer who is trying to debug a high-level language program. A better error report would locate the error at a particular line in the source program.

The general principle here is that error reports should relate to the source program rather than the object program. Another example of this principle is a facility to display the current values of variables during or after the running of the program. A simple storage dump is of little value: the programmer cannot understand it without a detailed knowledge of the run-time organization assumed by the compiler (data representation, storage allocation, layout of stack frames, layout of the heap, etc.). Better is a symbolic dump that displays each variable's source-program identifier, together with its current value in source-language syntax.

Example 9.4   Reporting run-time errors

Consider the Triangle program fragment of Example 9.3. Suppose that an out-of-range index is detected at (1). The following error report and storage dump are expressed largely in object-program terms:

```
Array indexing error at instruction address 1234.
Data store at this point:
```

address	content
...	...
200	74
201	97
202	118
203	97
204	10
...	...

This information is hard to understand, to put it mildly. It is not clear which array indexing operation failed. There is no indication that some of the words in the data store constitute an array. There is no distinction between different types of data such as integers and characters.

The following error report and storage dump are expressed more helpfully in source-program terms:

```
Array indexing error at line 45.
Data store at this point:
        name = ['J', 'a', 'v', 'a']
        i    = 10
```

Here the programmer can tell at a glance what went wrong.

□

But how can the source-program line number be determined at run-time? One possible technique is this. We dedicate a register (or storage cell) that will contain the current line number. The compiler generates code to update this register whenever control passes from one source-program line to another. Clearly, however, this technique is costly in terms of extra instructions in the object program.

An alternative technique is as follows. The compiler generates a table relating line numbers to instruction addresses. If the object program stops, the code pointer is used to search the table and determine the corresponding line number. This technique has the great advantage of imposing no time or space overheads on the object program. (The line-number table can be stored separately from the object program, and loaded only if required.)

The generation of reliable line-number information, however, is extremely difficult in the presence of heavily-optimized code. In this case, the code generator may have eliminated some of the original instructions, and substantially re-ordered others, making it very difficult to identify the line number of a given instruction. In the worst case, a single instruction may actually be part of the code for several different lines of source code.

To generate a symbolic storage dump requires more sophisticated techniques. The compiler must generate a 'symbol table' containing the identifier, type, and address of each variable in the source program, and the identifier and entry address of each procedure (and function). If the object program stops, using the symbol table each (live) variable can be located in the data store. The variable's identifier can be printed along with its current value, formatted according to its type. If one or more procedures are active at the time when the program stops, the store will contain one or more stack frames. To allow the symbolic dump to cover local variables, the symbol table must record which variables are local to which procedures, and the procedure to which each frame belongs must be identified in some way. (See Exercise 9.16.)

This problem is compounded on a register machine, where a variable might be located in a register and not in the store. It is also compounded for heavily-optimized code, where several variables with disjoint lifetimes may share the same memory location.

9.3 Efficiency

When we consider efficiency in the context of a compiler, we must carefully distinguish between compile-time efficiency and run-time efficiency. They are not the same thing at all; indeed, there is often a tradeoff between the two. The more a compiler strives to generate efficient (compact and fast) object code, the less efficient (bulkier and slower) the compiler itself tends to become.

The most efficient compilers are those that generate abstract machine code, where the abstract machine has been designed specifically to support the operations of the source language. Compilation is simple and fast because there is a straightforward translation from the source language to the target language, with few special cases to worry about. Such is the Triangle compiler used as a case study in this book. Of course, the object code has to be interpreted, imposing a significant speed penalty at run-time.

Compilers that generate code for real machines are generally less efficient. They must solve a variety of awkward problems. There is often a mismatch between the operations of the source language and the operations provided by the target machine. The target-machine operations are often irregular, complicating the translation. There might be many ways of translating the same source program into object code, forcing the compiler writer to implement lots of special cases in an attempt to generate the best possible object code.

9.3.1 Compile-time efficiency

Let us examine a compiler from the point of view of algorithmic complexity. Ideally, we would like the compiler to run in $O(n)$ time,[2] where n is some measure of the source program's size (for example, the number of tokens). In other words, a 10-fold increase in the size of the source program should result in a 10-fold increase in compilation time. A compiler that runs in $O(n^2)$ time is normally unacceptable: a 10-fold increase in the size of the source program would result in a 100-fold increase in compilation time! In practice, $O(n \log n)$ might be an acceptable compromise.

If all phases of a compiler run in $O(n)$ time, then the compiler as a whole will run in $O(n)$ time.[3] But if just one of the phases runs in $O(n^2)$ time, then the compiler as a whole

---

[2] The O-notation is a way of estimating the efficiency of a program. Let n be the size of the program's input. If we state that the program's running time is $O(n)$, we mean that its running time is proportional to n. (The actual running time could be $100n$ or $0.01n$.) Similarly, $O(n \log n)$ time means time proportional to $n \log n$, $O(n^2)$ time means time proportional to n^2, and so on. In estimates of algorithmic complexity, the constants of proportionality are generally less important than the difference between, for example, $O(n)$ and $O(n^2)$.

[3] Suppose that phase A runs in time an, and phase B in time bn (where a and b are constants). Then the combination of these phases will run in time $an + bn = (a + b)n$, which is still $O(n)$.

will run in $O(n^2)$ time.[4] In general, compilation time is dominated by the phase with the worst time complexity.

The parsing, type checking, and code generation algorithms described in Chapters 4, 5, and 7 do in fact run in $O(n)$ time. However, identification is often a weak link.

Assume that the number of applied occurrences of identifiers in the source program is $O(n)$, and that the average number of entries in the identification table is $O(n)$. If linear search is used, each identification will take $O(n)$ time, so total identification time will be $O(n^2)$. If instead some kind of binary search is used, each identification will take $O(\log n)$ time, so total identification time will be $O(n \log n)$. With clever use of hashing it is possible to bring each identification down to almost constant time, so total identification time will be $O(n)$, the ideal.

There are other weak links in some compilers. Some code transformation algorithms run in $O(n^2)$ time, as we shall see in the next subsection. An extreme case is the polymorphic type inference algorithm used in an ML compiler, which runs in $O(2^{2^n})$ time in pathological cases. (Fortunately these cases never arise in practice!)

9.3.2 Run-time efficiency

Let us now consider the efficiency of object programs, and in particular programs that run on real machines. Perhaps the most problematic single feature of real machines is the fact that they provide general-purpose registers. Computer architects provide registers because they speed up object programs. But compilers have to work harder to generate object programs that make effective use of the registers.

Example 9.5 Code generation for a register machine

The following Triangle command:

```
a := (b*c) - (d + (e*f))
```

would be translated to the following TAM code:

```
LOAD    b
LOAD    c
CALL    mult
LOAD    d
LOAD    e
LOAD    f
CALL    mult
```

---

[4] Suppose that phase A runs in time an, and phase B in time bn^2 (where a and b are constants). Then the combination of these phases will run in time $an + bn^2$. Even if a is much greater than b, the second term will eventually dominate as n increases.

```
CALL   add
CALL   sub
STORE  a
```

As we saw in Chapter 7, a simple efficient code generator can easily perform this translation. The code generator has no registers to worry about.

Now suppose that the target machine has a pool of registers and a typical one-address instruction set. Now the command might be translated to object code like this:

```
LOAD   R1  b
MULT   R1  c
LOAD   R2  d
LOAD   R3  e
MULT   R3  f
ADD    R2  R3
SUB    R1  R2
STORE  R1  a
```

Although this is comparatively straightforward, some complications are already evident. The code generator must allocate a register for the result of each operation. It must ensure that the register is not reused until that result has been used. (Thus R1 cannot be used during the evaluation of 'd + (e*f)', because at that time it contains the unused result of evaluating 'b*c'.) Furthermore, when the right operand of an operator is a simple variable, the code generator should avoid a redundant load by generating, for example, 'MULT R1 c' rather than 'LOAD R2 c' followed by 'MULT R1 R2'.

The above is not the only possible object code, nor even the best. One improvement is to evaluate 'd + (e*f)' *before* 'b*c'. A further improvement is to evaluate '(e*f) + d' instead of 'd + (e*f)', exploiting the commutativity of '+'. The combined effect of these improvements is to save an instruction and a register:

```
LOAD   R1  e
MULT   R1  f
ADD    R1  d
LOAD   R2  b
MULT   R2  c
SUB    R2  R1
STORE  R2  a
```

The trick illustrated here is to evaluate the more complicated subexpression of a binary operator first.

But that is not all. The compiler might decide to allocate registers to selected variables throughout their lifetimes. Supposing that registers R6 and R7 are thus allocated to variables a and d, the object code could be further improved as follows:

```
LOAD    R1  e
MULT    R1  f
ADD     R1  R7
LOAD    R6  b
MULT    R6  c
SUB     R6  R1
```

□

Several factors make code generation for a register machine rather complicated. Register allocation is one factor. Another is that compilers *must* in practice achieve code improvements of the kind illustrated above – programmers demand nothing less!

But even a compiler that achieves such improvements will still generate rather mediocre object code (typically four times slower than hand-written assembly code). A variety of algorithms have been developed that allow a compiler to generate much more efficient object code (typically twice as slow as hand-written assembly code). These are called **code transformation** (or *code optimization*[5]) algorithms. Some of the more common code transformations are:

- **Constant folding**: If an expression depends only on known values, it can be evaluated at compile-time rather than run-time.

- **Common subexpression elimination**: If the same expression occurs in two different places, and is guaranteed to yield the same result in both places, it might be possible to save the result of the first evaluation and reuse it later.

- **Code movement**: If a piece of code executed inside a loop always has the same effect, it might be possible to move that code out of the loop, where it will be executed fewer times.

Example 9.6   Constant folding

Consider the following Java program fragment:

```
static double pi = 3.1416;
...
double volume = 4/3 * pi * r * r * r;
```

The compiler could replace the subexpression '4/3 * pi' by 4.1888. This constant folding saves a run-time division and multiplication. The programmer could have written '4.1888 * r * r * r' in the first place, of course, but only at the expense of making the program less readable and less maintainable.

The following illustrates a situation where only the compiler can do the folding.

---

[5] The more widely used term, *code optimization*, is actually inappropriate: it is infeasible for a compiler to generate truly optimal object code.

Consider the following Triangle program fragment:

```
type Date = record
                y: Integer, m: Integer, d: Integer
            end;
var hol: array 6 of Date
...
hol[2].m := 12
```

The relevant addressing formula is:

$$\begin{aligned} address[\![\texttt{hol[2].m}]\!] \quad &= address[\![\texttt{hol[2]}]\!] + 1 \\ &= address[\![\texttt{hol}]\!] + 2 \times 3 + 1 \\ &= address[\![\texttt{hol}]\!] + 7 \end{aligned}$$

(assuming that each integer occupies one word). Furthermore, if the compiler decides that $address[\![\texttt{hol}]\!] = 20$ (relative to SB), then $address[\![\texttt{hol[2].m}]\!]$ can be folded to the constant address 27. This is shown in the following object code:

```
LOADL  12
STORE  27[SB]
```

Address folding makes field selection into a compile-time operation. It even makes indexing of a static array by a literal into a compile-time operation.

□

Example 9.7   Common subexpression elimination

Consider the following Triangle program fragment:

```
var x: Integer;   var y: Integer;   var z: Integer
...
... (x-y) * (x-y+z) ...
```

Here the subexpression 'x-y' is a common subexpression. If the compiler takes no special action, the two occurrences of this subexpression will be translated into two separate instruction sequences, as in object code (a) below. But their results are guaranteed to be equal, so it would be more efficient to compute the result once and then copy it when required, as in object code (b) below.

```
(a)  LOAD  x        (b)  LOAD  x
     LOAD  y             LOAD  y
     CALL  sub           CALL  sub        – computes the value of x-y
     LOAD  x             LOAD  -1[ST]     – copies the value of x-y
     LOAD  y             LOAD  z
     CALL  sub           CALL  add
     LOAD  z             CALL  mult
     CALL  add
     CALL  mult
```

Now consider the following Triangle program fragment:

```
type T = ...;
var a: array 10 of T;   var b: array 20 of T
...
a[i] := b[i]
```

Here there is another, less obvious, example of a common subexpression. It is revealed in the addressing formulas for a[i] and b[i]:

$$address\llbracket \texttt{a[i]} \rrbracket \quad = \quad address\llbracket \texttt{a} \rrbracket + (i \times 4)$$
$$address\llbracket \texttt{b[i]} \rrbracket \quad = \quad address\llbracket \texttt{b} \rrbracket + (i \times 4)$$

where i is the value of variable i, and where we have assumed that each value of type T occupies four words.

The common subexpression 'x-y' could have been eliminated by modifying the source program. But the common subexpression '$i \times 4$' can be eliminated only by the compiler, because it exists only at the target machine level.

□

Example 9.8   Code movement

Consider the following Triangle program fragment:

```
var name: array 3 of array 10 of Char
...
i := 0;
while i < 3 do
    begin
    j := 0;
    while j < 10 do
        begin name[i][j] := ' '; j := j + 1 end;
    i := i + 1
    end
```

The addressing formula for name[i][j] is:

$$address\llbracket \texttt{name[i][j]} \rrbracket \quad = \quad address\llbracket \texttt{name} \rrbracket + (i \times 10) + j$$

(assuming that each character occupies one word). A straightforward translation of this program fragment will generate code to evaluate $address\llbracket \texttt{name} \rrbracket + (i \times 10)$ inside the inner loop. But this code will yield the same address in every iteration of the inner loop, since the variable i is not updated by the inner loop.

The object program would be more efficient if this code were moved out of the inner loop. (It cannot be moved out of the outer loop, of course, because the variable i is updated by the outer loop.)

□

Constant folding is a relatively straightforward transformation, requiring only local analysis, and is performed even by simple compilers. For example, the Triangle compiler performs constant folding on address formulas.

Other code transformations such as common subexpression elimination and code movement, on the other hand, require nontrivial analysis of large parts of the source program, to discover which transformations are feasible and safe. To ensure that common subexpression elimination is safe, the relevant part of the program must be analyzed to ensure that no variable in the subexpression has been updated between the first and second evaluations of the subexpression. To ensure that code can be safely moved out of a loop, the whole loop must be analyzed to ensure that the movement does not change the program's behavior.

Code transformation algorithms always slow down the compiler, in an absolute sense, even when they run in $O(n)$ time. But some of these algorithms, especially ones that require analysis of the entire source program, may consume as much as $O(n^2)$ time.

Code transformations are only occasionally justified. During program development, when the program is compiled and recompiled almost as often as it is run, fast compilation is more important than generating very efficient object code. It is only when the program is ready for production use, when it will be run many times without recompilation, that it pays to use the more time-consuming code transformation algorithms.

For an industrial-strength compiler, a sensible compromise is to provide *optional* code transformation algorithms. The programmer (who is the best person to judge) can then compile the program without code transformations during the development phase, and can decide when the program has stabilized sufficiently to justify compiling it with code transformations.

9.4 Further reading

More detailed discussions of the major issues in programming language design and specification, and their interaction, may be found in the concluding chapters of the companion textbooks by Watt (1990, 1991). Interesting accounts of the design of a number of major programming languages – including Ada, C, C++, Lisp, Pascal, Prolog, and Smalltalk – may be found in Bergin and Gibson (1996).

A formal specification of a programming language makes a more reliable guide to the implementor than an informal specification. More radically, it might well be feasible to use a suitable formal specification of a programming language to *generate* an implementation automatically. A system that does this is called a ***compiler generator***. Development of compiler generators has long been a major goal of programming languages research.

Good-quality compiler generators are not yet available, but useful progress has been made. From a syntactic specification we can generate a scanner and parser, as described in Chapters 3 and 4 of Aho *et al.* (1985). The idea of generating an interpreter from a formal semantic specification is explored in Sections 4.4 and 8.4 of Watt (1991). Generating compilers from semantic specifications is the hardest problem. Lee (1989) surveys past efforts in this direction, which have succeeded in generating only poor-quality compilers.

A large variety of syntactic error recovery methods have been proposed and used in practice. One method, which is particularly suitable for use in conjunction with a recursive-descent parser, is described in Welsh and McKeag (1980).

Code transformation is a major topic in compilers. A detailed account is beyond the scope of this textbook. Instead, see the very extensive account in Chapter 10 of Aho *et al.* (1985). Although code transformation is now regarded as an advanced topic, surprisingly it was one of the first topics to engage the attention of compiler writers. In the 1950s, the writers of the first Fortran compiler went to extraordinary lengths to generate efficient object code, perceiving that this was the only way to attract hard-bitten assembly-language programmers to Fortran. The resulting compiler was noteworthy both for its Byzantine compiling algorithms and for its remarkably good object code!

Fortunately, our understanding of compiling algorithms – and of programming language design and specification – has developed a long way since those early days. In this textbook, and in its companions, we have tried to convey this understanding to a wide readership. We hope we have succeeded!

Exercises

9.1 Obtain a sample of ill-formed programs. (A first programming course should be a good source of such programs!) Compile them, and study the error reports. Does the compiler detect every error, and report it accurately? Does the compiler generate any spurious error reports?

9.2 Write a critical account of your favorite language processor's reporting of run-time errors and its diagnostic facilities. Does it detect every run-time error? Does it report errors in source-program terms? Does it provide a symbolic diagnostic facility?

9.3 Obtain a sample of well-formed programs, varying in size. Using your favorite compiler, measure and plot compilation time against source program size (n). Do you think that the compiler takes $O(n)$ time, $O(n \log n)$ time, or worse?

9.4 Obtain a sample of working programs. Using a compiler with a code transformation option, measure these programs' running time with and without code transformation. (If the compiler has several 'levels' of code transformation, try them all.)

9.5* Consider the following Triangle program fragment:

```
var a: array ... of Integer
...
i := m - 1; j := n; pivot := a[n];
while i < j do
  begin
  i := i + 1; while a[i] < pivot do i := i + 1;
  j := j - 1; while a[j] > pivot do j := j - 1;
  if i < j then
      begin
      t := a[i]; a[i] := a[j]; a[j] := t
      end
  end;
t := a[i]; a[i] := a[n]; a[n] := t
```

(a) Find out the object code that would be generated by the Triangle compiler.

(b) Write down the object code that would be generated by a Triangle compiler that performs code transformations such as constant folding, common subexpression elimination, and code movement.

Projects with the Triangle language processor

All of the following projects involve modifications to the Triangle language processor, so you will need to obtain a copy. (It is available from our Web site. See page xv of the Preface for downloading instructions.)

Nearly every project involves a modification to the language. Rather than plunging straight into implementation, you should first *specify* the language extension. Do this by modifying the informal specification of Triangle in Appendix B, following the same style.

9.6* Extend Triangle with additional loops as follows.

(a) A repeat-command:

```
repeat C until E
```

is executed as follows. The subcommand C is executed, then the expression E is evaluated. If the value of the expression is *true*, the loop terminates, otherwise the loop is repeated. The subcommand C is therefore executed at least once. The type of the expression E must be Boolean.

(b) A for-command:

```
for I from E₁ to E₂ do C
```

is executed as follows. First, the expressions E_1 and E_2 are evaluated, yielding the integers m and n (say), respectively. Then the subcommand C is executed repeatedly, with identifier I bound in successive iterations to each integer in the range m through n. If $m > n$, C is not executed at all. (The scope of I is C, which may use the value of I but may not update it. The types of E_1 and E_2 must be `Integer`.) Here is an example:

```
for n from 2 to m do
   if prime(n) then
      putint(n)
```

9.7** Extend Triangle with a case-command of the form:

```
case E of
   IL₁:  C₁;
   ...;
   ILₙ:  Cₙ;
   else: C₀
```

This command is executed as follows. First E is evaluated; then if the value of E matches the integer-literal IL_i, the corresponding subcommand C_i is executed. If the value of E matches none of the integer-literals, the subcommand C_0 is executed. (The expression E must be of type `Integer`, and the integer-literals must all be distinct.) Here is an example:

```
case today.m of
    2:    days := if leap then 29 else 28;
    4:    days := 30;
    6:    days := 30;
    9:    days := 30;
   11:    days := 30;
   else: days := 31
```

9.8** Extend Triangle with an initializing variable declaration of the form:

```
var I := E
```

This declaration is elaborated by binding I to a newly created variable. The variable's initial value is obtained by evaluating E. The lifetime of the variable is the activation of the enclosing block. (The type of I will be the type of E.)

9.9** Extend Triangle with unary and binary operator declarations of the form:

```
func O (I₁: T₁)  : T ~ E

func O (I₁: T₁, I₂: T₂)  : T ~ E
```

Operators are to be treated like functions. A unary operator application '$O\,E$' is to be treated like a function call '$O\,(E)$', and a binary operator application '$E_1\,O\,E_2$' is to be treated like a function call '$O\,(E_1,\,E_2)$'.

Here are some examples:

```
func -- (i: Integer) : Integer ~ 0 - n;

func ** (b: Integer, n: Integer) : Integer ~
   if n = 0
   then 1
   else n * (b ** (n-1))   ! assuming that n > 0
```

(*Notes:* The Triangle lexicon, Section B.8, already provides a whole class of operators from which the programmer may choose. The Triangle standard environment, Section B.9, already treats the standard operators '+', '-', '*', etc., like predeclared functions.)

9.10 ** Replace Triangle's constant and variable parameters by value and result parameters. Design your own syntax.

9.11 ** Extend Triangle with enumeration types. Provide a special enumeration type declaration of the form:

$$\texttt{enum type } I \sim (I_1, \ \ldots, \ I_n)$$

which creates a new and distinct primitive type with n values, and respectively binds the identifiers I_1, ..., and I_n to these values. Make the generic operations of assignment, '=', and '\=' applicable to enumeration types. (They are applicable to all Triangle types.) Provide new operations of the form 'succ E' (successor) and 'pred E' (predecessor), where succ and pred are keywords.

9.12 ** Extend Triangle with a new family of types, string n, whose values are strings of exactly n characters ($n \geq 1$). Provide string-literals of the form "$c_1 \ldots c_n$". Make the generic operations of assignment, '=', and '\=' applicable to strings. Provide a new binary operator '<<' (lexicographic comparison). Finally, provide an array-like string indexing operation of the form '$V[E]$', where V names a string value or variable. (*Hint:* Represent a string in the same way as a static array.)

Or:

Extend Triangle with a new type, String, whose values are character strings of any length (including the empty string). Provide string-literals of the form "$c_1 \ldots c_n$" ($n \geq 0$). Make the generic operations of assignment, '=', and '\=' applicable to strings. Provide new binary operators '<<' (lexicographic comparison) and '++' (concatenation). Finally, provide an array-like string indexing operation of the form '$V[E]$', and a substring operation of the form '$V[E_1:E_2]$', where V names a string value or variable. But do not permit string variables to be selectively updated. (*Hint:* Use an indirect representation for strings. The handle should consist of a length field and a pointer to an array of characters stored in the heap. In the absence of selective updating, string assignment can be implemented simply by copying the handle.)

9.13**   Extend Triangle with recursive types. Provide a special recursive type declaration of the form:

```
rec type I ~ T
```

where the type-denoter *T* may contain applied occurrences of *I*. (Typically, *T* will be a record type containing one or more fields of type *I*.) Every recursive type is to include a special empty value, denoted by the keyword nil. Do not permit variables of recursive types to be selectively updated. Example:

```
rec type IntList ~
      record head: Integer, tail: IntList end;

func cons (n: Integer, ns: IntList): IntList ~
   {head ~ n, tail ~ ns};

proc putints (ns: IntList) ~
   if ns \= nil then
      begin
      putint(ns.head); put(' ');
      putints(ns.tail)
      end;

var primes: IntList
...
primes := cons(2, cons(3, cons(5,
               cons(7, cons(11, nil)))));
putInts(primes)
```

(*Hint:* See Section 6.1.6 for a suggested indirect representation of recursive types. In the absence of selective updating, assignment can be implemented simply by copying the handle.)

9.14**   Extend Triangle with packages.

(a)   First make package declarations of the form:

```
package I ~ D end
```

This declaration is elaborated as follows. *I* is bound to a package of entities declared in *D*. The packaged entities may be constants, variables, types, procedures, functions, or any mixture of these. A packaged entity declared with identifier I_2 is named $I\$I_2$ outside the package declaration. Example:

```
package Graphics ~

   type Point ~
         record h: Integer, v: Integer end;

   func cart (x: Integer, y: Integer): Point ~
      {h ~ x, v ~ y};
```

```
        proc movehoriz (dist: Integer, var p: Point) ~
            p.h := p.h + dist

    end;

    var z: Graphics$Point
    ...
    z := Graphics$cart(3, 4);
    Graphics$movehoriz(7, z)
```

(b) Further extend Triangle with package declarations of the form:

```
package I ~ D₁ where D₂ end
```

A declaration of this form supports information hiding. Only the entities declared in D_1 are visible outside the package. The entities declared in D_2 are visible only in D_1.

9.15** Modify the Triangle language processor to perform run-time index checks, wherever necessary. (*Hint:* Add a new primitive routine `rangecheck` to TAM, as suggested in Example 9.3.)

9.16** Modify the Triangle language processor to produce run-time error reports and symbolic dumps along the lines illustrated in Example 9.4. You will have to modify both the compiler and the interpreter. (*Hint:* First, restrict your attention to global variables of primitive type. Then deal with procedures and local variables. Finally, deal with variables of composite type.)

9.17** Modify the Triangle compiler to perform constant folding wherever possible.

9.18** Modify the Triangle compiler to perform code movement in the following circumstances. Suppose that in the following loop:

```
while ... do ... E ...
```

the (sub)expression E is *invariant*, i.e., it does not use the value of any variable that is updated anywhere in the loop. Then transform the loop to:

```
let const I ~ E
in
    while ... do ... I ...
```

where I is some identifier not used elsewhere in the loop. (*Hint:* Implement this by a transformation of the decorated AST representing the source program.)

Answers to Selected Exercises

Specimen answers to about half of the exercises are given here. Some of the answers are given only in outline.

Answers 1

1.1 Other kinds of language processor: syntax checkers, cross-referencers, pretty-printers, high-level translators, program transformers, symbolic debuggers, etc.

1.4 Mini-Triangle expressions: (a) and (e) only. (Mini-Triangle has no functions, no unary operators, and no operator '>='.)

Commands: (f) and (j) only. (Mini-Triangle procedures have exactly one parameter each, and there is no if-command without an else-part.)

Declarations: (l), (m), and (o). (Mini-Triangle has no real-literals, and no multiple variable declarations.)

1.5 AST:

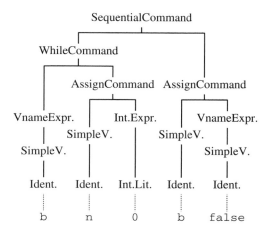

1.6   The value written is 10.

Answers 2

2.2   (a) Compiling and (b) running a Triangle program:

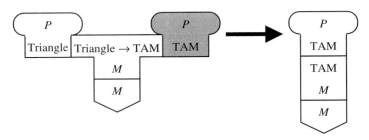

(c) Disassembling the object program:

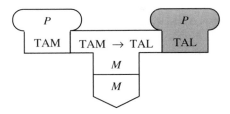

The purpose of the disassembler is to allow the programmer to read the compiler's object code.

2.4   (a) Compiling the TAM interpreter:

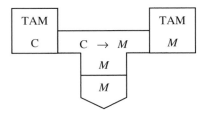

(b) Compiling the Pascal compiler:

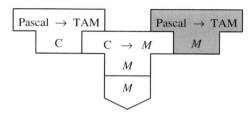

(c) Compiling and running a Pascal program:

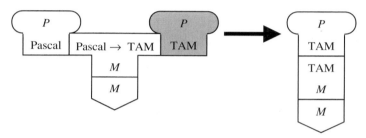

2.8 *Strategy 1:* Extend the C-into-RTL translator to become a C+-into-RTL translator, and compile it. Composed with the RTL-into-*M* translator, this gives a two-stage C+ compiler (similar to the given C compiler):

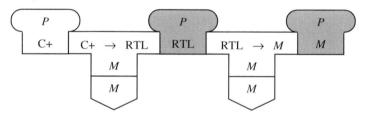

Strategy 2: Write a C+-into-C translator (a *preprocessor*) in C, and compile it. Composed with the two-stage C-into-*M* compiler, this gives a three-stage C+ compiler:

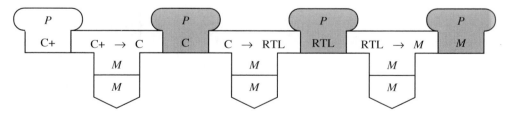

Strategy 2 requires more work, because the preprocessor must not only analyze the C+ source program, but also generate a C object program (requiring good layout if intended to be readable). Moreover the resulting compiler will be slower, being three-stage rather than two-stage. The advantage of strategy 2 is that the resulting compiler will be more modular: any improvements in the C-into-RTL translator will benefit the C+ compiler as well as the C compiler.

2.9 Write an initial version of the Utopia-1 compiler in C, and compile it using the C compiler:

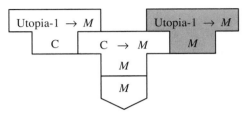

Then rewrite the Utopia-1 compiler in Utopia-1 itself, and compile it using the initial version:

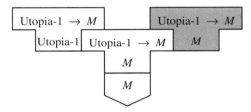

Extend the Utopia-1 compiler to become a Utopia-2 compiler, still expressed in Utopia-1. Compile it using the Utopia-1 compiler:

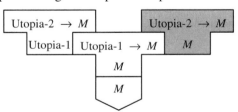

Extend the Utopia-2 compiler to become a Utopia-3 compiler, still expressed in Utopia-1. Compile it using the Utopia-1 compiler:

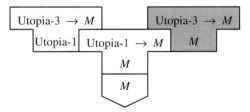

(Alternatively, the Utopia-3 compiler could be written in Utopia-2.)

Answers 3

3.3   The contextual errors are (i) 'Logical' is not declared; (ii) the expression of
the if-command is not of type *bool*; and (iii) 'yes' is not declared:

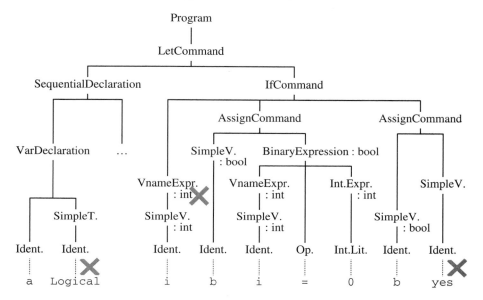

3.5   In brief, compile one subprogram at a time. After parsing a subprogram and
constructing its AST, perform contextual analysis and code generation on the
AST. Then prune the AST: replace the subprogram's body by a stub, and retain
only the part(s) of the AST that will be needed to compile subsequent calls to
the subprogram (i.e., its identifier, formal parameters, and result type if any).

The maximum space requirement will be for the largest subprogram's AST,
plus the pruned ASTs of all the subprograms.

3.6   This restructuring would be feasible. It would be roughly similar to Answer
3.5, although the interleaving of syntactic analysis, contextual analysis, and
code generation would be more complicated.

Answers 4

4.3   After repeated left factorization and elimination of left recursion:

Numeral   ::=   Digits (**.** Digits | ε) (**e** Sign Digits | ε)

$$\text{Digits} \qquad ::= \qquad \text{Digit Digit*}$$

4.4   (a)   {**C, J, P**}

        (b)   {**0, 1, 2, a, b**}

        (c)   *starters*⟦Digit⟧ = *starters*⟦Digits⟧ = *starters*⟦Numeral⟧ = {**0, 1, 2, 3**}

        (d)   *starters*⟦Subject⟧ = {**I, a, the**}; *starters*⟦Object⟧ = {**me, a, the**}.

4.9   Parsing methods (with enhancements italicized):

```
private void parseCommand () {
  int expval = parseExpression();
  accept('=');
  print(expval);
}

private int parseExpression () {
  int expval = parseNumeral();
  while (currentChar == '+'
         || currentChar == '-'
         || currentChar == '*') {
    char op = currentChar;
    acceptIt();
    int numval = parseNumeral();
    switch (op) {
    case '+':  expval += numval;  break;
    case '-':  expval -= numval;  break;
    case '*':  expval *= numval;  break;
    }
  }
  return expval;
}

private int parseNumeral () {
  int numval = parseDigit();
  while (isDigit(currentChar))
    numval = 10*numval + parseDigit();
  return numval;
}

private byte parseDigit () {
  if ('0' <= currentChar && currentChar <= '9') {
    byte digval = currentChar - '0';
    currentChar = next input character;
    return digval;
  } else
    report a lexical error
}
```

4.11   (a) Refine 'parse $X \mid Y$' to:

> **if** (currentToken.kind is in *starters*⟦X⟧)
>   parse X
> **else if** (currentToken.kind is in *starters*⟦Y⟧)
>   parse Y
> **else**
>   report a syntactic error

This is correct if and only if *starters*⟦X⟧ and *starters*⟦Y⟧ are disjoint.

(b) Refine 'parse $[X]$' to:

> **if** (currentToken.kind is in *starters*⟦X⟧)
>   parse X

This is correct if and only if *starters*⟦X⟧ is disjoint from the set of tokens that can follow $[X]$ in this particular context.

(c) Refine 'parse X^+' to:

> **do**
>   parse X
> **while** (currentToken.kind is in *starters*⟦X⟧);

This is correct if and only if *starters*⟦X⟧ is disjoint from the set of tokens that can follow X^+ in this particular context.

4.12   After left factorization:

> single-Command ::=   ...
> | **if** Expression **then** single-Command
>   (**else** single-Command $\mid \varepsilon$)
> | ...

The tokens that can follow a single-command are {else, end}. This set is not disjoint from *starters*⟦else single-Command⟧ = {else}, so the grammar is not LL(1). (In fact, no ambiguous grammar is LL(1).)

The parsing method obtained by converting this production rule would be:

```
private void parseSingleCommand () {
    switch (currentToken.kind) {
    ...

    case Token.IF: {
            acceptIt();
            parseExpression();
            accept(Token.THEN);
            parseSingleCommand();
```

```
        if (currentToken.kind == Token.ELSE) {
          acceptIt();
          parseSingleCommand();
        }
      }
      break;

    ...
    }
  }
```

Given (4.34) as input, `parseSingleCommand` would accept 'if E_1 then', and then call itself recursively. The recursive activation of `parseSingle-Command` would accept 'if E_2 then C_1 else C_2', and then return. The original activation would then also return.

This behavior is exactly what Pascal and C specify.

4.14 After eliminating left recursion:

Expression	::=	secondary-Expression (add-Operator secondary-Expression)*
secondary-Expression	::=	primary-Expression (mult-Operator primary-Expression)*

Parsing procedures (with AST enhancements in italics):

```
private Expression parseExpression () {
  Expression e1AST =
        parseSecondaryExpression();
  while (currentToken.kind ==
        Token.ADDOPERATOR) {
    Operator opAST = parseAddOperator();
    Expression e2AST =
        parseSecondaryExpression ();
    e1AST = new BinaryExpression(
        e1AST, opAST, e2AST);
  }
  return e1AST;
}

private Expression parseSecondaryExpression () {
  Expression e1AST = parsePrimaryExpression();
  while (currentToken.kind ==
        Token.MULTOPERATOR) {
    Operator opAST = parseMultOperator();
    Expression e2AST =
        parsePrimaryExpression();
```

```
        e1AST = new BinaryExpression(
                e1AST, opAST, e2AST);
    }
    return e1AST;
}
```

Procedure `parsePrimaryExpression` would be similar to the corresponding method in Example 4.12.

4.16 (a) Define an abstract class AST together with concrete subclasses NonterminalAST and TerminalAST:

```
public abstract class AST {
    public byte tag;

    public static final byte   // tag values
        IDENTIFIER        =  0,
        INTLITERAL        =  1,
        OPERATOR          =  2,
        PROGRAM           =  3,
        ASSIGNCOMMAND     =  4,
        CALLCOMMAND       =  5,
        ...
        CONSTDECLARATION  = 15,
        VARDECLARATION    = 16,
        SEQDECLARATION    = 17,
        SIMPLETYPEDENOTER = 18;
}

///////////////////////////////////////////////

public class NonterminalAST extends AST {
    public AST[] children;

    public NonterminalAST (byte tag,
            AST[] children) {
        this.tag = tag;  this.children = children;
    }
}

///////////////////////////////////////////////

public class TerminalAST extends AST {
    public String spelling;

    public TerminalAST (byte tag,
            String spelling) {
        this.tag = tag;  this.spelling = spelling;
    }
}
```

(b)   To display an AST:

```
public abstract class AST {
   ...

   public void display (byte level);
}

//////////////////////////////////////////

public class NonterminalAST extends AST {
   ...

   public void display (byte level) {
      for (int i = 0; i < level; i++)
         print("  ");
      switch (this.tag) {
      case AST.PROGRAM:
         println("Program");  break;
      ...
      }
      for (int i = 0;
                i < this.children.length; i++)
         this.children[i].display(level+1);
   }
}

//////////////////////////////////////////

public class TerminalAST extends AST {
   ...

   public void display (byte level) {
      for (int i = 0; i < level; i++)
         print("  ");
      switch (this.tag) {
      case AST.IDENTIFIER:
         print("Identifier ");  break;
      ...
      }
      println(this.spelling);
   }
}
```

4.18   This lexical grammar is ambiguous. The scanning procedure would turn out as follows:

```
private byte scanToken () {
   switch (currentChar) {
```

```
case 'a': case 'b': case 'c': case 'd':
   ...
case 'y': case 'z':
   takeIt();
   while (isLetter(currentChar)
            || isDigit(currentChar))
      takeIt();
   return Token.IDENTIFIER;

   ...

case 'i':
   takeIt(); take('f');
   return Token.IF;

case 't':
   takeIt(); take('h'); take('e'); take('n');
   return Token.THEN;

case 'e':
   takeIt(); take('l'); take('s'); take('e');
   return Token.ELSE;

   ...
   }
}
```

This method will not compile. Moreover, there is no reasonable way to fix it.

Answers 5

5.2   One possibility would be a pair of subtables, one for globals and one for locals. (Each subtable could be an ordered binary tree or a hash table.) There would also be a variable, the *current level*, set to either *global* or *local*. Constructor `IdentificationTable` would set the current level to *global*, and would empty both subtables. Method `enter` would add the new entry to the global or local subtable, according to the current level. Method `retrieve` would search the local subtable first, and if unsuccessful would search the global subtable second. Method `openScope` would change the current level to *local*. Method `closeScope` would change it to *global*, and would also empty the local subtable.

5.3   Constructor `IdentificationTable` would make the stack contain a single empty binary tree. Method `enter` would add the new entry to the topmost binary tree. Method `retrieve` would search the binary trees in turn, starting with the topmost, and stopping as soon as it finds a match. Method open-

Scope would push an empty binary tree on to the stack. Method closeScope would pop the topmost binary tree.

This implementation would be more efficient than the simple stack implementation, because it would replace linear search by binary search. In terms of time complexity, retrieval would be $O(\log n)$ rather than $O(n)$.

5.4 Constructor IdentificationTable would make the table contain a single (empty) column. Method enter would add the new entry to the leftmost column, and to the row indexed by the given identifier. Method retrieve would access the first entry in the row indexed by the given identifier. Method openScope would insert a new leftmost (empty) column. Method closeScope would remove the leftmost column.

This implementation would be more efficient than the simple stack implementation or the stack of binary trees, because retrieval would be essentially a constant-time operation. In terms of time complexity, retrieval would be $O(1)$ rather than $O(n)$ or $O(\log n)$. (This assumes that identifiers are hashed to index the table rows efficiently.)

5.7 Since each type is represented by an *object*, simply compare the object references. This will require changing the existing type checking code from using the equals method to using the '==' operator. For example, the code for visitAssignCommand in Example 5.11 would become:

```
public Object visitAssignCommand
                    (AssignCommand com,
                     Object arg) {
    Type vType = (Type) com.V.visit(this, null);
    Type eType = (Type) com.E.visit(this, null);
    if (! com.V.variable)
        ... // Report an error – the left side is not a variable.
    if (eType != vType)
        ... // Report an error – the left and right sides
            // are not of equivalent type.
    return null;
}
```

5.9   Undecorated AST:

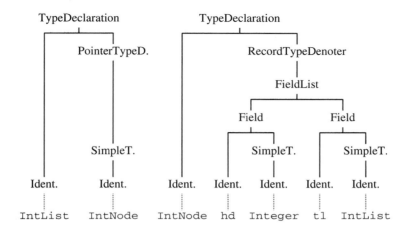

After elimination of type identifiers:

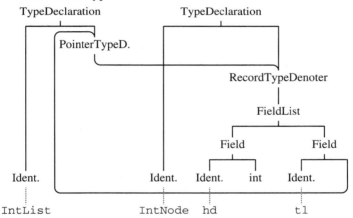

The AST has been transformed to a directed graph, with the mutually recursive types giving rise to a cycle.

The complication is that the `equals` method must be able to compare two (possibly cyclic) graphs for structural equivalence. It must be implemented carefully to avoid nontermination.

5.10   Consider the function call '*I* (*E*)'. Check that *I* has been declared by a function declaration, say 'func *I* (*I*′ : *T*′) : *T* ~ *E*″'. Check that the type of the actual parameter *E* is equivalent to the formal parameter type *T*′. Infer that the type of the function call is *T*.

Answers 6

6.3   Advantage of single-word representation:

- It is economical in storage.

Advantages of double-word representation:

- It is closer to the mathematical (unbounded) set of integers.

- Overflow is less likely.

6.5   (a)

(b)   Every T_{index} has a minimum value, *min* T_{index}; a maximum value, *max* T_{index}; and an *ord* function that maps the values of the type to consecutive integers. Thus:

$$size\ T = (u - l + 1) \times size\ T_{elem}$$
$$address[\![\ a[0]\ ]\!] = address\ a - (l \times size\ T_{elem})$$
$$address[\![\ a[i]\ ]\!] = address[\![\ a[0]\ ]\!] + (ord\ (i) \times size\ T_{elem})$$

where $l = ord(min\ T_{index})$ and $u = ord(max\ T_{index})$.

6.6   For two-dimensional arrays:

$$size\ T = m \times n \times size\ T_{elem}$$
$$address[\![\ a[i][j]\ ]\!] = address\ a + (i \times (n \times size\ T_{elem})) + (j \times size\ T_{elem})$$

6.8   Make the handle contain the lower and upper bounds in both dimensions, as well as a pointer to the elements. Store the elements themselves row by row (as in Example 6.6). If l, u, l', and u' are the values of E_1, E_2, E_3, and E_4, respectively, then we get:

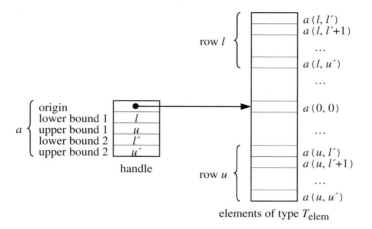

6.11   (a)   Evaluate subexpression '1 - (c * 2)' before 'a * b':

```
LOAD  R1  c
MULT  R1  #2
LOAD  R2  #1
SUB   R2  R1
LOAD  R1  a
MULT  R1  b
ADD   R1  R2
```

(b)   Save the accumulator's contents to a temporary location (say *temp*) whenever the accumulator is needed to evaluate something else:

```
LOAD    c
MULT    #2
STORE   temp
LOAD    #1
SUB     temp
STORE   temp
LOAD    a
MULT    b
ADD     temp
```

(In general, more than one temporary location might be needed.)

6.13   Address of global variable v_i is:

$$address\ v_i\ =\ size\ T_1\ +\ \ldots\ +\ size\ T_{i-1}$$

Only the addresses allocated to the variables are affected by the order of the variable declarations. The *net* behavior of the object program is not affected.

6.16   Let each frame consist of a static part and a dynamic part. The static part accommodates variables of primitive type, and the handles of dynamic arrays. The dynamic part expands as necessary to accommodate elements of dynamic arrays. The frame containing v would look like this:

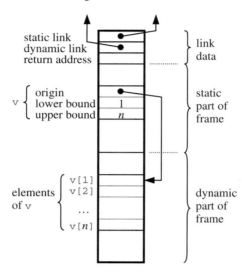

Since everything in the static part is of constant size, the compiler can determine each variable's address relative to the frame base. This is not true for the dynamic part, but the array elements there are always addressed indirectly through the handles.

6.17   There are three cases of interest. If $n = m+1$, S is local to the caller. If $n = m$, S is at the same level as the caller. If $n < m$, S encloses the caller.

(a)   On call, push S's frame on to the stack. In all cases, set Dn to point to the base of the new frame. (*Note:* If $n < m$, D($n+1$), …, and Dm become undefined.)

(b)   On return, pop S's frame off the stack. If $n = m+1$, do nothing else. If $n = m$, reset Dm to point to the base of the (now) topmost frame. If $n < m$, reset other display registers using the static links: D($m-1$) ← *content* (Dm); …; Dn ← *content* (D($n+1$)). (*Note:* If $n = m+1$, Dn becomes undefined.)

There is no need to change D0, D1, …, D($n-1$) at either the call or the return, since these registers point to the same frames before, during, and after the activation of S.

Advantages and disadvantages (on the assumption that D0, D1, etc., are all true registers):

• Nonlocal variables can be accessed as efficiently as local or global variables.

- The display registers must be updated at every call and return.

- The caller must reset the display registers after return, since S does not know where it was called from, i.e., it does not know m.

- Complications arise when S is an unknown routine (e.g., an argument), because then the caller does not know n.

6.19 (a)

Stack machine code Register machine code

```
LOAD  a            LOAD  R1  a
LOAD  b            LOAD  R2  b
LOAD  c            LOAD  R3  c
CALL  f            CALL      f
```

(b)

```
LOAD  a            LOAD  R1  a
CALL  g            CALL      g
                   STORE R0  temp
LOAD  b            LOAD  R1  b
LOAD  c            LOAD  R2  c
CALL  h            CALL      h
                   LOAD  R2  R0
LOAD  d            LOAD  R3  d
                   LOAD  R1  temp
CALL  f            CALL      f
```

6.23 The following algorithm uses an address translation table, in which each entry (a, a') consists of a heap variable's old address a together with its new address a' after compaction.

Procedure to compact the heap:
  calculate the new address of all heap variables;
  move and adjust all heap variables;
  adjust the heap top HT;
  adjust all pointers in the stack.

Procedure to calculate the new address of all heap variables:
  set the current new address newAddr to HB;
  for each heap variable hv, in order of distance from HB:
    subtract the size of hv from newAddr;
    add an entry for (address of hv, newAddr) to the table.

Procedure to move and adjust all heap variables:
  for each heap variable hv, in order of distance from HB:
    for each pointer p in hv:
      find an entry (p, q) in the table;
      replace p by q;
    find an entry (address of hv, r) in the table;
    copy hv to address r.

Procedure to adjust all pointers in the stack:
  for each pointer p in the stack:
    find an entry (p, q) in the table;
    replace p by q.

This algorithm assumes that the heap variables are linked (by hidden fields) in order of increasing distance from HB.

Answers 7

7.1 Code template (7.8e) gives rise to object code in which one jump instruction is executed per iteration. The code template of Exercise 7.1 gives rise to object code in which two jump instructions are executed per iteration, which is slower.

The code template of Exercise 7.1 is commonly used because it is suitable for one-pass compilation.

7.2 (a) *execute*$[\![V_1 , V_2 := E_1 , E_2]\!]$ =
          evaluate E_1
          evaluate E_2
          assign V_2
          assign V_1

   (b) *execute*$[\![C_1 , C_2]\!]$ =
          execute C_1
          execute C_2

   (c) *execute*$[\![$if E then $C]\!]$ =
          evaluate E
          JUMPIF(0) g
          execute C
       g:

   (d) *execute*$[\![$repeat C until $E]\!]$ =
       g: *execute* C
          evaluate E
          JUMPIF(0) g

(e) $execute[\![$repeat C_1 while E do $C_2]\!] =$

$\qquad$ JUMP h

$\quad g:\quad$ $execute\ C_2$

$\quad h:\quad$ $execute\ C_1$

$\qquad$ $evaluate\ E$

$\qquad$ JUMPIF(1) g

7.3 (a) $evaluate[\![$if E_1 then E_2 else $E_3]\!] =$

$\qquad$ $evaluate\ E_1$

$\qquad$ JUMPIF(0) g

$\qquad$ $evaluate\ E_2$

$\qquad$ JUMP h

$\quad g:\quad$ $evaluate\ E_3$

$\quad h:$

(b) $evaluate[\![$let D in $E]\!] =$

$\qquad$ $elaborate\ D$

$\qquad$ $evaluate\ E$

$\qquad$ POP(n) s $\qquad$ if $s > 0$

$\qquad\qquad\qquad\qquad$ where s = amount of storage allocated by D,

$\qquad\qquad\qquad\qquad\qquad$ $n = size$ (type of E)

(c) $evaluate[\![$begin C ; yield E end$]\!] =$

$\qquad$ $execute\ C$

$\qquad$ $evaluate\ E$

7.5   Selected encoding methods:

(a)
```
public Object visitSimAssignCommand
            (SimAssignCommand com, Object arg) {
    com.E1.visit(this, arg);
    com.E2.visit(this, arg);
    encodeAssign(com.V2);
    encodeAssign(com.V1);
    return null;
}
```

(c)
```
public Object visitIfOnlyCommand
            (IfOnlyCommand com, Object arg) {
    com.E.visit(this, arg);
    short i = nextInstAddr;
    emit(Instruction.JUMPIFop, 0,
        Instruction.CBr, 0);
    com.C.visit(this, arg);
    short g = nextInstrAddr;
    patch(i, g);
    return null;
}
```

(d) **public** Object visitRepeatCommand

```
                 (RepeatCommand com, Object arg) {
    short g = nextInstrAddr;
    com.C.visit(this, arg);
    com.E.visit(this, arg);
    emit(Instruction.JUMPIFop, 0,
            Instruction.CBr, g);
    return null;
}
```

7.7 (a) The most efficient solution is:

$$execute[\![\text{for } I \text{ from } E_1 \text{ to } E_2 \text{ do } C]\!] =$$

	evaluate E_2	– compute final value
	evaluate E_1	– compute initial value of I
	JUMP h	
g:	*execute C*	
	CALL *succ*	– increment current value of I
h:	LOAD -1ST	– fetch current value of I
	LOAD -3ST	– fetch final value
	CALL *le*	– test current value ≤ final value
	JUMPIF(1) g	– if so, repeat
	POP(0) 2	– discard current and final values

At g and at h, the current value of I is at the stack top (at address -1ST), and the final value is immediately underlying (at address -2ST).

(b) This solution requires the introduction of two new AST classes. The first is a Command AST used to represent the for-command itself. The second is a Declaration AST used to represent the (pseudo-)declaration of the for-command control variable. This is because the identification table stores Declaration ASTs as attributes.

```
public class ForCommand extends Command {
    ...
    // Declaration of control variable...
    public ForDeclaration D;

    // Subphrases of for-command...
    public Expression E1, E2;
    public Command C;
}

//////////////////////////////////////////////////
```

```
public class ForDeclaration
                extends Declaration {
  // The contextual analyzer links all applied occurrences of the
  // control variable to the ForDeclaration AST in the
  // corresponding ForCommand AST.
  ...
  public Identifier I;
}

//////////////////////////////////////////////////

public Object visitForCommand
                (ForCommand com,
                 Object arg) {
  short gs = shortValueOf(arg);
  com.D.entity = new UnknownValue(1,
                        gs + 1);
  com.E2.visit(this, arg);
  com.E1.visit(this, new short(gs + 1));
  short i = nextInstrAddr;
  emit(Instruction.JUMPop, 0,
       Instruction.CBr, 0);
  short g = nextInstrAddr;
  com.C.visit(this, new short(gs + 2));
  emit(Instruction.CALLop, Instruction.SBr,
       Instruction.PBr,
       address of primitive routine succ);
  short h = nextInstrAddr;
  patch(i, h);
  emit(Instruction.LOADop, 1,
       Instruction.STr, -1);
  emit(Instruction.LOADop, 1,
       Instruction.STr, -3);
  emit(Instruction.CALLop, Instruction.SBr,
       Instruction.PBr, address of primitive routine le);
  emit(Instruction.JUMPIFop, 1,
       Instruction.CBr, g);
  emit(Instruction.POPop, 0, 0, 2);
  return null;
}
```

The ForCommand visitor/encoding method first creates a run-time entity description for the control variable *I*, and attaches it to the corresponding ForDeclaration. Provided that the contextual analyzer has linked each applied occurrence of the control variable to the For-Declaration, the loop body *C* will be able to fetch (but not assign to) the control variable.

7.10 (a) Reserve space for the result variable just above the link data in the function's frame (i.e., at address 3 [LB]):

$$elaborate[\![\, \text{func } I \ (\ FP\ )\ :\ T \sim C\,]\!] =$$
$$\qquad \text{JUMP } g$$
$$e:\quad \text{PUSH } n \qquad\qquad \text{where } n = size\ T$$
$$\qquad execute\ C$$
$$\qquad \text{RETURN}\,(n)\ \ d \qquad \text{where } d = \text{size of } FP$$
$$g:$$

$$execute[\![\, \text{result } E\,]\!] =$$
$$\qquad evaluate\ E$$
$$\qquad \text{STORE}\,(n)\ \ 3\,[\text{LB}] \qquad \text{where } n = size\ (\text{type of } E)$$

(b)

```
public Object visitFuncDeclaration
                (FuncDeclaration decl,
                 Object arg) {
    Frame f = (Frame) arg;
    short i = nextInstrAddr;
    emit(Instruction.JUMPop, 0,
         Instruction.CBr, 0);
    short e = nextInstrAddr;
    decl.entity =
         new KnownRoutine(2, f.level, e);
    Frame f1 = new Frame(f.level + 1, 0);
    short d = shortValueOf(
         decl.FP.visit(this, f1));
    // ... creates a run-time entity for the formal parameter,
    // and returns the size of the parameter.
    short n = shortValueOf(
         decl.T.visit(this, null));
    emit(Instruction.PUSHop, 0, 0, n);
    Frame f2 = new Frame(f.level + 1, 3 + n);
    decl.C.visit(this, f2);
    emit(Instruction.RETURNop, n, 0, d);
    short g = nextInstrAddr;
    patch(i, g);
    return new Short(0);
}
```

```
public Object visitResultCommand
                (ResultCommand com,
                 Object arg) {
    short n =
          shortValueOf(com.E.visit(this, arg));
    emit(Instruction.STOREop, n,
         Instruction.LBr, 3);
    return null;
}
```

Answers 8

8.3   In outline:

```
public abstract class UserCommand {
  public abstract void perform
                    (HypoInterpreter interp);
}
//////////////////////////////////////////////
public class StepCommand extends UserCommand {
  public void perform
            (HypoInterpreter interp) {
      interp.step();
  }
}
//////////////////////////////////////////////
public class RunCommand extends UserCommand {
  public void perform
            (HypoInterpreter interp) {
    do {
       interp.step();
    } while (! interp.break[interp.CP]
         && (interp.status ==
             HypoState.RUNNING));
  }
}
//////////////////////////////////////////////
```

```java
public class ShowRegistersCommand
                extends UserCommand {
  ...
}

///////////////////////////////////////////////

public class ShowDataStoreCommand
                extends UserCommand {
  ...
}

///////////////////////////////////////////////

public class TerminateCommand
                extends UserCommand {
  public void perform
          (HypoInterpreter interp) {
     interp.status = HypoState.HALTED;
  }
}

///////////////////////////////////////////////

public class ToggleBreakpointCommand
                extends UserCommand {

  public short point; // The breakpoint address to toggle

  public void perform
          (HypoInterpreter interp) {
     interp.break[this.point] =
        ! interp.break[this.point];
  }
}

///////////////////////////////////////////////

public class HypoInterpreter extends HypoState {
  ...
  public static boolean[] break =
              new boolean[CODESIZE];
  UserCommand command;

  private void clearBreakpoints () {
     for (int d = 0; d < CODESIZE; d++)
        break[d++] = false;
  }
```

```
    private UserCommand interact () {
        ... //  Obtain a command from the user.
    }

    public void step () {
        // Fetch the next instruction ...
        HypoInstruction instr = code[PC++];
        // Analyze this instruction ...
        ...
        // Execute this instruction ...
        ...
    }

    public void emulate () {
        // initialize ...
        PC = 0; ACC = 0; status = RUNNING;
        clearBreakpoints();

        do {
            command = interact();
            command.perform(this);
        } while (status == RUNNING);
    }
}
```

8.6   (a) Advantages and disadvantages of storing commands as *text*:

• Loading and editing are easy.

• Commands have to be scanned and parsed whenever fetched for execution, which is slow.

Advantages and disadvantages of storing commands as *tokens*:

• Loading and editing are fairly easy.

• Commands have to be parsed whenever fetched for execution, which is moderately slow.

Advantages and disadvantages of storing commands as *ASTs*:

• Commands have to be scanned and parsed when loaded.

• Editing is awkward.

• Commands are immediately ready for execution.

(b) Answer implied by the above.

8.8   In outline:

```java
public class MiniShell extends MiniShellState {

   public MiniShellCommand readAnalyze () {
      // Read and analyze the next command from the user.
      ...
   }

   public MiniShellCommand readAnalyze
                     (FileInputStream script) {
      // Read and analyze the next command from file script.
      ...
   }

   public void execute (MiniShellCommand com) {
      if (com.name.equals("create")) {
         ...
      }
      else if (com.name.equals("call")) {
         File input = new File(com.args[0]);
         FileInputStream script =
               new FileInputStream(input);
         while (more commands in script) {
            MiniShellCommand subCom =
                  readAnalyze(script);
            execute(subCom);
         }
      } else  // executable program
         exec(com.name, com.args);
   }

   public void interpret () {
      // Initialize ...
      status = RUNNING;

      do {

         // Fetch and analyze the next instruction ...
         MiniShellCommand com = readAnalyze();

         // Execute this instruction ...
         execute(com);

      } while (status == RUNNING);
   }
}
```

Answers 9

9.5   In outline:

Common subexpressions are: 'i < j' at points (1); the *address* of a[i] at points (2); the *address* of a[j] at points (3); the *address* of a[n] at points (4).

```
var a: array ... of Integer
...
i := m - 1; j := n; pivot := a[n];
while i < j⁽¹⁾ do
    begin
    i := i + 1;
    while a[i]⁽²⁾ < pivot do i := i + 1;
    j := j - 1;
    while a[j]⁽³⁾ > pivot do j := j - 1;
    if i < j⁽¹⁾ then
        begin
        t := a[i]⁽²⁾;
        a[i]⁽²⁾ := a[j]⁽³⁾;
        a[j]⁽³⁾ := t
        end
    end;
t := a[i]⁽²⁾;
a[i]⁽²⁾ := a[n]⁽⁴⁾;
a[n]⁽⁴⁾ := t
```

Informal Specification of the Programming Language Triangle

B.1 Introduction

Triangle is a regularized extensible subset of Pascal. It has been designed as a model language to assist in the study of the concepts, formal specification, and implementation of programming languages.

The following sorts of entity can be declared and used in Triangle:

- A *value* is a truth value, integer, character, record, or array.

- A *variable* is an entity that may contain a value and that can be updated. Each variable has a well-defined lifetime.

- A *procedure* is an entity whose body may be executed in order to update variables. A procedure may have constant, variable, procedural, and functional parameters.

- A *function* is an entity whose body may be evaluated in order to yield a value. A function may have constant, variable, procedural, and functional parameters.

- A *type* is an entity that determines a set of values. Each value, variable, and function has a specific type.

Each of the following sections specifies part of the language. The subsection headed **Syntax** specifies its grammar in BNF (except for Section B.8 which uses EBNF). The subsection headed **Semantics** informally specifies the semantics (and contextual constraints) of each syntactic form. Finally, the subsection headed **Examples** illustrates typical usage.

B.2 Commands

A command is executed in order to update variables. (This includes input–output.)

Syntax

A single-command is a restricted form of command. (A command must be enclosed between begin ... end brackets in places where only a single-command is allowed.)

Command	::=	single-Command
	|	Command ; single-Command

single-Command ::=
  \| (empty)
  \| V-name := Expression
  \| Identifier (Actual-Parameter-Sequence)
  \| **begin** Command **end**
  \| **let** Declaration **in** single-Command
  \| **if** Expression **then** single-Command
     else single-Command
  \| **while** Expression **do** single-Command

(The first form of single-command is empty.)

Semantics

- The skip command ' ' has no effect when executed.

- The assignment command 'V := E' is executed as follows. The expression E is evaluated to yield a value; then the variable identified by V is updated with this value. (The types of V and E must be equivalent.)

- The procedure calling command '$I(APS)$' is executed as follows. The actual-parameter-sequence APS is evaluated to yield an argument list; then the procedure bound to I is called with that argument list. (I must be bound to a procedure. APS must be compatible with that procedure's formal-parameter-sequence.)

- The sequential command 'C_1; C_2' is executed as follows. C_1 is executed first; then C_2 is executed.

- The bracketed command 'begin C end' is executed simply by executing C.

- The block command 'let D in C' is executed as follows. The declaration D is elaborated; then C is executed, in the environment of the block command overlaid by the bindings produced by D. The bindings produced by D have no effect outside the block command.

- The if-command 'if E then C_1 else C_2' is executed as follows. The expression E is evaluated; if its value is true, then C_1 is executed; if its value is false, then C_2 is executed. (The type of E must be Boolean.)

- The while-command 'while E do C' is executed as follows. The expression E is evaluated; if its value is true, then C is executed, and then the while-command is executed again; if its value is false, then execution of the while-command is completed. (The type of E must be Boolean.)

Examples

The following examples assume the standard environment (Section B.9), and also the following declarations:

```
var i: Integer;
var s: array 8 of Char;
var t: array 8 of Char;

proc sort (var a: array 8 of Char) ~ ...
```

(a) `s[i] := '*'; t := s`

(b) `getint(var i); putint(i); puteol()`

(c) `sort(var s)`

(d)
```
if s[i] > s[i+1] then
    let var c : Char
    in
        begin
        c := s[i]; s[i] := s[i+1]; s[i+1] := c
        end
else ! skip
```

(e)
```
i := 7;
while (i > 0) /\ (s[i] = ' ') do
    i := i - 1
```

B.3 Expressions

An expression is evaluated to yield a value. A record-aggregate is evaluated to construct a record value from its component values. An array-aggregate is evaluated to construct an array value from its component values.

Syntax

A secondary-expression and a primary-expression are progressively more restricted forms of expression. (An expression must be enclosed between parentheses in places where only a primary-expression is allowed.)

Expression	::=	secondary-Expression
	|	**let** Declaration **in** Expression
	|	**if** Expression **then** Expression **else** Expression
secondary-Expression	::=	primary-Expression
	|	secondary-Expression Operator primary-Expression

primary-Expression	::=	Integer-Literal
	|	Character-Literal
	|	V-name
	|	Identifier (Actual-Parameter-Sequence)
	|	Operator primary-Expression
	|	(Expression)
	|	{ Record-Aggregate }
	|	[Array-Aggregate]
Record-Aggregate	::=	Identifier ~ Expression
	|	Identifier ~ Expression , Record-Aggregate
Array-Aggregate	::=	Expression
	|	Expression , Array-Aggregate

Semantics

- The expression 'IL' yields the value of the integer-literal IL. (The type of the expression is Integer.)

- The expression 'CL' yields the value of the character-literal CL. (The type of the expression is Char.)

- The expression 'V', where V is a value-or-variable-name, yields the value identified by V, or the current value of the variable identified by V. (The type of the expression is the type of V.)

- The function calling expression '$I(APS)$' is evaluated as follows. The actual-parameter-sequence APS is evaluated to yield an argument list; then the function bound to I is called with that argument list. (I must be bound to a function. APS must be compatible with that function's formal-parameter-sequence. The type of the expression is the result type of that function.)

- The expression '$O\ E$' is, in effect, equivalent to a function call '$O\ (E)$'.

- The expression '$E_1\ O\ E_2$' is, in effect, equivalent to a function call '$O\ (E_1,\ E_2)$'.

- The expression '(E)' yields just the value yielded by E.

- The block expression 'let D in E' is evaluated as follows. The declaration D is elaborated; then E is evaluated, in the environment of the block expression overlaid by the bindings produced by D. The bindings produced by D have no effect outside the block expression. (The type of the expression is the type of E.)

- The if-expression 'if E_1 then E_2 else E_3' is evaluated as follows. The expression E_1 is evaluated; if its value is true, then E_2 is evaluated; if its value is false, then E_3 is evaluated. (The type of E_1 must be Boolean. The type of the expression is the same as the types of E_2 and E_3, which must be equivalent.)

- The expression '$\{RA\}$' yields just the value yielded by the record-aggregate RA. (The type of '$\{I_1 \sim E_1, \ldots, I_n \sim E_n\}$' is 'record I_1: T_1, $\ldots$, I_n: T_n end', where the type of each E_i is T_i. The identifiers $I_1, \ldots, I_n$ must all be distinct.)

- The expression '$[AA]$' yields just the value yielded by the array-aggregate AA. (The type of '$[E_1, \ldots, E_n]$' is 'array n of T', where the type of every E_i is T.)

- The record-aggregate '$I \sim E$' yields a record value, whose only field has the identifier I and the value yielded by E.

- The record-aggregate '$I \sim E$, RA' yields a record value, whose first field has the identifier I and the value yielded by E, and whose remaining fields are those of the record value yielded by RA.

- The array-aggregate 'E' yields an array value, whose only component (with index 0) is the value yielded by E.

- The array-aggregate 'E, AA' yields an array value, whose first component (with index 0) is the value yielded by E, and whose remaining components (with indices 1, 2, $\ldots$) are the components of the array value yielded by AA.

Examples

The following examples assume the standard environment (Section B.9), and also the following declarations:

```
var current: Char;
type Date ~ record
              y: Integer, m: Integer, d: Integer
          end;
var today: Date;

func multiple (m: Integer, n: Integer) : Boolean ~
     ...;

func leap (yr: Integer) : Boolean ~ ...
```

(a) `{y ~ today.y + 1, m ~ 1, d ~ 1}`

(b) `[31, if leap(today.y) then 29 else 28,`
`    31, 30, 31, 30, 31, 31, 30, 31, 30, 31]`

(c) `eof()`

(d) `(multiple(yr, 4) /\ \multiple(yr, 100))`
`    \/ multiple(yr, 400)`

(e) `let`
`    const shift ~ ord('a') - ord('A');`
`    func capital (ch : Char) : Boolean ~`
`            (ord('A') <= ord(ch))`
`              /\ (ord(ch) <= ord('Z'))`

```
in
    if capital(current)
    then chr(ord(current) + shift)
    else current
```

B.4 Value-or-variable names

A value-or-variable-name identifies a value or variable.

Syntax

```
V-name    ::=   Identifier
          |     V-name . Identifier
          |     V-name [ Expression ]
```

Semantics

• The simple value-or-variable-name '*I*' identifies the value or variable bound to *I*. (*I* must be bound to a value or variable. The type of the value-or-variable-name is the type of that value or variable.)

• The qualified value-or-variable-name '*V*.*I*' identifies the field *I* of the record value or variable identified by *V*. (The type of *V* must be a record type with a field *I*. The type of the value-or-variable-name is the type of that field.)

• The indexed value-or-variable-name '*V*[*E*]' identifies that component, of the array value or variable identified by *V*, whose index is the value yielded by the expression *E*. If the array has no such index, the program fails. (The type of *E* must be Integer, and the type of *V* must be an array type. The type of the value-or-variable-name is the component type of that array type.)

Examples

The following examples assume the standard environment (Section B.9), and also the following declarations:

```
type Date ~ record
                m : Integer, d : Integer
            end;
const xmas ~ {m ~ 12, d ~ 25};
var easter : Date;
var holiday : array 10 of Date
```

(a) easter

(b) xmas

(c) `xmas.m`

(d) `holiday`

(e) `holiday[7]`

(f) `holiday[2].m`

B.5 Declarations

A declaration is elaborated to produce bindings. Elaborating a declaration may also have the side effect of creating and updating variables.

Syntax

A single-declaration is just a restricted form of declaration.

Declaration	::=	single-Declaration
	|	Declaration **;** single-Declaration
single-Declaration	::=	**const** Identifier ~ Expression
	|	**var** Identifier **:** Type-denoter
	|	**proc** Identifier **(** Formal-Parameter-Sequence **)** ~ single-Command
	|	**func** Identifier **(** Formal-Parameter-Sequence **)** **:** Type-denoter ~ Expression
	|	**type** Identifier ~ Type-denoter

Semantics

- The constant declaration 'const I ~ E' is elaborated by binding I to the value yielded by the expression E. (The type of I will be the type of E.)

- The variable declaration 'var I : T' is elaborated by binding I to a newly created variable of type T. The variable's current value is initially undefined. The variable exists only during the activation of the block that caused the variable declaration to be elaborated.

- The procedure declaration 'proc I (FPS) ~ C' is elaborated by binding I to a procedure whose formal-parameter-sequence is FPS and whose body is the command C. The effect of calling that procedure with an argument list is determined as follows: FPS is associated with the argument list; then C is executed, in the environment of the procedure declaration overlaid by the bindings of the formal-parameters.

- The function declaration 'func I (FPS) : T ~ E' is elaborated by binding I to a function whose formal-parameter-sequence is FPS and whose body is the expression E. The effect of calling that function with an argument list is determined as follows: FPS is associated with the argument list; then E is evaluated to yield a value, in the environment of the function declaration overlaid by the bindings of the formal-parameters. (The type of *E* must be equivalent to the type denoted by *T*.)

- The type declaration 'type *I* ~ *T*' is elaborated by binding *I* to the type denoted by *T*.

- The sequential declaration '*D*₁ ; *D*₂' is elaborated by elaborating D_1 followed by D_2, and combining the bindings they produce. D_2 is elaborated in the environment of the sequential declaration, overlaid by the bindings produced by D_1. (D_1 and D_2 must not produce bindings for the same identifier.)

Examples

The following examples assume the standard environment (Section B.9):

```
(a)  const minchar ~ chr(0)

(b)  var name: array 20 of Char;
     var initial: Char

(c)  proc inc (var n: Integer) ~ n := n + 1

(d)  func odd (n: Integer) : Boolean ~
          (n // 2) \= 0

(e)  func power (a: Integer, n: Integer) : Integer ~
          if n = 0
          then 1
          else a * power(a, n - 1)

(f)  type Rational ~
          record num: Integer, den: Integer end
```

B.6 Parameters

Formal-parameters are used to parameterize a procedure or function with respect to (some of) the free identifiers in its body. On calling a procedure or function, the formal-parameters are associated with the corresponding arguments, which may be values, variables, procedures, or functions. These arguments are yielded by actual-parameters.

Syntax

```
Formal-Parameter-Sequence
        ::=
        |    proper-Formal-Parameter-Sequence

proper-Formal-Parameter-Sequence
        ::=    Formal-Parameter
        |      Formal-Parameter , proper-Formal-Parameter-Sequence
```

```
Formal-Parameter   ::=   Identifier : Type-denoter
                    |    var Identifier : Type-denoter
                    |    proc Identifier ( Formal-Parameter-Sequence )
                    |    func Identifier ( Formal-Parameter-Sequence )
                              : Type-denoter

Actual-Parameter-Sequence
                   ::=
                    |    proper-Actual-Parameter-Sequence

proper-Actual-Parameter-Sequence
                   ::=   Actual-Parameter
                    |    Actual-Parameter , proper-Actual-Parameter-Sequence

Actual-Parameter   ::=   Expression
                    |    var V-name
                    |    proc Identifier
                    |    func Identifier
```

(The first form of actual-parameter-sequence and the first form of formal-parameter-sequence are empty.)

Semantics

- A formal-parameter-sequence 'FP_1, ..., FP_n' is associated with a list of arguments, by associating each FP_i with the ith argument. The corresponding actual-parameter-sequence 'AP_1, ..., AP_n' yields a list of arguments, with each AP_i yielding the ith argument. (The number of actual-parameters must equal the number of formal-parameters, and each actual-parameter must be compatible with the corresponding formal-parameter. The actual-parameter-sequence must be empty if the formal-parameter-sequence is empty .)

- The formal-parameter '$I : T$' is associated with an argument value by binding I to that argument. The corresponding actual-parameter must be of the form 'E', and the argument value is obtained by evaluating E. (The type of E must be equivalent to the type denoted by T.)

- The formal-parameter 'var $I : T$' is associated with an argument variable by binding I to that argument. The corresponding actual-parameter must be of the form 'var V', and the argument variable is the one identified by V. (The type of V must be equivalent to the type denoted by T.)

- The formal-parameter 'proc I (FPS)' is associated with an argument procedure by binding I to that argument. The corresponding actual-parameter must be of the form 'proc I', and the argument procedure is the one bound to I. (I must be bound to a procedure, and that procedure must have a formal-parameter-sequence equivalent to FPS.)

- The formal-parameter 'func I (FPS) : T' is associated with an argument function by binding I to that argument. The corresponding actual-parameter must be of the form 'func I', and the argument function is the one bound to I. (I must be bound to a function, and that function must have a formal-parameter-sequence equivalent to *FPS* and a result type equivalent to the type denoted by T.)

Examples

The following examples assume the standard environment (Section B.9):

(a)
```
while \eol() do
    begin get(var ch); put(ch) end;
geteol(); puteol()
```

(b)
```
proc increment (var count: Integer) ~
        count := count + 1
...
increment(var freq[n])
```

(c)
```
func uppercase (letter: Char) : Char ~
        if (ord('a') <= ord(letter))
            /\ (ord(letter) <= ord('z'))
        then chr(ord(letter)-ord('a')+ord('A'))
        else letter

...
if uppercase(request) = 'Q' then quit
```

(d)
```
type Point ~ record x: Integer, y: Integer end;
proc shiftright (var pt: Point, xshift: Integer) ~
        pt.x := pt.x + xshift
...
shiftright(var penposition, 10)
```

(e)
```
proc iteratively (proc p (n: Integer),
                    var a: array 10 of Integer) ~
        let var i: Integer
        in
            begin
            i := 0;
            while i < 10 do
                begin p(a[i]); i := i + 1 end
            end;
var v : array 10 of Integer
...
iteratively(proc putint, var v)
```

B.7 Type-denoters

A type-denoter denotes a data type. Every value, constant, variable, and function has a specified type.

A record-type-denoter denotes the structure of a record type.

Syntax

Type-denoter	::=	Identifier
	|	**array** Integer-Literal **of** Type-denoter
	|	**record** Record-Type-denoter **end**
Record-Type-denoter	::=	Identifier **:** Type-denoter
	|	Identifier **:** Type-denoter **,** Record-Type-denoter

Semantics

- The type-denoter 'I' denotes the type bound to I.

- The type-denoter 'array IL of T' denotes a type whose values are arrays. Each array value of this type has an index range whose lower bound is zero and whose upper bound is one less than the integer-literal IL. Each array value has one component of type T for each value in its index range.

- The type-denoter 'record RT end' denotes a type whose values are records. Each record value of this type has the record structure denoted by RT.

- The record-type-denoter '$I : T$' denotes a record structure whose only field has the identifier I and the type T.

- The record-type-denoter '$I : T$, RT' denotes a record structure whose first field has the identifier I and the type T, and whose remaining fields are determined by the record structure denoted by RT. I must not be a field identifier of RT.

  (Type equivalence is structural:

- Two primitive types are equivalent if and only if they are the same type.

- The type record ..., I_i: T_i, ... end is equivalent to record ..., $I_i{'}$: $T_i{'}$, ... end if and only if each I_i is the same as $I_i{'}$ and each T_i is equivalent to $T_i{'}$.

- The type array n of T is equivalent to array $n{'}$ of $T{'}$ if and only if $n = n{'}$ and T is equivalent to $T{'}$.)

Examples

(a) `Boolean`

(b) `array 80 of Char`

(c) `record y: Integer, m: Month, d: Integer end`

(d)
```
record
    size: Integer,
    entry: array 100 of
              record
                 name: array 20 of Char,
                 number: Integer
              end
end
```

B.8 Lexicon

At the lexical level, the program text consists of tokens, comments, and blank space.

The tokens are literals, identifiers, operators, various reserved words, and various punctuation marks. No reserved word may be chosen as an identifier.

Comments and blank space have no significance, but may be used freely to improve the readability of the program text. However, two consecutive tokens that would otherwise be confused must be separated by comments and/or blank space.

Syntax

Program	::=	(Token | Comment | Blank)*
Token	::=	Integer-Literal | Character-Literal | Identifier | Operator | **array** | **begin** | **const** | **do** | **else** | **end** | **func** | **if** | **in** | **let** | **of** | **proc** | **record** | **then** | **type** | **var** | **while** | **.** | **:** | **;** | **,** | **:=** | **~** | **(** | **)** | **[** | **]** | **{** | **}**
Integer-Literal	::=	Digit Digit*
Character-Literal	::=	**'** Graphic **'**
Identifier	::=	Letter (Letter | Digit)*
Operator	::=	Op-character Op-character*
Comment	::=	**!** Graphic* end-of-line
Blank	::=	space | tab | end-of-line
Graphic	::=	Letter | Digit | Op-character | space | tab | **.** | **:** | **;** | **,** | **~** | **(** | **)** | **[** | **]** | **{** | **}** | **_** | **|** | **!** | **'** | **`** | **"** | **#** | **$**

Letter	::=	a | b | c | d | e | f | g | h | i | j | k | l | m |
		n | o | p | q | r | s | t | u | v | w | x | y | z |
		A | B | C | D | E | F | G | H | I | J | K | L | M |
		N | O | P | Q | R | S | T | U | V | W | X | Y | Z
Digit	::=	0 | 1 | 2 | 3 | 4 | 5 | 6 | 7 | 8 | 9
Op-character	::=	+ | - | * | / | = | < | > | \ | & | @ | % | ^ | ?

(*Note:* The symbols space, tab, and end-of-line stand for individual characters that cannot stand for themselves in the syntactic rules.)

Semantics

- The value of the integer-literal $d_n...d_1d_0$ is $d_n \times 10^n + ... + d_1 \times 10 + d_0$.

- The value of the character-literal `'c'` is the graphic character c.

- Every character in an identifier is significant. The cases of the letters in an identifier are also significant.

- Every character in an operator is significant. Operators are, in effect, a subclass of identifiers (but they are bound only in the standard environment, to unary and binary functions).

Examples

(a) Integer-literals: 0   1987

(b) Character-literals: '%'   'Z'   ' '

(c) Identifiers: x pi   v101   Integer   get   gasFlowRate

(d) Operators: +   *   <=   \/

B.9 Programs

A program communicates with the user by performing input–output.

Syntax

Program   ::=   Command

Semantics

- The program 'C' is run by executing the command C in the standard environment.

Example

```
let
    type Line ~
            record
                length: Integer,
                content: array 80 of Char
            end;
    proc getline (var l: Line) ~
            begin
            l.length := 0;
            while eol() do
                begin
                get(var l.content[l.length]);
                l.length := l.length + 1
                end;
            geteol()
            end;
    proc putreversedline (l: Line) ~
            let var i : Integer
            in
                begin
                i := l.length;
                while i > 0 do
                    begin
                    i := i - 1;
                    put(l.content[i])
                    end;
                puteol()
                end;
    var currentline: Line
in
    while eof() do
        begin
        getline(var currentline);
        putreversedline(currentline)
        end
```

Standard environment

The standard environment includes the following constant, type, procedure, and function declarations:

```
type Boolean ~ ...; ! truth values

const false ~ ...;   ! the truth value false

const true ~ ...;    ! the truth value true

type Integer ~ ...; ! integers up to maxint in magnitude

const maxint ~ ...; ! implementation-defined maximum integer

type Char ~ ...; ! implementation-defined characters

func \  (b: Boolean) : Boolean ~
        ...; !  not b, i.e., logical negation

func /\ (b1: Boolean, b2: Boolean) : Boolean ~
        ...; !  b1 and b2, i.e., logical conjunction

func \/ (b1: Boolean, b2: Boolean) : Boolean ~
        ...; !  b1 or b2, i.e., logical disjunction

func +  (i1: Integer, i2: Integer) : Integer ~
        ...; !  i1 plus i2,
             !  failing if the result exceeds maxint in magnitude

func -  (i1: Integer, i2: Integer) : Integer ~
        ...; !  i1 minus i2,
             !  failing if the result exceeds maxint in magnitude

func *  (i1: Integer, i2: Integer) : Integer ~
        ...; !  i1 times i2,
             !  failing if the result exceeds maxint in magnitude

func /  (i1: Integer, i2: Integer) : Integer ~
        ...; !  i1 divided by i2, truncated towards zero,
             !  failing if i2 is zero

func // (i1: Integer, i2: Integer) : Integer ~
        ...; !  i1 modulo i2, failing unless i2 is positive

func <  (i1: Integer, i2: Integer) : Boolean ~
        ...; !  true iff i1 is less than i2

func <= (i1: Integer, i2: Integer) : Boolean ~
        ...; !  true iff i1 is less than or equal to i2

func >  (i1: Integer, i2: Integer) : Boolean ~
        ...; !  true iff i1 is greater than i2
```

402 Programming Language Processors in Java

```
func >= (i1: Integer, i2: Integer) : Boolean ~
          ...; ! true iff i1 is greater than or equal to i2

func chr (i: Integer) : Char ~
          ...; ! character whose internal code is i,
               ! failing if no such character exists

func ord (c: Char) : Integer ~
          ...; ! internal code of c

func eof () : Boolean ~
          ...; ! true iff end-of-file has been reached in input

func eol () : Boolean ~
          ...; ! true iff end-of-line has been reached in input

proc get (var c: Char) ~
          ...; ! read the next character from input and assign it to c,
               ! failing if end-of-file already reached

proc put (c: Char) ~
          ...; ! write character c to output

proc getint (var i: Integer) ~
          ...; ! read an integer literal from input and assign its value
               ! to i, failing if the value exceeds maxint in magnitude,
               ! or if end-of-file is already reached

proc putint (i: Integer) ~
          ...; ! write to output the integer literal whose value is i

proc geteol () ~
          ...; ! skip past the next end-of-line in input,
               ! failing if end-of-file is already reached

proc puteol () ~
          ...; ! write an end-of-line to output
```

In addition, the following functions are available for every type *T*:

```
func = (val1: T, val2: T) : Boolean ~
          ...; ! true iff val1 is equal to val2

func \= (val1: T, val2: T) : Boolean ~
          ... ! true iff val1 is not equal to val2
```

APPENDIX C

Description of the Abstract Machine TAM

TAM is an abstract machine whose design makes it especially suitable for executing programs compiled from a block-structured language (such as Algol, Pascal, or Triangle). All evaluation takes place on a stack. Primitive arithmetic, logical, and other operations are treated uniformly with programmed functions and procedures.

C.1 Storage and registers

TAM has two separate stores:

• *Code Store*, consisting of 32-bit instruction words (read only).

• *Data Store*, consisting of 16-bit data words (read–write).

The layouts of both stores are illustrated in Figure C.1.

Each store is divided into *segments*, whose boundaries are pointed to by dedicated registers. Data and instructions are always addressed relative to one of these registers.

While a program is running, the segmentation of Code Store is fixed, as follows:

• The *code segment* contains the program's instructions. Registers CB and CT point to the base and top of the code segment. Register CP points to the next instruction to be executed, and is initially equal to CB (i.e., the program's first instruction is at the base of the code segment).

• The *primitive segment* contains 'microcode' for elementary arithmetic, logical, input–output, heap, and general-purpose operations. Registers PB and PT point to the base and top of the primitive segment.

While a program is running, the segmentation of Data Store may vary:

• The *stack* grows from the low-address end of Data Store. Registers SB and ST point to the base and top of the stack, and ST is initially equal to SB.

• The *heap* grows from the high-address end of Data Store. Registers HB and HT point to the base and top of the heap, and HT is initially equal to HB.

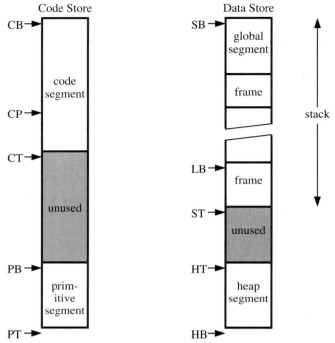

Figure C.1 Layout of the TAM Code Store and Data Store.

Both stack and heap can expand and contract. Storage exhaustion arises when ST and HT attempt to cross over.

The stack itself consists of one or more segments:

- The *global segment* is always at the base of the stack, and contains global data used by the program.

- The stack may contain any number of other segments, known as *frames*. Each frame contains data local to an activation of some routine. Calling a routine causes a new frame to be pushed on to the stack; return from a routine causes the topmost frame to be popped. The topmost frame may expand and contract, but the underlying frames are (temporarily) fixed in size. Register LB points to the base of the topmost frame.

Figure C.2 shows the outline of a source program in some block-structured language. Figure C.3 shows successive stack snapshots while this program is running:

(1)   The main program has called procedure P. Register LB points to the topmost frame, which belongs to P.

(2)   Procedure P has called procedure S. Register LB points to the topmost frame, which belongs to S; register L1 points to a frame belonging to P.

(3)   Procedure S has called procedure Q. Register LB points to the topmost frame, which belongs to Q; register L1 still points to a frame belonging to P.

(4)   Procedure Q has called procedure R. Register LB points to the topmost frame, which belongs to R; register L1 now points to a frame belonging to Q; register L2 points to a frame belonging to P.

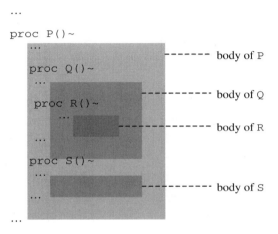

```
...

proc P()~
  ...                              ------- body of P
  proc Q()~
    ...                            ----------- body of Q
    proc R()~
      ...                          ------------- body of R
    ...
  proc S()~
    ...                            ---------- body of S
  ...
...
```

Figure C.2 Outline of a source program.

Global, local, and nonlocal data can be accessed as follows:

LOAD(n) d[SB]	– for any procedure to load global data
LOAD(n) d[LB]	– for any procedure to load its own local data
LOAD(n) d[L1]	– for procedure Q or S to load data local to P
LOAD(n) d[L1]	– for procedure R to load data local to Q
LOAD(n) d[L2]	– for procedure R to load data local to P

In each case an n-word object is loaded from address d relative to the base of the appropriate segment. Storing is analogous to loading.

In general, register LB points to the topmost frame, which is always associated with the routine R whose code is currently being executed; register L1 points to a frame associated with the routine R' that textually encloses R in the source program; register L2 points to a frame associated with the routine R'' that textually encloses R'; and so on.

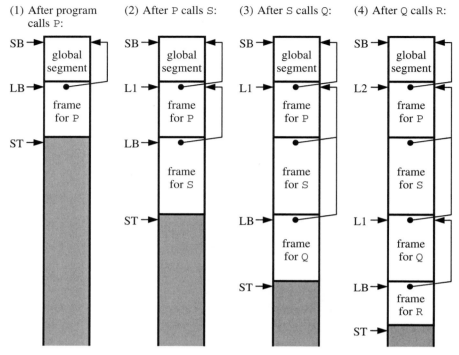

Figure C.3 Snapshots of the TAM stack (showing static links but not dynamic links).

All accessible data in the stack may be addressed relative to registers SB, LB, L1, L2, etc., as follows:

d[SB]	– for any routine to access global data
d[LB]	– for any routine to access its own local data
d[L1]	– for routine R to access data local to R'
d[L2]	– for routine R to access data local to R''

In each case an object is accessed at address d relative to the base of the appropriate segment. (In practice, registers L1, L2, etc., are used far less often than LB and SB.)

The layout of a frame is illustrated in Figure C.4. Consider a frame associated with routine R:

- The *static link* points to an underlying frame associated with the routine that textually encloses R in the source program.

- The *dynamic link* points to the frame immediately underlying this one in the stack.

- The *return address* is the address of the instruction immediately following the call instruction that activated R.

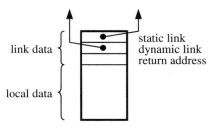

Figure C.4 Layout of a TAM frame.

There are sixteen registers, summarized in Table C.1. Every register is dedicated to a particular purpose. (No instructions use registers to operate on data.) Some of the registers are constant.

L1, L2, etc., are only pseudo-registers – whenever needed for addressing nonlocal data, they are dynamically evaluated from LB using the invariants L1 = *content*(LB), L2 = *content*(*content*(LB)), etc., where *content*(*a*) means the word contained at address *a*. This works because LB points to the first word of a frame, which contains its static link, which in turn points to the first word of an underlying frame, and so on.

Table C.1 Summary of TAM registers.

Register number	Register mnemonic	Register name	Behavior
0	CB	Code Base	constant
1	CT	Code Top	constant
2	PB	Primitives Base	constant
3	PT	Primitives Top	constant
4	SB	Stack Base	constant
5	ST	Stack Top	changed by most instructions
6	HB	Heap Base	constant
7	HT	Heap Top	changed by heap routines
8	LB	Local Base	changed by call and return instructions
9	L1	Local base 1	L1 = *content*(LB)
10	L2	Local base 2	L2 = *content*(*content*(LB))
11	L3	Local base 3	L3 = *content*(*content*(*content*(LB)))
12	L4	Local base 4	L4 = *content*(*content*(*content*(*content*(LB))))
13	L5	Local base 5	L5 = *content*(*content*(*content*(*content*(*content*(LB)))))
14	L6	Local base 6	L6 = *content*(*content*(*content*(*content*(*content*(*content*(LB))))))
15	CP	Code Pointer	changed by all instructions

C.2 Instructions

All TAM instructions have a common format, illustrated in Figure C.5. The *op* field contains the operation code. The *r* field contains a register number, and the *d* field usually contains an address displacement (possibly negative); together these define the operand's address (*d* + register *r*). The *n* field usually contains the size of the operand. The TAM instruction set is summarized in Table C.2.

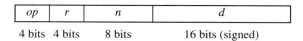

op	*r*	*n*	*d*
4 bits	4 bits	8 bits	16 bits (signed)

Figure C.5 TAM instruction format.

C.3 Routines

Every TAM routine must strictly respect the protocol illustrated in Figure C.6. Assume that routine *R* accepts *d* words of arguments and returns an *n*-word result. Immediately before *R* is called, its arguments must be at the stack top. (If *R* takes no arguments, *d* = 0.) On return from *R*, its arguments must be replaced at the stack top by its result. (If *R* does not return a result, *n* = 0.)

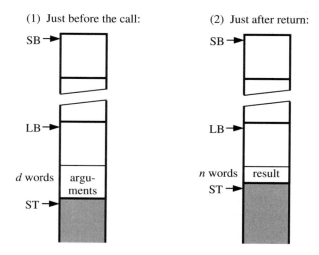

(1) Just before the call:

(2) Just after return:

Figure C.6 Stack layout before and after calling a TAM routine.

There are two kinds of routine in TAM:

- code routines

- primitive routines

A *code routine* consists of a sequence of instructions stored in the code segment. Control is transferred to the first instruction of that sequence by a CALL or CALLI instruction, and subsequently transferred back by a RETURN instruction. Figure C.7 illustrates the layout of the stack during a call to a code routine *R*.

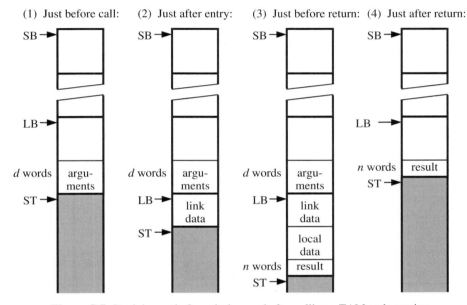

Figure C.7 Stack layout before, during, and after calling a TAM code routine.

(1)   Immediately before the call, *R*'s arguments (if any) must be at the stack top.

(2)   The call instruction pushes a new frame on top of the arguments and makes LB point to the base of that frame. The frame's static link is supplied by the call instruction. (The instruction 'CALL (*n*) ...' takes the address in register *n* as the static link. The instruction 'CALLI' takes the static link from the closure at the stack top.) The frame's dynamic link is the address formerly in register LB. The frame's return address is the address of the instruction immediately following the call instruction. At this stage the new frame contains only these three words.

(3)   The instructions of *R* may expand the topmost frame, e.g., by allocating space for local data. Immediately before the return, *R* must place any result at the stack top.

(4) The return instruction 'RETURN(n) d' pops the topmost frame and replaces the d words of arguments by the n-word result. LB is reset using the dynamic link, and control is transferred to the instruction at the return address.

Since R's arguments lie immediately below its frame, R can access the arguments using negative displacements relative to LB. For example:

```
LOAD(1)  -d[LB]          – for R to load its first argument (1 word)
LOAD(1)  -1[LB]          – for R to load its last argument (1 word)
```

A *primitive routine* is one that performs an elementary arithmetic, logical, input–output, heap, or general-purpose operation. The primitive routines are summarized in Table C.3. Each primitive routine has a fixed address in the primitive segment. TAM traps every call to an address in that segment, and performs the corresponding operation directly.

Table C.2 Summary of TAM instructions.

Op-code	Instruction mnemonic	Effect
0	LOAD(n) $d[r]$	Fetch an n-word object from the data address (d + register r), and push it on to the stack.
1	LOADA $d[r]$	Push the data address (d + register r) on to the stack.
2	LOADI(n)	Pop a data address from the stack, fetch an n-word object from that address, and push it on to the stack.
3	LOADL d	Push the 1-word literal value d on to the stack.
4	STORE(n) $d[r]$	Pop an n-word object from the stack, and store it at the data address (d + register r).
5	STOREI(n)	Pop an address from the stack, then pop an n-word object from the stack and store it at that address.
6	CALL(n) $d[r]$	Call the routine at code address (d + register r), using the address in register n as the static link.
7	CALLI	Pop a closure (static link and code address) from the stack, then call the routine at that code address.
8	RETURN(n) d	Return from the current routine: pop an n-word result from the stack, then pop the topmost frame, then pop d words of arguments, then push the result back on to the stack.
9	–	(unused)
10	PUSH d	Push d words (uninitialized) on to the stack.
11	POP(n) d	Pop an n-word result from the stack, then pop d more words, then push the result back on to the stack.
12	JUMP $d[r]$	Jump to code address (d + register r).
13	JUMPI	Pop a code address from the stack, then jump to that address.
14	JUMPIF(n) $d[r]$	Pop a 1-word value from the stack, then jump to code address (d + register r) if and only if that value equals n.
15	HALT	Stop execution of the program.

Table C.3 Summary of TAM primitive routines.

Address	Mnemonic	Arguments	Result	Effect
PB + 1	id	w	w'	Set $w' = w$.
PB + 2	not	t	t'	Set $t' = \neg t$.
PB + 3	and	t_1, t_2	t'	Set $t' = t_1 \wedge t_2$.
PB + 4	or	t_1, t_2	t'	Set $t' = t_1 \vee t_2$.
PB + 5	succ	i	i'	Set $i' = i + 1$.
PB + 6	pred	i	i'	Set $i' = i - 1$.
PB + 7	neg	i	i'	Set $i' = -i$.
PB + 8	add	i_1, i_2	i'	Set $i' = i_1 + i_2$.
PB + 9	sub	i_1, i_2	i'	Set $i' = i_1 - i_2$.
PB + 10	mult	i_1, i_2	i'	Set $i' = i_1 \times i_2$.
PB + 11	div	i_1, i_2	i'	Set $i' = i_1 / i_2$ (truncated).
PB + 12	mod	i_1, i_2	i'	Set $i' = i_1$ modulo i_2.
PB + 13	lt	i_1, i_2	t'	Set $t' =$ true iff $i_1 < i_2$.
PB + 14	le	i_1, i_2	t'	Set $t' =$ true iff $i_1 \leq i_2$.
PB + 15	ge	i_1, i_2	t'	Set $t' =$ true iff $i_1 \geq i_2$.
PB + 16	gt	i_1, i_2	t'	Set $t' =$ true iff $i_1 > i_2$.
PB + 17	eq	v_1, v_2, n	t'	Set $t' =$ true iff $v_1 = v_2$ (where v_1 and v_2 are n-word values).
PB + 18	ne	v_1, v_2, n	t'	Set $t' =$ true iff $v_1 \neq v_2$ (where v_1 and v_2 are n-word values).
PB + 19	eol	–	t'	Set $t' =$ true iff the next character to be read is an end-of-line.
PB + 20	eof	–	t'	Set $t' =$ true iff there are no more characters to be read (end of file).
PB + 21	get	a	–	Read a character, and store it at address a.
PB + 22	put	c	–	Write the character c.
PB + 23	geteol	–	–	Read characters up to and including the next end-of-line.
PB + 24	puteol	–	–	Write an end-of-line.
PB + 25	getint	a	–	Read an integer-literal (optionally preceded by blanks and/or signed), and store its value at address a.
PB + 26	putint	i	–	Write an integer-literal whose value is i.
PB + 27	new	n	a'	Set $a' =$ address of a newly allocated n-word object in the heap.
PB + 28	dispose	n, a	–	Deallocate the n-word object at address a in the heap.

(See notes overleaf.)

Notes for Table C.3:

- a denotes a data address
- c denotes a character
- i denotes an integer
- n denotes a non-negative integer
- t denotes a truth value (0 for *false* or 1 for *true*)
- v denotes a value of any type
- w denotes any 1-word value

Class Diagrams for the Triangle Compiler

This appendix uses class diagrams to summarize the structure of the Triangle compiler, which is available from our Web site (see Preface, page xv).

The Triangle compiler has broadly the same structure as the Mini-Triangle compiler used throughout the text of this book. It is discussed in more detail in Sections 3.3, 4.6, 5.4, and 7.5.

The class diagrams are expressed in UML (Unified Modeling Language). UML is described in detail in Booch *et al.* (1999). However, the following points are worth noting. The name of an abstract class is shown in *italics*, whereas the name of a concrete class is shown in **bold**. Private attributes and methods are prefixed by a minus sign (–), whereas public attributes and methods are prefixed by a plus sign (+). The definition of a class attribute or method is underlined. The name of a method parameter is omitted where it is of little significance.

D.1 Compiler

The following diagram shows the overall structure of the compiler, including the syntactic analyzer (scanner and parser), the contextual analyzer, and the code generator:

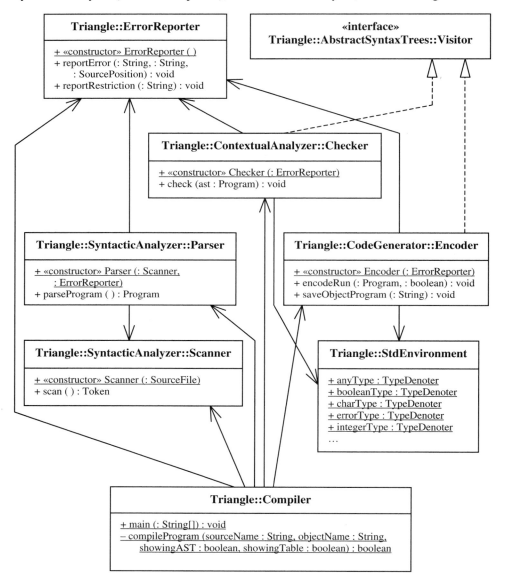

D.2 Abstract syntax trees

The diagrams in this section show the class hierarchy used in the representation of Triangle ASTs. Each major syntactic class is presented in a separate diagram. These diagrams show class names only, omitting constructors and methods.

   The following diagram shows the immediate subclasses of the AST class. Most of these are abstract classes representing the main syntactic phrases. Note that *Formal-Parameter* is a subclass of *Declaration* in order that formal parameters may be included in the identification table during contextual analysis.

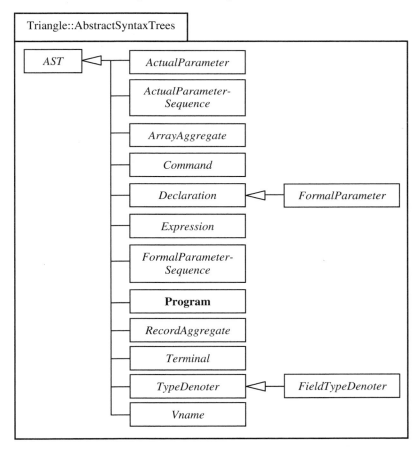

D.2.1 Commands

The following diagram shows the individual concrete classes for each form of command:

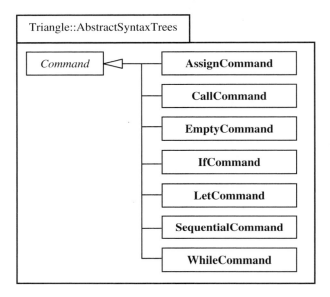

D.2.2 Expressions

The following diagram shows the individual concrete classes for each form of expression:

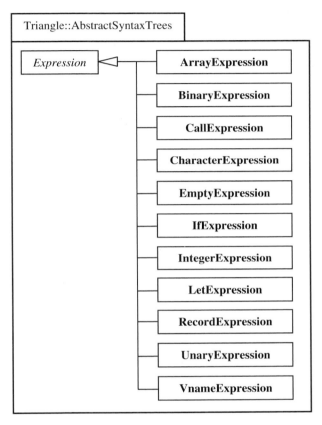

The following diagram shows the individual concrete subclasses for a record aggregate:

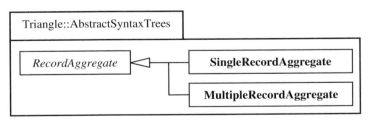

The following diagram shows the individual concrete subclasses for an array aggregate:

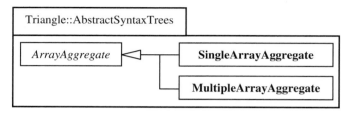

D.2.3 Value-or-variable names

The following diagram shows the individual concrete subclasses for each form of value-or-variable name:

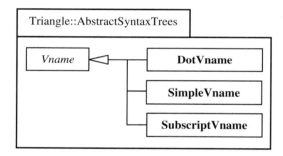

D.2.4   Declarations

The following diagram shows the individual concrete classes for each form of declaration:

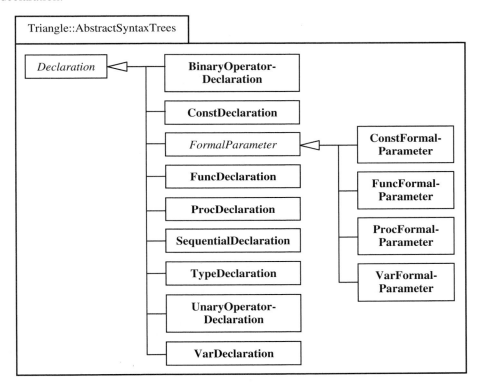

D.2.5   Parameters

The following diagram shows the individual concrete subclasses for each form of actual parameter:

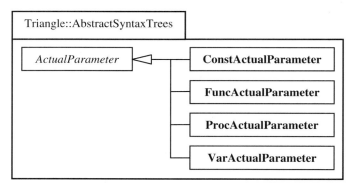

The following diagram shows the individual concrete subclasses for each form of actual parameter sequence:

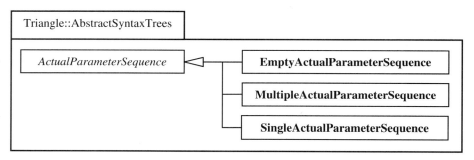

The following diagram shows the individual concrete subclasses for each form of formal parameter sequence:

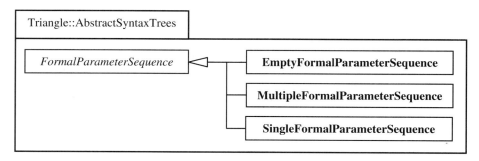

D.2.6 Type-denoters

The following diagram shows the individual concrete subclasses for each form of type-denoter:

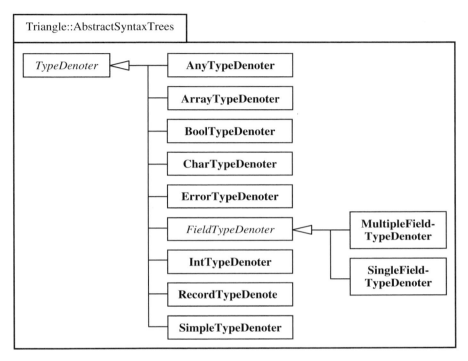

D.2.7 Terminals

The following diagram shows the individual concrete subclasses for each form of terminal node:

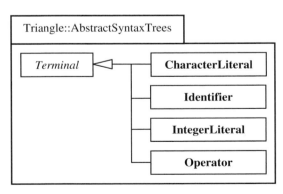

D.3 Syntactic analyzer

The following diagram shows the internal structure of the syntactic analyzer.

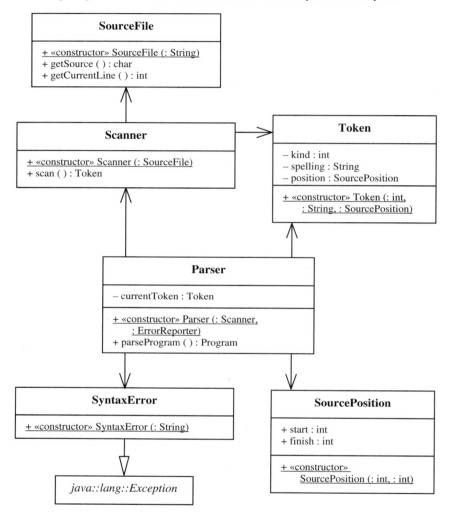

D.4 Contextual analyzer

The following diagram shows the internal structure of the contextual analyzer.

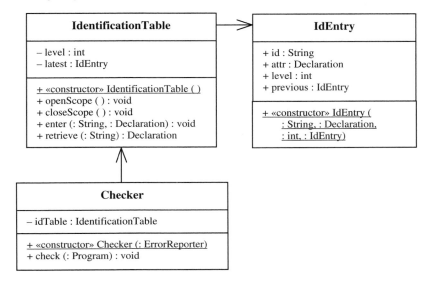

D.5 Code generator

The following diagram shows the internal structure of the code generator.

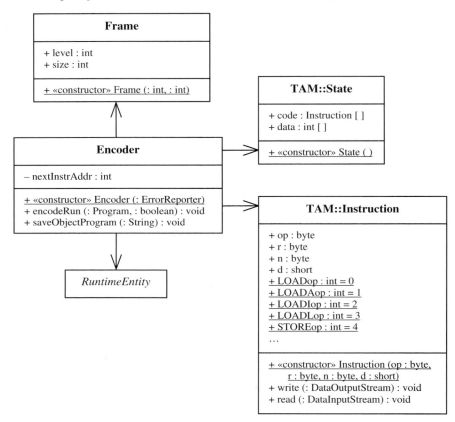

Bibliography

Adl-Tabatabai, A-R., Cierniak, M., Lueh, G-Y., Parikh, V., and Stichnoth, J.M. (1998) Fast, effective code generation in a just-in-time Java compiler, in *ACM SIGPLAN'98 Conference on Programming Language Design and Implementation*, ACM Press, New York, United States, pp. 280–90.

Aho, A.V., and Ullman, J.D. (1972) *The Theory of Parsing, Translation and Compiling*, Vol. I: *Parsing*, Prentice Hall, Englewood Cliffs, New Jersey, United States.

Aho, A.V., Sethi, R., and Ullman, J.D. (1985) *Compilers – Principles, Methods, and Tools*, Addison-Wesley, Reading, Massachusetts, United States.

Ammann, U. (1981) The Zürich implementation, in *Pascal – the Language and its Implementation* (ed. Barron, D.W.), Wiley, Chichester, England, pp. 63–82.

Appel, A.W. (1997) *Modern Compiler Implementation in Java*, Cambridge University Press, Cambridge, England.

Bergin, T.J., and Gibson, R.G. (eds.) (1996) *History of Programming Languages II*, ACM Press, New York, United States.

Booch, G., Rumbaugh, J., and Jacobson, I. (1999) *The Unified Modeling Language User Guide*, Addison-Wesley, Reading, Massachusetts, United States.

Cardelli, L. (1984) Compiling a functional language, in *ACM Symposium on Principles of Programming Languages*, ACM Press, New York, United States, pp. 208–17.

Dijkstra, E.W. (1960) Recursive programming, *Numerische Mathematik* **2**, 312–18; also in *Programming Systems and Languages* (ed. Rosen, S.), McGraw-Hill, New York, United States, pp. 221–7.

Earley, J., and Sturgis, H. (1970) A formalism for translator interactions, *Communications of the ACM* **13**, 607–17.

Fraser, C.W., and Hansen, D.R. (1995) *A Retargetable C Compiler – Design and Implementation*, Addison-Wesley, Reading, Massachusetts, United States.

Ganapathi, M., Fischer, C.N., and Hennessy, J.L. (1982) Retargetable compiler code generation, *Computing Surveys* **14**, 573–92.

Ghezzi, C., and Jazayeri, M. (1987) *Programming Language Concepts*, 2nd edn, Wiley, New York, United States.

Gosling, J., Joy, W., and Steele, G. (1996) *The Java Language Specification*, Addison-Wesley, Reading, Massachusetts, United States.

Hoare, C.A.R. (1972) Notes on data structuring, in *Structured Programming* (eds. Dahl, O.-J., Dijkstra, E.W., and Hoare, C.A.R.), Academic Press, London, England, pp. 83–174.

Hoare, C.A.R. (1973) Hints on programming language design, in *Proceedings of ACM Symposium on Principles of Programming Languages*, ACM Press, New York, United States.

Hoare, C.A.R. (1975) Recursive data structures, *International Journal of Computer and Information Sciences* **4**, 105–32.

Johnson, S.C. (1975) YACC: yet another compiler compiler, CS Technical Report 32, AT&T Bell Laboratories, Murray Hill, New Jersey, United States.

Jones, R., and Lins, R. (1996) *Garbage Collection*, Wiley, Chichester, England.

Kelsey, R., Clinger, W., and Rees, J. (eds.) (1998) Revised[5] report on the algorithmic language Scheme, *ACM SIGPLAN Notices* **33**, 26–76.

Lee, P. (1989) *Realistic Compiler Generation*, MIT Press, Cambridge, Massachusetts, United States.

Lesk, M.E., and Schmidt, E. (1975) LEX – a lexical analyzer generator, in *Unix Programmer's Manual 2*, AT&T Bell Laboratories, Murray Hill, New Jersey, United States.

Lindholm, T., and Yellin, F. (1999) *The Java Virtual Machine Specification*, 2nd edn, Addison-Wesley, Reading, Massachusetts, United States

McCarthy, J. (1963) Towards a mathematical science of computation, in *Information Processing 1962*, North-Holland, Amsterdam, Netherlands, pp. 21–8.

McCarthy, J., Abrahams, P.W., Edwards, D.J., Hart, T.P., and Levin, M.I. (1965) *LISP 1.5 Programmer's Manual*, 2nd edn, MIT Press, Cambridge, Massachusetts, United States.

Milner, R. (1978) A theory of type polymorphism in programming, *Journal of Computer and System Science* **17**, 348–75.

Sethi, R. (1988) *Programming Languages – Concepts and Constructs*, Addison-Wesley, Reading, Massachusetts, United States.

Standish, T.A. (1998) *Data Structures in Java*, Addison-Wesley, Reading, Massachusetts, United States.

Tennent, R.D. (1981) *Principles of Programming Languages*, Prentice Hall International, Hemel Hempstead, England.

Watt, D.A. (1990) *Programming Language Concepts and Paradigms*, Prentice Hall International, Hemel Hempstead, England.

Watt, D.A. (1991) *Programming Language Syntax and Semantics*, Prentice Hall International, Hemel Hempstead, England.

Watt, D.A. (1993) *Programming Language Processors – Compilers and Interpreters*, Prentice Hall International, Hemel Hempstead, England.

Welsh, J., and Hay, A. (1986) *A Model Implementation of Standard Pascal*, Prentice Hall International, Hemel Hempstead, England.

Welsh, J., and McKeag, M. (1980) *Structured System Programming*, Prentice Hall International, Hemel Hempstead, England.

Welsh, J., and Quinn, C. (1972) A Pascal compiler for ICL 1900 series computers, *Software Practice and Experience* **2**, 73–7.

Wilson, P.R. (1992) Uniprocessor garbage collection techniques, in *Proceedings of International Workshop on Memory Management*, Springer, Berlin, Germany.

Wirth, N. (1971) The design of a Pascal compiler, *Software Practice and Experience* **1**, 309–33.

Wirth, N. (1986) Microprocessor architectures – a comparison based on code generation by compiler, *Communications of the ACM* **29**, 978–90.

Index